Going With The Flow

Memories from the Feather River

To the Pacific Islands and Back

Paul Callaghan

Tellwell Talent
www.tellwell.ca

ISBN
978-0-2288-9085-0 (Hardcover)
978-0-2288-9084-3 (Paperback)
978-0-2288-9086-7 (eBook)

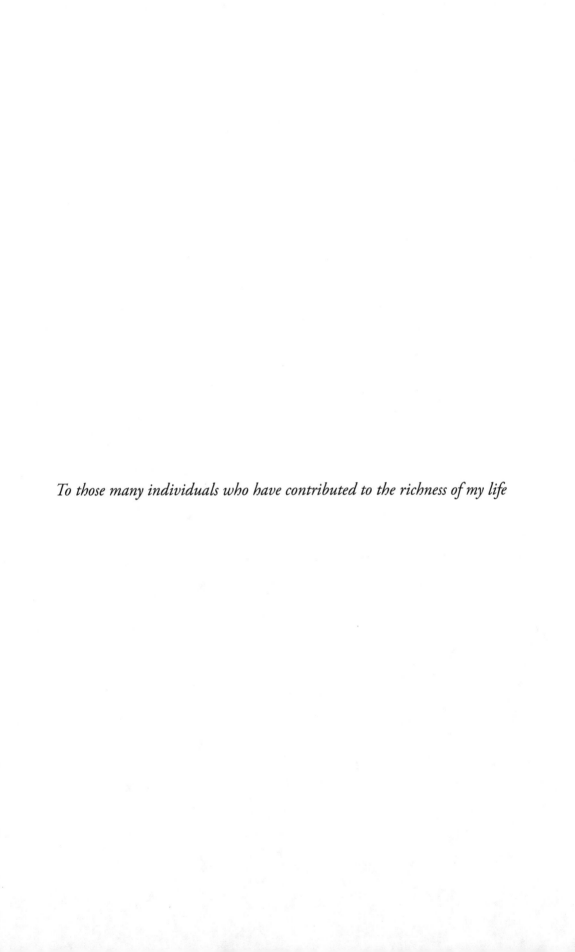

To those many individuals who have contributed to the richness of my life

Table of Contents

Acknowledgments

In addition to those who have contributed to the fabric of my life, I would like to thank Craig Severance for his thoughtful comments, and Susan Applegate and Margo Vitarelli for their studious commentary and valuable insights. Most especially, I would like to thank Suzanne Lee for her editing, cover design, and steadfast support during the many months of this creative effort.

Preface

As a teenager I sometimes pondered the questions: What will I be? Where will life take me? What will I be doing when I'm old? Old meant sixty in those days. My mother's advice was to get an education and the rest would take care of itself. She would say, "Open as many doors as you can, keep them open as long as you can, and enter the ones you feel are right for you. Listen to the little voice inside and try to make the best decisions as the choices unfold." My father would chip in, "And don't lose your integrity along the way, son—you know right from wrong. And don't get married too soon."

Well, the years have hurried by, and I've now negotiated eighty of them. Maybe there's still a few yet to go, but I'd like to stop for a moment and share some cherished memories—high points of the journey as I remember them.

I'm aware that my life has been relatively easy. Chance has bestowed on me sufficient food, clothing, shelter and money. Genetics has provided a reasonable level of intelligence and good health. My parents instilled beneficial social skills and values. I've had access to fine educational opportunities and decent health care. Few cultural barriers have blocked my progress, though I did live for many years as a minority in a brown man's world. That experience has provided an understanding and empathy for those who face cultural, racial and gender biases as part of their daily lives.

Not all has gone smoothly for me. There have been painful times. I've experienced learning difficulties, humiliation, divorce and rejection, prejudice and discrimination, failure and incapacity. In the long view of things, most of those difficulties have led to opportunities for further growth and success.

This book is simply an account of the life memories of an upper middle class, White, American male who lived during the intersection of the twentieth and twenty-first centuries. I have written it for my own self-satisfaction—a way of bringing closure to a satisfying life. Like other memoirs it's an attempt to preserve stories that otherwise would go untold and unremembered. It relates experiences that shaped my life, provided insight, and taught lessons. It recounts moments of satisfaction, pride, sorrow and humility. It recalls forks in the road, some chosen and some the result of happenstance. It attempts to honor individuals who guided and enriched my journey.

Though I have traveled through and lived in many beauteous places, there are no scenic photographs in these pages. It is the people in one's life that are most important. Nature's physical beauty will continue for eons, but people come and go in the briefest of lifetimes. These pages acknowledge individuals who contributed to my life's story, in the hope they will not be entirely forgotten. Of course, given this limited space, it's not possible to pay tribute to every person who influenced my journey. There are individuals and episodes that have been omitted, some purposely to protect privacy and avoid embarrassment, others inadvertently due to my oversight.

I hope the reader will bear in mind that memories are not always exacting and perceptions not always accurate, but I have done my best to relate my experiences as I remember them.

Prologue

I was born into a traditional, independent minded, politically conservative California farming community. Surrounded by oak-strewn hills, the Livermore Valley provides a Mediterranean environment situated just east of the San Francisco Bay Area. Prior to the gold rush the Valley was a Spanish land grant awarded to Don Roberto Livermore, an English-born Spanish citizen. After statehood, immigrants from several European countries settled in Livermore. Irishmen, Germans and Italians predominated, but there were also some original Spanish families and a sprinkling of Portuguese, Scandinavians and Eastern Europeans.

Sheep and cattle ranching, as well as vineyards and wine making, were the life blood of Livermore for a hundred years before I came along in 1942. By then the population had reached four thousand. All now Americans, they were united in the throes of a World War. The lone Japanese family had been shipped off to an internment camp. The only Chinese family ran the Yin Yin restaurant. A few Filipinos lived mostly in labor camps at the vineyards. There were no Blacks and no sign of the Indigenous people who had once called the Valley their home. My father, who was the local bank manager, expressed his view of racial differences quite succinctly when he said, "There are only two kinds of people in this Valley: Protestants and Catholics; among them are the hardworking and the lazy, those who pay their bills and those who don't." The possibility of a non-Christian philosophy never entered his mind.

As I grew and changed, so did Livermore. In 1952 a decommissioned World War II Navy air base on the edge of town was transformed into the Lawrence Livermore National Laboratory, and in 1956 Sandia National Laboratory moved in across the road from Lawrence. These research institutions brought with them an influx of residents with different values, experiences and expectations. The population grew to forty thousand. The pace of life quickened. Dial telephones replaced the hand operated switchboards and party lines. Housing developments began to erase pasture and vineyard. People with new perspectives transformed city boards, commissions and councils. Fresh business competition pressured old establishments. Dairy Queen, Royal Lanes, the Vine Movie Theater and Lucky Super Market opened. The renowned annual Livermore Rodeo was reduced to a shadow of its previous significance.

Although change was everywhere around me, I didn't notice it much. Other than some new, interesting classmates, my life and that of my friends remained seemingly unaffected. We had been together since the first grade. Each new person and thing became instantly part of our lives, as if they had always been there. Unlike our parents, we had neither perspective nor care as to what had gone before. The great war was over. Our relatives who had fought in it were home again and raising families. Optimism and opportunity surrounded us. We focused on the present, with a modicum of concern as to the immediate future, like "What's for dinner tonight?"

My parents taught by word and action that all endeavors should be approached with integrity, generosity and diligence. They emphasized the benefits of a good education, and they pushed me to reach out into the world, to do the unexpected, to take a chance, to have an adventure. They pointed out that those who put off adventure until later often lose the opportunity altogether. Much of their advice is encapsulated in this excerpt from a letter they presented to me on my fifteenth birthday.

> ... Employ deliberation and common sense, but let the wind blow you, and most of the time you will be swept down paths that lead to amazing adventure and opportunity. If the door is open to an exploit that may never again be available, think twice before passing it by. Life is full of barriers, but there is usually a way over or around. If not, there is nothing wrong with retreat. Sometimes retreat allows us to see new avenues that were previously overlooked. Don't marry at too early an age. When you have reached your thirties and have found a comfortable place that provides opportunity and stability for your wife and children, stay there and call that place home. Set an example of integrity, generosity and diligence for your children. Otherwise,

don't constrain or overly prescribe their path. Let them feel the wind. Encourage them to have their own adventures, to take a risk, to explore as you have done. If you do so, you will be proud of them, and also of yourself.

My mother and my father each had totally different but equally influential impacts on my life. In addition to a twenty-four-year disparity in their ages, they reflected vastly different personalities, backgrounds, and levels of formal education, yet their guidance was complementary. One's weakness was the other's strength. They seemed to understand this, and each supported and deferred to the other as needed. This symbiotic relationship was, of course, not perfect. I never saw any outward demonstration of affection between them. On the other hand, I never saw a disagreement build to more than words or last more than a day. They seemed to have a mutually beneficial, platonic relationship that lasted for thirty-two years until my father's death. After his passing, my mother never remarried or entertained another man.

My parents seldom hugged or kissed me as a child, but they were always there for me with support and guidance when needed. They treated me in a manner beyond my years. I knew I could count on them, and I wanted to please them. My world felt secure and stable, and the rules of conduct were clear. My mother spanked me a couple of times with her hair brush, and my father whipped me only once in the tool shed with his leather belt. In later years Mom told me that he cried afterward.

It is certain that an understanding of me and my life's path requires an understanding of my parents, so the first chapter of this book is devoted to each of them—my father first, since he was born first, and my mother second because she lived longer. After that we will get to stories about me and others who have influenced my time on this earth.

Chapter 1

Joe and Emma

For most of us, our lives are influenced for better or worse by our parents. Their values, strengths, and weaknesses have a profound impact on the choices we make and the paths we follow. Perhaps my parents produced me by accident, but I became the center of their lives and the glue that held them together. Their support was unwavering, each contributing differently to my life perspective. Their decisions regarding my welfare were approached in a spirit of compromise that led to a unified voice. Even though there may have been significant underlying disagreement, I was seldom aware of it.

I know little about the details of their lives before I came along, but here is what I do know.

*　*　*

My father, Henry Joseph Callaghan, Joe to his friends, came into this world near the wood stove of his family home in Livermore, California, on May 4, 1887. The house had fireplace heating, kerosene lighting, and no running water. It had been built in the 1870s by his father, Henry Callaghan, an immigrant from Donegal County, Ireland.

Joe's Mother, Sarah Ann (McCrory) Rodgers Callaghan, was an immigrant from Aghyaran, Tyrone County, Ireland. She and Henry had met in San Francisco and married there in 1878. Upon Joe's arrival there were already four children: James Edward (Ed) the eldest, Sarah Ann (Sadie), Florence, and Maud Mary. Little Joe was lucky that his sister, Sadie, was old enough to help care for him, because disaster struck within six months of Joe's birth. His father Henry was thrown from a wagon on his way home from the family sheep camp at Corral Hollow in the Livermore hills. Suffering from internal injuries and a broken collar bone, he lived only a few days.

Sarah Callaghan was left with a house, seven hundred acres of land, one thousand head of sheep, eight horses, one cow, two calves, farm equipment, five children (the oldest eight), and a $4,000 mortgage. But Sarah Rodgers Callaghan was made of tough stuff. She was healthy, competent, hardworking, and had her Catholic faith to sustain her. She hired men to run the sheep camp and ultimately rented out and eventually sold most of the hill land. She planted a vineyard on the thirty acres that surrounded the house and sold the grapes to the Concanon and Wente families who had small wineries nearby. Milk and eggs were peddled around town by the children, including Joe when he was old enough to accompany the others. She eked out pennies from her rabbits, pigs and lambs. At times she took in boarders. Every cent was made to count. The children wore shoes only when necessary. Sunday Mass was one of those times.

Despite their frugal lifestyle, Joe's mother brought into the family circle several orphaned or neglected children, giving them the same food and love she gave to her own children. Some of the boarders and household adoptees had a profound influence on Joe's life, and in later years served to expand his network of friends throughout the state. One such adoptee was Charley, who as a small child drifted into the household from parts unknown, likely at the behest of Father McKinnon, the Catholic priest.

Charley took the last name Callaghan and lived in the household until finishing the eighth grade. He then went to San Francisco, became a bellboy and operated a shoe shine stand at the Mark Hopkins Hotel. I know little of Charley's life, but somehow he ended up as an investor in the oil fields of southern California. There, going by the name Charles B. Callaghan, he became a wealthy man. I remember "Uncle Charley" as a kindly, white-haired, cigar-smoking gentleman who arrived once every year at our house in his chauffeur-driven Cadillac. He seemed to enjoy entertaining me on his knee while he talked with Mom and Dad. Before leaving, he always gave me a twenty-dollar bill, a huge sum of money for a child in the 1940s. Uncle Charley died, childless and unmarried, sometime in the 1950s. He left a goodly sum of money to Dad's sister, Maud, who had cared for him as a child, and the rest, several million dollars, he left to his long-time male secretary. Charley's burial site and other details of his economically successful life remain a mystery.

Front Row: James Edward (Ed), Frank, Henry (Joe) on sheep, Maud, Winnie, Florence, Monica, Mamie (wife of James Callaghan and mother of Frank, Winnie, and Monica). Back Row: Sarah Ann Callaghan (mother of Ed, Sadie, Maud, Florence and Joe), Sadie, Mr. & Mrs. Smith, Mr. & Mrs. Dun, James Callaghan (Joe's Uncle). At the Callaghan home on East Avenue, Livermore, c. 1899.

Joe Callaghan (seated left), youngest participant in the National Rifle Championships held in Camp Perry, Ohio, 1908

Joe Callaghan entered the first grade at Livermore Grammar School in 1894. Despite the two-mile walk from home, he liked school and excelled in mathematics. When guests visited, he was often paraded out to show off the speed with which he could add columns of four-digit numbers. To Joe's everlasting sadness his education was cut short sometime after the seventh grade. Family need dictated that he shoulder the role of an adult. There is no record of his ever having graduated from grammar school.

From an early age Joe had helped his uncles and brother herd sheep in the hills, sometimes being left alone to watch over the flocks on weekends and holidays. At thirteen he took to the fields, working ten-hour days in the summer heat on a hay press for a dollar a day. It didn't take long for him to realize that this work had no future, and in 1902, at fourteen, he was hired by the Livermore Commercial Company, the largest grocery store in town. There he worked for six years, carefully saving what money the family could spare from his salary, all the while making friends and establishing himself as a hardworking, honest and reliable young man.

In 1904 Joe joined the Livermore based Company I of the California National Guard. He soon rose to the rank of Sergeant and in 1906 was sent with Company I to patrol the streets of San Francisco after the great fire and earthquake. In October of 1907, he was commissioned Second Lieutenant. From the beginning of his service with the Guard he established himself as an exceptional marksman. In 1907 and again in 1908, Joe distinguished himself as the youngest member of the California Guard team at the National Rifle Championships in Camp Perry, Ohio. These were his first experiences traveling far from home.

At the age of twenty Joe had saved enough money to go into the grocery business on his own, so he opened the Valley Mercantile Company on Main Street in Livermore. Over the next ten years the business grew and flourished. He opened a second store, bought a van and provided home delivery. In 1910 he became a member of the Board of Directors for the Bank of Livermore. Joe's prospects as a young businessman in the Livermore Valley were looking up, when suddenly his life stood still.

The United States declared war on Germany, April 6, 1917. Being thirty years of age, in business, and a major contributor to his family's support, he wasn't called into service immediately. But in mid-summer of 1918 he received an induction notice with instructions to report immediately. This left him no choice but to sell his grocery business at a loss to those who would take advantage of his situation. Upon reporting at the induction center, he underwent a physical examination which determined that he had a hernia, so he was sent to the Fabiola Hospital in Oakland for corrective surgery. While convalescing there, the war ended and he was discharged from the hospital, never having officially been inducted into the military. Instead, he went home unsettled, without veteran status, his businesses gone, and few prospects for the future.

Though frustrated by this turn of events, Joe always had his share of Irish luck, and this time was no exception. The Bank of Livermore, where he had previously been a Board Member, had been reorganized into the First National Bank of Livermore. The new owners included his friend Carl Wente and Carl's sister, Frieda, who worked at the bank. When the bank's cashier was taken ill, Frieda asked Joe to take his place temporarily. The cashier never returned and Joe stayed on, once again becoming a member of the bank's Board of Directors. By 1924 he had risen to manager of what had become the American Bank. He remained as manager through subsequent name and ownership changes until finally the bank was purchased by Wells Fargo Corporation. Each owner recognized that Joe was critical to the bank's success. He knew the history and moral character of every family in the Livermore Valley. When Joe made a loan, it almost always got repaid on time.

The 1920s were wild and profitable times. Joe made lucrative investments in land and the stock market. He loaned the bank's money to a relatively unknown entrepreneur named Henry J. Kaiser, who was building a gravel pit near Livermore to supply concrete and fill for road construction. Joe married a beautiful young Portuguese lady named Rose Cabral from the nearby town of Brentwood and built her an impressive house with oak floors, three garages, and separate living quarters for his bachelor uncle, Michael (McCrory) Rodgers. Each year Joe hunted deer, elk and antelope with his friend Dr. George Therkoff, the local dentist. They often traveled into northern California, Oregon and Nevada on their quest for trophy antlers.

Dad told me a humorous story about one of those hunting trips. Apparently, he and Therkoff were traveling in a Stanley Steamer automobile on a rutted, lonely, dirt road, somewhere in Modoc County, northeastern California. They were lost, and the car was running low on the oil that fired its boiler. They spotted a house that appeared to be occupied. Upon driving into the front yard, Joe jumped out and approached a pipe-smoking, old woman who was sitting in a rocking chair on the porch. In his most polite tone he asked, "Excuse me, ma'am. We are lost. Can you tell me where this road goes?" She looked over her spectacles at him, took the pipe from her mouth, and said, "Sonny, it don't go nowhere. It stays right where it is."

Prohibition was in full force during the 1920s, and bank executives from the Bay Area regularly took the Southern Pacific train to Livermore for weekends of fun at Joe's place, where there could always be found liquor and a friendly poker game, with little chance of interruption by authorities. Joe admired these visitors because they were college-educated and worldly. He followed their stock tips and investment advice, feeling that they knew far more than he. Based on their advice, by the late 20s he had amassed a substantial stock portfolio. Several times he was offered bank executive positions in Oakland and San Francisco. He always turned them down. Perhaps he feared that his lack of education would hinder him in a more competitive environment. Perhaps he understood that his strengths lay with the people who respected him in the Valley that he loved and understood. In any case, his choice to remain in Livermore was fortuitous.

The smart tipsters and educated friends were of little help when the good times ended. The stock market crash of 1929 and the subsequent Depression of the 1930s took everyone down. Joe was no exception. He lost almost everything he owned. But his bank was solvent and his job secure, thanks to his shrewd and conservative lending practices. Since his first employment, Joe had contributed to the maintenance of the family home where he grew up and its occupants. In 1911 his sister Sadie had entered the Dominican order as Sister Mary Zita. His mother, Sarah, had died in 1925. His sister Maud had moved to San Francisco and married. His sister Florence had died in a freak kitchen fire, leaving two young sons, Arthur (Art) and Richard (Huff). They and their father, James Deck, still lived in the family home, along with Joe's brother Ed and his wife, Julia Flynn Callaghan, and her sister Mayme. With what money he had left, Joe continued to support the family home and household, especially the two young nephews whom he thought of as if they were his own sons.

In addition to his financial losses, Joe's marriage to Rose had not worked out. In 1930 he found a Catholic Bishop in Dallas County, Texas, who agreed to annul the marriage in return for a ten-thousand-dollar donation. That money was the last of his savings. Rose went her way, and no one ever mentioned her again. At the onset of the 1930s Joe found himself a poor man and a lonely bachelor. Many of those he had loved were gone. There remained only his beautiful house and forty-three years of memories, along with his optimistic, friendly personality and his Catholic faith.

As a rural agricultural community, the Livermore Valley was spared the worst of the Depression conditions that existed in urban areas. Families had some resources—cows, chickens, orchards, vegetable gardens, and above all, neighborly cooperation. The bank's main office in San Francisco didn't question Joe's judgment when it came to loans and credit. Many a family was given financial help, and most never forgot Joe's kindness. They came to him for advice on everything from the purchase of property, to the making of wills, to the settlement of family disputes. His integrity was well known. They trusted his decisions. After all, their mothers had been friends with Joe's mother, Sarah Callaghan. She had been respected by everyone in the Valley.

Throughout the 1930s Joe began carefully and thoughtfully to recoup his fortunes. He lived frugally, saving and investing his money. He studied the stock market with greater care than he had in the 1920s. This time he relied on his own judgment rather than that of others. His monthly bank salary was $375, a fine sum during Depression years. He bought rental units, made personal loans to individuals he knew, and purchased an interest in a 5-10-15 Cent Store in Oakland. Along with some others, he financially backed Maximilian Adalbert "Max" Baer, a Livermore boy who went on to become World Heavyweight Boxing Champion in 1934.

Not everything went as planned. In 1934 Joe was walking down Main Street to a meeting when a stomach ulcer that he'd been nursing for some time ruptured. He was rushed to the local St. Paul's Hospital, and a surgeon from San Francisco was summoned by telegraph. A day later when the surgeon arrived, Joe was unconscious and close to death. The surgeon operated, removing half of Joe's stomach and much of his upper intestine. Joe remained unconscious on the edge of death for another eight days, but Irish luck prevailed once again. He recovered and was back at work within a few months. The surgeon later told him that he had performed that same operation on ten other patients, and Joe was the first one to survive.

Dad sometimes spoke of a dream he had during the days when he was unconscious. He said he was walking barefoot across an unplanted field of soft dirt when he came to the bank of a river that he knew to be the River Styx. He sat on the bank while letting his feet and legs dangle in the water. It was warm and relaxing. A calm feeling swept over him. While enjoying the respite, he noticed a boatman poling his craft across the river, headed in his direction. He knew the boatman to be Charon. For a while he sat there enjoying the warmth and watching Charon come closer. Suddenly he said to himself, "No, I'm not ready to cross this river now. I have lots yet to do on this side." He stood up, turned his back to the river, and walked away without looking back. The doctor later said that the warm sensation was probably the blood beginning to flow back into his legs.

After his recovery, Joe continued to prosper, both economically and socially. He joined various societies, served on library and school boards, oversaw ticket sales for the annual Livermore Rodeo, hunted ducks and upland game, played golf, traveled with friends to Alaska and Hawaii, danced, partied, and every Wednesday night played poker with a group of friends. Their Wednesday night poker games continued for thirty-five years. In 1940 he sold the 5-10-15 Cent Store in Oakland and bought into the burgeoning movie theater industry as a partner of Gilroy Amusement Company, which owned a chain of theaters south of San Jose.

All seemed well on the surface of Joe's life, but underneath he sadly missed having his own family. He loved children and had spent considerable effort helping to raise his two motherless nephews, Art and Richard. Although Richard was doing well and attending the University of Portland, Joe was concerned about Art's passion to succeed as a bull and bronco rider on the rodeo circuit.

Just before noon one morning in late 1936, at the height of the Depression, Joe was in his office at the bank. His secretary, Jacqueline (Jackie) Nyquist, walked in and said, "Joe, there's a young lady outside who wants to meet with you. She says she's from the Alameda County Charities Commission. Do you want to see her now, or should I make an appointment for later? Don't forget, you have lunch today with Ralph Merritt."

"Yes, I know," Joe replied. "Make an appointment. I've got to get over to the Creamery and see Ralph about that housing loan for Coast Manufacturing and Supply."

In a minute or two he walked out of his office and saw an attractive, professionally dressed woman in her twenties standing in front of Jackie's desk. He smiled and nodded as he passed. So did she.

A few days later, promptly as scheduled, the same woman entered his office.

*　*　*

My mother, Emma Georgette Barham, was born at home on Apgar Street in Oakland, California on May 4, 1911. She must have been a well-disposed baby because within family circles she was forever known by the nickname "Cuddles," sometimes modified to "Cuddie." Her mother, Emma Regina Stoer Barham, was the youngest daughter of John Fredrick Stoer, a German immigrant who owned several businesses in Oakland and nearby Emeryville, as well as mining interests Montana and California. Emma Regina was well educated, having graduated in 1902 from the University of California, Berkeley, after which she taught at Oakland High School.

My mother's father, Courtney (Court) L. Barham, was born and spent his early years in Chico, California. Later his family lived in Red Bluff and on their ranch in Manton. Courtney's father, James Louis Barham, owned the Manton general store and at one point was the County Assessor of Tehama County. Courtney attended the University of the Pacific and graduated from the University of California in 1902, in the same class with his sweetheart, Emma Regina Stoer. For a time, Court taught school at various locations in California, before marrying Emma Regina and starting his banking career in Emeryville. There he managed and later owned the First National Bank of Emeryville and the Emeryville Savings Bank.

By the time my mother, Emma, was three years old her grandfather, John Fredrick Stoer, had died, and the Barhams moved into his three-story home in Emeryville, just across the street from her father's bank. Emma's sister, Janice, was born in that house on October 20, 1914.

When Emma reached school age in 1917, she attended Longfellow Public School in Oakland. There she excelled to the extent that she was allowed to skip the fourth grade, a decision that in later years she openly regretted. In 1923 Emma entered the prestigious Anna Head School for Girls in Berkeley, California. She took courses in Latin, French, Spanish, botany, mathematics, English literature, and European and world history. She competed in tennis, basketball and swimming, sang in choral groups, and studied art history and music. Her most satisfying activities centered on the dramatic. A thespian at heart, she sought parts in every theatrical performance. But more than anything else, she acquired from Anna Head a liberal world perspective, influenced by boarding students from elsewhere in the world. One such person was Estelle Booth, who had been born and raised of missionary parents in Yokohama, Japan. They remained lifelong friends.

Emma's view of her Anna Head's experience is summed up in this quote found among her notes:

What Heads education tried to do for me. "But you go to a great school, not for knowledge so much as for the arts and habits; for the habit of attention, for the art of expression, for the art of assuming at a moment's notice a new intellectual posture, for the art of entering quickly into another person's thoughts, for the habit of submitting to censure and refutation, for the art of indicating assent or dissent in graduated terms, for the habit of regarding minute points of accuracy, for the habit of working out what is possible in a given time, for taste, for discrimination, for mental courage and mental soberness. Above all, you go to a great school for self-knowledge." William J. Corey, A Great Eton Master."

In 1928 at the age of seventeen, Emma entered the University of California at Berkeley. Her father had sold his two banks and established the Barham Company, a personal loan, investment and insurance business located in Oakland near City Hall. The family had moved into a seven-bedroom, four-bath home in the exclusive Piedmont hills above Oakland. The house sported a three-car garage, maid's quarters, a patio with fountains and ponds, a tennis court, and a magnificent view of Oakland, San Francisco and the Bay. Emma drove a 1928 Essex Roadster convertible with rumble-seat, given to her as a high school graduation present by her grandmother, Emma Stoer. There were large formal parties with entertainment and dancing until the early hours of morning. Emma's sister, Janice, had a formal debutant gala that took the Bay Area society pages by storm.

Emma Barham driving her 1928 Essex, Janice Barham in the rumble seat, c. 1928

But Emma was different; she would have none of such society shows. She and her friends at Anna Heads, and subsequently at U.C. Berkeley, were involved with international and political affairs, women's rights, social justice, democratic activism and athletics. For some time, Emma was active in fostering racial and feminine equality through her positions of leadership in the Berkeley YWCA. Out of respect for her mother's wishes, Emma entered the 1928 fall sorority rush and was pledged to the Pi Beta Phi Sorority, but she never became an active member. Instead, she, with her friends Estelle Booth and Jaqueline Watkins, were among the first women allowed to live at International House—a campus residence that up until that time had been restricted to male foreign students. Emma and Jaqueline were also inductees into the Prytanean Honor Society, the oldest women's honor society in the United States, dating from 1902 at U.C. Berkeley.

Emma majored in Latin and Greek while minoring in drama and theater. Newspaper clippings attest to her participation as an actress, both at the University Theater and elsewhere around the Bay Area. One such clipping read,

> Little Theater's final production of the year, "The Twelfth Disciple," will open at 8:15 o'clock tonight in the International House Auditorium. Tonight's performance will be the west coast primer showing. Gorman Silen will play the part of Judas, the "twelfth disciple." Rachel, the girl to whom Judas is betrothed, will be played by Emma Barham. She is a member of Mask and Dagger, dramatics honor society, and appeared last year in "Ten Nights in a Barroom," "Interference," and "The Ticket-of-Leave Man."

Emma worked with such names as Nestor Paiva, Howard Banks, Carlton Morse, Marchael Raffetto and Barton Yarborough. The latter three asked Emma to join them in the production of Carlton's radio drama entitled, *One Man's Family*. Radio drama was all the rage, and Emma was about to graduate with little prospect of employment. She pleaded with her father, Courtney, to let her join the group, but he absolutely refused, saying that acting was neither a stable nor proper profession for his daughter. Emma couldn't bring herself to openly disobey her father. *One Man's Family* went on to become the longest-playing, uninterrupted dramatic serial in the history of American radio, running from 1932 to 1959.

With the Depression in full swing, one of the few stable and proper professions available to women was that of social worker. So in 1934, Emma, along with her friends Estelle Booth and Jacqueline (Jackie) Watkins, began graduate studies in the Curriculum in Social Service, Department of Economics, U. C. Berkeley. Here in what was to become the Graduate School of Social Work, Emma met three individuals who became role models and friends through the rest of her life. The first was Martha (Pattie) Chickering, who at that time was field supervisor for the Social Service Curriculum. The second was Catherine W. (Kit) Carson, a recent graduate of Bolt Hall Law School who had entered the social work curriculum to broaden her knowledge of that field. The third was a graduate instructor named Maurine McKeany. In the summers of 1936 and 1938, Pattie, Maurine and Emma, with their guide Onis Imus Brown, packed on horseback for five weeks at a time through the High Sierra Mountains, covering the John Muir trail from Glacier Point in Yosemite Valley to Giant Forest near Mount Whitney.

As soon as Emma, Estelle, Jackie and Kit received their Social Service certification, they were accepted to work at the newly established Alameda County Charities Commission, an agency that coordinated public and private relief efforts within the county. At that time in Alameda County the unemployment rate was approaching 25 percent. One in four families had no source of income. There were many hungry children. Emma's starting salary was $90 a month, with no benefits. She lived at home in Piedmont and using her own car, commuted daily to the Commission headquarters in Alameda. From there she used the Commission's vehicle to visit clients in the field. Initially she worked with clients on the Oakland waterfront. Then in 1936 she was assigned as Relief Agent to Murray and Pleasanton Townships, which included the rural towns of Dublin, Pleasanton, Livermore and Altamont.

On one cold, windy day she found herself driving east on US Highway 50 on her way to an eleven o'clock meeting with Mr. H. J. Callaghan, the manager of the First National Bank of Livermore. Being new to the district, it was customary to make courtesy calls at local institutions such as the courts, law enforcement, emergency services, banks and charitable organizations.

As she left the main highway and entered Livermore on L Street, she wondered what kind of man this H. J. Callaghan would be. She had only glimpsed him three days earlier as he left his office. He was well dressed, balding, with gold rim glasses, but good looking for his age—in his forties, she thought. His passing smile had seemed quite welcoming. At least she hoped it had been, because she needed all the help she could get. These country folks were not her kind of people, and she knew nothing of farming and farm animals, or anything about the interpersonal human relationships that crisscrossed this valley.

Emma Barham, Jacque Watkins, Estelle Booth, social workers, 1933

In their attempts to receive the much-coveted county relief benefits, people could easily deceive her about their financial affairs. Only a person like Mr. Callaghan might know the true state of their lives. She hoped he would be willing to help her.

Across the street from the bank stood the city's towering flag pole, its Old Glory streaming in the stiff north wind. She parked, reviewed her countenance in the mirror, and buttoned her fur-collared wool coat before stepping out into the wind. The bank's heavy metal door thumped closed behind her as she crossed the lobby's expansive marble floor. After announcing herself to the secretary, she took a seat on the cold marble bench near the manager's office door. It wasn't long before she was told that Mr. Callaghan would see her. "Just walk right in," said the secretary.

* * *

Upon entering she saw Joe seated behind a leather-padded, oaken desk that was illuminated by two green glass desk lamps. Two deer heads with massive antlers hung behind him on the dark mahogany-paneled wall. The high ceiling supported a large French Empire chandelier—*the crystals are a bit dusty*, she thought. Gas light fixtures protruded from the walls around the room, but they clearly hadn't been used for some time. Most light came through the brocade-curtained picture window that faced onto Main Street. As she walked across the well-used oriental carpet toward his desk, she thought, *His baldness accentuates his good looks. I hope he's not as stodgy as his surroundings imply.*

He stood as she approached. "Thank you for seeing me, Mr. Callaghan. I know you're busy, but I wanted to stop by and introduce myself." She handed him a card that read, "Miss. Emma G. Barham, BA, SSC, Social Worker, Alameda County Charities Commission."

After momentarily examining the card, he said, "Please have a seat, Miss Barham. How can I help you?"

She sat on the front lip of one of the two heavy oak chairs that faced his desk. If she sat any farther back, the chair would consume her and her feet couldn't reach the floor. *Those chairs are designed for men*, thought Joe. *I've got to remind Jackie to get something more suitable for women.*

Her wavy, brunette hair curled inward just below her ears. She wore flashy black and white oxfords. The grey, V-necked dress extended well over her knees. Other than a wristwatch, she wore no jewelry. Her smile was pleasant but controlled, her expression businesslike. There was an air of sophistication and self-assurance about this woman that asserted itself as she spoke. "As you can see from my card, Mr. Callaghan, my name is Emma Barham, and I've been assigned as the Charities Commission Relief Agent for Murray and Pleasanton Townships. Since I'm new to this area, I would hope to call upon you from time to time for advice and assistance in determining client eligibility."

"Murray and Pleasanton Townships are pretty big places and include some pretty rough country. There are a lot of families out there who need help these days," he said. "Are you the only agent assigned here?"

"Yes, I'm the only case worker for this area. And I can come to the Valley only four days a week. On Fridays I must remain in the Oakland office to write my reports. I was hoping you might take a look at this list of applicants and help me decide where the needs are greatest."

"You have a car I assume, maps and address?" he asked.

"Yes, the Commission provides me with a car, but I expect that the location records are not all up to date.

"I suspect that's right," Joe said. "Some people live far up in the hills and are probably not on any map. They might come into town only once a week to pick up their mail and provisions. You'll find it hard to reach them." *This gal is going to need a lot of help*, he thought. *I hope she can ride a horse, sweat a bit, and tolerate some dirt on those fancy two-tone shoes.*

Chapter 2

The Beginning

I never talked with my mother or father about their four-year courtship, but I suspect that as a city girl, Emma had much to learn of country ways and people, and Joe probably provided much help and advice. He knew the family background and financial status of every family in the Valley, and in those days, there were no privacy laws or regulations. I know they worked together on Emma's welfare cases and ate lunch together at the Golden Rule Creamery near the Bank. That probably led to a friendship, then evening dates followed by weekend outings and summer trips to the Barham vacation cabin on the Feather River near Chester in Plumas County. Gradually a serious and permanent relationship emerged.

One thing I am sure of is that Joe learned in a hurry that Emma was not a conventional city girl. She had a tough, down-to-business streak, similar to that of Joe's mother, Sarah. Emma could ride a horse, sweat, and get dirty. She did so when meeting with isolated clients in the mountains of the Hamilton Range southeast of Livermore. Joe was probably pleasantly surprised by that.

On November 30, 1940, they flew to Reno, Nevada, where they were married in the office of William McKnight, District Judge of Washoe County. Forgoing a honeymoon, they flew back on the same day. I don't think that either of them had ever flown in an airplane before. Joe was fifty-three and Emma twenty-nine. Despite their age difference, they had similar political and social views and a mutual empathy that allowed their dissimilar backgrounds to serve as complementary strengths rather than disruptive weaknesses. In addition to a mutual distaste for large weddings, they shared the same birthday, the fourth of May.

Both Emma and Joe were concerned about the appearance and propriety of Emma being the bank manager's wife while at the same time determining welfare relief eligibility for Valley residents, most of whom were also bank clients. The Charities Commission offered to assign Emma elsewhere in the Bay Area, but that would have entailed longer hours and a daily commute. In the end Emma conceded to the expected norm of those days. She resigned from her position at the Charities Commission and settled into Joe's Livermore home as a housewife.

During 1941 the couple plunged into one social event after another, from formal dinners, open houses, and cocktail parties to weekend trips and festivities at Castlewood Country Club (the William Randolph Hurst estate in Pleasanton). Joe's group of friends was much older, but for the most part they welcomed Emma graciously. However, full acceptance among the wives presented several challenges. For one thing, these rural women were masters of baking, broiling and stewing. They could dress and cook all manner of farm animals and wild game. Their pies, cakes and cookies were divine. Emma knew almost nothing about meal preparation and planning. She had always lived in a house with cooks and kitchen help. Her mother, Emma Regina, was a fine cook but had done little to teach Emma more than how to boil water.

Emma Barham and Joe Callaghan at the Golden Gate Exposition, 1939

Additionally, these Livermore Valley women sewed and knitted their own clothes, quilted, and when necessary, patched and mended the family wardrobe. Emma had never sewn a stitch in her life. There had always been seamstresses available in Piedmont. The Barham house did have a separate sewing room, but it was seldom occupied, other than by her mother's lady friends as they crocheted and gossiped in rocking chairs during afternoon tea.

With typical resolve, Emma set to work learning how to cook, sew and knit. Often she called on the phone or drove to Piedmont to get advice and assistance from her mother and the Piedmont household staff. Joe was a good natured "guinea-pig" for Emma's experimental cooking efforts. He once in later years confided in me that the effort "at times required some fortitude." His patience paid off, however. Within a few years Emma became a master cook and seamstress who could hold her own among the best. Joe loved cake, and for the rest of their married lives he could count on a freshly baked cake being under that stainless-steel cake dome on the kitchen sideboard.

Another challenge for Emma and Joe in the Livermore social circle had to do with differing political views. Most of the Valley's elite were large landholders and professionals who had been somewhat isolated from the Depression's social and economic impacts. They were politically conservative and detested President Roosevelt and his New Deal policies. Emma's family had always been Liberal Democrats, and her social work experiences had reinforced a belief in the necessity of government-sponsored welfare and assistance. Joe did his best to avoid any personal political nametag, but his childhood and work experience, coupled with his strong religious beliefs, gave him deep respect and concern for the "hard-working," the "underdog," and those "down-on-their-luck" through no fault of their own.

At social gatherings, Joe and Emma were forced to quietly endure verbal assaults on beliefs that they held dear, assaults from those they respected and people whose friendship they valued. After everyone had gone home, I can imagine my mother saying, "Joe, how can they not understand that if people are forced into poverty by conditions beyond their control, and if nothing is done about it, this country could have a revolution like they did in Russia? It happened there, and it can happen here. Roosevelt is just trying to do something about things before it's too late."

And I can imagine my father replying, "Thanks for keeping quiet, Emma. Politics is not something worth losing a friend over. They're good people. They just grew up with a silver spoon in their mouth and can't see beyond the hills of this Valley."

On December 7, 1941, everything changed forever. Like the rest of America, Joe and pregnant Emma sat by the radio listening to reports of the Japanese attack on Pearl Harbor and President Roosevelt's address to the nation as war was declared on Japan, Germany, and Italy. The Great Depression ended almost overnight. Joe's nephews, Art and Richard Deck, went off to war. Like others on the West Coast, Joe and Emma installed blackout curtains, as the possibility of enemy night air attacks loomed. They planted a vegetable garden to help with the war food production. Along with everyone else, they endured the rationing of everything from sugar and meat to eggs and gasoline. In addition to his work at the bank, Joe became Alameda County Chairman for the War Chest Campaign to sell war finance bonds.

A wave of anti-Japanese feeling spread across the nation, and on February 19, 1942, President Roosevelt signed Executive Order 9066 that forced all Japanese to evacuate the West Coast of the United States, irrespective of their immigration status, nationality, or loyalty to America. There was only one Japanese family in the Livermore Valley. Mr. George Yamauchi, his wife, Yoshi, their two children and aged parents farmed vegetables on leasehold land owned by a long-time Livermore resident named Gats Wagner.

Over the course of several years George Yamauchi had borrowed money from Joe's bank and had always made timely payments on his obligations. Their family grew produce that was sold in several Valley markets. They had never been anything but model citizens, and now they were being given thirty days to sell everything they owned and report with one suitcase each to a train in Oakland that would carry them to an internment camp in Colorado.

Irrespective of skin color, nationality, or religion, Joe judged a person's character based on three factors: Did they work hard, were they honest, and did they pay their bills? As far as he was concerned the Yamauchi family set an excellent example on all three counts, so Joe quickly and quietly set about protecting their interests. He personally paid off their bank loan and made an oral agreement with George to pay the money back whenever that was possible in the future. When the Yamauchi family left for Colorado, Joe put bank seals on their farm buildings and equipment, telling the community that the bank was owed money and was taking possession of buildings and equipment as collateral. By doing so, he prevented the vandalism and theft that certainly would have occurred, given the hostile tenor of the times. To help with the cold of Colorado, Emma knitted wool sweaters for the Yamauchi children and sent them frequent care packages that made their life a little brighter.

George and Yoishi Yamauchi, 1984

Three years later when the Yamauchi family returned, Joe had preserved almost everything at their farm and in their home. He had even managed to collect some revenue by subleasing some land to other farmers. Unfortunately, in the War's aftermath, anti-Japanese discrimination continued. Mr. Wagner refused to renew the Yamauchi's lease agreement, and stores refused to buy their produce. Much to Joe's sorrow, the Yamauchi family was forced to leave the Livermore Valley. They settled with other Japanese families in the Central Valley town of Lodi. There George became a successful businessman selling farm supplies and operating a labor camp for migratory farm workers. Each year without fail George and Yoshi Yamauchi arrived at our house bearing gifts of fruit and vegetables. After Joe's death, George and Yoshi continued to visit Emma, putting flowers on Joe's grave as they passed the cemetery. This annual Yamauchi pilgrimage continued until their old age made the trip impossible. My father never forgave Gats Wagner and certain people in Livermore for their treatment of the Yamauchi family.

*   *   *

In those months of world turmoil, I was growing, nestled comfortably in Mom's ever-expanding belly. Dad and Mom hoped that I might poke my head out sometime near the fourth of May. That way the three of us could have the same birthday. But for me, things were warm and cozy. I was in no hurry to exit into the bright unknown.

Mom and Dad had no idea whether I was a boy or a girl. In those days there was no way of telling ahead of time. Mom thought I would be a boy and favored the name Joseph. Dad favored the name Paul but bet one dollar with Mom that I'd be a girl. If that were the case, they agreed to call me Sharon. I was not given a vote on the matter.

In an effort to encourage my arrival, Dad regularly took Mom and I for a fast drive over the Seven Sisters. These seven adjacent hills made for quite a roller-coaster ride. I loved it. I'm pretty sure Mom didn't. Anyway, I remained ensconced well into spring, finally slithering into this world at eight thirty in the morning on Saturday, May 30, 1942, in St. Paul's Hospital, under the sure-handed guidance of Dr. Paul E. Dolan. He was the local doctor specializing in people; however, the community being small, he was equally adroit at doctoring farm animals should the need arise.

I'm told that I weighed something over eight pounds and had a huge earlobe on the left side. Mom was horrified. So much to my discomfort, Dr. Dolan cut it apart, giving me a smaller one. Circumcision was no fun either, but I guess in those days most boys had to go through that. Dad lost his bet as to my gender but got his way on the name Paul. Most people thought I was named after Dr. Dolan and the hospital. That was not true, though Mom and Dad never disabused anyone of the idea. Mom didn't have much breast milk, so I went on the bottle after only three weeks. That lack of breast-feeding and its associated maternal intimacy may have contributed to my detachment and reserve. I was not a hugger or toucher until I acquired those traits in later life.

Mom was thirty-one years old when I was born. She had no previous experience with babies, so the frequency of her long-distance phone calls to Grandma Barham in Piedmont grew exponentially, as did Dad's monthly phone bill. But Dad didn't seem to mind. He passed out cigars and proclaimed that he personally had closed every bank in America on the occasion of my birth. He was right about that, because May 30 was Memorial Day, a national holiday at the time. The gang of men at Dad's Wednesday night poker club put on a rousing party for us, presents and all. Mom and I left early. Dad stayed later for a few hands and a congratulatory drink or two.

Paul and Emma Callaghan, 1942

Over the next three years I grew pretty fast, oblivious to the war effort, rationing, war bonds, shortages, air raid alerts and blackouts. I had no idea that some things were not being made at all, such as automobiles, bicycles and typewriters. I was totally unaware that rationing stamps were required to purchase gasoline at 19 cents a gallon, bread at 9 cents a loaf, milk at 20 cents a quart, prime rib at 32 cents a pound, or that the average salary in America was $2,400 a year, the minimum wage 30 cents an hour, the national speed limit 35 miles an hour. I didn't realize that we had blackout blinds on our windows for fear of Japanese nighttime attacks. I just grew in my self-centered world while Mom washed a lot of dirty diapers and fed me copious amounts of Gerber and Heinz baby food, so much that I strenuously resisted switching to more substantial foods that required chewing. By fourteen months I was walking but at three years still sucking my thumb and clinging to my "baga," an old, worn-out diaper used for chewing and hugging.

In 1944 my cousin Randy Cramer came to live with us for six weeks while his brother, Jim Cramer, was being born. I remember nothing of Randy's visit, but Mom's notes in my baby book tell the story: "One continuous squabble, fought the whole time, Paul does not know how to play with other children. Want to forget the whole episode."

At the time I was also oblivious to current events that would significantly impact my future life. On February 17, US forces attacked Truk Lagoon, on June 15 they struck Saipan, and on July 2 they retook the island of Guam. In September of 1944, when Randy and I were being our most discordant, the battle for Palau began on the island of Peleliu. The US 1st Marine Division had seven thousand dead and wounded there. The Japanese defenders lost thousands more. The waters ran red with blood, and the mother of my future wife barely escaped through that violence and mayhem.

My earliest memory is of being in my highchair and looking out through the breakfast room window into the intersection where 4th and H Streets join Livermore Avenue. The street was filled with people. Some I recognized as neighbors; others I did not know. "Mommy," I said, "what are those people doing out there?"

She replied, "Paul dear, I hope you can remember this day for the rest of your life. They just announced on the radio that World War II is over. Everyone is celebrating." Whenever Mom called me "Paul dear," it usually marked something momentous or important, so although I was not quite three-and-a-half years old, I have never forgotten that scene.

* * *

During my first six years Dad spent less time with his golf and hunting and a lot of time with me. After work he sometimes took me to the train station to see the steam locomotives. I loved seeing the huge drive-wheels slowly begin to turn as the steam puffed and the smoke billowed. Dad knew some engineers and firemen. They sometimes hoisted me up into the cab where I sat in the engineer's chair and felt the heat from boiler fire. I even got to pull the whistle cord and ring the bell.

Another early memory is of sitting on Dad's shoulders as we watched the rodeo riders pass our house. The Livermore Rodeo had been held every June since 1918. My great uncle, John James Callaghan, was an original founder, and by the 1940s the Livermore Rodeo had become one of the largest such events in California. Dad was in charge of ticket sales. His records show that paid attendance ran well over fifteen thousand people in those years. On opening day, upwards of five hundred riders passed our house headed out Livermore Avenue to the rodeo grounds. Some Vaquero riders and their horses were adorned in silver from their stirrups to their sombreros. Sometimes they waved to me and made their horses walk sideways and bow. There were also horse drawn wagons and coaches, some with six horse teams. Rodeo weekends were exciting times. Dad and I each had silver banded, black cowboy hats, and Mom wore her cowgirl boots and riding pants with a silver belt buckle.

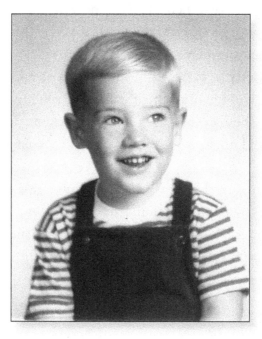

Paul Callaghan, 1945

In the later part of 1945, Dad bought from his brother and sisters their family home and the surrounding fifty acres of vineyard, barns and corrals. Uncle Ed, Aunt Julia and her sister Mayme had been living there, but Ed wasn't well and could no longer maintain the property. Dad paid him $15,000, and the three of them moved into a house at the corner of 5th and M Streets. Dad also paid $15,000 to Aunt Maud who lived in San Francisco, as well as $7,500 each to Art and Richard, the sons of his deceased sister, Florence. His oldest sister, Sadie, had joined the Dominican Order of nuns and taken an oath of poverty, so he donated a sizable sum to the Catholic Church in her name. Dad then sold the old family house and set about improving the remaining property. I haven't been inside that Callaghan house since Dad sold it, but it still exists as an Historic Site at 3062 East Avenue in Livermore.

Upon returning home after a full day's work at the bank, Dad frequently donned his work clothes and headed out to work at what we called "the ranch." Some afternoons and most weekends I accompanied him. In fact, until I started school, I went almost everywhere with Dad in his 1940, "four-on-the-floor" Ford pickup.

At the ranch he tore down the largest of two barns and all the corrals, leaving only one barn and two work sheds for storage of equipment and tools. I often played in the barn while he worked. There were many treasures in that place: drawers and shelves of nuts, bolts and screws; tools of every shape and size; anvils; vices; and a drill press with which I learned to drill holes in lots of things, much to Dad's periodic chagrin. Dad kept his tractor there too. I loved pretending to start the engine using the heavy metal crank on the front and then climbing up over the steel tracks to the operator's chair, where I imagined driving as I maneuvered the steering levers to-and-fro.

In the barn there was also a treadle-operated sharpening stone. By pumping the pedals, I could get the stone spinning at quite a clip. Sparks flew as I ground steel scraps. Once I did a superb job of grinding all the teeth off one of Dad's hand saws. He was not happy, and we agreed that from then on, I would consult with him before grinding.

Horse team harnesses hung on the barn walls. We didn't have any horses, but Dad explained to me how the various parts fit together on the horse's body and connected to the wagon. The barn also contained various machines for the capping, corking and labeling of bottles. Dad said they were used during prohibition when he had to make his own liquor. Although he never elaborated further, I suspect that he was involved in a level of production that far exceeded his personal needs.

It was scary fun to watch the black widow spiders that lived in the dark nooks and crannies. I was forbidden to play with them. But I poked them with sticks and fed them flies and ants when Dad wasn't around. I learned much about a lot of practical things while playing and watching Dad work on projects in and around that old barn.

There was a huge pepper tree that grew near the watering trough. It served no purpose and shed an abundance of seeds and leaves, so Dad wanted it gone. He worked for weeks digging a pit around the roots and removing branches. He then used a hand screw auger to drill a series of holes from the exposed roots up the trunk. With the help of some friends, he filled the holes with black powder and connected blasting caps and a fuse. When he lit off the charge, he made me stay far away in the cab of his pickup on 7th street. The resulting shock wave and mushroom cloud were impressive. Afterward I saw the tree split in half on its side, having been blasted completely out of the ground.

In 1947 Dad replanted half the vineyard with a German variety of Riesling grapes. One by one the old vines had to be pulled out and the remaining roots killed. The new rows were then marked and subsoiled. I rode with Dad on the tractor as it struggled in its lowest gear to pull that deep-subsoil knife through the gravelly ground. After the wild vines were planted and took root, each one had to be pruned and grafted with Riesling buds from the German cuttings. Then there was endless root maintenance with stinky carbon bisulfide, watering, fumigating, weeding, pruning and disking. Dad did it all after work and on weekends, with me tagging along.

In September of that year, I started kindergarten at the public grammar school on 5th street. I recall the experience as not being completely comfortable. For some reason I felt a bit different from the other kids, not a lot different, just not quite in sync with everyone else. For one thing, I had seldom before associated with children my age; for another, the school was just a block from our house, so unlike the others, I walked home for lunch. Also, I was far sighted and the only one of my classmates to wear glasses. Moreover, I was not by nature a competitive person, often deferring to others and not uncomfortable playing alone. Perhaps my uneasiness was mostly in my head. My classmates never seemed to notice, and I have no memory of bad treatment. Other than a sense of not quite fitting in, my only substantive memory of kindergarten is walking around a maypole holding colored streamers. I certainly had no inkling that twenty-three more years of education were in store for me.

*   *   *

I was allowed to ride my tricycle and scooter unattended, so long as I didn't cross any streets and let Mom know when I departed and returned. That meant that I was restricted to the sidewalks of our block, bordered on four sides by 4th, 5th, H and I Streets. Along that route I had several regular stops. Next door lived the Mahovich family. Their son, Butch, was four years older than me and sometimes tolerated my presence when he was home from school. The walls of his bedroom were plastered with pictures of fighter and bomber aircraft, and models of Japanese Zeros and flying tiger P-40s hung from his ceiling as if they were engaged dogfights. I loved visiting his room, and Mrs. Mahovich could usually be counted on for a cookie on days when Butch was away at school. Another regular stop on my route around the block was Mrs. Walters. Her contribution to my wellbeing frequently consisted of angel food cake with vanilla frosting.

In the event that neither of these two regular stops answered their doorbells, my depressed blood-sugar and dopamine levels dictated that I break the rules and scurry across I Street to visit Mrs. Tubbs. Frieda Tubbs was the sister of Dad's friend Ernest Wente. She really liked me and could almost always be counted on for tasty edibles. I liked her too. She had the reddest rouge-colored cheeks and talked to me as if I were a grownup. In the event that Mrs. Tubbs wasn't home, all bets for food were off, because my next stop was at the home of her neighbor, Mr. Hampson. He was an interesting widower who could usually be found tinkering in his workshop, but he was not a reliable source of food.

Joseph H. Hampson was a retired civil engineer who had spent his career in design, construction and maintaining of the Hetch Hetchy Project, a two-hundred-mile-long aqueduct system that supplies water from the Sierra Nevada mountains to cities in the San Francisco Bay area. His wife had died when I was quite young, so he was a frequent dinner guest at our house. Mr. Hampson traveled a lot and brought presents for me: a boomerang from Australia, a shark's tooth from Tahiti, a boar's tusk from New Guinea. He spent a year in his workshop building a forty-inch-high scale model of a sailing sloop as a present for me. The hull was hand carved from a block of redwood. The keel was of steel and lead, the rigging of nylon cord. Mom sewed the sails from tough linen cloth. The result was a beautiful craft with teak-colored deck, white sides and a red waterline. It even included a cradle for display in my bedroom.

The problem was, where to sail her? Lake Merritt in Oakland would have been most appropriate, but that was a far drive, so Dad suggested a seepage pond at the bottom of an abandoned gravel quarry owned by the Kaiser Sand and Gravel Company. On the appointed day, the three of us drove to the quarry. Neither Dad nor I knew anything about sailing, and I suspect neither did Mr. Hampson. When we launched the boat, she kept turning into the wind until her sails luffed and she drifted back to shore. Dad and Mr. Hampson then fiddled with the rudder and mainsheet before launching her again. This time she took off, quartering into the wind like a true sailing ship. Across the pond she flew, straight as an arrow. I was so excited—that is, until she hit the cliff, bowsprit first, on the opposite side of the quarry. There she remained, becalmed, with no possibility of retrieval. The two adults were completely unprepared, having apparently not considered this possibility. I became a bit emotional. My sailboat was lost. As he always did, Dad fixed things. Striping down to his jockstrap, he dogpaddled to her rescue. He wasn't a good swimmer. That sailboat never again sailed and never received a name. When I left for college, she still resided on her cradle in my bedroom. Her subsequent disposition is a mystery. I hope she found a home with people who knew how to sail her.

Of course, my neighborhood forays were in time reported to my parents, and Mom took steps to curtail the frequency of my visits. "Paul dear, we don't want you to become a neighborhood pest. You may visit the neighbors only once each week. Ring the doorbell once. If they don't respond, leave immediately. If they do respond, politely ask if you are disturbing them. Never enter unless you are invited to do so, and under no circumstances ask for food. If they offer something to eat you may accept; otherwise, do not bring up the subject of food, and do not overstay your welcome. Whenever they appear busy, you thank them and leave. Oh! Look both ways and be careful when you cross I Street. If you ever go further than Joe Hampson's house, you're in big trouble."

I tried to follow Mom's instructions. The part about not mentioning food was the most difficult.

* * *

In those days Dad regularly listened on the radio to the Friday Night Fights while lying on his bed in the dark. I often snuck into the bedroom and lay beside him with my head on his arm. Usually I went to sleep before the fight was over, but one Friday night in December of 1947 things were different. The next day I was scheduled to have my tonsils removed at the hospital. Mom and Dad had said it would be an easy thing, but I wasn't so sure and a bit anxious.

As I settled down beside Dad, I heard the bell ending the round. That meant I could talk. Dad didn't like me talking unless it was between rounds. "Who's fighting?" I asked.

"Oh, they just finished the eighth round. It's the heavy weight championship. Joe Louis, the champion, is fighting a guy named Jersey Joe Walcott."

"Who's winning?" I asked.

"Well, it sounds to me like Walcott has gotten the best of it so far. But you can never count Joe Louis out. He's knocked out a lot of men in the later rounds." Just then the bell rang again. I knew it was time to be quiet.

When the next round ended, I mustered the courage to say, "Daddy, I'm scared about tomorrow. Will it hurt a lot?"

"Don't you worry son," he said, "It might be a little hard to swallow for a couple of days afterward, but nothing more than that. You're a big man. I know you'll do just fine. Doctor Dolan said I can be in the operating room with you. Everything will be okay. Don't worry."

"Will they put me to sleep?" I asked. "I'm really afraid if they put me to sleep."

"Don't worry. They're not going to put you to sleep," he said just as the bell rang for the next round.

Of course, the next day they did put me to sleep. It was my first realization that people do lie, even trusted parents. I was incredulous. How could my daddy have lied to me? It concerned me more than the lingering sore throat from the tonsillectomy. At the time I didn't realize it, but this incident marked the end of my infancy and the beginning of childhood. Never again would I hold absolute certainty and trust in the assertions of others.

*   *   *

I entered Sister Angelica's first grade class at St. Michael's Convent School in the fall of 1948. Dad was a devout but liberal Catholic, who felt that the nuns could provide me with a superior level of religious training, moral character and self-discipline. Mom was not a proponent of any religion and had attended church only for a brief period in her youth when she was baptized a Unitarian. At the time she married Dad, she was very much an agnostic and would have been happy to see me attend public school. However, in March of 1945 they had solemnized their civil marriage before a Catholic priest at Corpus Christy Church in Piedmont. Among other things, Mom had promised the priest to raise me a Catholic, and my parents had agreed that the first eight years of my education would be in Catholic school. After that, Mom could influence my educational choices in whatever way she wished.

Mom took such agreements seriously. I doubt the priest or Dad had any idea how fervently she would fulfill her promise to raise me a Catholic. When I started school, she immediately joined the St. Michael's Mothers' Club and began studying Catholic history, doctrine and liturgy. As one of the most well-educated mothers, her liberal influence at times proved exasperating to the nuns. She was instrumental in organizing the mothers' lobby for less restrictive uniform requirements, coeducational activities, and tuition subsidies for low-income parishioners. She organized weekly hot dog and spaghetti feeds that raised money for school supplies and provided petty cash for the nuns' personal needs. One of her most laudable accomplishments was the establishment of professionally taught weekly dancing lessons, during which the St. Michael's boys and girls were allowed to actually touch each other.

In those days the Catholic Mass and liturgical rituals were conducted in Latin. Being a Latin and Greek major, Mom knew every word. To their consternation she at times corrected the pronunciation of our Irish priests, and it wasn't long before she became the unofficial Latin tutor for several prospective altar boys. In later life I discovered that she had, on several occasions, corresponded with the Archdiocesan Bishop regarding matters having to do with St. Michael's School and the Livermore Parish.

I heard Dad and Mom talking after dinner one night. Dad was saying, "Emma, just let it go. It's not worth the effort. They're going to send those Christmas seals home with those children no matter what you think or do."

"I don't care, Joe. It's wrong. They send home those Christmas labels, envelopes and pledge cards with every child and require them to return at least five dollars. Some families can't afford five dollars, so their kids go door to door selling Christmas Seals. Of course, the kids go straight away to neighbors who find it difficult to say no, even though they may not want to support the Catholic Church. I don't want Paul knocking on the doors of our neighbors. They won't feel they can say no to him, especially because of your position in the community. It just isn't right. And on top of that, the nuns give prizes to the kids who sell the most, so every child is out there ringing doorbells. Three children came by our front door after school today."

"All right, Emma," said Dad, "I see your point. I'll give Paul five dollars, and I'll explain why we don't want him selling door to door. But please don't storm over to St. Michael's and unload on Sister Allice or Father O'Donnell. They're just doing what the Diocese tells them to do. And please, no letters to the bishop."

Mom's full involvement in my Catholic education was, on the whole, beneficial; however, at times her participation was embarrassing. For example, our family pew in St. Michael's Church was located well toward the front, near a stained-glass window that had been donated by my grandma, Sarah. Everyone could see us as we walked down the center aisle to get there. On Sundays Mom regularly attended Mass with Dad and me. She said it was her responsibility to do so as part of her agreement to raise me as a Catholic.

It was normal practice for parishioners entering the church to bless themselves with holy water from the fonts by the door, to walk up the center aisle and genuflect before entering their pew, and then to kneel for some time before sitting. My mom did none of that. She did not bless herself with holy water, she did not genuflect when entering the pew, and she did not kneel or stand. In fact, she did nothing but sit for the entire service, irrespective of what the rest of the congregation did. I was mortified by her behavior, feeling throughout the whole Mass that every eye was upon us. Why couldn't my mother act like the other mothers and the nuns who were sitting just across the aisle?

From her sitting position, she ensured that I paid attention, did not fidget, and was opened to the proper page of my daily missal. When we returned home, she quizzed me about the messages of the gospel and homily. Only much later in life did I realize that this period of embarrassment was actually a time of teaching. Mom was showing me that it's all right to be different. It's all right to stand up (or in this case sit down) for strongly held beliefs, even if you are a minority of one, so long as you do it with dignity and respect for the beliefs of others. Mahatma Gandhi was one of her most admired heroes.

Chapter 3

Saint Michael's

Despite an inkling that this might be a dream, it seemed so real that I allowed it to continue. On the schoolyard's asphalt court, Mom and Sister Alice were playing a furious, one-on-one game of basketball. Mom's defense was spectacular. Sister Alice was becoming increasingly frustrated. As they twisted and turned, Sister's belted rosary beads struck Mom again and again. Blood ran down Mom's face and arms, but her focus never faltered. Sister Alice was unable to break through for a clean shot, not on Mom's watch … One side of the volleyball court was lower than the other. Players on the downhill side faced black lettering on the net that read "Culpa" (guilt or fault). The uphill side players faced lettering in gold that read "Virtus" (virtue). The downhill players had their feet shackled … The unfenced, weed-filled baseball field with its dilapidated wooden backstop was occupied by a single player at home plate. He hit rocks into the outfield in an attempt to strike a stray dog …

I had reached the head of the challengers' line and would next face Richie Rochin, as soon as he dispensed with Tommy Boggini. Richie was "king of the hill" at tetherball and, for that matter, every other sport. Boggini lasted less than a minute. When I stepped into his place, Richie hammered the ball. It flew erratically at me. I missed. Richie hammered it again and again as the rope wound round and round the pole just above my reach. Those in line chided, "Hey, Mayor Plumpfront, four-eyes. Can't you jump?" Back at the end of the line I hid my hurt. I hated to be called Mayor Plumpfront, a character from the afternoon radio show, *Big John and Sparky*. Why did I have to wear glasses, be fat and uncoordinated, the first to sit down in spelling bees, unable to read aloud? The two boys in front of me turned to leer. One said, "Look at him. He's such a loser. Let's see if he can cry." I broke for the safety of Sister Redempta's classroom door, but try as I would, my legs could only move in slow motion. At any second, those boys would be on me. Oh! God help …

The faint light from the hallway reflected through my open bedroom door. Dad's silhouette was saying, "Time to wake up, little man. It's six o'clock, and Mass starts at seven. Breakfast's ready."

A bad dream, I thought. My heart was pounding.

"I'm awake," I said. "Don't turn on the light, Dad. I'll get up."

"All right, son. Hurry up. It's warm in the kitchen."

My parents never heated the house at night, and each morning it took several hours for the hot water radiators to warm February's cold. I climbed out from under my covers and hurried into the salt and pepper corduroy pants, blue shirt, and dark blue V-neck sweater of my St. Michael's School uniform.

Feeling for the rosary beads in my pocket, I stepped into the dim hallway and hurried toward the far end where light flooded through the opaque glass of the kitchen door. I dared not look back, but my senses were attuned to what lurked there. The source of my fear was Eddie, who was somehow embodied in a grotesquely carved wooden chair that occupied the guest room at the far end of the hallway. From its place at a writing table, the chair-back faced directly down the hall. I was certain it was alive, and at times I had seen it move. Now I could feel its evil eyes watching my back from the darkness.

I can't remember how that chair became known as Eddie. Perhaps my father christened it. His brother, Ed, had died recently. In any case, I had been afraid of that chair for as long as I could remember. When I was little, I couldn't enter the hallway without accompaniment. Lately Mom and Dad had been helping me to overcome my fear. They stood at the kitchen door with words of encouragement as I faced Eddie and walked down the hall to my room. It was becoming easier. In daylight I could now do it on my own, but I still had trouble when it was dark and my back was turned, like now.

With relief, I reached the crystal knob on the kitchen door and entered into warmth and safety. The windows were steamy from the percolating coffee pot. Dad was using a bread knife to saw chunks from a stale loaf of French bread.

"Good morning, little man," he said. "Your cereal and toast are on the table. Do you want orange juice or milk or both?"

"Can I have hot chocolate?" I asked.

"Sure, but it'll take me a minute or two, so go ahead and get started."

I took my seat at the dining room table, poured some cream from the creamer, applied a couple of heaping teaspoons of sugar, and devoured the bowl of banana-topped Cheerios. I didn't care for bananas, but I knew better than to complain. "Eat what's put in front of you. Bananas are healthy for a growing boy," would certainly have been the response. Dad made breakfast. Mom usually stayed in bed until after I left for school, but sometimes she'd get up and cook something special, like hotcakes.

About the time I finished the cereal, Dad brought my chocolate along with his two bowls of black coffee and hunks of stale bread. He drank his coffee in bowls, saying how he didn't like hot coffee, it cooled faster in bowls, and he didn't see how Mom could stand drinking that boiling hot stuff.

"Well, little man," he said as he sat down. "It's six thirty. That gives you half an hour before Mass begins. Who's the priest this week?"

"I think it's Father Hennessy," I said.

"Ah, Five-Star Hennessy," he muttered. I had no idea what that meant, but in later years I understand that Five-Star Hennessy is a top-of-the-line brandy.

"Who's serving with you?" he continued.

"David," I replied. David Dutro was one of my two best friends. Leo Andersen was the other. We were altar boys and frequently served at the 7:00 a.m. weekday Mass before school. Mom had taught us the Latin responses. She knew Latin and Greek and Catholic Church history better than the priests or nuns. She had also translated some songs in our hymnal so that my friends and I might know what we were singing. Such efforts were usually accompanied by her declaration, "By God, no one will ever accuse me of not doing my best to raise you as a Catholic."

Dad dunked his bread into the coffee. I did the same, dunking my toast into the chocolate. Mom would have reminded us that dunking was impolite and that under no circumstances should it be done in public or at someone else's house. She would also have reminded Dad that he was setting a bad example. But Mom was not here, so we guys could act as we pleased.

"You've only got twenty minutes, little man," said Dad. "Finish up. Don't forget to brush your teeth, and don't forget your catechism."

At that moment my heart sank. I realized that I had left the catechism on the writing table in the guest room—behind Eddie! Every evening after the dishes were done, Mom helped me with homework in the guest room. Last night

Mom had been quizzing me on catechism questions. When we came to the last question, "Can non-Catholics go to heaven?", the answer of course was "No." I knew that question and answer would upset Mom, and it did. It bothered me too. It seemed unfair that my mother couldn't go to heaven, but I put it out of my mind and hurriedly went to my room, forgetting the catechism. Now, in order to retrieve it, I had to walk the entire length of the hall, right up to Eddie.

"Dad, will you watch me go down the hall?" I asked.

"You don't need me to do that, son. Just leave the kitchen door open and turn on the hall lights. I'll be right here. You can call to me if you have a problem. That's just a chair, son. It can't hurt you. You know that," he said.

With determination I started down the hallway. The lights made it easier, but Eddie was ahead, staring at me from the grayness of the guest room. I passed my parents' room and the dining room entrance and the entrance to my room, all the time getting closer to that evil chair. As I passed the wall niche that held the telephone, I realized that the kitchen door behind me was slowly closing. I had forgotten to secure it to the baseboard latch. My connection to Dad and the kitchen was being cut off. The guest room door and Eddie were now only twenty feet in front of me. The carved eyes were burning into my chest; my heart was thumping.

The bathroom on the right offered sanctuary. Rationalizing the need for personal hygiene, I ducked through the doorway to safety. There I brushed my teeth, combed my flat top using Pomade, urinated, anything to delay the inevitable faceoff with Eddie.

It wasn't long before Dad's voice resounded down the hall. "You better get going, son. You'll be late for Mass."

He must be standing in the kitchen doorway, I thought. I bounded into the hallway, ran into the guest room without looking at Eddie, grabbed the catechism, and ran back down the hall to the kitchen.

"Good! You made it," said Dad. "Here's your lunch." He handed me a paper bag with my name written on it. "Do you have two-bits for milk?" he asked.

"Yes, and I've got a dime for licorice at recess," I replied.

"Good. Have a nice day, son; say a prayer for me at Mass, and say hello to Sister Zita when you see her."

"I will, Dad," I said as I hurried out the back door into the frosty cold dawn.

*   *   *

35

Running the two blocks on 4th Street to St. Michael's Church, I entered the sacristy with five minutes to spare and hurriedly pulled on my cassock and surplice. David had already prepared the altar. Father Hennessy in his vestments faced the credence praying. We stood behind him waiting. When he turned toward us, he looked at me. With a friendly Irish smile and a slight brogue, he said, "Paul, it surely would be nice if-yu'd get here a wee-bit earlier from now on."

"Yes, Father," I replied, my head bent in humility.

We followed him out into the sanctuary and took our places kneeling on the bottom step of the altar. David had the bell side. That meant he served the wine and rang the bell. I served the water. Father Hennessy liked a full chalice of wine and a drop or two of water. He always consumed the entire contents before Mass ended.

During communion I was responsible for holding the gold inlaid paten-plate under the chin of each communicant as Father placed an unleavened wafer of eucharist bread on their outstretched tongues. To my knowledge, no wafer or crumb had ever fallen off onto the paten, so as we moved along the line of communicants my attention drifted to other matters. We altar boys kept a running dialogue among ourselves as to the color and shape of parishioners' tongues. Mr. Kelly's tongue was a horrible purple color. Mrs. Mahovich's had arguably the reddest tongue. There was a clear consensus that Mr. Raboli had by far the longest tongue. However, as yet there was no agreement on the fattest tongue, the largest mouth, or the worst breath. The distinction of most gold teeth was also as yet unresolved, although, in my opinion, Mr. Concannon was well in the lead.

Father Hennessy and I moved methodically down the rail of kneeling communicants. Tongue after tongue protruded and retracted, taking with it the body of Christ, my paten firmly placed under each chin. When we reached Mr. Sweeny the aroma of liquor was quite apparent. His protruding tongue shook a bit. Father placed the wafer and muttered the obligatory, "Corpus Christi." For a moment Mr. Sweeny delayed retracting his tongue. When he finally did so, the wafer caught on his upper front tooth and flipped into the air, landing on the edge of my paten. There it teetered for an instant before dropping to the red carpet. My heart pounded.

Father Hennessy had already moved on to the next gaping face. When my paten failed to appear under that chin, he turned his attention back toward me. Mr. Sweeny was rising to leave, having no idea that he had not retained the body of Christ. I was frozen in place and mortified beyond expression. The Eucharist, the Body of Jesus, had fallen to the unclean rug. It was my fault—no doubt a sacrilegious mortal sin. Overcome with guilt, I had no idea what to do. I just stood there and pointed at the wafer on the rug. Once Father Hennessy realized what had happened, he bent over, picked up the wafer, and popped it into his own mouth. We then proceeded onward down the rail of communicants, as if nothing had happened.

I was sure that I'd get a scolding after Mass. During the closing prayers I knelt on the hard altar steps and prayed fervently for God's forgiveness. He apparently heard me. Nothing was ever said by Father Hennessy or anyone, save for David, who spread the word among the altar boys. This disclosure brought me some temporary notoriety among a peer group in which I was normally quite inconspicuous.

*   *   *

When I emerged from sacristy into the sunlight, I noted that the student Safety Patrol, with stop signs and police whistles, was still on duty at the intersection. Wishing to avoid their slow procedures I hurried directly across the street toward the schoolyard. Upon reaching the curb I saw Sister Zita, standing at the schoolyard gate waiting to intercept tardy students. She had seen me, so there was no choice but to proceed.

As I approached, she said, "Master Paul, do you not understand that jaywalking is both against the law and dangerous?"

"Yes, Sister," I said. "I'm sorry. I was in a hurry to get to assembly."

Looking me straight in the eyes while holding me at arm's length, one hand on each of my shoulders, she said, "I'm sure you've heard that haste makes waste. Don't let me see you do that again, or I'll have to inform Sister Alice."

Everyone was afraid of the principal, Sister Alice, but I wasn't afraid of Sister Zita. Her words were sometimes gruff, but I knew she liked me. She wasn't a teacher like the other nuns. She often had yard duty during recess and frequently worked in the bookstore, where she sometimes gave me a piece of licorice on days when I forgot my money.

"Come here," she said, pulling me to her and giving me a big hug. "How's your dad?"

"He's fine," I said. "He said to say hello."

"God bless him. Say hello to him from me too. Now you'd better get a move on."

I was unaware at the time that Sister Zita was actually my aunt, my father's eldest sister, Sadie. My parents' decision not to tell me was probably well advised. Had I known, I likely would have bragged to my classmates and perhaps put Sister Zita in a difficult position.

The bell had rung and students were already assembled by grade, gender, and height on the asphalt-covered playground in front of the flag pole. I stepped into my regular place among the fourth-grade boys, behind Tommy Boggini and in front of Richard Flanagan.

The area where we stood was fenced and contained the usual playground equipment in addition to bicycle racks and drinking fountains. The restrooms were separated, boys at one end of the yard and the girls at the other. Along the back fence was a row of picnic tables to accommodate student lunches. Other than ice cream and candy from the bookstore, there was no food service. Everyone brought their own lunch. Girls and uncool boys used lunch boxes and thermoses. Cool guys rode their bikes to school and brought their lunch in brown paper bags. Mom and Dad said I could ride my bike when I got into fifth grade.

We stood at attention while the flag was hoisted by members of the Safety Patrol. Patrol members, fifth graders and above, no girls allowed, were responsible for directing pedestrian traffic at the intersections in front of the school. They got out of class early to do their work, and they wore yellow insignia on their sweaters that showed their rank. I hoped to join the Patrol when I reached the fifth grade.

As the flag hit the top of the mast, Sister Alice conducted our rendition of the national anthem followed by the Pledge of Allegiance. She then made a few announcements while other nuns inspected our ranks for uniform and hygiene infractions. The only announcement worth noting was that the bookstore would be closed today during recess. Alas, I would have to forego my Big Hunk candy bar.

When Sister Alice blew her police whistle, we marched single file, boys first, up the stairs of the Dominican convent toward Sister Redempta's fourth-grade classroom, a place where I excelled at almost nothing. I could hardly read. My spelling was atrocious. My long division and multiplication were labored. I couldn't hear pitch or understand musical notation. My handwriting was acceptable so long as one ignored the spelling.

As to strengths, I had reasonably good deportment, proper speech and annunciation, and a relatively accomplished vocabulary. That was because Mom had read to me every night since I could remember. I loved the books she read, things like *The Wind in the Willows, Little Lord Fauntleroy, Deer Slayer*, and *Last of the Mohicans*. She made sure that I understood all the words. When I didn't, her explanations entailed profuse synonyms and a discourse on Latin or Greek derivations.

Whenever I was called upon to read aloud in class, my heart raced so fast that I could barely see the page, let alone the words. During reading sessions, Sister usually called on students in front and then worked her way back. I sat near the back wall. While awaiting my turn, I tried to anticipate and review those paragraphs that would most likely fall to me. That task required constant adjustment as those ahead of me read more or less. By the time my turn arrived, I'd paid no attention to the story, the plot, the characters, or anything else. If my calculations proved faulty, I was forced to read an unprepared passage, having no feeling for its context. My reading aloud was so torturous for everyone, including Sister Redempta, that I was sometimes skipped over or given a short paragraph or asked a vocabulary definition, which I was fortunate to almost always know.

Sister Redempta was a patient, kindly old lady with years of teaching experience, but like other Dominican nuns, she could be intimidating in her black and white habit with its black leather belt, from which hung a fifteen-decade-long rosary and an oversized crucifix. The black glass beads of Sister's rosary made a tinkling noise that gave warning of her approach. She maintained absolute order. Anyone who misbehaved was sent to Sister Alice, who doled out corporal punishment with Little Nellie, a foot-long wooden ruler, or Big Nellie, a stiff yardstick.

I was not a trouble maker and never visited Sister Alice. My difficulties were mostly to do with reading and spelling, but in general I was a slow learner. The other students seemed not to notice, a circumstance for which I was thankful. My parents hired a tutor, a spinster school teacher, Delya Lord Davis, who lived next door to our house along with her lifelong companion, Mildred Lovell, also a school teacher. Delya Lord pounded phonetics and grammar rules into my head to such an extent that I could sound out most words if given enough time. Unfortunately, phonetics seemed of little use when it came to spelling. I once wrote an entire essay using the letters "ov" in place of the preposition "of." I often "fot" the good "fite"; tied the "not"; played in the "gras" among the "leves"; lived in a "dreme"; and ate when it was time to "ete."

Choir practice presented additional challenges. I loved listening to music, and I liked to sing, once I had memorized the words. Sadly, I was a slow memorizer, and to make matters worse, our hymnal was configured so that the lyrics were separated into syllables, each relating to musical notes on the staff above. I simply could not sound out the syllables fast enough or recognize the words in time to keep up with the music; furthermore, it didn't help that most lyrics were in Latin. Over time I became adept at appearing to sing when I was not.

I had difficulty memorizing multiplication tables and was slow at addition and subtraction. Long division, which we were arduously learning, required a considerable amount of all three procedures. We were forbidden under pain of a knuckle lashing to count on our fingers, so I devised a secret way of counting in my head that did not involve any finger motion. Sister never knew. My way was accurate, but not fast.

Catherine Ferrario sat two rows in front of me. I had been in love with her since the second grade, but she never knew, and by now it was clear that she didn't care to know. In second and third grades we had been about the same height. Now she was taller than I—not a good situation. She got top grades. I almost never did. I wasn't good enough at anything to impress her, or any girl for that matter, so I gave up and busied myself as an altar boy, a Boy Scout, a friend to all and enemy of none.

My parents were undoubtably concerned about my reading difficulties, but they never once let me feel that any of it was my fault. If there was fault it lay with the nuns who persisted in using sight-reading methods instead of phonics. I was always told that I was as smart or smarter than the other kids, so I pressed on, coping as best I could without any major self-esteem problems.

Against all professional advice, Mom continued to read to me, so my vocabulary continued to improve. Over time my reading did get a bit better thanks to Delya Lord's phonetics, and I learned tricks about how to hide my weaknesses and emphasize my strengths. Another thing that I had going for me, but didn't realize it at the time, was that my father was the local banker, a stalwart community citizen and a large church contributor. Also, Mom gave the nuns no leeway and was probably the bane of their existence. Against their wishes, she sometimes took me out of school for reasons that she considered important, like the symphony in San Francisco, theater performances in Berkeley, trips to the desert, a week of snow skiing in winter. Sister Alice tangled with Mom several times on issues like coeducational dancing lessons and gender inclusive class parties. Sister Alice did not come out well. Mom didn't tolerate foolishness on the part of those she felt should know better. Anyway, to my knowledge, Mom had not lately caused any ripples in the placid order of Dominican pedagogy. I learned the word pedagogy from my Grandpa Barham, who had been a teacher before becoming a banker.

Upon taking my seat in the classroom, the day began as usual, the first subject being religion. Sister read questions from the catechism. When called upon, we each stood beside our desk and recited the answer verbatim as memorized. In short order she called upon me. That was good. I hated the suspense of waiting.

"Paul Callaghan, please stand."

"Yes, Sister," I replied as I stood up, my left hand subconsciously fiddling with the empty inkwell that occupied the upper right corner of the desk.

"Please stop playing with your inkwell," she demanded.

I jerked my hand back beside my body and waited.

"What is actual sin?" she asked, her gaze locked upon me like a raptor intent upon its prey.

"Actual sin is any willful thought, word, deed, or omission contrary to the law of God," I replied

"How many kinds of actual sin are there?" she probed.

"There are two kinds of actual sin—mortal sin and venial sin," I responded.

"And what is mortal sin?" Her eyes flashed to my hand, which was again moving toward the inkwell.

Quickly reacting, hands to my side, I answered, "Mortal sin is a grievous offense against the law of God."

"And why is this sin called mortal?" she continued.

This was a hard question, but last night Mom had helped me to memorize it, even though I could tell that she wasn't happy about the words. "This sin is called mortal because it deprives us of spiritual life, which is sanctifying grace, and it brings everlasting death and damnation on the soul. When the soul is sent to Hell it is dead forever, because never again will it be able to do a single meritorious act."

"Very good, Paul. So what things are necessary to make a sin mortal?" quarried Sister.

"To make a sin mortal three things are necessary: a grievous matter, sufficient reflection, and full consent of the will," I replied.

"And before you sit down, what does the word grievous mean?"

"It means very bad or serious. My mother says that it probably comes from a French word that is based on the Latin word 'gravis,' which means heavy or weighty."

"All right, Paul, thank you. That'll be enough. You may sit down. Next, Richard Burk …"

Sister apparently didn't appreciate my elaboration regarding the origin of grievous, but at least now I could relax for the rest of religion period. I was off the hook for today. Sister never called on anyone twice, especially if they had answered properly.

I drifted into a daydream about trout fishing. We had a cabin on the North Fork of the Feather River. My grandma had taught me to trout fish, and last Christmas she had given me a fly-tying vice and a kit of materials to make my own fishing flies. I envisioned my grey hackle fly with its yellow body, floating just in front of that red rock in the river below our cabin. As the current was about to carry it around the rock there was a flash of gold and silver. The surface broke beside the fly. I jerked and felt the rod tip bend as the hooked fish dove for cover. The fight was on. I stripped line to get the proper tension. The fish, at least a two-pound rainbow, remained in front of the rock for only an instant as it came to grips with its predicament. Then it headed straight for submerged willows that protruded from the opposite bank. I couldn't let it reach those willows or it would surely tangle the line and escape. There was no choice but to apply more pressure than the three-pound monofilament leader was designed to accommodate. At that instant, the fish jumped, flipped in midair, and ran down stream to a deep pool. I followed over the slippery wet rocks while trying to maintain tension on the line …

"Paul Callaghan," Sister was saying, "can you help Kirsten with her answer?"

She was calling on me again. She never did that. Panicked, I stood up and said, "I'm sorry, Sister, I didn't hear the question."

Her eyes dug into me. "Attention is required during the entire religion class, not just when you are asked to recite. Stop fiddling with your ink well!" I jerked my hand to my side. She continued. "The question to Kirsten was, 'Which are the chief sources of sin?' Can you help Kirsten with the answer?"

There was a moment of uneasy silence while I gathered my thoughts and shifted into rote memory mode. Kirsten stood by her desk, facing me with a scowl that Sister Redempta couldn't see. "The chief sources of sin are seven in number: pride, covetousness, lust, anger, gluttony, envy, and sloth; they are commonly called capital sins," I answered.

"Good. Can you help Kirsten with the meaning of sloth?"

"All I can remember is that sloth is like laziness," I said.

Sister was less than pleased. "Catherine Ferrario, can you help Kirsten and Paul with the meaning of the word sloth?"

Catherine stood and faced both Kirsten and I. Without missing a beat, she said, "Sloth is committed when we idle our time and are lazy; when we are indifferent about serving God; when we do anything slowly and poorly and in a way that shows we would rather not do it. They are slothful who lie in bed late in the morning and neglect their duty. Slothful people are often untidy in their personal appearance, and they're nearly always in misery and want, unless somebody else takes care of them."

Catherine was so smart and so beautiful. I really didn't mind being corrected by her. In fact, my day was the better for it.

"Thank you, Catherine," said Sister. "Now the three of you may sit. And Paul, pay attention during the entire religion class, and while you're at it, reflect on the meaning of sloth to see if it might apply in any way to you."

That directive did provoke my serious reflection and concern, since one of Mom's friends often called me "lead butt," in reference to my sometimes less than energetic behavior.

* * *

After religion class, Sister passed out the results from last month's reading and vocabulary tests. My reading comprehension was scored at second grade level. During the allotted time I had managed to read only five of twenty-four readings. It was at least somewhat consoling that I had not missed any questions on the material that I managed to read. Time was the problem. If I were allowed more time, I was sure I could do better. Whenever I tried to rush, things got all confused.

As to vocabulary, I missed five out of fifty words. That was a twelfth-grade level according to the score sheet. I was pretty sure I was the highest in the class. Sister never mentioned class rankings, but I had overheard Catherine and some other girls comparing notes. None of them were close to twelfth-grade level. Even so, it was irritating to note that my reading and spelling problems caused me to miss two vocabulary words that I actually knew. When Sister went over the list, she pronounced the word faux pas as "fō ˈpä" and the word elite as "əˈlēt." The minute I heard them I knew their meanings. Faux pas was a mistake, and elite meant high class or important. Mom often used both those words.

Using Delya Lord's phonetics, it had sounded to me like "fox paw" might be a name for a plant or flower, or an animal print in the snow, or a smart move in chess. Foxes were thought to be smart characters. Based on phonetics the word "elite" sounded like it should mean to step down or land. It was disheartening to miss vocabulary words that I knew just because I couldn't read them properly.

Such was life in the fourth grade, and for that matter the fifth, sixth, seventh and eighth grades as well. I never felt completely accepted by the group, yet I never felt completely unaccepted. I was different but not enough different to be bullied or ostracized. Of course, I wanted to be like everyone else, and I worked hard at it.

*   *   *

In the fourth grade there was one person who was enough different to be ostracized and bullied. His name was Elbert R. Jepsen. He was a slow learner, probably not much slower than I, but somehow less able to cover it up. One day five or six of us boys were eating lunch at a table near the schoolyard fence. Elbert ate alone at a nearby table. Some in our group started teasing him. I no longer remember what was said or who said it, but as the heckling continued Elbert became increasingly red-faced and agitated. Our group ended up following him around the school yard yelling "Red Hot Fire Engine," which drove him to be more upset. Eventually Elbert was rescued by Sister Zita, who hugged him as she lectured us all, while giving me a particularly withering look of reproach and disdain.

Elbert didn't stay in our fourth-grade class for long. I believe he transferred to the public school, where I hope he received better treatment. In any case, I haven't forgotten how I got swept up in that crowd and how poorly Elbert Jepsen was treated by others and me. I can still feel Sister Zita's piercing look into my soul as she arrived to rescue Albert. To this day the memory of that event causes me to question the wisdom of participating in any emotionally-charged group action, no matter the apparent worthiness. If I knew where to contact Elbert Jepsen, I would offer my belated apology and tell him that his pain served to teach me a lesson of life-long value.

*   *   *

Once or twice a week, Dad walked with me the three blocks to school. It required only a slight deviation from his regular morning walk to the bank. When I was young, we held hands all the way to the St. Michael's School intersection. As I grew older, hand-holding was discarded, and Dad obligingly went his own way before we reached the school intersection. I had informed him that fourth graders and older kids ride their bikes to school. If they walked, there was no need for parental supervision. My dad was so much older than the other dads. The last thing I wanted was peer teasing about my grandfather walking me to school.

One day when I was eleven years old, Dad asked if he could walk with me on the way to school. He hadn't done so for several months, and I had thought our days of walking together were over. His request surprised me, but I knew it must be important to him, so I said yes, despite preferring to walk by myself. In my mind, we stood out like sore thumbs as we crossed Livermore Avenue together, me in my St. Michael's uniform and he in his double-breasted suit with fedora hat. No one in Livermore ever went to work in coat and tie except my dad and Judge Manley Clark.

As we passed by Dr. Dolan's house on 4th Street, Dad said, "You know, Paul, this will be the last day I walk to the bank. They're retiring me as of tomorrow."

"Does that mean you won't be working at the bank anymore?" I asked.

"Yes, that's about it all right. From here on out I'll have to find something else to do while you're at school."

"So I won't be going to the bank after school anymore?" Usually when Mom was out of town, I walked to the bank after school. There I had a secret hiding place above the safety deposit boxes in one of the vaults. Hidden away, I stayed out of sight doing my homework, or daydreaming until the bank closed and the tellers had balanced their books. Sometimes, against Dad's instructions, I peered down at clients while they opened their deposit boxes. The bank employees knew I was there, but the clients never had a clue. Dad made sure that he had me in tow before locking the vaults at night, because the vaults were on timers and could not be reopened until the next morning. If I were inside, it would be a long, hungry night.

"Yes, no more hiding in the vaults. Anyway, you're too old for that now."

"Wow, are you going to work somewhere else?" I asked.

"I've got the vineyard to take care of and plenty to do around the house. Ernie and I will be doing a lot of hunting next fall. I've joined the Gustine Gun Club that he and Ralph Merritt belong to." Ernest Wente was Dad's best friend.

"Can I go hunting with you?"

"You can when you get a little older. Next year you can take your hunter safety classes and get a license. After that, we'll see about hunting."

At that point we had reached the intersection of 4th and McLoed, where Dad went on his way to the bank and I proceeded to St. Michael's. Just then Richard Flanigan came by on his bicycle. He waved and yelled, "Hurry up, Callaghan. You'll be late."

"Dad, why can't I ride my bike like the other kids?"

"They live farther from school. You only have three blocks to walk. Walking is good for you. As I've said before, when you're twelve, you can ride your bike. Not before."

I wouldn't be twelve until May 30. School would be out for the summer in early June. What a bummer, but I knew better than to argue further with Dad when he used that tone of voice.

"Goodbye, little man. Have a nice day," he said as he turned down McLoed Street. I hurried on to school, wishing he wouldn't call me "little man."

That afternoon I arrived home to find Mom and Aunt Myrtie talking over some sewing in Mom's bedroom. With a peanut butter and mayonnaise sandwich in hand, I plopped down on Mom's bed to listen to their conversation.

Aunt Myrtie immediately acknowledged my arrival. "Good afternoon, Master Paul. How was your day at school? I see you have sufficient sustenance to tide you over until dinner." She used big words. I liked that, but I wasn't excited about the title "Master." None of my friends ever got called that.

Before I could respond, Mom said, "Paul, keep that plate under you. I don't want crumbs on my bed."

"Yes, Mom."

They ignored me and continued their conversation.

Aunt Myrtie (Myrtle E. Harp) was the librarian at Livermore's Carnegie Library. She lived by herself just a block from us on Livermore Avenue, and she was a frequent visitor to our house, often staying for dinner. Though she was much older than Mom, they hit it off on an intellectual basis, both being voracious readers, lovers of ancient history, and speakers of Latin. Dad told me that Aunt Myrtie's mother, Sarah, had been the town librarian before Aunt Myrtie took over. Between them they had served Livermore for more than fifty years. Aunt Myrtie had known Dad for many years prior to Mom's arrival, so Mom relied on her to fill in historic events about the Valley, its residents, and Dad's previous life and marriage.

Myrtle E. Harp, Livermore librarian, 1955

Aunt Myrtie was a walking encyclopedia of books and authors as well as a font of Livermore Valley news and gossip. Her father, Erastus Moses Harp, had been a gold prospector and miner, living his life in and around Sierra mining towns. Every so often he appeared in Livermore with gifts for his wife and daughter. He never stayed long. On one such occasion he gave Aunt Myrtie a harp-shaped gold nugget. She treasured it, and upon her death in 1959, she willed it to me, along with some other nuggets. I eventually had a jeweler make a pendant of the harp nugget. Sadly though, it has disappeared from my life. I know not how or when it departed. A few of the other nuggets remain in my possession to remind me of Aunt Myrtie.

As I munched on my sandwich, their conversation was about Dad. Aunt Myrtie was saying, "He has managed that bank through several ownerships for thirty years. He knows every client personally and their family history. In fact, he knows the family histories of almost everyone in this Valley. It's unconscionable that they would let him go."

"I know Myrtle. The employees are like family to him. He is so depressed about the situation.

"He'll certainly be missed by the community. For years families have come to him for advice. He has been the executor of their wills and the arbitrator of their disagreements. They trust his integrity and fairness. Without Joe at the bank, things won't be the same anymore."

"Myrtle, I think the problem boils down to the fact that Joe made loans based upon character and intuition. He treated people as individual human beings. Wells Fargo wants things done by the corporate rule book. Paperwork and formulas determine who does and does not get a loan. Customers are just numbers, their importance based solely on the size of their accounts and their potential contribution to corporate profits. Accounting rules and procedures take the place of employee integrity and pride. The simple fact is that Joe is to be pushed aside and replaced with impersonal, rule-following robots who know little about their customers and who never make exceptions. It's killing him. In a way, it's good that he's leaving. If he stays, he'll likely have a heart attack."

"On Thursday he had those San Francisco executives over for cocktails. I slaved making hors d'oeuvres with only last-minute notice. What a bunch of uncouth pigs. After only a few drinks, one of them made a pass at me, asking if I was satisfied married to such an older man with little formal education. With Paul here, I can't repeat the entirety of what I said to him about his emaciated brain and gauche behavior, but I let him know that Joe was twice the man he could ever be and in no need of a liquor bottle to prop him up. For the rest of the evening whenever I glared at him, he cowered, tail between his legs. The next day they informed Joe that he would be retired at sixty-five."

"That's awful," said Aunt Myrtie. "But Joe has to forget that bank and get on with his life. There's lots for him to do around town. He's got the vineyard, and many people will continue to seek his help and advice. I've been trying to get him on the library board for years, but he always says, 'You need college educated people on that board, not slow readers like me.' Emma, maybe you can convince him that we need brains, experience, and community contacts on the board, much more than we need formal educations."

"Is Dad going to be all right?" I asked. They both looked at me, having forgotten I was in the room.

"Sure, dear. Don't worry. He'll be fine," said Mom.

I did worry, at least for a while. I was the only kid among my peers with a father who was retired and old enough to be my grandfather. On one hand, I loved him and didn't want his retirement, whatever that was, to affect our relationship. On the other hand, I was at times embarrassed about his age. In the end, both these concerns turned out to be of little consequence. Dad was always around when I needed him, and I was increasingly able to help out as he got older. Also, I became skilled at nurturing intergenerational relationships, an ability that served me well throughout later life.

*   *   *

It never occurred to me that my upbringing was more advantageous than that of my classmates. Family finances were never discussed in front of me. Our three bedroom, two-bath, stucco home wasn't outwardly ostentatious. Our appliances were old. Mom did the laundry in an aged, leaky, ringer type machine and hung wash outside on a clothesline to dry. She drove a 1941 Dodge coupe. Dad walked to work and drove a 1940 Ford pickup. The 1939 Chrysler New Yorker was kept in the garage and used only on special occasions. We had no television until I was in the seventh grade. Nothing in our lives was ostentatious. My twenty-five-cent-per-week allowance remained firmly in place during the first six years of school. St. Michael's uniform dress code didn't allow differences in attire. I walked or road my bicycle to and from school, as did my friends. My bicycle was an old rehab, similar to theirs. Yet, as previously noted, I always felt just a bit out of sync with my classmates, though I barely sensed the issue and never dwelt on it.

In later life I came to understand the reason for that slight feeling of misfit. As a child I had advantages and experiences that were beyond the reach of my classmates. My parents were older, more financially secure, and in my mother's case, better-educated than most parents in our community. I attended plays and concerts. Mom read to me nightly from the likes of Robert Louis Stevenson, Kenneth Grahame, Lewis Carroll and James Fenimore Cooper. I traveled to snow ski in winter and visited the desert during spring. We were members of Castlewood, the William Randolph Hurst Golf and Country Club in Pleasanton. I was often the only child at formal dinner parties. We owned a mountain cabin where I spent summers trout fishing, hiking and camping. My parents' closest friends were older, well-educated professionals, and members of the area's political and economic elite. My father was the bank manager. His cousin, Richard M. Callaghan, was the City of Livermore Attorney. Another cousin, Leo R. Callaghan, owned and operated the Valley's sole mortuary. As an only child who went everywhere with my parents, I grew up associating with those people and knowing them personally. We weren't wealthy, but we were well off, and I was advantaged, though my parents tried never to let me perceive that advantage. It was years before I came to understand that their intentional downplay of our family's economic status was in part designed to help me better find my social bearings.

Chapter 4

Framers and Shapers

After Mom got married, she continued to maintain close relationships with several of her female college friends as they pursued their careers. Some were university professors, others attorneys and social service professionals. None of them ever married or had children, so I was the lucky recipient of their attention and tutelage. Now in my old age, I realize the seeds of maturation these women sprinkled on my youth. They all chose professional life over marriage. It was one or the other for most women in those days. Few men could tolerate a well-educated, working spouse. These ladies taught me by their example that: those who are different often make a difference; leadership and competency are not the province of males alone; challenging the accepted norms can be costly and difficult, but perseverance makes the path easier for those who follow; nature's solitude provides a place of refuge; what really counts is the service you provide for those in need. No one could have been more blessed with such loving "aunties," all of whom contributed immensely to the richness of my life.

*   *   *

Martha (Patty) Chickering, Aunt Patty, was born into a prestigious and wealthy Bay Area family in 1886. Her father, William Henry Chickering, headed a prominent law firm in San Francisco. She graduated from U.C. Berkeley in 1910 and subsequently held positions with the Associated Charities of Oakland, the Red Cross and the YWCA. Between 1913 and 1918 she established YWCA sponsored Institutes to assist the assimilation of immigrants in San Francisco,

Fresno and Honolulu. Subsequently, she lived for an extended time in Poland, where she headed the YWCA's Polish relief efforts after World War I.

Martha (Patty) Chickering, 1933

By 1934, when Mom entered the Social Service Graduate Program at U.C. Berkeley, Patty had become the program's head of curriculum and field work. Mom admired Patty's socially progressive ideas and staunch individualism. They became fast friends and politically active compatriots. Being Sierra Club members and loving the out of doors, they frequented Soda Springs, where Patty's family had a summer home. They also visited Yosemite, sometimes sleeping on the ground under the stars and at other times settling into the fashionable Ahwahnee Hotel. As Mom put it, "The polarization of life was important to Patty."

Several times Mom invited Patty to the Barham family cabin on the Feather River near Chester, California. Patty so enjoyed these visits that in 1937 she asked my grandfather, Courtney Barham, to build her a simple three-room cabin on an adjoining vacant lot. There she relished her summer solitude for several years.

Following graduate work at the University of Chicago, Patty received her Ph.D. in economics and was thereafter instrumental in building a fully accredited graduate School of Social Work at U.C. Berkley. In those times, the mores of academia were such that Patty believed a man with academic and scholarly research experience should head the school. This was not a popular view among the female faculty and Patty's female friends. They had fought a long battle for women's suffrage and were now staunch women's rights activists. But Patty believed that the students deserved the best School of Social Work that a great university could offer. Putting pragmatism before emotional and personal feelings, she recruited Dr. Harry Cassidy from the University of British Columbia to be Dean. Thereafter, Patty settled into a supportive teaching roll.

In 1939 Patty took leave from the university to become Director of the California State Board of Social Welfare, a position she held until 1945. In 1946 she retired as an honored Emeritus Professor and moved to an isolated home in the Mojave Desert, near Victorville, California. There she lived by herself until age 102.

I have fond memories as a child of visiting Aunt Patty's desert home. Much to the nuns' unhappiness, Mom took me out of school to make the trip. I learned more from Aunt Patty than I could have in any classroom. On Jeep rides, we chased jackrabbits, observed coyotes, poked slow moving tortoises, and viewed miles of spring-blooming desert plants. Aunt Patty knew the taxonomy and habits of them all. Tracks and scat were her forte. I loved swimming in her concrete water storage pool and learning how the windmill worked to pump water. Mostly I just enjoyed being with this stately, white-haired lady who seemed to know everything and be interested in teaching it all to me. The lines in her wizened face are etched in my memory.

*   *   *

Catherine W. (Kit) Carson was an only child born in 1914 to George C. and Gertrude Carson of Grass Valley, California. I know little of her early life, but by 1939 Kit had graduated from U.C. Berkley with a bachelor's degree in economics, finished a law degree from Bolt Hall Law School, one of two women in her graduating class, and completed certification as a social worker. For a brief time, she worked at the Alameda County Charities Commission before accepting a position as Deputy District Attorney for Alameda County, a position she held until 1946, when she joined a private law firm in Modesto, California.

Kit opened her own practice in Modesto in 1952 and was appointed Stanislaus County Inheritance Tax Appraiser in 1959. As the county's only practicing woman attorney, she offered clients a mixture of social work and law, always with an eye to helping "hard working regular people." Often her only payment was the satisfaction of making someone's life a little better.

Catherine W. (Kit) Carson, 1955

Liberal progressive politics was her love. She was a member of the county and state Democratic Central Committees and a state delegate to the 1964 Democratic National Convention.

Of all Mom's friends, Kit was my favorite. She smoked cigarillos, drank straight bourbon on the rocks, barbequed her steaks rare, and talked with a sprinkling of cusswords sufficient to ensure her acceptance into any old-boys' club. Much to Mom's discomfort, I quickly adopted some of Kit's depraved verbiage. Upon her departure from our house, I was usually subjected to an uncomfortable period of linguistic cleansing.

During and shortly after law school, Kit worked as a part time riveter in a Naval aircraft facility in Alameda, California. It was said in our family that she was the model used for the famous World War II poster of "Rosie the Riveter." I have no proof of that, but the likeness to Kit at a young age is striking.

Kit taught me useful phrases like, "Anything worth doing is worth overdoing" and "never up, never in." I didn't fully appreciate the later phrasing until some years later. She called me "lead butt"—I was a bit slow and overweight in those days. Kit and my dad got along famously. They saw eye to eye on almost everything and frequently talked business, politics, or religion over a bourbon highball. Kit prepared and administered Dad's will and handled all our family legal matters. She often stopped at our house in Livermore on her way back and forth between Modesto and the Bay Area. I looked forward to every visit. And as I grew older, her advice and counsel always captured my full attention.

At the relatively young age of fifty-nine, on May 4, 1974, Kit Carson passed from this world, a victim of lung cancer and no doubt the vagaries of her lifestyle. I was attending graduate school in Hawaii and was unable to attend her memorial service, but Kit's death affected me deeply. She had been a pillar of support in my life. For several years Kit had played first base on a Modesto women's softball team. She was number 12. Her warmup jacket still resides on a hanger at my cabin, waiting to provide warmth to some visitor on a frosty mountain morning.

*   *   *

Maurine McKeany was born in Porterville, California, on December 18,1905. She and her mother, Effie Hodges McKeany, moved to Berkeley, where Maurine graduated from Berkeley High School in 1923. By 1936 she had received a B.A. and M.A. in Economics (with Honors) from U.C. Berkeley, was Phi Beta Kappa, and had acquired a secondary teaching credential as well as Social Work certification.

Maurine McKeany, 1953

When Mom entered the social work program at U.C. Berkeley in 1934, Maurine was already a lecturer. She, Mom and Aunt Patty Chickering belonged to the Sierra Club and enjoyed hiking, skiing and pack trips together. But the glue that cemented their friendship was a mutual desire to resolve Depression-era social problems having to do with workers' rights, women's rights, family stability and migrant assimilation. Franklin D. Roosevelt was their hero, and they championed his "New Deal" policies.

Like Aunt Patty, Maurine remained in academia. She received her Ph.D. in Social Service Administration from the University of Chicago and was for many years Associate Dean of the School of Social Welfare at U.C. Berkeley. Her interest in child welfare and public assistance policy led to research and widely disseminated publications on the topics of absent fathers and aid to dependent children. After retirement in 1970, she was awarded the title of Emeritus Professor.

Maurine was part of almost all my childhood summers. For a month or longer she regularly vacationed at our Chester cabin. With her Lieca 35mm camera, she introduced me to photography. By the fourth grade I had learned about focus, f-stops, shutter speeds, depth of field, ISO film speeds and the operation of a hand-held light meter. On our forest walks I helped Maurine as she took pictures of interesting plants and creatures. In the fall when I was back in school, she mailed the prints to me as a reminder of the natural beauty we had experienced together.

One summer Maurine asked if I would help with her research about aid to fatherless dependent children. Thinking how terrible it would be not to have a dad, I took the assignment seriously. Each morning for a week I added long columns of numbers by hand, two pages for each of the forty-eight states. Maurine then showed me how to use my long division skills to calculate an average. She explained that the average number was a best representation of all the numbers. I'm sure that Maurine rechecked my calculations upon returning to Berkeley, but that summer my addition and long division skills significantly improved, and I gained a rudimentary appreciation of applied statistics.

Maurine often accompanied Mom and I on ski trips. She was there as support for my first skiing efforts at Pacific House, age six, and on the rope tow hill at Mineral, age seven and eight. Several times as a child and as a teenager Maurine invited me to authentic meals at Japanese and Greek restaurants in San Francisco and to formal luncheons at the Faculty Club on the Berkeley campus. She was always interested in providing experiences that broadened my perspective.

Maurine passed away on May 20, 2001, at age ninety-five, but she lived to see me receive my Doctorate in Economics and become a university professor—an accomplishment toward which she made a significant contribution.

*　*　*

Francis Estelle Booth, "Hankie" to her close friends, was born of American parents in Yokohama, Japan, in 1909. Estelle's father, Frank S. Booth, was the son of Reverend Eugene S. and Emilie (Stelle) Booth, Christian missionaries who arrived in Yokohama in 1880, the year Frank was born. For forty years Reverend Booth was principal of Ferris Seminary for Women, now Ferris Jogakuin University, in Yokohama.

Francis Estelle Booth, 1950

Estelle spent her first twelve years in Japan. After that she attended school in Switzerland for a time before becoming Mom's classmate at Anna Head School for Girls in Berkley. Because Estelle was a boarding student with no nearby relatives, the Barham household provided surrogate family support. Estelle and Mom became close friends, and Estelle celebrated holiday festivities and spent summer vacations with the Barhams.

Upon completing her B.S. in Psychology at U.C. Berkley, in 1934 Estelle entered the graduate Curriculum of Social Service along with Mom. Upon receiving her Social Service certification, Estelle, like Mom, was employed by the Alameda County Charities Commission. She remained at the Commission for several years, during which time she completed her M.S. degree in Social Work.

Estelle's father Frank lived his entire life in Japan and was by all accounts a businessman with interests in the Japanese fish processing and canning industry. His import-export firm was named Sale Frazzar. It's likely that he remained in Japan during WWII, but his wife, Lilly Foster Booth, immigrated to California to live with Estelle. She never returned to Japan.

In the late 1950s Estelle moved to Nashville, Tennessee, where she established an acclaimed program for homebound senior citizens. Her book *How to Work with the Hard-to-Reach Elderly* is still used today. Upon returning to California, she was employed by the San Francisco Senior Center (SFSC), the oldest non-profit senior center in the United States. The Center Director, Florence Vickery, asked Estelle to organize and manage a downtown branch of SFSC, located in an area south of Market Street, where numerous seniors lived with few resources in decrepit hotels and boarding houses. Under Estelle's leadership the Downtown Center flourished and was the first California institution to receive funding under the *Older Americans Act* of 1965. Estelle retired in 1972, but the Downtown Senior Center still serves thousands of San Francisco's homebound and immobile elderly.

Hankie regularly appeared at our Chester cabin in the summers of my childhood, usually espousing some socially beneficial idea. One year it was dishwashing sanitation. I had to wash and carefully rinse each item in boiling water. Another year it was healthy whole wheat bread making. I kneaded lots of brown, seedy dough and spent hours watching the thermometer on our kerosene stove oven. Another year it was solar ovens. We tested several aluminum foil creations and cooked whole meals on the cabin porch. Another year she was absorbed with adobe construction. I hauled water from the creek and mixed buckets of grass-infused mud, which we formed into sun dried bricks. The project was a failure because volcanic soil did not lend itself to brickmaking, but the rock and mud foundation that we built near the outdoor toilet was visible for many years before eroding to a memory.

After retirement Estelle moved to Sonoma, California. There her interests turned to ecology. She attended courses on the subject at Oxford University and founded the Sonoma Ecology Center. While living in Sonoma she met the elusive love of her life, John W. Page. They were married in 1984 and lived together at Friends House in Santa Rosa until Estelle's death in January of 1999. Hankie was present at family gatherings and major turning points in my life, always in the background with words of wisdom and encouragement, interested in my story and my future.

I regret that I don't know the origin of the nickname "Hankie," and the specifics of Estelle's Japanese connections remain an intriguing mystery. At Anna Head School and at U.C. Berkeley she always had sufficient spending money. Her tuition, room and board were always paid in full. Her father, Frank, arrived from Japan on several occasions with gifts for Estelle, Mom and the Barhams. After a week or two he would return to Japan. Just prior to WWII Estelle's mother arrived to live with her in Berkeley, bearing the name Lilly Booth Foster. In 1957 Frank Booth was found murdered in Kamakura, Japan. After her father's death Estelle never spoke of her father or their life in Japan—not to Mom or me, or anyone else as far as I know.

*   *   *

Jacqueline Adele (Jacque) Watkins was born in Dallas, Texas, in 1911, to Halbert E. and Adele Watkins. Halbert held various positions in South America, both in private business and in public service. For several years he was US Commercial Attaché at the US Consulate in Caracas, Venezuela and Buenos Aires, Argentina. Later he was chief accountant at the Department of Commerce in Washington, D.C.

Jacqueline Adele (Jacque) Watkins, 1953

Jacque and her mother moved to Berkeley in 1925. After finishing high school, Jacque entered U.C. Berkeley, where she became deeply involved in social and political affairs—writing regular columns for the *Daily Californian*, holding membership in Mortar Board, Prytanean Society, Torch and Shield, and Theta Sigma Phi. She was instrumental in organizing the first cooperative housing for women on the U.C. campus, now called Stebbins Hall.

Jacque's father, Halbert, died suddenly in 1932 on his way from Washington, D.C. to Berkeley. After his death Jacque's mother moved to Sonoma for a time and then to Coronado in southern California. There for many years, she was the social secretary for the actress Spring Byington.

Upon graduation Jacque entered the graduate Social Work Curriculum along with Mom and Estelle. After receiving her Social Service certification, Jacque briefly worked for the Alameda County Charities Commission. But her real interests lay in sports, fitness and ecology. She moved to Point Richmond on the San Francisco Bay. There she could kayak and swim on a regular basis, becoming an avid bird watcher and Audubon Society member.

For several years Jacque worked with the Richmond Red Cross and the California Employment Service, while at the same time teaching tennis and other sports at Mills College. Then in 1952 Jacque joined the City of Berkeley Recreation and Parks Department. Over the next twenty years she helped organize a city-wide program for senior citizens, the California Specialists on Aging, the East Bay Coordinating Council of Senior Citizens Clubs, the city-wide tennis program, and a recreation program for handicapped and mentally challenged children.

During the summers of my childhood Jacque appeared at our Chester cabin along with Kit and Estelle. When Mom and the three of them got together it was an exciting time for me. Often I was the center of attention, and there were lots of fun choices of things to do. In those days we all slept under the stars on the cabin porch. I was sent to bed early, but my bed was positioned so that I could watch what was going on inside the cabin through the pane glass of the door. I snuggled down under my blankets, watching them inside in the firelight as they talked and laughed. It was comforting to know they were there, because on the other side of the porch railing was nothing but the starlit forest and the sound of the river in the canyon below. Inevitably I fell asleep before they came to bed. By morning there was usually frost on our covers. Jacque and Mom were always the first up. Kit was next, but Hankie and I remained under the covers until the sun had hit the breakfast table. We then ran inside together to put on our clothes in front of the crackling fire.

When I was an infant, Jacque wrote a poem that for years remained tacked on the wall of our Chester cabin. I copy it here in her memory:

<u>Sierra Psalm</u>

O' Spirit of Nature
Give unto me
Strength of mighty mountains
Graciousness of a tree
Quiet dignity of the rock
Industry of a bee
Warmth of mellow sunshine.
All this I ask of Thee
And with the giving of thy gifts
Add the solvent of humanity—

Jacqueline Watkins
Chester, Summer 1942

Jacque died of cancer at age sixty-two on May 6, 1973, just a year before Kit. At the time I was away at graduate school in Hawaii. The two of them often arrived and departed together in my life, and they did so in death as well.

*   *   *

My dad had one close friend. They spent much time together, and I was often along for the ride. Ernest August (Ernie) Wente was born in Livermore three years after Dad, on June 9, 1890. The Wente family had immigrated to the Napa Valley from Hanover, Germany, in 1870. After working at the Charles Krug winery for several years, Carl Heinrich Wente moved his family to Livermore in 1883. There he started his own vineyards and winery, often buying additional grapes from the vineyard of my grandmother, Sarah Callaghan. Dad and Ernie, and Ernie's brothers and sisters, Carl, Herman, Carolyn and Frieda, attended Livermore Grammar School and grew up together in the close-knit farming community.

Ernest August (Ernie) Wente, 1958

The Wente family had more resources than struggling Sarah Callaghan, so the Wente children were able to stay in school while Dad had to work, dropping out of grammar school before graduation. Herman Wente ultimately graduated from U.C. Berkeley, and Ernie was one of the first students at U.C. Davis when it opened in 1909. After graduation they both remained with the family wine business in Livermore. Their brother, Carl, graduated from Stanford University and went into banking. In the 1950s he was for a time President of the Bank of America.

After high school Frieda Wente worked for the Bank of Livermore and was responsible for bringing Dad into the banking business when he was at loose ends after WWI. Frieda married a local businessman and one-time Mayor of Livermore named George Tubbs. They lived in a house on 4th Street, around the block from our house. In the early 1950s as I peddled my trusty tricycle through the neighborhood, Mrs. Tubbs, as I was required to call her, could usually be counted on for a cookie. Upon the death of George Tubbs in 1957, Frieda married Dad's cousin, Richard M. Callaghan, who was then the City Attorney for Livermore.

Aside from the winery and vineyards, Ernie owned a cattle ranch on the southeast side of town. There he and his wife, Bess, lived in a sprawling, vine-covered home at the end of Wente Street. The grounds included corrals, saddle shops, hay barns, machine shops, and George's house. George was the caretaker, a jovial overweight fellow. I never knew his last name.

When I was young, Dad and Mom sometimes left me with Ernie and Bess overnight. I loved that. They had a huge king-sized bed and let me sleep between them. In early morning, Ernie, whom I always called Mr. Wente, took me on his shoulders for morning chores in the barnyard, while Bess cooked a farm breakfast with fresh eggs on toasted homemade bread.

As I got older, so long as I checked in with Ernie or Bess or George, I pretty much had the run of the place. From the eighth grade through high school, I spent many hours in the vineyards hunting jackrabbits with my 20 gage Winchester Model 12 shotgun. They were destructive vineyard pests, and Ernie was happy that I reduced the population. As time passed, I became known to the Mexican vineyard workers as "the rabbit kid," because they often skinned and cooked my kills.

The ranch property had two reservoirs in the hills behind Ernie's home. One was entirely concrete and served as a swimming pool when the water was fresh in the spring. The other was created by an earthen dam in a side canyon of Dry Creek. It contained bass and bluegills, so I became a pretty good bass fisherman using poppers and plugs amid the weeds and lily pads. On hot fall evenings, Dad, Mr. Wente, and I hunted doves and quail in the hills near water holes.

Ernie was a heavy featured, powerfully built, giant of a man. His hands were larger than any I have seen. His palm could engulf the hands of most adults, and he used only his thumb and forefinger to shake hands with young people. He preferred to be outdoors, close to the earth, doing physical labor. He was a farmer and rancher at heart, not a businessman, salesperson, or vintner. Those things he left to others in the family. Once a year Ernie and Bess held an "open house" party. Seventy or eighty of Livermore Valley's old-guard elite descended on the ranch. Except for me, there were seldom any children, so early on I was given the job of dispensing beer from the keg tap. By age twelve I had mastered the whole operation and spent the day delivering mugs of frosty brew to party goers, a skill that ultimately proved useful during fraternity life in college.

Ernie was a hardworking, no-nonsense, politically conservative German Protestant, in many ways the opposite of my dad, who was a flexible, easy going, politically liberal Irish Catholic. Strangely though, and to my benefit, the two men got along famously. I don't know why Ernie treated me so kindly. Maybe it was just because he and Dad were best friends. Maybe it was because he missed having a young person around. His own son, Karl, was older and at that time fully involved in managing the family businesses, and Karl's children were not yet old enough to spend time with their grandfather. I suspect also that Ernie had been a stern disciplinarian and taskmaster in the raising of his own son. This was so because Karl was the only child among all three Wente brothers capable of taking over the family businesses. Ernie couldn't fail with Karl. The stakes were too high. On the other hand, I was a child with whom Ernie could relax, have fun, and not worry so much about how I would "turn out." That was Joe's problem, not his. Whatever the case, I much admired Mr. Wente and hung on his every word.

I was there in Ernie's study that night in the late 1950s when Ernie and Dad plotted how they might raise money for a new Livermore Valley hospital. The old St. Paul's Hospital was inadequate to serve the growing population. Frequently patients were required to travel to Oakland for medical treatment. Because the Wente family had large land holdings, they were interested in keeping hospital costs off the property tax rolls. Ernie thought that many in the farming and business community felt similarly and would prefer to donate rather than be taxed. Together Dad and Ernie created a list of prospective donors and the amounts they would be asked to contribute. Ernie said, "Joe, I'm not the right person to approach most of these people. You are. You should do this for the good of our Valley. Ralph Merritt has agreed to help. He can reach some people that you can't." Over the next year, Dad and Ralph Merritt formed a nonprofit corporation and collected several million dollars from local families and businesses. Matching that money with federal grant funding, they built Valley Memorial Hospital on land donated by Kaiser Industries, a company that had gotten its start in the Livermore Valley.

In 1981 I returned to Livermore for my twentieth high school reunion. The day before the reunion I paid an unannounced visit to Ernie, whom I had not seen for ten years. My arrival woke him from his afternoon siesta in the huge leather recliner that had always occupied his front room. He was happy to see me and anxious to hear about my life. We talked into the late afternoon, when he asked if I'd like to stay with him. Of course, there was no refusing that offer, so we had a wonderful visit over the next three days. He told me how Bess had died in 1969, how he still missed her, and how he now had a live-in cook/housekeeper, but she was away for the weekend, so we had to fend for ourselves. That we did in style, with leftovers and an unmarked gallon jug of red wine from the cellar. "Never mind that white wine; this is the best wine we make," he said. "I drink a glass or two every day. It keeps me going."

During my visit I was reminded of Ben Franklin's adage: "Early to bed and early to rise makes a man healthy, wealthy, and wise." Ernie got me up at five o'clock every morning to help him feed hay to horses and cattle and collect eggs from the chicken coops. After breakfast on Saturday morning, Alfred Sakau, then ninety-seven years of age, arrived on horseback to visit Ernie, having ridden through the hills from his Dry Creek ranch. I listened while the two old friends sat in the sun talking about the weather, their health and their cattle. I only regret not having taken their picture. They were the last of their generation.

Ernie seemed impressed with my university teaching and fisheries management work in the Pacific. "Joe would be proud of you if he were alive," he said. "But you know, it was our hope that when you finished your M.B.A., you'd come to work for us at the winery. Joe never said anything to you about that because he wanted you to make up your own mind about your own life, and you did, and that's good, and you seem to be doing well." Ernie never mentioned his son, Karl, who had died suddenly of cancer late in 1976. I think the pain of loss was still too great. At that point there was none of his generation left except his sister, Frieda Tubbs Callaghan. Ernie had to devote all his last remaining energy to readying his three grandchildren to take over the family businesses.

Before leaving the next day, I took Ernie's picture standing in his vegetable garden behind the house. He stood on the porch and waved as I drove away. I waved back. He died a year later at age ninety-one. One of his grandchildren now lives in that house. I've never been back.

A couple of years later I visited Frieda and my cousin Richard Callaghan. Frieda was the last Wente of her generation. She controlled all Wente family holdings. Over dinner she shared with me their long-term business plans for Wente vineyard expansion and entry into the entertainment business. She said that Ernie had not been in favor of moving into the restaurant and entertainment businesses. She too yearned for the old days when making wine didn't require tasting rooms, restaurants and concerts. But as she put it, "The grandkids are in charge now. Richard and I don't have long on this earth."

Richard died in 1985, a year after my visit, and Freda in 1986. I cannot forget her cookies and her smile, dominated by rouge-covered cheeks. Ernie was the only one of his brothers and sisters to have a child, and Karl passed away relatively early in life. I suspect that Dad, Ernie and Freda hoped I might choose a career with Wente Brothers Wines. I will always wonder where life might have taken me had I done so.

Chapter 5

The Cabin

From my first year of life through high school, I never spent a summer in Livermore. As soon as school was out and the Livermore Rodeo was over, Mom piled me into her 1942 Dodge Coupe, and we headed north to our mountain cabin on the North Fork of the Feather River, under the shadow of Mt. Lassen. Because of this ritual, there was no Little League baseball for me and none of the summer activities that were common to my classmates. I missed out on their experiences while gaining exposure to a different world that was beyond their reach. At the time I didn't recognize the value of this tradeoff and regretted the loss of summer fun with friends. In later life I've come to realize the benefits and appreciate my parents' foresight.

In the 1940s and 1950s the trip from Livermore to the cabin involved an eight-hour drive, all of it on two lane roads. We left Livermore at three or four in the morning, "To avoid the valley heat," Mom said. But it was unclear to me that we avoided much heat. Once the sun rose, things got pretty warm. Cars in those days weren't air conditioned. Probably the more important reason for an early departure was that it allowed for our arrival in early afternoon, with sufficient daylight remaining to get the cabin opened and livable before nightfall.

I slept while Mom drove the Vasco Road from Livermore to Byron and Brentwood. She woke me as we crossed the San Joaquin River in Antioch and the Sacramento River in Rio Vista. I liked seeing the big bridges, and I wondered how long it had taken some of that Sacramento River water to travel the hundreds of miles from our Feather River swimming hole at the cabin.

After Rio Vista we motored north up Highway 99 through endless farmland and small towns—Dixon, Winters and Dunnigan, Arbuckle, Williams and Maxwell, Willows, Orland and Corning, then finally Red Bluff. Between the towns were Burma-Shave signs that passed too quickly for my dyslexic reading skills, but Mom read aloud: "Cost so small, Coolest, Smoothest, Shave of all; Burma-Shave was such a boom, they passed the bride, and kissed the groom." Life was simple in those times.

The Dodge coupe had a static-jammed AM radio that required frequent adjustment, so we seldom used it. FM radio had not yet come into widespread use, and cassette/CD players and electronic game technologies were only a dream in the mind of some engineer. As a youngster I curled up in the passenger seat or on the floor—no one had yet thought about seatbelts for passenger cars. There I would slip into a deep meditative state. Call it "Peter Pan Land" if you like—a state of daydreaming that embodied wonderful adventures, scary villains, and all-powerful heroes. Often I was the center of action: saving friends, hitting home runs, outsmarting opponents, overcoming mystical creatures. In these fantasies I suffered no failures, only self-confident successes and glorious outcomes. The monotonous drone of road noise and the hot wind from open windows faded into the background as I escaped into my fantasy world. From time to time, I exited my dreams in order to keep track of our progress, but for the most part, time disappeared and the long, hot trip up Highway 99 to Red Bluff seemed almost enjoyable.

When I was about ten years old, something happened on our annual trek to the cabin. It changed things forever. Most years Mom and I made the trip alone, but on this particular spring day both Dad and Mom were driving separate vehicles. I was riding with Dad in his green 1951 Chevrolet pickup, loaded with rolls of linoleum and buckets of glue and paint for cabin improvements. Whenever Dad came to the cabin, he stuck around until Mom ran out of jobs for him; then he went back to Livermore to tend to our house and his beloved vineyard. He always returned each fall to transport me back to school, while Mom remained at the cabin by herself until at least mid-October.

We had just passed Dunnigan and were on our way to Arbuckle. Mom was driving ahead of us in her Dodge. I had settled as usual on the passenger side floor. When I tried to enter my dream world fantasy, I found it difficult. Ultimately, I gained some halting access, but not anything like the deep immersion of times past. After a few minutes I surfaced again, and this time there was no going back.

It seemed that the door had been closed and locked. For an hour or more I tried to gain access to "Peter Pan Land" but with little but momentary success. Road noises, excitement, anticipation and real-world thoughts seemed to overshadow and crowd out the dream-world fantasies. At that point I somehow knew this was the end of my dream-world days. I could no longer escape reality. From here on out there was no hiding. I have never forgotten that moment when I climbed back up onto the bench seat of that pickup and looked at the passing farmland. That trip to Red Bluff seemed to take forever, as did all subsequent trips. An important phase of my childhood had ended.

*   *   *

Red Bluff marked a turning point in the trip. From there on things became more interesting, and my anticipation and excitement built as we got closer to our goal. It was often a hundred degrees or hotter in Red Bluff, so we hurriedly bought gas and ate our sandwiches in the shade beside the Sacramento River. Eastward out of Red Bluff, Highway 36 wound its way through oak-covered hills and valleys. The green grasses and wildflowers of spring already showed signs of the inevitable summer brownness to come. As far as one could see, dark volcanic boulders were strewn amid the oak trees like sprinkled peppercorns. They had been ejected eons ago from the eruptions of nearby cinder cones. I marveled at the size and abundance of these rocks. It must have been an amazing sight when those glowing hot bombs came hurtling from the sky to be scattered on the knolls and fields all about us.

At the Dales there was a crossroad that led to the town of Manton. As we passed that intersection, Mom invariably launched into the story of my grandfather, Courtney Barham, and how he had spent his youthful summers working on their family's ranch in Manton; how he rode on horseback the thirty miles from his home in Red Bluff to the ranch; how he and Indian Bob had cleared the manzanita bushes to make tillable land; and how they had subsisted on rabbit, squirrel, doves, rattlesnake, beans, oats and corn meal. I imagined the difficulties of riding a horse in that heat through these rocky hills and eating rattlesnake, beans and cornbread for breakfast, lunch and dinner. Grandpa Barham was always a giant in my mind.

As we gained altitude, the temperature gage on the car's dashboard moved closer to the red mark. If the radiator boiled or we got a vapor lock in the fuel line, there was no choice but to stop, open the hood, and let things cool down. Mom hated having to delay, so she drove carefully and we usually avoided trouble.

On the twenty mile stretch of curvy road between Paynes Creek and Mineral, the fir, pine and cedar trees gradually replaced the oak and digger pines of the lowlands. The damp, fresh, green smells of spring blew through the open windows, and Mom became excited about the wildflowers, especially the blooming cyanosis and dogwood. As the road became steeper and winding, I became less concerned about flora and more concerned about getting carsick. I hated getting nauseous, as I often did along this stretch of road. When my stomach started churning, it usually helped to kneel on the passenger seat facing backward, looking out the rear window. If that didn't work, Mom stopped the car and let me walk a bit.

I was excited when we reached Mineral. It was the last stop before going over Morgan Summit, the highest part of our trip. For two winters when I was seven and eight years old, Mom and her friend Maurine McKeany brought me to Mineral for a week of snow fun. There I had my first downhill skiing experiences with the help of a rope-tow that operated on the hill below the water tanks. To this day I hold a clear memory of disaster averted on that hill. I was holding on with both hands to the rope as it whisked me up the hill. At the top I let go and tried to scoot off to the side, as I had done before; however, it turned out that my open parka had become wrapped around the rope, which tended to rotate a bit as it went along. I was jerked into the air—skis, poles and all—headed straight for the pulley system anchored high on a pine tree. About fifteen feet up, Irish luck kicked in and the coat gave way. I dropped into a soft snow drift. Had I been carried into that pully system, I certainly would not be writing these words.

Beyond Mineral, my excitement level increased even further as we passed the melting snow banks on the top of Morgan Summit and twisted our way down the other side, across Mill Creek to Childs Meadow. According to Mom, Mr. Childs had been a friend of my great-grandfather, James Louis Barham. She never said more than that, and we didn't usually stop there, preferring to hurry on the twenty-two miles to Chester.

Once in Chester we bought groceries at the Corner Store, where Mom had a charge account. After that we bought a hundred-pound block of ice from the ice man on Gay Street. Mom had him cut it into four pieces so it was easier to lift into our icebox at the cabin. From Chester it was eight miles over a rough, dirt road to Willow Creek, where we turned off onto a blazed trail through the forest that everyone in our family called "Grandpa's Road." He had built it in the 1920s. It no longer exists, though my mind can still retrace its path.

When the Dodge finally came to a stop near our cabin steps, I was out and up onto the porch. Mom was close behind. The smell of the pine forest and the sounds of rushing river water confirmed that we were once again where we belonged. Gone were thoughts of missed Little League baseball, rodeo weekend, and the doings of my classmates in Livermore. The cabin's eight-foot-wide porch extended around three sides of the building. From there we could look down on the river below and determine what of its course had changed during the winter. Was the waterfall above the swimming hole as full as it should be? Had trees fallen across or been washed down? Had there been any change in the old growth forest that stretched to the sky across the river from the cabin? We stood there, Mom and I, each quietly savoring the forest scents, drinking in the view, listening to nature's music. We had left behind the turmoil and din of urban life. Chipmunks and golden-mantled ground squirrels chirped their warnings as a red-tailed hawk glided overhead in observation of our arrival. Similarly, grey tree squirrels and Steller's jays chided their concern at our presence in their territory. Once again, we were back in our mountain world.

Paul and his dog Sox on the cabin porch, 1950

During those minutes of reincarnation, I connected with familiar landmarks. There was the Jeffrey pine by the front porch. At about twenty feet from the ground its trunk forked into two almost perfectly symmetrical halves, each the reverse image of the other. This was a unique occurrence, as most forked pines were unbalanced to one side. This tree was perhaps two hundred years old at the time of my childhood. We have grown older together. During that time the right fork has gained some slight size advantage over the left, due to better sun exposure. Near the base of the forked Jeffrey, overlooking the river gorge, was a rock outcropping, the end of an ancient lava flow. In some years a marmot family called that place home. They sunned themselves on the rocks and introduce us to their babies, who grew into adults as summer progressed.

Another landmark was the tamarack pole crossbar between two adjacent yellow pines. It had been placed there long before our arrival by hunters who used it to hang and dress their game and to secure food above the reach of predators. The two pines had been notched about twenty feet above the ground and the cross pole spiked into place. Years of disuse had caused the pole to become moss-covered and rotten. Eventually, as I grew older, the winter snows broke it down, leaving only the scar marks and spikes on the trunks of those two pines. Now after eighty years, even the scars have disappeared. All that remains are my memories and those spikes that are embedded somewhere under the bark. In the future, some sawyer in a lumber mill will discover them, much to his unhappiness. Or alternatively, the earth might reclaim the iron after those trees eventually fall to the forest floor.

My first minutes on the cabin porch included an appraisal of the tiptop of the oldest and tallest yellow pine in the area. With a diameter of five feet and a height in the hundreds, it stood along our entrance road, its crest visible from the porch. When I was young its tiptop was forked, each side sprouting green needles. As the years passed, the fork withered and the debarked greyness of death gradually crept downward. In some years, it appeared that the old tree held its own, with no apparent change. In other years, more top branches succumbed to the grayness. In the 1970s the Forest Service marked that tree for cutting with a ring of white spray paint around its trunk. They said it was valuable prime timber, and if not harvested it would soon die of old age. Mom disagreed. She scraped off the government's white marking with a garden hoe and colored over the damaged area using paint that she had matched to the tree's bark. It was never cut and lived on for another sixty years, finally succumbing to pine beetles in my seventy-eighth year. For several years it stood needleless, in austere dignity, a testament to four hundred years of life that has spanned freezing winters, volcanic eruptions, lightning storms and forest fires. Its story is not finished. In death it will provide shelter to forest creatures long after I have departed this earth. I'm glad to have known it and other inhabitants of the surrounding forest.

In that regard, I must admit to having one-way conversations with our cabin and much of the flora, fauna and land that surrounds it. Those conversations continue to this day, bringing me considerable peace of mind and clarity of thought.

* * *

The cabin is situated at the confluence of Willow Creek and the North Fork of the Feather River at about five-thousand-feet elevation. For centuries that location was the site of Maidu Indian summer encampments. There was no gold in this northern watershed, so the forty-niner hordes paid no attention to the place. Sometime in the early nineteenth century there was said to have been a trapper's cabin, but to my knowledge, the Bullard family of Red Bluff was the first to construct anything substantial on the site. In the 1880s they built two log buildings and some tent platforms for sleeping. They regularly used the place every summer until sometime in the 1920s, when their main building burned to the ground. After that they came only sporadically, and they ultimately abandoned the site, leaving behind a functional, single-room log cabin that we maintained and used for storage. The heavy snows of 1952 crushed the roof, and we never rebuilt it. The log walls stood well into the 1970s but eventually turned to dust. Its location now remains only in my memory.

In 1928, Grandpa Barham, with his construction crew from Oakland, built a cabin about two hundred yards upstream from the Bullard location, overlooking the big pool we call the "swimming hole" or "big hole." From then on, Mom and her whole family, including Great Aunt Theresa in her wheelchair, along with cooks and maids and friends, spent every summer there. In 1937 Mom's friend Patty Chickering asked Grandpa Barham to build her a cabin near the spot where the Bullard building had burned. He did so, hand-hewn rock fireplace and all, for a cost of six hundred dollars. In time it turned out that Patty seldom used the place because she lived far away near Victorville in the Mojave Desert. So as time passed, Mom and I spent summers in "Aunt Patty's cabin" to avoid the congestion and noise at the Barham household. In 1946 Dad bought the cabin from Aunt Patty for seven hundred dollars, and from then on it became ours. Mom subsequently spent every summer there for the next sixty years.

The building was single wall, uninsulated construction, with exposed beams and no running water. It had three rooms, a loft, and surrounding porch. The kitchen had a kerosene stove, a sink with drain, and two externally ventilated coolers that were designed to capture and hold the cold night air. Pans hung on the walls, and metal bins protected whatever food Mom left behind over the winter. Next to the kitchen was a dressing room that contained shelves, a clothes hanger bar and a mirrored washstand. This room was mouse-proofed with tin and wire screen so that bedding could be stored there without fear of little creatures making homes in our blankets and mattresses. The living room had a rock hearth and fireplace, an icebox, crockery water dispenser and kerosene lights. A ladder on one wall provided access to the loft. As a child I loved the loft. It was my hangout place. Most nights we slept outdoors on the porch under magnificent star filled skies. Only when it stormed did we move inside, and then I got to sleep up in the loft.

Mom hauled water in buckets from Willow Creek. She said it was good exercise, but as I got older, water hauling became one of my summer jobs. I was about ten when I learned that a gallon of water weighed eight pounds. When Dad arrived in the fall to pick me up for school, I announced that during that summer I had hauled fifty-six thousand pounds of water from Willow Creek. Mom said not to tell anyone or they might think my parents were abusing their child. When I returned to Livermore, I of course told everyone who would listen.

In the mid-1960s Mom finally relented and had a tank-house built out of used lumber that she managed to extract from friends at Pacific Gas and Electric Company. From then on, a Briggs-and-Stratton powered pump moved water from Willow Creek into the tank, a canvas-covered, galvanized water trough. From there it flowed by gravity into the cabin—running water, a revolutionary step forward in our lives.

The sewer system remained rudimentary for several more years. The kitchen and dressing room sinks drained into a covered sump. The sump was roofed with dirt-covered boards so that the forest floor appeared completely natural, that is until a passing bear caught the scent of bacon grease and fish entrails. Almost every spring and sometimes during the summer we had to recover the sump after a bear ripped it apart in search of edibles. Our toilet facilities consisted of two wooden sitting holes over a pit situated about eighty yards from the cabin.

Initially there was no roof or walls. During the summer, privacy was provided by a swath of burlap wrapped around the frame. Mom said that the intense sunlight provided sanitation, though it certainly didn't deter the flies. Toilet paper and reading materials were stored in an old metal bread box so that chipmunks and other rodents couldn't use them for nesting material.

Over time, the burlap walls were replaced with wood, and a roof was installed. A pully and weight mechanism automatically closed the door to help reduce the fly problem. At one point some guest placed a sign on the door that read, "Emma's Place." I learned to plan my bowel movements during daylight hours. A trip to the outhouse by flashlight through the dark, shadowy forest on a cold, moonless night was a fearsome undertaking. At night I urinated off the porch edge, always leaning far out from the railing. Mom hated to see wet stains on the porch boards. Before getting back into bed, I always took a minute to marvel at the Milky Way, spread out overhead as a background to nearby stars and planets. At an early age and still today, I wish that I had been born in the future so that it might be possible to visit those worlds. It was super exciting to see those first satellites drift overhead in the late 1950s.

Each fall as Mom closed the cabin for the winter, she threw powdered lye into the toilet pit in order to extend its life, but eventually the hole filled to the point where a new one had to be dug. When Mom was in her early eighties, the Plumas County Health Inspector visited our cabin and said that she could no longer use our outdoor pit toilet. We referred to it as an "outhouse" or "two-holer." He said that she must immediately install a "code approved" septic tank. Mom, being a tactful and persuasive person, invited the inspector onto the cabin porch "to see her river view," after which she plied him with hot coffee and homemade chocolate chip cookies. Subsequently he agreed that, due to her age and limited means, she could keep the outhouse until the pit was full, but then she must install a proper septic tank. That reprieve was all Mom needed. The next summer she dug a deep hole beside the old one and then used a friend's four-wheel-drive pickup to pull the old outhouse over the new hole. She then carefully filled the old hole, spreading pine needles over the surface to make it look as natural as possible. The inspector never discovered the truth, even when he returned in subsequent years for more coffee and cookies.

I was living in Guam during those years when Mom was dealing with the inspector and slyly digging her the new hole. An excerpt from one of her weekly letters to me reads as follows:

… Every morning when it is still cool, I dig a little bit more on the new toilet hole. I am making good progress. But today I had a disaster. After digging for about an hour I decided that I was thirsty and had other things to do back at the cabin. When I tried to climb out, I couldn't make it. It was too deep. Just as in the old proverb, "I had dug myself into a hole." There was no choice but to pull some dirt back down so that I could climb out. In the end I had to pull back almost all of what I had accomplished. That's my dumb move story for today. Tomorrow I'll definitely put the ladder in the hole before starting …

*   *   *

Our initial invigorating arrival on the cabin porch was short-lived. Afternoon shadows had begun creeping, and Mom would say, "All right, Paul dear, time to get going. You sweep the porch while I open the shutters and take out the log supports." She called me "dear" a lot. The older I got, the less I liked it.

Paul and Dad Joe at the Big Hole, 1945

Hinged wooden shutters covered all windows and doors, and seven debarked tamarack trunks were wedged between roof trusses and the floor in order to transfer winter snow loads away from the walls toward the floor joists and foundation. In the years prior to our current global warming, it wasn't uncommon for the cabin to be buried in fifteen to twenty feet of snow during mid-winter. When we arrived in early June, snow drifts still occupied shady places throughout the forest, their moisture supporting an abundance of ravenously hungry mosquitos.

The real work began once the shutters were opened, the tamarack braces removed, and the porches swept. The ice that we had brought from Chester had to be lifted into the icebox. Buckets of water had to be hauled from Willow Creek. Luggage and groceries had to be unpacked and stowed, beds made with several layers of wool blankets, lamps and stove filled with kerosene, firewood and kindling stockpiled. Mom tried to make the work fun. We competed to see who might be first to spot snow plants poking their red asparagus-like tops out of the pine duff. At Willow Creek we looked for tiger lilies and other early spring flowers. Interesting birds and animals provided an excuse for respite and observation.

Our tasks on arrival included a trip to Domingo Springs. Mom loaded five-gallon, glass water bottles into her Dodge for the three-mile dirt road journey. The spring was, and still is today, a marvelous place of God's creation. Every minute hundreds of gallons of ice-cold water gush from lava rocks at the base of giant pines and aspens. A crystal-clear pool forms the headwaters of Domingo Creek, which meanders through the adjacent meadow on its way to join the Feather River. The water has flowed continuously for centuries, its source unknown. During my lifetime the rate of flow has never changed.

Until I was older, Mom never let me help with the water bottles for fear they might break. She filled them while I searched for Indian arrowheads. The Springs had been a site of Maidu Indian encampments, and relics remained scattered over the surrounding area. By the time Mom loaded the bottles into the Dodge and gathered some watercress for our salads, I had usually wandered far down the creek on my quest for arrowheads. Having found some broken pieces, there was always hope that the next patch of earth might yield an undamaged specimen. I loved this pastime and spent countless hours each summer pursuing it in various locations up and down the river. Being loathe to abandon my search, I responded slowly to Mom's calls—that is, until her tone required immediate action. At that point further delay was not an option. Upon returning to the car, Mom always reveled in my success as I showed off my booty. Throughout my life Mom's enthusiasm and interest in my undertakings made a significant contribution to my self-confidence and success.

Back at the cabin Mom hefted those bottles onto the porch and up into our ceramic olla water dispenser, the storage vessel for our drinking water. We used water from Willow Creek only for cooking or for dishes and bathing. Our first night's dinner was usually something simple like Campbell's soup and toasted cheese sandwiches, eaten in front of a crackling fire. As we did for the entire summer, we washed our hands and faces in a basin on the kitchen side porch, mixing hot water from a kettle with cold from the water buckets. We brushed our teeth while leaning over the railing, rinsing with a cup of cold water. The towels, cups and toothbrushes were hung on nails along the cabin wall.

Then it was into flannel pajamas and my bed on the porch, a WWII army-surplus cot with plenty of wool covers over flannel blanket sheets. The surrounding treetops were silhouetted against a black sky that contained billions of twinkling stars. The Big Dipper was high in the north, its spout pointing to the North Star. The sound of the river, its rapids swollen with spring runoff, dominated all forest sounds. Sleep came quickly.

As I grew older and stronger, I took over more of the workload, but for all intents and purposes, this is how my summers began every year until I went away to college. Memory of those times, the solitude, sounds and smells, have sustained me throughout my life, providing an anchor in times of turmoil.

*   *   *

The Swift family cabin was located on Domingo Creek, about a quarter mile walk from our cabin. George and Mary Swift had three children. Cameron (Cam) was two years older than I. Carol was my age, and Dean was three or four years younger. Like Mom and I, they came every year from their home in Benicia and stayed throughout the summer. No other cabins had occupants with children that stayed the whole summer, so Cam and I became close friends. We both loved to flyfish and spent hours together tying elegant creations that mimicked real world insects. Cam was lucky to have a father and uncles who were accomplished trout fishermen. My Grandma and Grandpa Barham were good fishers, and they taught me much about the art of trout fishing; however, I probably learned the most about flyfishing from Cam. Critical skills include camouflage body positioning and casting techniques that present a natural appearance to the fly as it floats on the water. Techniques differ greatly between fast-moving streams and placid beaver ponds. Cam was particularly skilled, and I became pretty good myself.

Over the years I grew to know every rock, trail and crossing place along the river within fishing distance of our cabin. As I got older, I ventured further down the canyon toward Chester, often returning well after dark with a catch of German brown and rainbow trout, wet to the waist and shivering. In those days the limit was fifteen, but I never paid much attention to limits. Mom had this rule: "If you catch'm, you clean'm. I'll cook'm." So after peeling off my wet clothes, I set to work cleaning, salting and wrapping by kerosene light, all the while anticipating a hot bowl of soup and a sandwich in front of the fire.

Sometimes Cam and I took extended, all-day fishing expeditions, far up the river to where it became Rice Creek, or down river to the place where Warner Creek joined. We had names for some of our favorite fishing locations: Lake's hole, White's hole, Evan's beach, Eva's hole, the hatchery. We hiked to the headwaters of Willow Creek, fished in Willow Lake, and camped there overnight. Trout fishing was the center of our lives, and all else revolved around it.

The swimming pool below Grandpa's cabin was referred to as the "big hole." It provided a community gathering spot on hot summer afternoons. Over eons the river had cut down through an ancient lava flow, leaving a small waterfall and a twenty-foot-deep streambed surrounded on both sides by lava rock, which in places towered thirty feet above the water. At its downstream end the pool widened beside a grassy meadow that we called "the beach." Every afternoon people from nearby cabins came to the "big hole" for swimming fun, conversation and gossip. Cam was an athletically fit, wiry guy and a beautiful diver. When he pushed off in a swan dive from the highest rocks, his body seemed to defy gravity as it floated down into a knife-edged entry that produced only churning bubbles. I didn't have the courage to attempt those high dives, so I became a confirmed jumper whose body plummeted feet-first like a sack of barley. My cannonball entries could throw sheets of water over the surroundings.

The river was cold, always near fifty-six degrees. We kids didn't seem to mind the cold as we explored all parts of the pool with diving masks and fins, at times trying to spear trout with three-pointed frog spears. Mom had a rule that when our lips turned blue, it was time get out and warm up. A few minutes lying prostrate on the hot lava rocks stopped the shivering and warmed the innards. Then it was back into the water for renewed fun and adventure. We floated throughout the pool and down the rapids sitting in innertubes that we paddled using pie pans as oars. Mom was a fierce caretaker of her favorite kitchen pie pans. Woe to me if any were missing.

The forest and its waterways were our playground and in many ways our teacher. We made friends of chipmunks and golden mantled ground squirrels by feeding them sunflower seeds. Some ate while sitting in our hands. For several summers, Mrs. Swift (we were required to address adults by title and last name) got us involved in butterfly and moth collecting, an undertaking in which even little Dean could participate. Our bug nets at the ready, we searched forest and meadow for elusive specimens, which we killed in jars laced with carbon tetrachloride and then mounted, wings outstretched, into derelict cigar boxes.

We watched the water ouzels bob and dip in the rapids as they caught minnows and waterborne insect larvae. We found their nests on rock faces overhanging the water and watched as they raised their young. We learned about the habits of forest birds using Cam's ten power binoculars. We discovered a hunter's deer blind, a platform built high up between two trees overlooking a well-traveled deer trail. Railroad spikes created a ladder up one of the tree trunks. It became our secret hideout and fort. From there we saw the comings and goings of many forest creatures. Further discoveries included red ant hills that sent out a million ant armies to attack their more docile black neighbors. For amusement we tossed carpenter ants to their annihilation on the red ant hills. We placed captured ants into the dusty funnel cones of antlion nests in order to watch the ensuing battles, the outcomes of which were not always certain.

At the age of ten I was allowed to wear a six-inch blade knife in a scabbard on my belt. That knife and I were seldom separated. It endured being thrown at targets and sometimes used as a hammer. It cleaned fish, cut fishing lines and leaders, bent hooks, chopped trails through willows, whittled carvings, opened cans and got poked into mysterious places. I religiously sharpened it and still possess it today.

Barring exceptional circumstances and fishing trips, we were required to be home at our own cabins by mealtimes. Mom didn't allow swimming for at least one hour after eating, so after lunch I frequently walked to the end of our entry road and waited on a stump near our mailbox. Yes, despite not having running water or electricity, we did have five-day-a-week mail service. Our mailbox was nailed to a tree beside the road. A contract mailman picked up mail at the Chester post office and delivered it to mountain residents scattered over a large area. His route included our cabins and Warner Valley up to the National Park boundary. He normally arrived shortly after lunch in his dust-drenched, faded orange pickup. I have long since forgotten the postman's name, but he was a congenial, accommodating fellow. Mom and Mrs. Swift sometimes gave him grocery lists, which he filled on his own time and delivered the next day as he passed.

Occasionally the mail contained a letter from Dad to me or Mom. That was a happy day. Also, Mom ordered postal delivery of the *San Francisco Chronicle*. It arrived a few days late. The Sunday paper showed up on Tuesdays. Save for what news we could pick up on our weekly trips to Chester, that paper was our only window into the outside world. While walking back toward the cabin, I checked out the front-page headlines. My dyslexic mind appreciated the big print and orderly columns. I never enjoyed comics. Reading their irregular and abbreviated scripts was more work for me than it was worth. Mom usually read the front section before her afternoon swim. The rest she consumed by kerosene light in the evenings, sometimes reading articles aloud to me as she went along. I haven't forgotten her elation with the headlines that said the armistice had been signed and the Korean War was over. That was toward the end of July, 1953. I was eleven years old.

In 1955 Dad hired some carpenters to build a one-room extension onto the fireplace end of our cabin. It functioned as a tool shed and later as a bunkhouse for me and school friends that I invited to the cabin. David Dutro and Leo Andersen were regular summer visitors, but others like Wally Walker and Richard Flanigan also made appearances. Mom limited their stay to three weeks, saying that it was all she could handle of teenage boys who ate everything in sight and thought they were invincible. Her speeches to new arrivals went something like this: "I intend to deliver you boys back to your parents well fed and in one piece, so I expect you will at all times give me your full attention. There will be morning chores. When I make a rule, I expect you to obey it. When I ask you to do something, I expect it to be done quickly. Rule number one is, no one goes beyond sight of this cabin without telling me where you are going." She made quite a few additional rules as well while at the same time keeping us enthusiastic and filled with wholesome food. We seldom took baths. Mom said that the forest's volcanic dust was "clean dirt" and daily swimming was enough. But every so often we were forced to take a shower with soap at Grandpa's cabin, where there was hot running water from a propane boiler.

Aside from the Swift children, several young people my age sometimes spent time in various nearby cabins. Mike Ratto and his younger brother, Jeff, occupied a cabin across from us on Willow Creek. Jan Jensen and his brother, Eric, lived up the river near the Swifts. Valery Smith and her two sisters lived where Domingo Creek joined the river. Sue Sequara occupied a cabin just up the river from my grandparents. She was a blonde goddess. In her presence I found it difficult to stammer a complete sentence. One summer when I was about sixteen, Sue's older brother, Paul, arrived in his own car with a girlfriend. The Sequara parents, wanting a chaperone, required that Sue accompany Paul and his girlfriend whenever they went cavorting at night to Chester town or Lake Almanor. A couple of times Sue invited me along to keep her company on these excursions. I found myself in the back seat of Paul's car with this gorgeous creature as we explored the Lake Almanor nightlife. I was so self-conscious and timorous that, from my perspective, nothing seemed to have gone well. I have no idea how Sue felt, other than to observe that she never suggested future outings. In any case, I wish that I had been more confident and relaxed.

Most afternoons everyone gathered at the "big hole." In addition to Carol Swift, the Smith girls and Sue Sequara, other young ladies sometimes arrived from cabins along Willow Creek or from Chester and Lake Almanor. Hoping for attention, some of us boys showed off. I just ogled and dreamed. My friend Leo was a diver on the Livermore High swim team. Both he and Cam Swift attracted much attention with their high dives. At one point, Leo did a pike summersault off the highest rocks, some thirty plus feet above the water. It attracted considerable attention, but Mom had forbidden diving from that spot, and unfortunately for Leo, she happened to be watching from Grandpa's cabin porch. When Leo surfaced, a shriek of doom echoed through the forest: "Leo Anderson, you get up here right now." He had attracted attention all right, but not exactly the kind he had set out to achieve. I don't know what Mom said to Leo, but he remained a bit sheepish for a few days. Several years later when I was away at college, a young man from Chester was showing off by diving from that same spot. An inadvertent misstep made him a quadriplegic for the rest of his life.

Each summer my cousins, Jim and Randy, and their parents, Janice and Jerry Cramer, arrived for a two or three week stay with Grandpa and Grandma. That cabin became full of action, so I spent much time there. When not swimming, we three boys played hearts and Monopoly by the hour on the back porch and reveled in Grandma's buttermilk pancakes served to us through the kitchen window. I was astonished at the loving affection that Jan and Jerry Cramer openly displayed.

Paul on the cabin porch railing, the North Fork of the
Feather and Big Hole in the background, 1956

They seemed never to argue, and they did everything together, with lots of kissing and loving along the way. Their intimacy made me feel that something must be wrong with my family. Mom and Dad never acted lovingly and sometimes argued, while frequently going their separate ways. I thought Randy and Jim were lucky to have parents like that, and I was sure that, somehow, I was deprived. Later in life I came to understand that there are no perfect marriages, and one should never judge the quality of marital relationships based on superficial appearances. Marital strengths and difficulties are both obscure and intricate. Through compromise and mutual respect, my parents melded their differences into a cooperative and functional relationship that served our family well. I profited immensely from their union.

*   *   *

During summers at the cabin, I interacted with some memorable individuals, each of whom contributed in their own way to my growth and maturity. One such person could be found every morning, excepting Sundays, bundled in layers of warm clothing, on the topmost rocks above the swimming hole, fishing rod in hand. Her name was Mina Andersen. Her husband, Paul Andersen, had for many years been the maintenance supervisor for the Plaza Building in Oakland, the same building that housed Grandpa's Barham Company. For several years the Andersens had occupied the Barham cabin each fall after Grandpa and Grandma had departed for Piedmont. Mrs. Andersen cleaned and Mr. Anderson did minor repairs and prepared the cabin for winter. In subsequent years the Andersens had built their own cabin on the east side of Willow Creek near where it joined the river. They were both immigrants with heavy accents, he Norwegian and she Swedish. I wish I knew more of their story. On the surface they seemed like night and day. He was gaunt and agile, she rotund and plodding, he stern and exacting, continuously smoking a pipe, she gentle and welcoming, always sporting a smile. They were approachable neighbors but largely kept to themselves, their three children having grown and moved on. I was possibly one of their few frequent visitors. Mrs. Andersen's hot cinnamon rolls, fresh out of her wood stove oven, were a tempting attraction. She called them *kanelbulle*.

Upon reflection, there may have been a bit of friction, or at least unease, between my Grandpa Barham and Mr. Andersen. After building their own cabin the Andersens remained cordial in passing but never visited or socialized with the Barhams, even though the Barhams had provided the initial opportunity for the Andersens to discover our Feather River location. It's possible that Mr. Andersen was or had been a debtor client of Barham Company; however, I suspect that Grandpa, being quite class conscious, felt that Mr. Andersen was a working-class immigrant who had been provided the privilege of occupying the Barham cabin in return for maintenance and winterizing assistance. Grandpa likely thought it audacious of Mr. Andersen to have used that introduction as an opportunity to move into our mountain neighborhood. Mom went out of her way to engage with Mrs. Andersen, making sure that she knew of community happenings and showing interest in her children's health and activities. I suspect Mom was trying to compensate for what she knew to be her father's prejudice.

Each day when I awoke, there was Mrs. Andersen, fishing in the same place and in the same way, sitting on those high rocks near the falls, above the deepest part of the swimming hole. Mountain mornings are cold, yet she regularly walked in the grey dawn from her cabin across the log bridge on Willow Creek, past our cabin and Grandpa's cabin, to her perch on those rocks. Sometimes when the sun had reached her location, I went down to the "big hole" and talked with her. She was always welcoming and let me observe her catch and fishing technique, which involved using heavy lead weights to sink a baited hook to the bottom. There it remained until a fish came along to munch on the tempting combination of hellgrammites and nightcrawlers. At certain times each summer there were spawning runs of German brown and rainbow trout. During those days Mrs. Andersen caught a lot, sometimes two or three big fish a morning. At times when the big fish weren't running, she caught nothing. I asked her one day why she bothered to fish on cold mornings when there were no fish to catch. She replied in a Swedish accent that I am not skilled enough to reproduce: "Paul, it's not the catching that's important. It's the fishing. I see the sunlight every morning; first it shines on the ridge top, then it creeps down the mountain toward me. I see the ouzels awake to feed their babies. Sometimes I see deer and other night animals looking for a place to rest by day. Sometime ducks bring their children over the falls and into the pool. Sometimes eagles and osprey fly past. I don't care if I catch fish, but I do care about my morning fishing."

Often, I saw Mrs. Andersen wading in Willow Creek with a bucket, collecting her hellgrammites (Dobsonfly larvae) and other insect larvae for bait. During the spawning runs, I often joined her on the rocks in the early mornings. Sometimes I netted her fish in order that she didn't have to climb down from her perch. When the sun's warmth reached us, we often conversed, mostly about me, Mom and the weather, but never about Mrs. Andersen. During heavy fish runs, we caught more fish than we could use, so she taught me the art of cold smoking using dry aspen and green willow wood. Her husband had built a smoker from a discarded steel ice container and a chimney pipe. With Mom's help we built a similar smoker at our cabin, and I became quite proficient.

At this writing, the Andersen cabin remains, dilapidated and seldom used, in the forest above Willow Creek, its brick chimney in disrepair, its porch boards broken by winter snows. After Paul and Mina passed away, the Andersen children and grandchildren took little interest in the old place. The fact that it still remains standing gives testament to the fine workmanship of the man who built it. I hope at some point it can be revived by a loving owner. Even now when I walk by what remains of the back porch, I can still hear Mrs. Andersen's warm greeting and the smell of those cinnamon rolls. I suspect that her spirit is still comfortably perched on that rock above the "big hole" watching the sunlight progress down the ridge to the river. When I sit on my cabin porch in the mornings, I still find myself looking for her.

* * *

A bit upstream on Willow Creek from the Andersen cabin lived Fred and Jeannette Righter. Their cabin was somewhat more polished than others, having insulated double walls and the first propane refrigerator in the area. Fred was a boisterous, outgoing, cigar-smoking, retired soap salesman. For years he had driven the highways and byways of western states for the consumer products division of U.S. Borax Company. He operated on only two levels: full-speed ahead and full stop. He knew everything there was to know about soap and could easily be enticed to expound on the subject. His wife, Jeannette, was a city girl and a bit of a floozy, but she could rein in Fred when he got carried away. They were both in their sixties and had no children. Always addressing each other as "honey," they were a bit eccentric but warm hearted, welcoming and generous to all neighbors.

Mr. and Mrs. Righter were frequent attendees at the swimming hole in the afternoons. They both enjoyed swimming in the cold water, Jeannette floating on her back, and Fried jumping from the rocks in an attempt to make the biggest possible splash. He couldn't swim well, his style being more akin to a dog-paddle than a stroke. Once or twice every summer, when the number of children at the swimming hole was highest, Mr. Righter arrived with a roll of shiny silver quarters. Without a word, he would start tossing those coins, one at a time, into the pool. We all went crazy jumping and diving from the rocks, our eyes focused on those silver specks scattered among the rocks and gravel of the river bottom. Mr. Righter seemed to enjoy our frenzied response as much as we did. Our parents endured the practice, hoping it didn't occur too often. Twenty-five-cents was a lot of money in those days.

The Righters often fished on lakes in the surrounding area where boat rental facilities were available. I sometimes watched Fred meticulously caring for his twenty-horsepower Evinrude outboard, having no idea at the time how important outboard motors would become in my future life. At least once every summer, the Righters, Mom, and I traveled to Bucks Lake, near Quincy, for camping and fishing. The trip was harrowing for both Mom and me. She feared Fred's driving, and I feared getting car sick. During years on the road as a salesman he had developed quite a lead foot. His approach on curvy mountain roads was to maintain a straight line wherever possible. "The shortest distance between two points," he said. Jeannette didn't drive and remained oblivious as Fred flew along, puffing billowing clouds of cigar smoke in his Pontiac Safari V-8.

After negotiating the twisting, uphill dirt road to Bucks Lake, we rented a boat, installed Fred's outboard, and transported Mom, food and camping gear to the far shore. There she set up camp while we three trolled for lake trout. With three lines playing out from the stern, care had to be taken to avoid entanglements. In those days we had no global positioning or fish finder technologies. Positioning and depth were a matter of guesswork and experience. From the time we set out to the time we returned, Mr. and Mrs. Righter squabbled about one thing or another—our location, direction, speed, line length, lure configuration, turning radius. It seemed strange to me that every sentence of their incessant bickering started and ended with the endearing word "honey." I thought, *How can two people call each other "honey" as frequently as they do yet argue as much as they do?* Whenever a fish was lost or gear tangled, blame had to be assigned and acknowledged or the Fred vs. Jeannette Honey dialogue erupted into full bloom. I sat where I was told, fished where I was told, kept my mouth shut, and usually caught more fish than either of them. If she wished, I exchanged lines with Mrs. Righter, but still I caught more fish.

The Bucks Lake trip was always fun. Mom was an excellent camp cook, and the star-filled nights were exceptional. We survived Fred's driving and usually arrived home with several limits of big lake trout. That meant numerous days of smoking and gifting to neighbors. I will never forget Fred Righter's flamboyant, gung-ho, fast driving, cigar-smoking kindness. At one point I spent a month constructing, painting, and rigging a twenty-mule-team Borax wagon model that he gave me. Dad helped mount it on a long board. It hung around our house for years, but somewhere along the way it vanished from my life. Like Fred and Jeannette Righter, it remains only in my memory. Their cabin has changed hands twice over the years, but to me it will always remain the Righter cabin.

*   *   *

Norman Isherwood had a reputation among surrounding neighbors as a grumpy, nasty old man who did not like children. In early spring, as soon as the snow melt allowed, he and his wife arrived at their cabin, a quarter mile upstream from us. They remained throughout the summer and fall until the snows fell once again, living as much as possible off the land. Mrs. Isherwood gathered wild berries, greens and tubers. Mr. Isherwood fished for trout before, during, and after the legal fishing season. He shot deer as he needed the meat, irrespective of official hunting seasons. He maintained a feeding pit into which he threw edible scraps and garbage for the purpose of attracting bears. In late fall he shot one of the unsuspecting creatures, both for its meat and its lard. Mom said that when he rendered the fat, she could smell it all the way to our cabin. By that time of year, I was long gone, back to school in Livermore.

I always gave Mr. Isherwood's cabin a wide birth whenever I walked up river to fish or visit the Swift kids. However, I never actually saw the man, even at a distance, until I was about eight years old. That night we had just finished eating dinner on Grandpa Barham's cabin porch that overlooked the big swimming hole. Someone had anchored an innertube in the center of the pool so that young, weak swimmers like me might have a resting place as we swam across. Apparently, Mr. Isherwood felt that the innertube and its rope anchor-line were an obstruction in one of his favorite fishing spots. Our family had been of the mind that swimming activities at the "big hole" took precedence over fishing activities. Mrs. Andersen had not complained, though she probably wasn't altogether happy about the tube's presence. Mr. Isherwood, however, clearly disagreed with the policy of swimmer's preference.

The homemade pie a la mode had just settled into my stomach, and Grandpa was licking the edge of his freshly-rolled after dinner Bull Durham cigarette, when a resounding blast emanated from the pool area, followed by another and then another. I looked toward the pool just in time to see the inner tube surrounded by foam on its way to the bottom. Mr. Isherwood, gun in hand, his wife beside him, stood on the rocks above the pool. His 12-gauge shotgun had unequivocally eliminated the obstruction to his fishing activities. Swimmers did not have priority so long as he was calling the shots.

That event, as well as his letters to the editor complaining about fish and game regulations, marked Mr. Isherwood as a fierce contrarian, not a person to be trifled with. Cabin owners did their best to avoid him—that is, except Mom. She was impressed with the man, feeling that the articulate nature of his writings reflected a person of considerable depth. She was curious to know about his background and took every opportunity to interact with him. One early morning two or three years after the shooting incident, she saw from our cabin porch that Mr. Isherwood had hooked a big trout and was having difficulty landing it. She grabbed a net off the cabin wall, ran down to the river and netted the fish for him. That fish turned out to be a six-pound rainbow trout, the largest caught in any California river that year. In fact, Mr. Isherwood held the state record for several subsequent years.

One morning when I was about eleven, I worked up the courage to speak with him while he was fishing at the "big hole." The conversation went something like this:

"Hello Mr. Isherwood. Have you caught anything today?"

"You're Emma Callaghan's son?"

"Yes, sir."

"What's your name?

"Paul, sir."

"Look in that creel over there." He gestured toward a wicker creel behind him. It was filled with grass and ferns, but nestled amid the greens lay a nice fish, a German Brown, about two pounds.

"Wow, nice fish," I said.

"I see you fly fishing in the evenings. I'll bet you catch some nice ones yourself," he said.

"Yes, but I catch mostly little ones. Mom thinks they're better eating."

"Do you tie your own flies?" he asked.

"Yes, my grandma gave me a fly-tying vice and bobbin for Christmas. I get feathers and hooks by mail order from Herter's. Cam Swift and I tie flies together a lot. He's really a good fly fisherman."

"Yes, I see you walking up to the Swift cabin quite often. You boys haven't been playing around with my ram, have you? Someone's been fooling with it, and I don't appreciate that." His voice had taken on a sinister tone.

I knew exactly what he meant. The source of water for his cabin was a hydraulic ram pump on Domingo Creek. We kids thought the ram was an amazing machine. It pumped water with no engine or power source. The force of water flowing downstream in a big pipe pushed water uphill in a smaller pipe to his tank house. Water spurted out a valve on top of the ram, then stopped, then spurted, then stopped, continuously all day and night. It was a machine with a heartbeat. And we enjoyed pushing on the valve with a stick to stop the heartbeat and watch the water just spurt out. However, sometimes when we stopped playing with it, the ram's regular heartbeat did not return, and we ran away in fear of Mr. Isherwood's wrath, should he catch us.

"I don't know about that," I said. "Cam and I just tie flies and sometimes play chess or checkers and hearts, but hearts requires three players, so Carol Swift has to agree to play, and she usually doesn't." He was clearly unmoved by my mendacious and evasive response, but he let it stand unchallenged.

"And you sometimes play in my deer blind on the old CCC road behind the Swift cabin, don't you?"

"Yes, sir." I was shocked that he knew of our hideout and that he was the one who had built it. "But we take care of it."

"Yes, including carving your initials into the roof braces. Please don't fall off that platform. It's a long way down, and I don't want your parents blaming me for having constructed a dangerous attraction."

I didn't answer. He checked his bait and recast it into the deepest part of the pool before observing, "You say you play chess?"

"Yes, sir. I play with Cam and some of my friends back in Livermore, but no one in our family plays. I've tried to teach Mom, but she isn't good at remembering how the different pieces move."

"Would you be willing to play chess with me?" he asked. "I'm always interested in a game."

"Sure!" I said.

"If it's agreeable with your mother, come to my cabin around eleven tomorrow morning. We'll play some chess and have lunch together. Does that sound satisfactory?"

"Yes, sir. Should I bring my chess board and pieces?"

"No. That won't be necessary. I have a board."

When I told Mom, she was delighted that I had made headway in getting to know Mr. Isherwood, but she reminded me to be on my best behavior, not to stay too long, and to return there only when invited.

He had a chessboard all right. It and the pieces were hand-carved marble. During that summer we played chess on the back porch of his cabin two or three times a week, for sessions lasting several hours. The rules were that he must move within five seconds. I could have all the time I needed to contemplate my moves. I never won a match the entire summer. Toward the end we did have one draw, but I suspect that he purposely allowed that to happen. He taught me chess notation and gave me homework problems. For example, "Beginning on position B1, move the knight so that it lands on every square of the board at least one time, and record the list of your moves." When I had accomplished that in one hundred six moves, he said, "All right, now see if you can do it in less moves, trying not to land on the same square twice." That kept me busy for many nights. On one afternoon toward the end of summer, he cleared the board except for one knight in position B1. "All right," he said, "you record my moves. I'll show you the

Knight's Tour." He moved that knight around the board, landing on sixty-four different squares in exactly sixty-four moves.

When I returned to Livermore that fall, I had no problem beating my friends in chess. Mr. Isherwood had shown me that the first step in learning is to gain perspective as to the extent of one's ignorance. When something appears simple, it's often that we don't comprehend its intricacy. With regard to chess, he showed me that excellence requires complete competitive immersion and a level of mental acuity that is likely beyond my reach. That next summer I concocted polite excuses for rejecting his invitations, and I hardly ever played chess again, but to this day I hold much respect for those who do. Inadvertently, Mr. Isherwood introduced me to a bedrock concept of economic theory—all choices have opportunity costs. I was unwilling to take time away from other enjoyable pursuits because the value of what I would give up was too great. The costs of becoming a really competent chess player outweighed the benefits. Perhaps if Mr. Isherwood had made the learning a little more enjoyable and a little less onerous, I might have pursued chess further. In any case, my father's philosophy has provided a guide throughout my lifetime: "It is better to be a jack of all trades than a master of one."

*   *   *

Those first eighteen summers at the Chester cabin provided insights that have influenced my entire life. I learned to appreciate solitude. As Mom put it, "Learn how to be alone. It can be invigorating, and it allows you to perceive more of what is around and inside you." I learned to entertain myself, to appreciate and respect nature and its seasonality, to make do with less and live with meager amenities. I learned the worth of patience, planning and persistence, the value of routine and the satisfaction of physical accomplishment. My mother's friends, Maurine McKeany, Kit Carson, Jacque Watkins and Estelle Booth broadened my perspective and provided an enduring appreciation for the capability of women.

As of this writing, only five of our once youthful group still maintain and use their family cabins. My cousins Jim and Randy Cramer inherited Grandpa Barham's cabin through their mother, Janice. They and their children spend varying amounts of time there each summer. Carol Swift inherited her family cabin and lives there for much of each summer. She is now a retired science teacher and a talented stained-glass artist. Her brother Cam is retired from being Curator of Ichthyology at Los Angeles Museum of Natural History. He now lives in South Carolina. Dean, their younger brother, is a landscape architect living in Scotland. Jan Jensen inherited his parents' cabin, where he regularly spends the summer months from snow melt to snow fall. In the winters he resides in Chester. Over the years, Jan has been of great assistance to our family. He remains a valued helper and friend.

I still maintain our cabin. It remains much as it was, though it now sports propane lights, stove and refrigerator, as well as an indoor toilet and septic system. The playing card, checkers, and Monopoly games of my youth still remain on the shelves, as do cigar boxes full of collected obsidian artifacts. Fishing gear still hangs on the wall. The rock fireplace has seen many fires. There is still no hot running water. Barely visible on a doorjamb are penciled marks and dates that show my progression of height as I grew into manhood. Another jamb bears similar, but more legible, marks for my children. Every so often while sitting on the cabin porch during the summer months, I hear the shouts of glee as young swimmers and divers splash in the "big hole." It's reassuring to know that a new generation has pulled themselves away from their electronic devices long enough to enjoy a most miraculous place.

Chapter 6

Teenage Years

My time in the sixth, seventh and eighth grades at St. Michael's School was filled with those common difficulties associated with puberty. Parental limits seemed more restrictive. My voice deepened. I grew taller, faster. Hair started growing everywhere. Pimples disrupted my complexion. I became self-conscious as other guys grew more competitive and girls seemed more attractive. Along with this, the ever-vigilant nuns intensified their efforts to ensure separation of the sexes.

In staunch opposition to the nuns, Mom maintained a firm commitment to coeducation. In earlier years she might have taken her appeal for integration to the relatively liberal parish priests, Father O'Donnell and Father Egan, for whom she had considerable respect. Regrettably, they had been reassigned and replaced by Father William Hennessy, an older Irish conservative. Mom considered him to be a hopeless ignoramus, so she rallied members of the St. Michael's Mothers Club to take on the more tractable school principal, Sister Allice.

Mom's initial objective was a small concession having to do with our regular Friday square dance classes. She didn't see why ballroom dance instruction couldn't also be provided. At Mom's approach, Sister Allice was uncooperative and dismissive, stating that ballroom dance lessons were against church policy, since they facilitated close physical contact between boys and girls, potentially leading to sins against chastity. Mom was undeterred. Soon Sister Allice received a resolution passed unanimously by the Mother's Club, along with funding to cover the additional instruction. Though not without some trepidation, I was soon able to put my arm around the waist of Catherine Ferrario and float momentarily in heavenly bliss on the dance floor. During my years at St. Michael's, Sister Allice learned that being dismissive of Mom was not a course of action without consequence.

*   *   *

My parents' approach to the vagaries of puberty and the pressures of teenage stress was to keep me fully engaged in activities, many of which departed from the norm of my classmates. There was coin and stamp collecting as well as wine bottle label collecting. I built airplane and ship models, did copper engraving, painted by the numbers and constructed jigsaw puzzles. I'm sure I was the only one in the seventh and eighth grades who regularly listened to classical music or played chess for a summer with a ranked master, or received duplicate bridge lessons from the world renown Charles Henry Goren. I was also kept busy with snow skiing, shooting, hunting, trout fishing and fly tying, with a bit of biking and tennis thrown in. It's worth noting, however, that recreational reading was never on my list of enjoyable activities. I read what was required or necessary for self-improvement, but I never thought of reading as a pleasurable pastime. It was hard work. I feel that way to this day.

Much to my regret, I was never encouraged to take music lessons. Apparently, Mom had been forced to endure several years of repugnant piano lessons and recitals as a child, so she vowed to protect me from that same fate. Consequently, my music education was limited to listening. We had no television until I was in the seventh grade, so I missed out on the Howdy Doody era, save for limited exposure at the homes of friends whose families owned televisions. I undertook most activities alone or with my parents and their friends. Mom and Dad seldom hired babysitters, so I accompanied them to cocktail parties and gatherings where I was the only young person among adults whose children were already grown. I learned to dress properly, in coat and tie when necessary. By the sixth grade I could tie a half Windsor knot and politely maneuver a silent butler around a crowded room without disturbing hors d'oeuvre plates, cocktail glasses, or party participants. I was known as Joe Callaghan's polite, well behaved young son, and I learned how to deal effectively with older people. These skills served me well in later life when it came time to interact with elder supervisors, academics and politicians.

*   *   *

I hung around a lot with Dad at the ranch vineyard. Since his retirement from the bank, Dad spent much of his time at the ranch doing odd jobs, building things and tending to the vineyard. He had modified a portion of the barn into a one-bedroom apartment. The occupant was an Italian man named Angelo Maffa. Angelo was one of Dad's attempts at social rehabilitation. It was well-known around the Valley that Angelo was an exceptionally good pruner and vineyardist. Unfortunately, he was also a homeless alcoholic, locally referred to as a "wino" because he drank sweet wines like port and sherry. No one wanted to hire Angelo, but Dad believed that everyone deserves a chance to restart their lives, so he offered Angelo the apartment, utilities included, and a dollar an hour wages if he would sober up, help with the vineyard, and do odd jobs as requested. A dollar an hour was an acceptable wage back in the early 1950s.

Despite some improvement, Angelo still drank a lot. Dad allowed him to make his own wine in one corner of the barn, thinking that the home vintage might be better for Angelo than store-bought port and sherry. At the end of each harvest season, Dad gave Angelo a half ton of grapes. I watched as Angelo crushed them by foot, using rubber waders in an open half barrel. When he got out, he did so by climbing out of the waders, leaving them behind in the barrel so as not to introduce contamination from the barn's dirt floor. In this way the entire half ton of grapes was mashed in batches and transferred to a larger, open topped, five-hundred-gallon barrel for fermentation. Eventually the brew was filtered and moved to small kegs and an assortment of glass and ceramic containers. At times during the year our barn smelled like a winery, or more appropriately, a vinegar factory. Dad said that Angelo's wine was pretty bad, but I liked it. If I knocked on Angelo's door when Dad wasn't around, I could count on being offered a glass of wine and a hunk of French bread, so long as I gave Angelo the rabbits that I'd shot in the vineyard. Angelo's rabbit stew was lots better than his wine.

My first lessons in finance and economics occurred during grape harvesting. Each worker used a chalk marker to place a unique personal symbol on the wooden boxes they had filled with grapes: "A" for Mrs. Azevedo, "R" for Mr. Rodriguez, etc. The vines weren't trained on wire trellises as they are today. Each bush stood alone. Workers slid the empty wooden boxes under the vines and cut the grape stems with a hook knife so that the bunches fell into the box without damage. It was backbreaking stoop labor in the hot sun. The filled boxes were carried to the end of each row and stacked. Twice daily Charley Gardella arrived with his truck to haul the harvest off to the winery. As each box was lifted onto the truck bed, Dad recorded it in his little black book under the name of the appropriate worker. If he saw crushed or broken grapes or a poorly filled box, he noted that too. The workers were paid somewhere between twenty and thirty cents per box, depending on the richness of the harvest, the price of grapes at the winery, and the availability of workers. At the end of each day every worker received an envelope containing a check, or sometimes cash, in payment for their previous day's work. It was my job to write names on the envelopes, tally each worker's number of boxes, multiply that by the price per box, and fill out the checks for Dad's signature. When I was young, ten or eleven, Dad checked my work. As I got older, he didn't need to do that anymore. I should note that a skilled and strong worker could harvest fifty boxes in an eight-to-ten-hour day. Depending on the going rate per box, that translated into between ten and fifteen dollars. In the 1950s, that was a decent wage for a day laborer. Also, when the harvest was complete, Dad paid bonuses to the workers who showed up every day and did a good job as recorded in his black book.

At some point Dad and Angelo had a falling out. Angelo disappeared into the mists of my past. He probably regressed to his previous life on the streets and in bars. Ernie Wente's comment to Dad was, "I told you so." I'm probably the only one alive now who remembers Angelo, but I'm glad I knew him.

* * *

Dad kept two Brittany Spaniel hunting dogs, Brit and Susie, in pens at the ranch. They both had fancy registered names, but Brit and Susie are all I can now recall. My job was to change their water, clean their pens and feed them. In reality, Dad and Angelo did most of that, but at least once a day I rode my bicycle the eight blocks from our house to the ranch to check on the dogs. I liked them and they liked me, but Dad made it clear that they were strictly working dogs, not pets. Dad didn't allow doggie treats unless it was a reward for proper behavior. I learned a lot watching him teach those dogs to sit, lie down, stay put, and come to his whistle. When he and I exercised them in Dry Creek, he sometimes brought along a shotgun to pepper some quail so that the dogs might become used to the noise and learn about birds.

The hard part was teaching the dogs to point. For that, Dad fashioned a bundle of dry pheasant skins and feathers. This he tied to the end of a long string that was in turn attached to a bamboo pole. Using the pole, he flipped the bundle of feathers to one side of the yard. The dog charged after it, but just before the dog reached the feather bundle, Dad flipped it away in another direction. Each time the dog charged the bundle, Dad flipped it away. All the while he kept talking to the animal, using simple words like "no," "hold," "okay," "good dog." After a while the animal's inbred senses caused it to try slowly sneaking up on the bundle. As the dog inched forward, Dad voiced calming approval, "good dog," and a warning, "hold, hold." If the dog made a lunge for the feather bundle, it was jerked away to the gruff sound of "no!" Eventually the dog learned to hold a point and not to charge that bundle of feathers until Dad said "okay."

Only after the dogs could hold on point did Dad start teaching them to hunt and fetch at his command. After six months of daily work, he could hide that bundle of feathers around the barn yard and tell the dogs to "hunt." In short order they would find the imitation prey and hold a staunch point until Dad said "okay, fetch." Only then did they bring it to him. When they acted well, he lavished them with praise and rewards. He never hit them unless they chased after rabbits. Their world must be centered on birds, not furry creatures. They knew that tracking furry smells was wrong, but sometimes they just couldn't resist. When a dog returned from a rabbit chase, it cowered in front of Dad, tail between its legs, while he gave a stern lecture and maybe a tap on the nose.

In later years when Susie and Brit had passed on, Dad trained another Brittany pup named Happy. He lived in the back yard of our Livermore house, and much to Dad's discomfort, Happy became Mom's pet. Dad and Happy hunted together until Dad was well into his eighties and could no longer chase after pheasants. Even then Dad could open the back door of our house in late afternoon and say to Happy, "Go get the paper." Happy scampered around to the front where the newspaper boy had tossed the evening paper, fetching it back to Dad's hand. After Dad's passing, Happy became Mom's companion, spending summers with her at the cabin and winters in Chester. He is buried below the cabin on the point above where Willow Creek enters the river.

*   *   *

When I was quite young, Mom drove me twice a week from Livermore to Hayward for professional swimming lessons. Because of that, my swimming and diving form was well developed at an earlier age than most children in Livermore. So in the sixth grade, I was asked to join the Livermore Valley Swim Team. That competitive swimming experience lasted less than two years before I decided that the daily chlorine baths and competitive pressures were not worth the potential rewards. When it became clear to me that my effort to improve stopwatch times was benefiting the coach and the team rather than me, my competitive swimming days ended. That experience taught me that I was not a fan of group endeavors. For better or worse, that attitude has prevailed throughout my life. I have no desire to sacrifice for the team. I like to compete against myself, and I can be a fearsome self-critic and taskmaster, but I do not care about being the best. If I happen to come out ahead of others, that's fine, but winning isn't my objective. I just want to keep getting better in the hope of becoming competent enough at a particular skill to understand what perfection looks like and what's required to reach that level. When the costs and sacrifices needed for further improvement outweigh the personal satisfaction gained, I'm onto something else. Limited as I am by capacity and opportunity, my objective is to be a "Jack of all trades, master of none, though oftentimes better than some."

That same attitude held sway during my two-year stint with the Boy Scouts of America. Records indicate that I was a patrol leader, reaching the rank of Star and holding merit badges in public health, coin collecting, citizenship, scholarship, cooking, skiing, fingerprinting and horsemanship. However, it became clear to me that my experiences at the Chester cabin had provided me with more out-of-doors knowledge than most of the scouts and troop leaders. I felt certain that I could reach the top rank of Eagle if I wanted to spend the time to do so, but there were more interesting opportunities available, so I said goodbye to the Boy Scouts. In retrospect, I'm amazed that I could obtain a merit badge in anything to do with horsemanship. Aside from a couple of uncomfortable experiences at a private summer camp, my only horse-riding involvement had been on Ernie Wente's ranch, and that was a calamity worth recounting.

Mom and Dad felt that since we lived in a farming-ranching community, I should know about horses and riding. To that end, Dad prevailed upon his friend, Ernie Wente, to take me with him when he tended his cattle. For several weekends I accompanied Mr. Wente on rides over the hills behind his home, into what was known as Dry Creek, where he and Alfred Sakau raised cattle. On this particular Saturday, the objective was to cut out two bulls from the herd and drive them back over the hills to the corrals at the ranch house. We got the bulls separated and moving up a draw that led to the top of a ridge. Ernie yelled, "Paul, you ride on that side of the draw, and I'll take this side. Keep them moving, but don't push them. Let them go at their own speed. They don't like going uphill, and they don't like leaving the herd. If they turn around on us in this narrow draw, they're going back, and there's nothing you can do about it. Just get out of the way and let them go."

As the bulls plodded along, Ernie periodically cracked his bull whip, and we both kept talking and yelling at the massive creatures. Near the top of the draw at the steepest incline, the bull on my side stopped. No amount of yelling could get him going. Suddenly he turned and came straight at my horse as it desperately attempted to get out of the way on the steep hillside. I went into the air, tumbling across the narrow trail in front of the oncoming bull. Seeing the success of its compatriot, Ernie's bull turned and did the same. Irish luck once again saved me from what could have been a deadly experience. I lay crumpled at the bottom of the draw but was unhurt other than scratches and a bruised ego. My horse was long gone on his way home, and I had a sizable hike back to the ranch house. Mr. Wente told Dad that he didn't want to be responsible for more riding experiences, and I have never since spent much time around horses.

* * *

There were eighteen of us in Sister Agnes's 1956 eighth grade graduating class, eight boys and ten girls. I was far from an outstanding student. A review of my report cards from the sixth, seventh and eighth grades reveals As in religion, deportment, courtesy, and application. My grades in real subjects reflect a hodgepodge of Cs and Bs. I don't remember our graduation, but an article in the *Livermore Herald* newspaper, dated June 15, 1956, indicates that I and Catherine Ferrario were given scholarship awards by the Young Men's Institute, a Catholic fraternal organization. If my grades were worthy of a scholarship award, I hate to think what the grades of other boys in my class must have looked like.

Mom lobbed one last coeducational grenade into the nun's morality battle. She hosted a daylong party at Castlewood Country Club for our entire eighth grade graduating class, with swimming, dancing, music, and food. She even invited Sister Agnes and Father Hennessy. They didn't show, nor respond to the invitation. In later years I've had several classmates tell me how they still remember that day. It was their first experience being in such a prestigious place, free of religious and close parental supervision.

Father Hennessy did everything in his power to have me sent to Bellarmine College Preparatory High School, a Jesuit run boarding school in San Jose. I was somewhat enthusiastic and Dad was amenable, but Mom, as she would say, put her foot down. "Joe, Paul has spent the last eight years in Catholic school getting a religious grounding. I respect the Jesuits, and I have no doubt that Bellarmine can provide a much better education than Livermore High, but you and I have an agreement, and I expect you to stick by it. It's time for Paul to be exposed to a secular, coeducational environment. He'll stay here and go to Livermore High School. You can tell Father Hennessy, or I will, that Paul is not going to Bellarmine." Dad capitulated and I entered Livermore High along with my fellow St. Michael's classmates.

Here I would like to bring up an issue that may have crossed the minds of readers. In recent years there has been considerable social and legal ferment regarding sexual abuse and pedophilia within the Catholic Church and also within the Boy Scouts of America. During my membership in both organizations, I can think of instances that might have been conducive to such untoward activity, but I have never personally experienced nor heard from my peers about such happenings.

*   *   *

At the time, Livermore High School had a student body of seven hundred or so students, most of whom were White. Aside from one Chinese student whose family ran the local Chinese-American restaurant, and a couple from the Philippines and Guam, the only students of color were from Mexican families that had resided in the Valley for generations. There were no junior high schools in Livermore, so freshmen came directly into high school from eighth grades at St. Michael's or the much larger Livermore Elementary School. High school was a big adjustment for me—my own locker, a sea of unfamiliar faces, separate classrooms, different teachers for different subjects. Initially there was some hazing of freshmen by seniors, but I kept my head down and managed to avoid problems.

Students at Livermore High were divided into two academic tracks: noncollege and college preparatory. At Mom's insistence I was enrolled in the college preparatory curriculum. During freshmen year I received Cs in Latin, Bs in English, algebra, social science and woodshop, and As in physical education. My grades remained substantially the same over the next three years, a few Cs, mostly Bs, and a few As.

Throughout high school I can't remember any courses that I particularly enjoyed. For me, school was a task that had to be undertaken as a rite of passage to adulthood and an obligation of family pride. There were, however, four courses that stand out in my memory and have influenced my life. Mr. Kenneth Teberg taught a course in physiology. I received only a grade of C, but I learned much about the human body that has proven useful over the years. Mr. Robert Anderson taught a course in public speaking that provided the foundation for a lifetime of prepared and impromptu discourse. Ms. Jo Ann Brennan, a meek and less than self-confident teacher who had trouble maintaining classroom order, taught geometry, a course that cemented my lifelong appreciation for logical rigor in all things. Finally, there was Mrs. Anne Trudeau, who taught Latin, a course that I suffered through at Mom's behest. After two years of declensions and conjugations being scrawled on butcher paper with marker pen and plastered on the walls of my bedroom, my final grade was a C-. Likely it was awarded out of sympathy for my mother's efforts rather than my ability. That experience fostered a fear and distaste of foreign language learning that has lasted throughout my life. The weightiest responsibility of teachers and parents is that they can affect the rest of a young person's life without ever realizing it.

As teenagers do, I savored one particular rite of passage to adulthood: the acquisition of my driver's license, accomplished with relative ease thanks to a driver education class taught by Mr. Clancy Crew, a man of steel nerves and unshakable optimism in the face of manifest inattention and ineptness. Dad and Mom made it quite clear that I could not have my own car, but I was free, upon good behavior, to use one of our three family cars. Generally, I was a responsible and conservative driver, but on occasion I did test the limits of our 1956 Buick Special. One such test involved running the Seven Sisters, part of the Greenville Road that roller-coastered its way over seven consecutive hills. The idea was to see if the Buick could fly like in the movies. It did, and I and my passengers survived. In 1962 a car full of teenagers was not so lucky. They all died or were badly injured. Subsequently, the county reengineered the road, removing all the humps, and the Seven Sisters passed into Livermore's historic folklore.

My athletic activities in high school were limited. I tried out for football, but after getting knocked around for a couple of months, I came to the conclusion that spectating was much preferable to playing. As a freshman I was manager of Coach Nevin McCormick's track team. During that season I discovered I could throw the discus and javelin farther than most others, so I earned a letter in track and field in four consecutive years, one year as manager and three as a competitor. That qualified me for membership in Block L, the only male athletic organization on campus.

Initiation into Block L provided my first personal experiences with hazing and racial discrimination. The initiation ceremony took place at night in the gymnasium, with only one or two coaches as observing chaperones. We initiates were stripped to our underwear and subjected to a series of strenuous and humiliating tasks; however, one individual in particular was subjected to inordinate humiliation, among other things being forced to eat sheep's testicles. That person was John (Juan) Aflague, whose parents had recently immigrated from the Pacific Island of Guam. His features were a bit more Asian than Spanish, and he was one of two or three ethnically unique athletes in our school. That night he suffered disproportionately, though he was a talented athlete and a first-string basketball and baseball player. At the time I didn't know him and had no idea that years later I would be greeted with kindness and acceptance by his cousins and grandparents in Guam.

Despite having no memory of it, a January 20, 1957, newspaper clipping indicates that as a freshman I was a member of Livermore Teen Club, and in my junior and senior years, I belonged to the Hi-Y Club, an affiliate of the YMCA. Other than those two groups, I didn't participate in any high school social organizations. I didn't attend homecoming dances, picnics, or parties. I did admire several girls but was far too shy to approach them. I watched from the sidelines as other boys succeeded where I had feared to tread. I never had a date with a girl from Livermore until the end of my senior year. At that point someone told me that Elaine Clark was one of a few girls remaining without a date to the senior prom. Her locker was near mine, so I worked up the courage to ask her. She said yes, and from then on we attended senior functions together. That summer I went away, as usual, to the Chester cabin, and in the fall I entered the University of Colorado. Elaine attended San Jose State University, so we didn't see each other again until a brief meeting at our only high school class reunion in 1980. She is now an artist living near the town of Fortuna on the California coast.

Aside from timidity toward the opposite sex, one big reason for my lack of participation in high school activities was that I seldom remained in Livermore on the weekends and never during the summers. At those times I was pursuing activities that were not the norm of Livermore teenage life. In the summer I was at the cabin involved in fly fishing, hiking and other mountain pursuits. In the fall I hunted with Dad. In the winter I skied with Mom. That left only spring for track and field. There was little time left for school events and organizations. Among the student body I had friendly acquaintances but no close friendships. I was just there, not in any way outstanding, a so-so athlete and student, just one of seven hundred, pretty much doing my own thing.

*   *   *

The Gustine Gun Club, a subsidiary of the Gustine Land and Cattle Company, was incorporated in 1906 and is located on West Duck Club Road near the Old Santa Fe Grade in the marshy grasslands of California's Merced County. It encompasses some two thousand acres of private land that lies in the center of the Pacific Flyway, a route of north-south waterfowl migration between Alaska and Mexico. The property abuts a vast area of wetlands that includes the Great Valley Grasslands State Park and the San Luis National Wildlife Refuge. The Club complex includes a clubhouse with dining and lounge facilities. A centrally located toilet and shower facility is surrounded by a village of ramshackle buildings, each belonging to one or more of the sixty members. Dad's membership included a one-room shack that was just large enough to contain a bunk bed, wash basin, refrigerator, and wood stove for heating. The community toilet facilities were across the road.

Seventy-five duck blinds were scattered throughout the club's vast flooded acreage. The blinds consisted of concrete barrels sunk into grass-covered islets just above the water line. Each blind was numbered and was marked with a vertical white pole that could be seen from a distance. Some were single blinds having only one barrel, while others were double blinds sporting two adjacent barrels. Graveled levee roads led from the clubhouse grounds to a few designated parking areas. From there, footpath levees led deeper into the swamp. At various points along these paths, arrows with blind numbers pointed across the water toward the designated blinds. A full-time caretaker and his wife lived at the club, managed water levels, and oversaw the maintenance of levees, blinds, and grounds.

On Saturdays from October through mid-January, Dad and I and the dogs departed Livermore around five in the morning. Our initial destination was a farmland property near Hilmar on the Merced River where Ernie Wente, Dad, and some other men maintained a pheasant hunting club. There we hunted pheasants and other upland birds before moving on to the Gun Club in preparation for the Sunday duck hunt. I can still sense the excitement of our dogs holding on point as Dad walked up behind them saying, "Good dog, Hold, hold," his training having come to fruition. I can still feel the explosion of wing beats and feathers as one or two, or sometimes three, pheasants erupted into the air from under Dad's feet, the crack of shots and the happy tail-wagging dogs as they retrieved the downed prey. Few collaborations between man and animal are more beautiful to watch than upland game hunting.

We frequently hunted pheasants together with Ernie. His dog was a large and somewhat inept German shorthair pointer named Herman. Ernie had named the dog after his brother, Herman, who was a wine sommelier with a superb sense of smell. I guess Ernie hoped that his brother's sense of smell might somehow be transferred to the dog, along with the name. Unfortunately, things didn't work out that way. Herman was often disruptive and uncontrolled, more interested in rabbits than pheasants. Sometimes he crashed through the middle of our dogs when they were on point, scattering pheasants in all directions. Dad was loath to say anything to his friend Ernie, so we and our dogs tried to ignore Herman's bad behavior. Ultimately, Herman fell victim to his own hyperactive nature. He was chasing a jackrabbit in front of Ernie's house in Livermore. Apparently oblivious to the milk delivery truck that had just parked in the driveway, Herman ran headfirst at full speed into the front left wheel of the stationary truck. That was the end of Herman. He killed himself on the spot.

Throughout the morning we tromped through frost-covered fields and tule-filled drainage ditches. By early afternoon we had usually downed five or six pheasants and regrouped at the car for late lunch. I wish I had better appreciated those times with Dad as we sat on the tailgate of our Chevrolet station wagon eating Mom's sandwiches and discussing the morning's excitement, especially the few that got away. In those days I had no idea that memories of that time would provide solace for a lifetime.

From the Pheasant Club it was only a half-hour drive to Gustine. Upon reaching our Gun Club shack, Dad usually took a siesta while I gutted, washed, and stored the pheasants in our refrigerator. The next day when we returned to Livermore, they'd be skinned and packed for freezing. We ate and gave away a lot of pheasants and ducks in those days.

Dad and I never cooked in our shack. We usually ate dinner at the house of Ernie Wente, Ralph Merritt, Glen Smallcomb and Ray Atwater. Their place was relatively luxurious compared to other buildings on the Club grounds, and they often brought guests, so there were bunk beds enough to sleep eight people. Our dinners and the preceding cocktail hours were accompanied by considerable lighthearted and boisterous fun. Ernie was sometimes accompanied by his brother, Carl.

Paul with pheasants, Brit the Brittany, and Dad Joe
at the Gustine Gun Club, c. 1966

In those days, Carl was president of the Bank of America and chairman of the California State Fish and Game Commission. His presence resulted in an extended cocktail hour and appearances by various Club members with banking or hunting and conservation interests. Ralph Merritt was president of Coast Manufacturing and Supply Company. It operates today as Hexcel Corporation. Glen Smallcomb and Ray Atwater owned a chain of Chevrolet dealerships on the peninsula between San Francisco and Palo Alto. Being the only young person at these gatherings, I kept a low profile, speaking only when spoken to, and helping out when asked.

During the evening's activities I managed to make one or two trips to the household restroom. That was partly because our shack had no toilet facilities, but mostly because the restroom walls were hung with risqué calendars displaying nude ladies in a variety of positions. Before leaving the room, I made sure that each was opened to the correct month, even though the years had long since outdated.

After dinner I was sometimes sent to the clubhouse to find out what blinds had been assigned for the next morning's shoot. Blind numbers were drawn randomly using a machine similar to a bingo number generator and then posted on the clubhouse wall beside the member's name. Some blinds were historically more productive than others, so the draw was taken seriously and closely overseen by the Club elders, President George Fink and Vice-President Fuller Lyman.

When the draw was completed, there was always horse trading and the modification of blind assignments to accommodate special circumstances. For example, some blinds were more comfortable and easily accessed. These were reserved for older hunters in their eighties and nineties. Sometimes a member with a guest drew a blind that couldn't accommodate two hunters, so it could be exchanged for a double blind at another location. Seldom did all sixty members attended a shoot, so usually there remained sought-after blinds that hadn't been drawn or assigned. That's when the horse trading could get a bit contentious. But Mr. Fink maintained order. All changes had to be approved by him, and he was not a personality to be trifled with. His most distinguishing characteristic was a lower jaw that protruded far forward of his upper one. Once he made a decision on blind assignments, that was the end of discussion. Often when I returned to the Wente household with a list of blind assignments, some members rushed over to the clubhouse to obtain Mr. Fink's approval for a modification.

At four in the morning the Club's siren sounded to alert members that breakfast was being served in the clubhouse. We dressed in our cold, dimly-lit shack: wool socks, long underwear, pants, turtlenecks and sweaters. I wore hip boots anchored to my belt, and Dad wore chest-high waders with suspenders. Once dressed, we headed to the food and warmth of the clubhouse. The fog was sometimes so thick that the clubhouse porch lights were barely visible as we stepped outside. The breakfasts were scrumptious and always the same: fried eggs, bacon, sausage, fried potatoes and freshly baked biscuits, all served on platters. I could take all I could eat. Oatmeal could be scooped from a caldron and covered with brown or white sugar before being splashed with fresh milk sent directly from the Gustine Creamery.

By five-thirty we had donned our camouflage hunting parkas, loaded the car with guns, ammunition, and decoys, and started driving to the parking area nearest our assigned blind. From there it was all footwork. We carried two dozen decoys, one hundred rounds of 12-guage magnum ammunition, shotguns, flashlights, and walking sticks, an essential aid for swamp slogging. From the parking area we walked along a footpath-wide levee until we came to our blind pointer, a stake indicating our blind number and the direction we should take out into the swamp. I usually led the way with both our flashlight beams trying to find the elusive white blind marker pole. On cold mornings we sometimes broke a quarter inch of ice with each step. To keep our route on line during foggy mornings, we used a compass reading taken from the blind pointer at the levee. It was a relief when our flashlight beams finally illuminated the blind's white marker pole. Once there, my job was to submerge the barrel lids and the pole marker deep underwater, so as to hide them from the ducks' excellent vision. Then I put the shell bags and guns into the blinds and sometimes placed a lit can of Sterno under the stools to warm and dry the damp barrels. Meanwhile, Dad set the decoys out so that they resembled a naturally feeding flock.

Some club members used dogs to retrieve their downed birds, breeds that were larger and could tolerate the cold, like standard poodles and Labradors. Our Brittiany spaniels were too small to endure the harsh conditions, so much to their disappointment, we left them behind in the car or at the clubhouse. We retrieved or downed birds by hand.

At the crack of dawn, we were hunkered down watching nature unfold around us. V-shaped flights of geese and ducks crisscrossed the sky above. Teal rocketed past as they buzzed our decoys. Flights of sprig and mallard whistled and quacked as they looked for a place to settle. At exactly one-half hour before sunrise the Club's siren wound up to its highest note and guns around us begin to pop. We sat in our blinds, back-to-back, each watching our respective half of the marsh while keeping each other informed as to potential targets. Dad let me shoot first on incoming flights, but I was a horrible shot in those days, and he frequently had to "clean up," as he put it. We tried to shoot only the best eating ducks: mallard, sprig (pintail) and widgeon, but due mostly to my over exuberance, we often ended up with some spoonbills and a teal or two. Occasionally a cinnamon teal and gadwall also found their way into our pile. On some days, snow geese or Canadian geese passed overhead, close enough for us to bang away at them. If one or two fell from the sky, I'd be up and out of the blind in a hurry to retrieve them, lest they sneak away wounded among the tules. The limit in those days was fifteen ducks of any species, per hunter. We almost always accomplished that by late morning and headed back to the clubhouse.

The Gustine Gun Club was exclusively a man's world. Wives appeared only once a year for the annual coot (mud hen) shoot and picnic. The total membership was limited to sixty. Applicants had to be sponsored by existing members and were subject to anonymous "blackball." Shoots were held only on Wednesdays and Sundays. Upon payment of a fifty-dollar guest fee, members were allowed one guest per shoot, but the same guest could only be invited once per season.

An exception was made for the children of members. I was allowed to shoot as Dad's guest throughout the year, but it cost him fifty dollars each time I did so, not a small sum of money in the 1950s. Most members were in their sixties or seventies, so their children were grown and involved in other pursuits. I was the only school-aged regular guest. Being surrounded by elders was nothing new for me. I was good at it, and because of that, some members took a liking to me.

One such person was an energetic man in his fifties named Ray Cann. Ray was a voracious hunter, shooting pheasants with us on Saturdays, ducks on Sundays and Wednesdays, and anything else he could find to shoot on the in-between days. He taught me about snipe hunting. Yes, there truly are such birds. Their full name is Wilson's Snipe *(Callinago delicata)*. A marsh and wetlands dweller throughout North America, the snipe is well camouflaged with a body about the size of a morning dove; however, its breast muscles are larger and much better eating than those of a dove. When flushed from its marsh-side feeding grounds, it chirps with surprise and flies erratically at speeds up to sixty miles per hour, a target hard to hit. Mr. Cann taught me that if I knelt down and remained motionless, the snipe would circle far around and return to see what had been the cause of its fright. This time it presented an easier target. On Sunday afternoons, after the duck hunters had retired, my joy was to accompany Ray as he walked the Gun Club wetlands after snipe. Although Dad was tired and anxious to go home after the morning's duck hunt, he usually allowed me a couple of hours snipe hunting with Mr. Cann. These were memorable times. Both Mom and Dad had to admit that the resulting baked snipe breasts were exceptional fare.

Before moving on from my hunting days, I'd like to relate an incident that remains to this day seared in my memory. It was a frosty Sunday morning in 1958; I was sixteen years old. Dad and I were running a little late and had just climbed into our blind barrels when the clubhouse siren sounded. It was time to shoot and we weren't yet completely organized and ready. I grabbed three magnum 12-gauge rounds from my satchel and jammed them into the Remington Model 58. When I looked up, a lone mallard was beating his way at full throttle in a straight line that would take it directly overhead. There was no time to think. In one motion I rose up, focused both eyes on the mallard's chest, subconsciously allowed for a proper lead and pulled the trigger. At that instant Dad stood up in front of the discharging barrel. If he had been one inch taller or my gun barrel one inch lower, my life would have become an eternity of remorse and guilt. We both instantly realized what had happened. Dad just sat down in his blind and said nothing for a while. I did the same, even though several flights came in over our decoys. Eventually Dad looked over at me and said, "Try to take things a little slower from now on, son. No old duck is worth having a shooting accident." Nothing else was ever said, but to this day, I can still see his brown Duxbak hunting hat just below my barrel as I pulled the trigger. Our Irish luck prevailed that day. Oh, by the way, that mallard flew off unscathed.

*   *   *

During my grade school years at St. Michael's, Mom took me out of school for a week of snow skiing every winter. As I got older, she added more weekends to our winter ski schedule. By the time I was in high school, weekends of skiing stretched from mid-January through Easter vacation. We were regular patrons at Edelweiss resort above Twin Bridges on US Highway 50. Rooms that included breakfast and dinner were twenty dollars a night. The chairlift was four dollars a day or seventy dollars annually. During Easter break Mom dropped me off for the week, and I was allowed to stay in the crew dormitory above the kitchen for eight dollars a night, including two meals. I loved hanging out with the staff and ski patrol guys.

The ski school director was a German immigrant named Hans Ludwig "Lutz" Aynedter. An architect by profession, he had been German downhill champion in 1946, but World War II and a stint in Rommel's Africa Corp had robbed him of his best competitive years. That loss and his military experiences were likely responsible for his often-harsh temperament and heavy alcohol consumption. Lutz had a unique rhythmic, almost waltz like, style of skiing that he passed on to others for $3.50 an hour. I last skied in 2018 in Vail, Colorado. At the time, friends told me that I was easy to find on the mountain side because of my rhythmic style. Upon hearing that, I thought, *Perhaps there's still a little bit of Lutz Aynedter left inside this old body of mine.*

After immigrating from Germany in 1950, Lutz opened a ski school at Strawberry Lodge, later renamed The Edelweiss. As the popularity of that area grew, he started a junior ski racing team known as the Red Hornets, sometimes referred by other teams as the Highway 50 gang. I was ecstatic when Lutz invited me to join the Red Hornets, though I knew that his invitation was more likely a result of Mom's valued patronage than my ski racing potential. The best team members were local kids who attended nearby schools. Lutz held practices on weekdays after school and on weekends. Only a few Red Hornets were "flatlanders" like me, showing up only on weekends and holidays. Team practices involved setting up and running a slalom course of bamboo poles. Lutz ran the course first. At the bottom he waited for each of us to follow, one after another. The best skiers, like the Sabich family—Spider, Pinky, and Mary—went first. By the time my turn came, the course was rutted and my descents were, at best, unconfident and labored.

Lutz Aynedter, Edelweiss managers Bunny and Ken Cotton, c. 1959

Lutz was never encouraging and often made sarcastic remarks. "Callaghan, I set a flush with the intention that you go through the gates, not over the top of them." Despite my less than spectacular racing skills, I continued to practice regularly with the team whenever I was at the Edelweiss. Only once did Lutz angrily order me off the hill "for a rest." We were running a simulated downhill race and I crashed, head over skis, in a sixty-mile-an-hour eggbeater cloud of snow, the impact of which was so severe that my orthodontic retainer flew out of my mouth and was never seen again. The retainer cost Mom over a hundred dollars to replace, and my ego never recovered. It was clear that I was not cut out to be a downhill racer, or any kind of racer, for that matter. I was too conservative. Over the years I've skied in several slalom and giant slalom races, never placing in most of them, but three fraternity brothers and I did win the University of Colorado Intramural Team Ski Championships in 1962.

There was one girl, perhaps two years younger than I, who regularly accompanied me at the back of the pack, despite the fact that she was a local resident and an accomplished slalom skier. Her name was Judy Frasinetti. Often we two were the last skiers to come down Lutz's practice courses. Judy always provided encouragement and well wishes before I pushed off. I was grateful for that, since my self-confidence was never high. Judy stood out as a modest, kind, caring person. I wasn't surprised when in 1961, the year after I went off to college, she won the Sacramento Bee's annual Silver Ski Giant Slalom, the biggest race in the Tahoe area. I was further not surprised when, years later, I discovered that Judy had become a Catholic nun and worked with Mother Teresa in India. Life takes funny turns, but kind people usually remain so and are remembered for their caring.

In retrospect, I can see that our skiing forays were Mom's way of introducing me to a world outside the mundane Livermore scene. Skiers at The Edelweiss came from San Francisco and elsewhere around the Bay Area. They were largely professionals and intellectuals with eclectic tastes and interesting backgrounds. Dr. Diamond, a well-known San Francisco psychiatrist, often arrived with his wife and their five children, some of whom were also on the Red Hornet team. Then there was Dr. Mike Gibbons, a distinguished-looking Bay Area bachelor and Edelweiss investor. He and Mom may have known each other in earlier times or simply had friends in common, but Dr. Mike took me in tow. He led and I followed down the steepest runs, through the trees, taking chances I would not have taken on my own. Following behind Dr. Mike did much to improve my all-terrain skiing and confidence.

Mom and I made friends with the Hibbard family from Walnut Creek: Frank, Lettie, Butch and Jim. Frank, the father, was an electrical engineer and weekend ski patrolman at the Edelweiss. His oldest son, Butch, and I were both on the Red Hornet team and became inseparable ski partners. Our moms worked together as gate keepers during ski races and otherwise helped to support Red Hornet activities. Mom and I and the Hibbard family spent several days together camped out on various runs at the 1960 Squaw Valley Olympics. We watched as a German girl named Heidi Biebl edged out the American, Penny Pitou, for a win in the women's downhill. Little did I know at the time that some years later I'd be skiing in Germany with some of Heidi's compatriots from the German Olympic team. That same year the Hibbard family moved to Indiana. Mom continued to correspond with Lettie for many years, but I've never seen Butch again and know nothing of his whereabouts. His little brother, Jim, visited Mom in Chester in the 1980s. He had become a civil engineer and was consulting on a project to review the integrity of the Lake Almanor Dam.

On some holidays and during spring break, a busload of girls from Burke, a private San Francisco girls' school (Katherine Delmar Burke School), arrived at the Edelweiss. There were few skiers among them. Most stayed on the bunny hill and played in the snow, mindful of their chaperon's vigilance. However, in the evenings they took over the jukebox and turned out the lights in the Edelweiss basement. The fact that I was shy and danced poorly made little difference. Those girls knew how to get a guy warm and fuzzy and keep him that way all evening. Slow, close dancing was their specialty, and they kept funding the jukebox with songs like "You Send Me," "Come Softly to Me," and "All I Have to Do Is Dream." However, no matter what happened in that dimly-lit basement, the next morning they didn't know your name or recognize your existence. At nightfall their memory seemed to temporarily improve once again.

The Burke girls provided my introduction to the realities of female manipulation as well as wealth and class discrimination. I had a friend who worked at Edelweiss by the name of Ray Dushane. He helped service and operate the chairlift. Ray was nineteen and good looking, with Elvis Presley style hair, a black leather jacket, and a souped-up 1957 Chevy. At some point during the winter, he had become involved with a Burke girl and thought he was in love. She had given him only a street address, not a phone number. Ray was determined to contact her and asked me to accompany him to San Francisco. I said yes because I wanted to ride in his fine Chevy machine.

In late afternoon on a Sunday, after four hours of driving from the Edelweiss, we ended up in front of a home in the Marina District. This residential area looked pretty upscale to me, and I wasn't sure we should be knocking on doors dressed as we were in ski clothes. Ray was not to be dissuaded. I stood by his side as he pressed the doorbell.

The girl's name has long since departed my mind, so for the sake of this writing, let us call her Diana Pope. When the door opened, a gentleman in black coat and bow-tie appeared before us.

"Good afternoon, may I help you?" he said.

"I'd like to see Diana Pope, if she lives here," said Ray.

"Mother or daughter?" came the dry, unemotional reply.

"Oh, ah, I guess daughter," replied Ray.

"And whom might I say is calling?" droned the man.

"I'm Ray Dushane. I work at the Edelweiss Ski Lodge."

"And who is your compatriot?"

At that point I replied, "I'm Paul Callaghan, just a friend of Ray's."

"And the purpose of your visit?"

I could see that Ray was not at ease with this interrogation, so I continued. "We've just come to say hello to Diana—a social visit."

"Please wait a moment," said the gentleman as he closed the door in our faces.

After inordinate time had passed, the door reopened and a woman stood there. "I am Mrs. Pope, Diana's mother. I understand that you two young men have come to visit my daughter. Unfortunately, she is indisposed at the moment and unable to meet with you. May I ask, how do you know Diana?

"I work at the Edelweiss Ski Resort on Highway 50. She was there with girls from Burke school. We had a good time together and became friends," said Ray.

"I see. Have you driven all the way from the Edelweiss today, just to see Diana?"

"Yes."

"That's too bad. I'm so sorry. I suggest that next time you call ahead to ensure Diana's availability."

"I would have called, but I don't have her phone number," said Ray.

"Then I suggest you correspond with Diana by mail and perhaps she will provide it, or not, as she sees fit. Drive safely on your return trip. Good afternoon."

The door closed. Ray moved to ring the bell again. I stopped him. Perhaps Diana never knew we were there. Or perhaps she did know but couldn't bring herself to face Ray and disabuse his expectations. Mrs. Pope had been polite but in no way encouraging, and she was clearly not enamored by her daughter's choice of relationships. Ray had spent a lot of gas money for nothing. We both learned a lesson about the reliability of weekend relationships with rich girls from Burke.

In my senior year I had occasion to ride up in the chairlift with a girl from San Francisco named Sue Werchek, not a Burke. We skied and had lunch together that day. She returned to Edelweiss on several succeeding weekends and we began a correspondence. In those days if you wanted to keep in touch with someone, you did it through expensive long-distance phone conversations or by the US Postal Service. Sue lived in Golden Gate Heights, and I made three or four trips to San Francisco on dates that we arranged by mail. In each case we were required to meet and talk with her parents before departing. Fronting my best manners in a sport coat and tie, I apparently passed those inspections. We were allowed to depart together on various adventures. Sue's favorite was Haight-Ashbury. There we poked around art shops and listened to street music. Sue thought I was quite a naive country boy. She was right about that.

Although her parents were pleasant, they remained aloof. I had no idea they were practicing Jews—that is, until on one of my visits Sue asked that we meet in the lobby of the Mark Hopkins Hotel. When I arrived, she ushered me to the obligatory parental inquisition. Her parents were seated at one end of the head table at a Bar Mitzvah party in one of the hotel's ballrooms. I had no idea what a Bar Mitzvah was. I just knew I'd been thrust into a throng of people dressed differently, men wearing skullcaps, dancing to unfamiliar music, and singing in an unfamiliar language. It was a long walk from the back of that room to the front. I felt many eyes was upon me, though that was probably not the case. Once we reached Sue's parents, they happily dismissed us with the standard questions about where we were going and when we intended to return. That was my first experience being an outsider in an unfamiliar social setting. It was eye opening to realize that there existed a complex social-religious world of which I knew nothing. Understanding would take years of focused effort, should I decide to do so.

Our relationship didn't last much longer. The distances and differences between us were too great, but I haven't forgotten Susie Werchek and wonder where life took her and where she might be today.

When the Edelweiss chairlifts closed on Sunday afternoons, Mom and I headed for home. It was hard to stay awake on the three-hour drive. I sometimes fell asleep. Mom, with her thermos of coffee, never did. On Monday morning I was the only student in high school with a sunburned face and white shadows around my eyes from ski goggles. My classmates had no understanding or regard for the adventures of my weekend, and I knew nothing of theirs.

Some of Lutz Aynedter's Red Hornets went on to skiing fame and notoriety. Chief among them was Valadimir Peter "Spyder" Sabich, who competed in the 1968 Olympics and was twice champion of the world professional ski circuit. He later died of gunshot wounds administered by a female companion. Lutz himself was murdered under mysterious circumstances in 1965. The Edelweiss resort closed for lack of snow in 1963, the first signs of a warming planet. It never reopened. Its chairlift was sold to a ski area in Oregon. The owner-managers, Ken and Bunny Cotton, moved to manage Breckenridge ski area in Colorado. The Edelweiss lodges were ultimately burned to the ground by the US Forest service. Nothing but a parking lot and memories exist today.

* * *

Paul Callaghan at High School Graduation, 1960

In 1960 I graduated from Livermore Joint Union High School, twenty-third in my class of 188, having attained no exceptional awards or accomplishments. My self-esteem at the time was pretty low. In my mind, the fact that I was ranked twenty-third said more about the relatively poor academic ability of my fellow graduates than it did about my capabilities. The college board entrance exams, along with tests administered by guidance counselors, indicated that I should choose an outdoor career such as agriculture or forestry, and not be concerned with college. Mom would have none of that "drivel." With her help I completed applications for the Universities of California, Oregon and Colorado. The University of California at Berkley rejected me outright. The Universities of Oregon and Colorado accepted me on condition that I take their English and math placement exams prior to registration. I decided to try Colorado, since the skiing was better there and the legal drinking age was eighteen rather than twenty-one. Mom was happy about my choice. She wanted me to attend a large, multifaceted university that was far enough away so that I could never arrive home on the weekends with a load of laundry. Dad never said a word about the high out-of-state tuition. Both he and Mom were happy that I had been accepted somewhere and could continue to advance my education. I was just excited to have an opportunity to be on my own.

Chapter 7

College

In August of 1960, Mom drove me from Chester to the Reno airport. There I boarded a TWA flight to Denver, followed by a bus ride to Boulder. As the plane descended over the Rocky Mountains toward the Denver airport, it hit an air pocket. The passengers were strapped into their seats, but a stewardess standing in the aisle a few rows in front of me first hit the ceiling and then the floor. I can still see it happening in slow motion. Our plane landed safely, but the stewardess broke her arm, and several passengers got a dowsing from flying drinks. That incident instilled a lifelong understanding as to the value of seatbelts.

For three days I lived in the Boulder Hotel while meeting with advisors and taking math and English placement tests. That trip to Boulder was my first solo journey away from home, my first airplane ride, my first bus ride, and the beginning of life on my own. I felt apprehensive but also invigorated and liberated from parental oversight and the expectations of small-town Livermore society. With the placement tests behind me, I felt the exuberant thrill of my own life opening up before me.

A few weeks later in early September 1960, Dad and Mom delivered me and my luggage to Willard Residence Hall on the University of Colorado, Boulder campus. The gravity of that moment was marked by a flurry of hugs, kisses, photographs and best wishes for my "new life." Dad gave me a hug as he said, "We raised you to do the right thing. Just keep doing it, and your life will work out just fine." Mom's last words were something like, "There are envelopes, stamps and note paper in your suitcase. We expect one letter a week. It needn't be a long letter, just enough to let us know you're alive and well." Such demonstrations of affection and concern were an unusual occurrence in our family, so I knew this must be a momentous occasion. I waved goodbye as they drove off toward the Flatirons on their way to Estes Park. In later life Mom told me that both she and Dad shed some tears upon leaving me; however, I was excited to be on my own and begin this college adventure.

My dorm room was split into two identical halves by an aisle leading from the door to the only window. Each side had a built-in closet, drawers, bed, bookcase and desk with chair. I chose the left side because the window lighting was better. I was unpacking when my roommate arrived. His name was John Baker Howell. Born and raised in Denver, he had graduated from South High School. As he unpacked, I could discern that John was a city boy, not a skier, back packer, athlete or outdoors person. But he turned out to be a quiet, pleasant, studious roommate. We got along well, and he introduced me to his friends from the Denver area. At least half of our dorm's residents were from Colorado, and many were John's acquaintances from high school. Others were from all over the United States. At that point, a person's origin made little difference. We were naive freshmen trying to understand how the university system worked and how to adjust to a life different from what we had previously known.

Dorm cafeteria food posed an adjustment for us all. I thought it was fine, but for others it was a constant topic of complaint. The coin-operated laundry facilities and associated pecking order were for me a challenge, but I lost only a few socks before adapting. The communal bath facilities were similar to those I had experienced in high school P.E. classes, but some dorm residents were clearly bothered by the lack of privacy. Our rooms had no telephones, so incoming calls were impossible. Outgoing calls could be made on coin-operated pay phones in the lounge area, but the waiting lines were long and filled with homesick or ill prepared residents. Initially my only complaint was in regard to late night noise. Official rules about quiet hours did exist, but during our first week they were poorly observed. Thankfully, when the resident advisor, David Arthur "Sosh" Socier, arrived, things quieted down. Dave was an interesting guy who was able to maintain order under what could only be described as difficult conditions. He went on to become a well-known and respected sports columnist for the *Pueblo Chieftain* newspaper.

Our first big hurdle was fall class registration—a chaotic, all manual event held in the University Field House. Freshmen had last priority for class selection, so by the time I was allowed to register, the available course and time selections were limited. My placement exams indicated that I could enroll in college algebra, Math 101, but I was also required to take EN002, remedial composition, also known as "bonehead English." Until I successfully completed that English course, my subject choices were restricted. Somehow, after standing in lines and often retracing my steps, I secured a full schedule of fourteen credit hours. My course load consisted of College Algebra, Remedial English Composition, Geology, Economic History of the Western World and Physical Education. The next challenge was to find books and the appropriate classrooms on the correct day and time.

The story of my first day in "bonehead English" class is worth relating. I had searched out the classroom location prior to the first day, so I arrived early to the small room that held twenty chairs with writing pads, arranged in five rows of four. One student already sat in the fourth row, so I took a seat behind him. As students filtered into the room, they filled up seats in front, leaving me seated alone in the back row. Then four very large fellows entered the room. I assumed they were athletes because of their size and manner. All four proceeded into my row. The largest, with dreadlocks, said, "Dude, you're sit'n in our seats. You best move somewhere else." Discretion being the better part of valor, I moved to the only remaining seat in the front row, just as the professor arrived. He was a hunchbacked old fellow with glasses that appeared three quarters of an inch thick. It was likely that he couldn't see the back row, and those guys seemed to know it. They never participated or were called on throughout the whole semester, and I became enlightened as to the importance of athletics on the C.U. campus.

On top of registration and the first week of classes came fraternity rush week. My grandfather, Courtney Barham, had been a member of Alpha Tau Omega (ATO) fraternity during his days at U.C. Berkeley. He valued that experience and wanted me to pledge at the ATO house in Colorado. In anticipation he had given me his diamond fraternity pin and written a letter of introduction. For the first two days of rush week, freshmen candidates attended coat and tie open house functions at various fraternity houses. At the time there were more than twenty fraternities on the C.U. campus. I visited only six or seven.

During most visits, one or two brother-members gave me a tour of their house and grounds, introduced others, answered questions and enquired about my background. At some fraternities I was asked to provided written information regarding my state of residence, my religion, my father's profession, my ethnic background, my source of college funding, my pastime and recreational activities, and so on. Their objective was to determine whether I could fit in and make a contribution to their group. My objective was to determine whether or not I liked the fraternity, and if so, to make a decent impression in the hopes of being invited to return on subsequent days. Lists of return invitations were posted at a central location on campus. If a return invitation was not forthcoming, that meant rejection. In most fraternities, rejection, known as a "blackball," required only one negative vote from any member.

On the third day I was invited back to four fraternities: ATO, Delta Tau Delta, Phi Delta Theta, and Phi Kappa Tau. I was most impressed with Delta Tau Delta, as they had several skiers with whom I seemed to relate. However, by the fifth day I received final bids from only Phi Delta Theta and Phi Kappa Tau. Both Delta Tau Delta and my grandfather's fraternity had rejected me. My small town naiveite, limited high school activities and reserved personality were probably to blame.

Disheartened though I was, I feared spending my entire college career on my own, living in dormitories or boarding houses. My roommate, John Howell, was also participating in rush week and intended to join a fraternity, as did several of my dormitory acquaintances. It seemed that fraternity life could offer the social and academic support I needed in this new and challenging environment, so I had only two choices. They both were located walking distance from campus and, ironically, across the street from each other. I have no memory of why I chose one over the other, but in the end, I pledged to Psi Chapter of Phi Kappa Tau (ΦΚΤ), often referenced as Phi Tau.

Phi Kappa Tau Fraternity House in winter, 1963

Per university policy, I lived in the dormitory throughout my freshman year. As a Phi Tau pledge, I was encouraged to spend time at the fraternity house. Weekend work duties and pledge meetings were mandatory, as was the memorization of names, majors and contact information for all active members and fellow pledges. Pledges were assigned phone duty on a round-the-clock schedule and expected to answer incoming calls, alert recipients and take messages. Six hours of phone duty could be taxing.

As if fraternity obligations weren't enough, I started dating an attractive, brown-eyed, brunette freshman from Hallett Residence Hall named Ann Lynn Frohberg. She was my first ever steady girlfriend. Like most freshmen, I didn't have a car, so our dates involved studying together at the library, smooching in the stairwells of campus buildings, and walking hand-in-hand through the snow for a beer and hamburger at the Sink, a famous Boulder landmark.

Ann was from Birmingham, Michigan, a city girl as naive about university life as the rest of us freshmen. Our first big fraternity party was the annual Phi Tau Viking Party. Invitations were limited and highly sought after on campus. Viking costumes were required. I invited Ann with no idea what to expect. It took a week of artistic labor to turn the ground floor and basement of our fraternity house into a cave, with bandstand, dance floor and bar.

Under police escort, dates were picked up at residence halls and sorority houses by a band of torch-carrying Vikings on horseback. Girls were carried out by their dates and thrown into horse drawn wagons filled with hay. When this band of Viking horsemen and wagons reached the fraternity house, a walkway of torch lights led into the Viking cave. What went on inside that cave appeared from the outside to be a raucous, drunken melee overlaid with rock and roll music. Actually, it wasn't nearly as bad as it appeared, though there were a few out of control brothers and sisters. Ann and I drank rum coolers and snuggled behind a bale of hay while watching the antics and listening to the music. The dance floor was packed and the cave lighting dim. We danced a bit, but after our third rum and Coke, it was appealing to just lie in the hay. By university regulation, two faculty chaperones were required. If they were present, we never saw them, and I'm sure that the Boulder City fire marshals were never consulted regarding all that paper fascia, straw and hay in association with alcohol and cigarettes. My pledge father and fraternity watchdog, Ken Dulany, gave Ann and I a ride back to the residence halls in time to meet Hallett Hall's 1:00 a.m. closing hour.

Other Phi Tau parties were held during freshman year as well. Besides a formal Christmas party with tree and presents for all, there was a gambling party that featured blackjack and craps tables, as well as real slot machines, programed to recoup just enough to pay for equipment rental. Little imagination is required to visualize the dress and décor for the pajama party—bathrobes were allowed. For the Congo party, the house interior became a simulated African jungle. Brothers wore breechcloths and painted their bodies. Some came dressed as missionaries or explorers. The all-black band was named "Daddy Hascle." In retrospect, I wonder what they thought of these rich White boys and girls making fun of African stereotypes. At the time I thought nothing of it. Thankfully my perception and understanding has evolved. By year end, both Ann and I felt that fraternity social life was a leap forward from our high school days.

Of course, there was a price to be paid for fraternal brotherhood. Pledges like me were required to participate in house cleanup and grounds maintenance. We were not full members and could be "blackballed" at any time by one negative vote of any member. So we were constantly careful not to alienate senior brothers. Whenever an active member questioned a pledge about fraternal or personal matters, the correct answer had better be forthcoming or the result would likely be a "boarding." Most active members had in their rooms a half inch thick wooden paddle board with the Greek letters ΦΚΤ engraved on it. A pledge could receive a loud and painful swat on the buttocks for the most minor infraction. I clearly remember one such event.

"Pledge Callaghan, what's my name?"

"Jim Ross, sir."

"It is James, not Jim. What is my middle name?"

"I'm sorry, I don't know, sir."

"Assume the position." That meant bend over and hold your ankles. I prepared for a torturous swat. The anxiety built as he wound up for a crackling forehand shot. I closed my eyes and clenched my teeth in anticipation, but the shock never came. He tapped my butt with the board and said, "You have ten minutes to find out my middle name. You better know it when I ask you again. Get a move-on."

Jim Ross, like most brothers, was a fair minded and reasonable guy. He went on to be the commander of a nuclear submarine and had a career in nuclear submarine construction. There were, however, some brothers who were best avoided if seen with a paddle in hand. One such person was Richard (Dick) Wise, nickname "Ivan." When he hit you, the letters ΦΚΤ appeared clearly on the rosy red cheeks of your derriere. Several times I was Ivan's victim, as I was notoriously bad at name memorization. Ivan went on to become a well-known and respected Colorado attorney.

By the end of my freshman year, I and sixteen of my pledge class had completed "hell week" and been initiated as full-fledged Phi Tau brothers. During "hell week," pledges lived in the fraternity basement, slept on the floor, and were subjected to intense physical and mental hazing. We were required to attend our classes and study hours while wearing burlap sacks under our clothing next to our skin. Sleepless nights were filled with interrogations as to Greek and Phi Tau history and ritual. Anyone who inadvertently fell asleep was taken outside in their underwear to play in the snow. Food was scarce and suspect. Outlandish food coloring and hot spices hid the true identity of offerings. Some in our group de-pledged, leaving the fraternity forever. Most of us endured the experience, forging close bonds and, in some cases, lasting aversions. Few of our "hell week" experiences would likely be allowed today.

Given the life adjustments and distractions of my freshman year, it's a wonder that I survived academically. In retrospect, much credit goes to my parents' foresight. They didn't allow me to have a car or ski equipment during freshman year, and they made it clear that they were confident in my capabilities and expected me to succeed. I wanted to please them, and I felt that if I succeeded in my freshman year, they might allow the car and skis in my second year. I was also lucky that my roommate, John Howell, was a quiet, organized, somewhat studious fellow. He pledged to another fraternity, Phi Gamma Delta, and like me had a girlfriend from a nearby residence hall. We faced similar challenges, yet our room remained an organized and quiet place for study and sleep, without distractions. After freshman year, John and I went our separate ways and have had little contact over the years. I believe he still lives in the Denver area.

Somehow, I was able to balance class and study time with fraternal obligations and social commitments. By the end of freshman year, I had received twenty-eight hours of course credit, with a C+ average. For many people that might be viewed as a less than satisfactory result. For me, and I believe for my parents, it was a momentous accomplishment. In my mind I had never shown academic prowess and had little self-confidence when it came to matters of schooling. Many of my freshmen peers seemed much smarter and accomplished than I, yet lots of them fell by the wayside that year. I managed to hold on, validating my parents' faith in me. Never mind that I barely passed "bone head" English and received a D grade in English composition. I had survived both courses, and my B grades in two semesters of Geology bolstered my self-confidence. There was hope that I could graduate from college, though I had no idea what I wanted to do in life and absolutely no incentive other than graduation for my parents' sake. Students with a C average could graduate. That was fine with me. I made that my goal.

In the fall of 1961, I moved into the fraternity house, and my girlfriend, Ann, moved into a nearby boarding house. The cost for room and board and fraternity dues was ninety-two dollars a month. My roommate was David Kipp, a Colorado resident. Being low in seniority, our room was located next to the second-floor lavatory. Dave was a political science major and completely absorbed with the ideas of Senator Barry Goldwater. Our year together was my first exposure to intellectual conservative thinking. When I rode the California Zephyr train home for Christmas, I brought with me some of those conservative ideas, as well as some ideas from Professor Grubs' economics class about the demand and supply of marijuana, and how its legalization might be less costly for society than punitive measures. Mom was pleased that I was being exposed to "a rich soup of ideas." Dad was probably a bit concerned, but he didn't show it. They were both just happy that I was making progress, happy enough to let me return to Colorado with my ski equipment. The car was yet to be earned.

*　　*　　*

That winter and spring I skied in earnest at places like Winter Park and Arapahoe Basin, reveling in Colorado's powder snow. It was so much better than the norm in California. At times Ann accompanied me on double or triple dates, six people and ski equipment jammed into and on top of some fraternity brother's two-door coupe. Foggy windows were the norm. Ann had not previously skied, so equipment rentals and lessons were a bit torturous, but by the end of our sophomore year she was coming down the easier runs with a semblance of grace. Obligingly, she often gave me time to fly off on my own for a rock and roll on the advanced slopes. After-ski bar hopping and pizza on the way home to Boulder were the capstones to every ski trip.

That year I got a job as a hasher in the Kappa Kappa Gama (KKΓ) sorority house. A fraternity brother, Raymond A. Smith, was the head hasher there. Mrs. Clancy, the cook, loved Ray and trusted his opinion, so I got the job. A hasher helps prepare and serve food, clear tables and wash dishes. In return, hashers receive free meals and sometimes collect gratuities for helping around the house. Lunch and dinner were served formally to between sixty and seventy girls. Breakfast was an informal buffet. Their stern housemother sat at the head table. Woe be it to any hasher who didn't serve with his left hand from the left and clear with his right hand from the right. I learned much in that job about food preparation and formal service, including how to carve meat and decorate food. While doing odd jobs around the premises, I was surprised to learn that girls can be slovenlier than boys. My fraternity brothers had disheveled rooms, and our bathrooms were far from a paragon of cleanliness, but what I saw at the KKΓ house let me understand that girls can be even worse.

I also learned how obnoxious and petty some rich girls could be, especially to those whom they considered inferior. However, the sorority girls knew that to annoy the hashers was to invite retaliation. If a girl was particularly irritating, we sometimes took things into our own hands during days when the housemother was absent. Pitchers of ice water inadvertently spilled down the backs of offensive sisters. Super-hot pepper sauce found its way onto the plates obnoxious sisters. Under Ray's leadership one weekend when both the cook and housemother were absent, we tied and gaged a girl, placed her on a bed of three dishwasher trays, and ran her entire body through the operating Hobart dishwasher. Of course, it was filled with ice water, some dry ice added for effect—so much for her cashmere sweater. Apparently her sisters weren't altogether unhappy about our action, so little was said about it.

Ray Smith was a skier, so on one weekend when we both had the day off, we headed for the slopes, arriving at Winter Park just as the lifts opened. Ray had a silver 1960 Corvette convertible. It had no ski rack, so we ran the skis from the passenger side footwell up through the slightly open canvas roof. That caused a cold draft throughout the car, requiring the wearing of full ski garb for the two-hour ride. That inconvenience was quickly forgotten the minute my skis hit the slope.

We skied the day through, barely stopping for a snack of candy bars, cookies and coke. When the lifts closed, we headed back down Hwy 40. Along the way we stopped at a popular bar in Idaho Springs. There we downed two pitchers of beer and a couple hamburgers with fries. It was close to midnight when we proceeded on to Boulder, feeling no pain and dressed in full gear to ward off the cold from the open roof.

Somewhere near Golden I awoke to Ray swearing and the vision of a barbed wire fence post coming at me in the headlights. For what seemed like a long while my body was being shaken like a ragdoll by unseen forces amidst the sounds of crunching metal and shattering glass. I knew what was happening, and I knew my fate was in the hands of a higher power. My only emotion was one of hope.

The next thing I knew, I was lying on my back looking up at stars that twinkled in the blackness. Not a sound was audible. I wondered if I was alive. Slowly I moved one finger, then a toe, then one limb after another. When I sat up, I realized that there was something resting on my shoulders around my neck. It was the right-side passenger window frame with the remaining glass pointing in toward my neck. I lifted it off over my head and struggled to my feet. I was standing in a field of stubble. Ten yards away the completely trashed car was lying on its back, wheels still spinning, radio still playing. I found Ray about thirty yards away. He was on his back, unconscious, with blood running from his nose. As I was bending over him, car lights flashed over us. Vehicles had stopped on the road, which was now some distance away. A woman was running across the field toward me. Her words have been imbedded in my memory: "Are you all right? That was the most spectacular accident I've ever seen." I told her I was okay but not sure about my friend. However, within moments, I began shaking uncontrollably. People were rushing up. The woman said, "You had better lie down."

I dimly knew that policemen were on the scene and I was being loaded into an ambulance. Ray and I both were taken to Denver General Hospital. A doctor called my parents to reassure them that I was all right and would likely be released the next morning.

A fraternity brother fetched me back to Boulder. For a week I had aches and pains throughout my body. Some black and blue marks lasted much longer. Ray had a concussion and was released a day later. His beautiful car was a total loss. My beloved Head skis and Scott poles looked like pretzels. The police report indicated that the accident happened on a slight curve at the end of a long straightaway. Their estimate was that the car left the road at well over one hundred miles an hour, flipped once end for end, and rolled five times. When I later saw it at the junk yard, the fiberglass body was shattered into pieces no bigger than a foot in diameter. We must have been ejected soon after the car left the road. There was no roll bar, so had we been wearing seatbelts, we would likely have died. I went out the passenger side window, since its frame ended up around my neck. Our thick clothing had protected us against glass and other sharp objects. That night Irish luck was again on my side, and the leprechauns must have protected Ray as well.

When I took the train home for spring vacation, Dad and Mom came up with the money for new skis and poles. They also allowed me to drive back to Boulder in our family's 1956 Buick Special. Their reasoning was that if I were going to die in a car accident, it was better that I die driving my own car rather than as a passenger with someone else. I was thankful for their trust in me and pledged that there would be no drinking and driving—well, maybe just a little. I was overjoyed to have my own wheels that could facilitate skiing on my schedule rather than that of others.

*   *   *

In the summer of 1962, my fraternity brother, Neil Dunbar, stowed away on a freight train from Denver to California, just for the excitement and adventure of doing so. When he arrived at my house in Livermore, Dad got us both jobs at the Alameda County Fair Grounds in nearby Pleasanton. It was one of the largest county fairs in California, sporting two weeks of pari-mutuel horse and harness racing, a carnival, and exhibition halls filled with everything from cakes and pies to vibrating massage chairs. The farm animal competitions and livestock auctions attracted participants from throughout northern California.

For a month Neil and I worked in the poultry section. Prior to the fair's opening we painted and set up hundreds of wire cages. Once the chickens arrived, we installed markers that described the species, ownership and registration number of each inhabitant. I had no idea that there existed so many breeds of chickens. Their owners were responsible for feeding. Neil and I were responsible for water and waste disposal. "What goes in must come out," and it did in atrocious form and odor. The exhibit area was roofed but otherwise open air. Every night the cages had to be cleaned and the concrete floor hosed down. Fans at either end of the building provided circulation to cool the birds and reduce the odor. Both Neil and I concluded that chicken farming was not high on our list of potential lifetime occupations.

After the fair ended, Neil and I drove to the Chester cabin. There we were joined by another fraternity brother, Joe Beerer, and my cousin, Jim Cramer. Mom helped us plan, purchase and prepare the food for a two-week backpack trip. The four of us then drove south to Bishop, California, where we began our trek from North Lake, hiking with sixty-pound packs, into the central Sierra over 12,800-foot Lamarck Col, camping our first two nights on the treeless granite of Darwin Bench. From there we worked our way along the Muir trail and over 12,000-foot Muir Pass, then down into the Kings River Canyon before climbing up again into Dusy Basin. All along the way we cooked over an open fire, enjoying meals of golden trout caught in nearby streams and lakes. On one layover day in Dusy, I went trout fishing while the others climbed a small granite mountain on the Basin's southern perimeter. There they built a cairn and christened the pinnacle "Phi Tau Tower." Years later Jim Cramer and my son returned to that spot and could find no sign of a cairn or any marker. So much for Phi Tau Tower's prominence among Sierra highpoints.

We eventually hiked out to civilization over 12,000-foot Bishop Pass to Bishop Lake. During our thirteen-day wilderness trek, we saw but two other human beings. That same route today is so well traveled that it requires registration arrangements, permits and entry fees. Fires are not allowed. Fishing is restricted to catch and release.

A brief digression. During my lifetime, population growth has strained nature's carrying capacity worldwide. I have been fortunate to experience some pristine environments, but I am not optimistic as to their continued survival unless human population is significantly reduced. The population, technical aptitude, and affluence of human beings continues to expand, and with them the degradation of both renewable and nonrenewable resources. Efforts to protect, conserve and manage these scarce resources are laudable, but often the effort serves only to shift burdens and benefits from one social group to another in unforeseen ways, leading to unforeseen consequences.

After hamburgers, french fries and milkshakes at Jack's Restaurant and Bakery in Bishop, we drove back to Livermore via Yosemite Valley. Dad knew a train yard foreman in the nearby town of Tracy. With that man's help, Neil Dunbar and Joe Beerer were able to hide away on a freight train bound for Denver. I wanted to join them, but my car couldn't drive itself back to Boulder for the fall semester, so I was forced to miss out on an adventure. Though in all honesty, the automobile seemed more inviting than a drafty freight car rolling across the Utah-Nevada desert and through the Rocky Mountains. Mom and Dad were doubtless relieved at my choice.

* * *

Two important happenings occurred in my junior year at Colorado. First, I found that I couldn't register for classes unless I declared a major. I had never given much thought to a major, but I realized that I had already completed five courses taught by the economics department: Economic Principals 1 and 2, Economic

History of the Western World 1 and 2, and Economic Geography. Never mind that I had C grades in all of them. Those courses represented more credit hours than I had amassed in any other subject, so I declared an economics major, with no idea what additional courses were required, and no particular fondness for the subject. Little did I appreciate the lifelong ramifications of that decision.

The second major happening was that I was elected fraternity treasurer. That meant I was the business manager for everything to do with the organization, including cooks, food, janitors, supplies, repairs and grounds maintenance. I paid all wages and bills, maintained all bank accounts and records. I collected all rents, dues and fees from brothers. The president, Neil Dunbar, and I reported directly to a board of alumnae elders in Denver. They owned the property and oversaw legal, income and property tax matters. That managerial responsibility provided the most worthwhile learning experience of my college career.

Sororities and fraternities were required to have a housemother. Strange as it seems, no one ever thought of a housefather. Our housemother was a lady in her late sixties or early seventies, Mrs. Goldie Ish. She lived in a one-bedroom apartment on the ground floor. Goldie had been a housemother in several fraternities over the years since her children had grown and moved on. It was not an easy job, but she had the drill down pretty well—dress appropriately, be a figurehead at meals and functions, do what the fraternity officers tell you to do, and otherwise stay out of sight as much as possible. Neil and I knew she was a lonely old lady. I still feel guilty that I didn't visit her more often. I know she wanted to be closer to some of us, but we were young bucks with horns and egocentric agendas. At times some brothers were verbally unkind to Mrs. Ish. Being experienced with older people, I was the one to soothe her feelings. She was particularly distraught on the afternoon that President Kennedy died, because she felt that some brothers were not showing sufficient respect. There were some more conservative brothers who were upset at being faced with Lyndon Johnson as president, but most were simply ambivalent, feeling that the whole episode had little impact on their personal lives. I spent several hours that day in Mrs. Ish's apartment, watching the television news with her. She was a sincere and well-intentioned lady. I hope things eventually worked out well for her.

Life at the Phi Kappa Tau house was similar to that portrayed in the movie *Animal House* starring John Belushi. Our fraternity brothers were better dressed and more sophisticated, but otherwise resembled the movie characters in many ways. Nicknames abounded. There were Mouse, Boo, Worm, Double-u, Doc,

Duls and Ivan, just to name a few that I can still remember. Mouse was a member of the Serendipity Singers, a folk group that went on to some degree of fame. They periodically practiced in our basement. Boo and Worm were brothers who came from a Chicago crime family. Their mother, Big Mama, ran a collection agency. Boo and Worm drove a black Jaguar XKE, which Phi Tau pledges were frequently required to polish. There was a brother named Mike O'Hanlon who ran a betting pool during final exam weeks. The first-place money from the pool went to the brother who could log, with witnesses, the most hours of sleep during the week. Mike held the record and also managed to graduate with honors.

Stairwell of Phi Tau brothers, Paul, 2nd from lower left corner

At one-point, Phi Tau, with the help of hashers, stole all the silverware from seven sorority houses on the same day. The girls were told that if they wanted their silverware, they must come to the Phi Tau house and serenade the brothers. They came all right, in such a mass of angry girls that it was thought best to return the silverware without the need for singing. The problem was that some flatware got intermixed, and the sororities were still sorting things out for some days afterward.

There was considerable alcohol consumption in the house, but drugs were not part of the scene as far as I know. There was pressure on everyone to dress well, be courteous, get good grades, participate in university activities, and generally be a credit to the fraternity. In that regard we had brothers who were members of academic honor societies, officers in campus governance, and members of the track, gymnastics, wrestling and lacrosse teams. The whole idea of Phi Tau life was to cause a little trouble for notoriety's sake and have some fun doing it.

Three theme parties were scheduled for the year that Neil and I were officers: the Viking party, a high school party to remind everyone of our past lives, and the purple passion party. Purple passion was a punchbowl drink composed of grape juice and grain alcohol, much of which was purloined from the university's chemistry lab. In order to avoid damage to our fraternity house from the inebriated hordes, the party was held outdoors in the mountains west of campus. It didn't take much purple passion to relax even the most well-intentioned date. In short order, the university had become alarmed and sorority girls had been advised to avoid the Phi Tau p.p. party; therefore, in our junior year, under Neil Dunbar's leadership, the party was transformed into a more sedate Polynesian/Hawaiian luau costume-party, held at our house. As a result, both female attendance and our fraternity's image improved.

My roommate during junior year was, Joseph Schonthal III, a passionate and emotional, Chicago born and raised Jewish fellow. Across the hall from us lived Ernest John Saliba, a passionate and emotional person of Arab-American heritage, who also hailed from the Chicago area. Throughout the year they carried on a good natured, but at times overly exuberant, Arab-Israeli war. The hallway was referred to as the Gaza Strip. The weapons of choice included firecrackers, water balloons, and water guns, so there was periodic collateral damage to those noncombatant brothers occupying adjacent rooms. No third-party peace-keeping efforts seemed to make any impact on the tit for tat conflict. During those two semesters, I learned more than I ever wanted to know about a disagreement in a faraway land that I otherwise would have ignored.

In our senior year Neil Dunbar and I lived together in a basement two-room suite that included a bath and wet bar. The entire suite was painted a glossy black enamel. Playmates of the Month adorned the walls of the entry and minibar. It was a real man cave. Neil was a serious, conservative engineering student with excellent study habits. Unfortunately, his positive influence was insufficient to save me from a fall semester that included eight credit hours of F grades in beginning Spanish and statistics.

Part of the reason for that debacle stemmed from my fear of foreign languages, a remanent of high school Latin difficulties. Part was sheer laziness and too much skiing. Also, that year Ann had dropped out of school and gone home to Michigan. She had never been much of a student and had difficulties concentrating. Though she had promised to return, I was free to try some new possibilities. I attended the C.U. Homecoming Dance with an Alpha Phi named Gigi Brikner. Gigi was from Hawaii, an exotic place in my mind. The occasion was particularly memorable because the homecoming queen, Mary Mothershed, was the first Black girl to ever be crowned homecoming queen at C.U., and the orchestra that night was conducted by Louis "Satchmo" Armstrong, one of history's finest entertainers.

During Thanksgiving break, 1963, I and a fraternity brother, Bob Clark, drove straight through the 1,300 miles from Boulder to Birmingham, Michigan. Our stay in the Frohberg's home allowed me to meet Ann's parents and her younger two brothers, Jim and Bill, and her sister, Marylin. Ann's father was an executive with the Rinshed Mason Paint Company, a supplier to General Motors and Ford autobody coatings. As a perk their family had third baseline seating for Detroit Tiger baseball games and a fifty-yard box at Detroit Lions football games. On Thanksgiving Day, we saw the Detroit Lions and Green Bay Packers battle to a 13-13 draw. Dinners at the Bloomfield Hills Country Club provided an insight as to the Frohberg's social status and expectations. I felt I could fit in, if need be, but that was not the lifestyle to which I aspired, and there were no decent ski hills nearby.

Ann did return to Boulder the next semester. She lived with a roommate in a nearby apartment and got a job as a salesperson in the local Handcock Fabrics store. Our relationship continued, and despite my subconscious misgivings about her family's expectations, I proposed to her in the spring of 1964, diamond ring and all. She accepted. We didn't set a date for the wedding, but our plan was to get married after I graduated. That semester I retook the Spanish class and this time passed with a grade of C. There was really no choice, as two semesters of a foreign language were required for graduation. I was running out of time. Either I passed Spanish or I didn't graduate. During Easter vacation, Ann and I drove home to Livermore so that she could meet my parents. I explained to Dad and Mom that I was twenty-one credit hours short of graduation and needed to attend both summer school and the fall semester in order to graduate. They were supportive, though a bit reserved about the marriage idea.

In the summer of 1964 I took four courses, a heavy load for summer school. All were upper division Business School courses that could be accepted as electives by the Economics Department. I had never taken business courses before because Dad had often said, "Never be a banker," and I had equated business school with banking. For the first time I found myself studying subject matter that interested me. There was no skiing. Neil had graduated. I had our suite to myself. The Phi Tau house was relatively empty and quiet, so I managed to get three Bs and an A in Financial Institutions. Perhaps Business School was the place for me. Perhaps I just focused for the first time. I'll never know what happened, but I experienced a great awakening, even though it came a bit late in my college life.

There was a cost to that summer of fervent study, or depending on one's viewpoint, a benefit. I neglected Ann to the point that she gave me back the ring and called off our engagement. I was heartbroken but determined to graduate, as I had promised my parents. I knew how much it meant to them, and I was determined not to let them down. After summer school four courses remained: Monetary Policy, Labor Economics, Public Finance Administration, and the dreaded part two of Beginning Spanish. If I passed them, I graduated.

Despite a little skiing on the side, I immersed myself in fall semester studies, partly as a way of assuaging the pain of Ann's rejection and partly because I wanted to be done with college and move on to something else, though I had no idea what that might be. My hard work paid off. I passed those courses with three Cs and a B in Monetary Policy. The degree was finally conferred in June of 1965. My transcripts indicate that I was ranked 716 out of 818 bachelor degree graduates, and my overall grade point average was 2.22. I was clearly not a paragon of academic success, but I had accomplished what my parents wanted and was done with school forevermore, or so I thought.

My time at the University of Colorado proved most worthwhile. By luck and divine intervention, I managed to overcome self-doubt and survive opportunities for academic and physical self-destruction. In addition to a grounding in property management, my fraternity experience broadened my perspective and deepened my understanding of individuals from different parts of America who held views dissimilar to mine. Most of all, I secured a Bachelor of Arts in Economics degree. I didn't bother to attend graduation ceremonies, and at the time had little appreciation for its value; however, that degree was the ticket to my future. It opened many doors that otherwise would have been closed to me. My parents knew the risk of sending a small-town child into the tumult of a large, faraway university. They hoped it would work out for the best, and with luck, it did.

Chapter 8

Europe

Dad and Mom had planned to finance a trip to Europe as a wedding present for Ann and me. When our marriage plans were terminated, they offered the same trip to me as a Christmas/graduation present. Of course I accepted, with the understanding that they just give me the money. I would do my own trip planning. Lots of American college students were traveling to Europe in those days, hitchhiking and boarding in youth hostels. I didn't want a planned itinerary with hotel reservations that required adherence to schedules. My heart was set on skiing as much as possible, and that required flexibility. They gave me four thousand dollars for Christmas under the proviso that I would graduate.

Mom's distant cousin, Joan Curry, owned and operated The San Francisco Travel Service on Montgomery Street in San Francisco. It was located next door to the ostentatious office of well-known defense attorney, Melvin Belli. In passing I marveled at the facade and furnishings. Whenever he won a lucrative case, he hoisted a skull and crossbones flag on his building's outrigger flagpole. Little did I know that years later I would be a witness for the plaintiff in a malpractice suit against Mr. Belli.

During that Christmas vacation, with Joan's help, I spent the entire $4,000 and $578 of my own money to purchase airline tickets, an all-Europe Youth Hostel Pass, and a slate-grey Porsche 1600 SC Coupe with British racing green leather interior, for delivery in Brussels, Belgium. That price also included Belgian registration, international driver's license, and European car insurance, along with homebound shipment from Antwerp to New York in mid-June. I could tell that Dad was not happy with my use of the money, but he said nothing. Mom thought I had been a bit extravagant, but also said nothing.

I returned to Colorado, into the teeth of final exams week, knowing that I must pass all four courses with a grade of C or better in order to graduate. On the Sunday before my first final, I sat in the Phi Tau dining room, nursing my coffee and glazed donut in contemplation of a full day of study at Norlin Library. The words over that library entrance remain embedded in my mind: "He who knows only his own generation remains always a child." *No child for me*, I thought. *I will pass these exams and graduate.*

I was jolted from my stupor as a fraternity brother, Dick Wasem, sat down across the table from me, his overly large coffee cake spewing sugar and crumbs in all directions. *Ed the janitor will be overjoyed*, I thought sarcastically.

"Callaghan, you're graduating this semester, aren't you?"

"I hope so," I said. "I've got twelve credit hours of exams this week."

"Then what are you going to do?"

"I'm off to Europe, skiing."

"When are you leaving?"

"Right after my last final. I'm driving to California and leaving from S.F."

"Cool! I wish I was going. By the way, my sister Jori is leaving for Europe around the first of May. Maybe you two could get together. She's a cool cat. You might like her company. I know she's a little nervous about being alone over there. She'd probably like some company. Right now, she's in Anaheim. You want her address and phone number?"

"Sure," I said, but my mind was elsewhere. Female company in Europe was not on my immediate agenda.

"Give her a call and say I recommended you contact her." He wrote the information on the back of a napkin and flung it my direction.

"Thanks, Dick. I'll give her a call when I get to California. Right now, I'm off to the library for some serious booking."

"Yeah, do that, but sometimes you can study too much."

"No, I can't. Not this time. It's my last hurrah. I've got to graduate or my parents will kill me."

"Have at it. But be sure and give Jori a call. I'd feel better if she was traipsing around Europe with you rather than some unknown joker."

I slipped the napkin into my notebook and headed off to my favorite carrel at the library.

*   *   *

The TWA flight from San Francisco to New York was uneventful. A three-hour layover at JFK turned into six because the Icelandic Airlines flight was delayed. Then in the mid-Atlantic, one engine of the DC-6 failed in rough weather. As I peered out the window into the blackness, the wing tip light rhythmically blinked red. Every so often a bolt of lightning lit up the entire wing, and the sick outboard engine with its feathered propeller was thrust into my awareness. We limped into Rakovic on three of four engines. It took another several hours to make repairs before we were again airborne to Brussels. Adrenalin and anxiety kept me awake for much of the trip. I would need to negotiate a big, unfamiliar airport and city, reach my hotel, and pick up my car, all without knowing a word of any European language or having any idea of European custom or culture. Michelin maps and guide books provided my only aid and comfort. I consulted them assiduously.

The taxi dropped me at the hotel, along with ski equipment and suitcase. I had no Belgian money and paid the driver in US dollars. Upon miscalculating the exchange rate and underpaying, the driver's loud language was infused with the words *merde* and *Americain*. I next probably overpaid the bellboy, since he left my room with a smile on his face. Upon flopping into bed, I remained there for the rest of that day and night while subsisting on leftover airplane food.

In the morning, with help from the front desk, I acquired some local currency and made a phone call to the car dealer, who said that the Porsche was being prepared and would be available the next morning. I had a whole day to play tourist in Brussels. Being afraid to attempt public transit, I wandered the city streets on foot in consultation with my guidebook. After visiting a couple of churches, some government buildings and a museum, hunger drove me into a bakery and subsequently a wine and cheese shop. The pastries were tasty. My meals that day and the next consisted of wine, cheese and bread. By that evening my feet hurt, and I fell into bed with little appreciation for what I had seen, but satisfied that I had survived my first day in Europe.

The next morning, I and my gear arrived by taxi at the Porsche dealership. When the paperwork was complete and the gas tank filled, a kindly, English-speaking employee helped me load and secure my skis on the rack over the engine compartment. Off I drove into the streets of Brussels. My objective was Spangdahlem Airforce Base in Germany, my only guide an open Michelin map on the seat beside me.

My cousin, Randy Cramer, was an army officer stationed at Spangdahlem. He spoke some French and German and had considerable European experience, so I hoped to hang out with him for a few days in order to get my "feet on the ground" before venturing south to Bavaria. Seeing Randy's face that afternoon was a relief. Though I didn't admit it, the prior four days had been stressful. Happily, the next four days under Randy's tutelage provided a delightful rest. I slept at his apartment in the officers' quarters, and while we tipped a few beers in the nearby town of Trier, Randy provided some useful advice about how to navigate Germany and deal with Germans.

During my stay at Spangdahlem, I met a girl named Solveig who was working in the Officers' Club coat check room. She gave me her home address, and in those days my testosterone levels were such that I drove the hour and a half to her home town of Walheim. She wasn't home when I arrived, but a neighbor, Herr Ernst Batz, invited me to lunch in his home while I waited. Herr Batz was a teacher who wanted to practice his English. He also turned out to be a stamp collector, so I forwarded his name and address to Dad and Mom. Mom and Herr Batz maintained a correspondence for many years thereafter. Solveig eventually arrived home, but I have no recollection as to our time together. Somehow I made it back to Spangdahlem in the early morning hours. Randy let it be known that he thought my behavior was a bit imprudent. He was right. I never saw nor heard from Solveig Dultgen again.

After rest and food, complements of the US Army, I felt ready to move on. As a parting gift, Randy gave me his allotment of gasoline stamps. When presented at gas stations in Germany, they allowed American military personnel to purchase fuel at reduced prices. I had no problem passing myself off as being in the American military. The station attendants took one look at me and my Porsche with skis on the back rack and never bothered to ask for identification.

* * *

My first stop in Bavaria was the village of Oberammergau, where I stayed in a small hotel and skied for a couple of days at nearby Garmisch-Partenkirchen. The skiing there was satisfactory, but the weather wasn't cooperating and the place was filled with a lot of American military guys. I had hoped to meet and ski with local Germans, so I decided to wander on and see what materialized.

After a couple of hours driving through the snow-covered Bavarian countryside with its narrow, icy roads and winter, dreary towns, I found myself in a village with buildings scattered along the shore of a long lake. According to my map, the place was called Schliersee. People were skiing on a hill with a T-bar poma-lift. There were no military license plates on the cars parked along the roadside across from the lift. This was clearly not a tourist frequented ski area, so I pulled off the road to get my bearings. A sign in the driveway to my right said *"Gasthaus – Zimmer Frei"* and below that *"Haus am Spiessbach."* **Good**, I thought, *maybe I can ski here this afternoon and stay the night if they have a vacancy.* I walked down the driveway of packed snow and knocked on the door. A matronly lady with a food-stained apron, whom I judged to be in her forties, answered the door with a smile and said, *"Gruss gott."*

"Haben sei ein Zimmer?" I asked. That was my first attempt at using the German from my guide book.

"Ja, ich habe einen ..."

I understood that she did have a room, but I didn't understand the rest of her somewhat long discourse. Subsequently I deduced that she didn't normally rent rooms during winter. Having no inkling of that, I plodded onward.

"Can I see the room?" I asked, pointing to my eyes and then into the house.

"Do *kommst ins haus.*" With a slight frown she motioned me inside into a vestibule, where it was clear that I should remove my shoes. Luckily, I was wearing zippered after ski boots.

"Bist du ein amerikanischer soldat?"

"No, I'm not in the military. I'm on holiday for ski fun," I said.

She appeared to understand my English and led me up the tiled stairs of an impeccably clean interior. Potted plants filled the corners, and vines were interlaced through the railing of the second-floor landing that looked out over the lake and functioned as both lounge and dining area. Overhead a chandelier made of deer horns hung from the heavy wood beams. The tiny, narrow room she showed me brought back memories of my college freshman dormitory. A window at the far end shed light on a single bed, desk and chair. A suitcase stand and armoire filled the remaining space. I suspected she had shown me the smallest, undesirable room, but that was fine with me. It was all I needed.

"Was kostet?" I asked.

"*Neon mark mit fruhstuck,*" was the firm reply. A quick calculation told me that translated into $2.25 a night, including breakfast. *Not bad*, I thought.

"*Gut*, I'll take it." I had no idea of the German words for that, but she seemed to understand and stuck out her hand.

"*Reisepass,*" she said.

I fished out my passport from the inner pocked of my parka. She looked carefully at my picture and name before saying, "*Paulo. Das ist ein gutter name. Hedi ist mein name. Willkommen im Haus am Spiessbach.* How many day you stay?"

"One week if the skiing is good."

"*Ah gut. Der schnee ist jetzt sehr gut.*"

We shook hands, and I noted the roughness of hard work in Hedi's grip. After parking the Porsche near the front door, I unloaded my gear and skied on the hill across the road for the rest of the day.

That evening I was sitting at a table on the landing, eating my bread, cheese and wine, when Hedi appeared along with a man who was perhaps in his late-forties or early-fifties, and two young girls that I judged to be perhaps eight and ten. The man's balding head topped a smiling, weather-beaten face.

With the clear intention of introducing them, Hedi said, "*Mein mann Hans Stangl unt unsere tochter, Susanne unt Sabine.*"

I arose, took a step toward them, and said, "*Guten abend Herr Stangl.*" We shook hands. He had a fearsome grip, but I realized that there was only a stub of an arm below the shoulder on his left side. *Probably a war-related amputation,* I thought.

Hedi continued in understandable English. "Hans will go for *skifahren* tomorrow *um* Spitzingsee. He likes you to accompany him."

I had no idea what or where Spitzingsee was, but if it had skiing, I was happy to go, so with a smile I replied, "*Ja, ich gehe. Vilen dankeschon.*" Hans seemed happy with that response, and the four of them departed down the hallway.

We left early the next morning in my Porsche. It appeared Hans was eager to ride in it. The Spitzingsee was a mountain lake at a higher elevation than Schliersee. When we disembarked and donned our gear, I was amazed at Hans's self-sufficiency, strength, and dexterity. Using his right arm in conjunction with his teeth and the stub of his left arm, he could accomplish almost anything that a two-armed person could do. In the following days I learned that he was an enthusiastic sailor and compressed-air diver on Schliersee during the summers.

Some of his friends told me that Hans was an accomplished mountain climber who could support his entire body weight from a rope clenched in his teeth, and before the war, he'd been one of Germany's top skiers.

I might note that during the time I associated with these people of southern Bavaria, never once did they talk about the war or their experiences during it. I'm sure that many of them had served in the German military and some were still sympathetic to Nazi ideals, but they treated me as a friend and companion, a sportsman, as they said. Our conversations, such as they were, never ventured into political, social, or religious issues, although they seemed to appreciate my being a Catholic.

Hans Stangl and Porsche 1600 SC, Spitzingsee, Germany, 1965***

I soon harbored no doubts as to Hans's skiing ability and community respect. When he talked to the lift operators, they clearly knew him well. We both skied for free that day, and ski we did. The T-bar lifts were long and stacked so that it took three separate rides to reach the mountain top. From there lifts ran down the backside as well. This was exactly what I had hoped for—a completely local ski area. If there were any non-Germans around, they kept a low profile. The snow was fresh, and we skied in unbroken powder through the trees and on open slopes. Hans took the lead, since he knew the place well. I followed, in wonder at the dauntless way he attacked the hill. His right turns were a bit smoother than his left, but his strength and confidence overcame all else.

Sometime after noon, Hans led the way down one flank of the mountain to some buildings nestled in a high mountain valley. He said the place was called Firstalman. We entered a bar filled with jovial skiers, some of whom wore masks and odd costumes. Those who greeted Hans were interested to know who he had brought along with him. They had a special slang word for non-Bavarians, people from the flatlands, something like "*briez.*" I was told it had something to do with pigs, but I should ignore it because it didn't apply to me. Over and over Hans explained that I was an American guest in his house, a sportsman, and not a military. There we ate and drank beer that was served in one-liter steins with lids. After consuming sausages, fried potatoes and a liter of beer, I was ready to get back out to the slopes. Hans was clearly not ready. It turned out that one of his reasons for taking me skiing was to get away from Hedi for a few beers with his friends in celebration of Fashing. I soon learned that Fashing was Bavaria's Mardi Gras, and we were in a special part of Bavaria known as Allgau, where the celebration was exceptionally jubilant.

Noting my reticence to consume more potent beer, Hans suggested that I drink *radiermass*, a fifty-fifty mixture of beer and lemonade. By the time I had finished one, he had downed his third liter of beer. For several hours we sang and cavorted with the raucous group. An accordion and mandolin made music that was frequently drowned out by boisterous singing. All were inebriated and having a joyous time. I'm sure I was the only foreigner there.

As twilight advanced, Hans led the way on crusty snow down a forest trail that led back to our car. He was feeling no pain. When we reached home after dark, Hedi was clearly unhappy with him. I, not wanting to get caught up in family discord, went to my room and stayed there.

Over the next several days, with Hans and Hedi's guidance, I visited several ski runs around Schliersee. One night Hans and I joined a group that was packing the outrun of a jumping hill in the neighboring village of Neuhaus. When the work was finished, we watched until almost midnight as boys as young a twelve flew through the air on the fifty-meter jump. I met one teenage jumper named Hans Bauriedl who wanted to speak English, so he invited me to dinner at his parents' home the next night.

"You try *springen*. I give you *meine sprungski*," he said. "Put your *angst* in your back pocket and fly."

Despite his insistence, there was no way I could work up the courage. Those guys might fly through the air, but not me.

Toward week's end the municipality of Schliersee held a slalom race for guesthouse residents. To Hans's and Hedi's delight, I won the race. That evening they and the girls accompanied me to the town meeting hall, where the mayor presented me with a Schliersee Bayer Alpine ribbon, a plaque, and a gift certificate for Sporthaus Schuster in Munich. The next day Hans and I drove to Munich in the Porsche. After having a beer or two, he helped me purchase a pair of lederhosen and a Bergen backpack that was specially designed to be worn while skiing. The lederhosen have long since disappeared. The plaque went on the wall near the front door of Haus am Spiessbach. To this day I still possess that Bergen pack.

*   *   *

When it came time to leave Haus am Spiessbach, Hans suggested that I visit a friend, Anderl Prinzing, who lived in the village of Karanzegg near Oberstdorf. It was about a three-hour drive to the west over icy mountain roads. When I got there, I found that Karanzegg was a tiny hamlet, but it had a nice-looking mountain with a chair lift. Locals directed me to the Prinzing Haus, which was within walking distance of the ski lift. I presented a note of introduction to Frau Prinzing, the only one home at the time. She spoke enough English to let me know that her family never rented rooms, but because of Herr Stangl's request, she would provide me with a room and two meals a day. However, she warned me that the bedroom was on the second floor and difficult to heat. What she didn't tell me was that the second-floor bathroom had only cold water and was impossible to heat, and that each morning I'd find an ice sheet on my toilet water. I thanked her and said that I'd be on the ski hill and return when the lift closed.

By early afternoon, I'd been up the lift a couple of times and was resting in a sunny spot at the edge of a run when I chanced to look uphill. Far away, a tiny dark speck was carving giant, drawn-out, S-shaped turns that traversed the full width of the hill. The speck was traveling at such a high rate of speed that puffs of powder snow stretched out far behind. *Whoever that is, he must be a downhill racer with legs of steel,* I thought. *He's purposely traversing the roughest, mogul strewn terrain at high speed, and his skis seldom leave the snow.* Every racer knows that skis pressing on the snow are faster than skis that are airborne. Closer and closer came the hurtling body. The final sweeping arch was carved so that I got showered with snow as the skier came to a full stop in front of me.

Under the yellow tinted goggles, I could detect the friendly smile of a girl. Her wavy dark hair was held away from her face by a red headband that covered her forehead and ears. Skiing as she did, I could imagine the attractive, buff body that must reside under her stretch pants and wool turtleneck. "Are you the Paul who comes from Herr Stangl?" she asked.

"Yes," I said.

"You live at our house. I am Christa Prinzing. My father is Herr Anderl Prinzing. My brother is Gerhard. Come, we ski," she said as she pushed off with a skating motion, straight down the fall line. In the fall line I could do a decent job of keeping up with her. None of that high-speed cross hill mogul traversing for me.

We made several runs together that afternoon before she disappeared, saying something in German that I didn't understand. For the next twelve days we skied together every day, and I ate breakfast and dinner with her family. Their questions about my life in America were unending, and their hospitality was exceptional. Christa's brother, Gerhard, was a bit reserved toward me, but he expressed certainty that his BMW could outrun my Porsche and wanted to give it a try. With humor I avoided the challenge. High speed in all activities was his thing. He went on to take seventh place in the men's downhill at the 1968 Olympics.

My state of mind at the time is summed up in this quotation from a March 5, 1965 letter to my parents:

> Christa is a wonderful girl who just took second place to Heidi Biebl in the German Alpine Championships. Every morning she and I ski together. I am better now than I have ever been in my life. Christa says, "Here, Paul, take these skis, they're too long for me," and she hands me a pair of Kastle downhills. She and her brother must have 30 pair between them. Yesterday she took me on a guided tour through the Kastle ski factory. I strap the long-thong bindings and we start up the lift. When we reach the top, we take the #1 run for a warmup, no turns allowed [as I recall, #1 was a two-mile-long, well-groomed intermediate run]. Then we work up to #3 and #4 to cap off the morning. My legs have become tree trunks of muscle, and I'm in excellent shape. I think now I can keep up with Christa on any slope and condition.

That last thought was overstated, but skiing with Christa greatly improved my stamina and self-confidence. She was a fine person, always encouraging and upbeat, and seemingly happy to have someone to train with. I know we enjoyed each other's company.

There was just one problem, Christa had a boyfriend, Ekke Trost, from the nearby hamlet of Blaichach. When he heard that I was on the scene, he started showing up for evening meals. I found him to be a fine fellow, and we got along well, but his arrival brought me back to reality regarding the possibility of closer relations with Christa.

One thing stood out to me. The world of Allgau was staunchly patriarchal. Christa paid absolute attention to the wishes of her father and showed much deference to her brother and Ekke. She couldn't allow herself to outshine either one of them, on the ski hill or elsewhere. Her trophies and awards were in back of the family showcase. Gerhard's were in front. Gerhard seemed to have few responsibilities other than ski training and racing. Christa had to plan her training around household chores and family responsibilities. I saw that Anderl lauded his son's accomplishments, while never seeming to mention those of his daughter. Christa was destined to be a house frau for Ekke, and that's the way it would be. I believe that I brought a breath of fresh air into her life. I followed her down the hill, paid attention to her, thanked her for helping me, and generally reflected an attitude of gender equality and respect that was something uncommon in her family life.

Ekke Trost and Christa Prinzing, Karanzegg, Germany, 1965

That brief experience with both the Stangl and Prinzing families provided my first immersion into another culture. Unbeknownst to me, it was preparation for future events. Much went on that I didn't understand, but I was exceptionally well treated. Why, I'm not sure, but I suspect I was the first respectful, civilian, non-competitive, fun loving, American skier that had entered their lives. They understood that I had no agenda other than ski adventure, and I drove a Porsche, so I was likely from an affluent American family.

At any rate, in mid-March Christa went off to race in Spain, and Gerhard went to Norway. Before leaving they invited me to meet them in Val d'Isere, France, in April. They said the spring skiing there would be excellent, and I could have some fun while they worked on a ski movie with Willy Bogner, the ski clothing entrepreneur. Also, Ekke asked me to join him and his brother and their father, Aquilin Trost, on their late March ski venture to Colfosco in Italy. My calendar was becoming full.

After Christa departed, I remained at the Prinzing house while making day trips to ski in Oberstdorf. The skiing there was good, but I found the place too commercialized and crowded with packed gondolas and long lift lines. So I said goodbye to Karanzegg and headed east, staying as much as possible away from large centers of population. My objective was Innsbruck, Austria, where the Olympics had been held the year before. The following quotation comes from a mid-March 1965 letter to my parents:

> I am staying in a small pension in Gutzens above Innsbruck. The room and breakfast cost me less than $2 a day. I ski every day on the Lizum, where the Olympic women's downhill was run. I hope you don't think I am spending too much time skiing. I'm sure that I have seen more of Europe and its people than most Americans ever get a chance to see. I have stuck to the back roads, the poor sections, and the quiet places, and it has paid off. I have met wonderful people and done interesting things … I may not have seen the great museums and historic tourist traps, but I will see the real people, become an excellent skier, and have many fond memories to look back on … In fact, I think I will remember the friendly people of Allgau all my life. They are simple and wonderful. For my part, I could settle down in Bavaria tomorrow and never go home to America. Life moves so slowly, and yet everyone is well fed and happy, and life to these people is interesting and fun.

I was having such fun skiing at the Lizum that I decided to reward myself with a meal at a fine restaurant. I settled on one in central Innsbruck that appeared upscale enough to fulfill my self-reward needs, but not demanding enough to quibble over my ski attire. I couldn't decipher most items on the menu, but the waiter suggested a red wine that turned out to be quite good, and I pointed to the most expensive item listed under the heading *Rinder*. I had learned that *rinder* meant beef, so I expected at least pot roast, if not steak.

Soon after pouring my wine, the waiter appeared with a tray of condiments and a plate containing a pile of ground raw meat. With a flourish he proceeded to separate an egg yolk from its white by pouring it back and forth between the two shell halves. The yolk was then plopped into a dimple atop the raw meat, and the creation was placed in front of me, along with a side of cooked vegetables. With the help of several unknown condiments and the entire bottle of wine, I was able to down the mixture and drive back to Gutzens, having learned that *pferdefleisch tartare wit ei* was not on my favorite cuisine list.

This understanding was further confirmed the next day when I came down with severe stomach cramps. After a day in bed, I saw an Austrian doctor, who gave me pain medication and said, "Lots of people get food poisoning. It will go away in a day or two." The pain medication allowed me to ski but did nothing to alleviate the underlying cause, so the discomfort continued to increase. I was about to try a hospital in Innsbruck when fate once again came to the rescue. I met a British doctor and his nurse wife who were on a skiing holiday. He gave me some antibiotics that improved my condition greatly. I wish I could recall their names. They were kind to help out a fellow traveler in distress.

With improved symptoms I and my Porsche were off again over the Brenner Pass into the Dolomite Mountains of Northern Italy. There I met Ekke and his father and brother in a mountain village called Colfosco. If I were to pick the highlight of my skiing time in Europe, it would be that week spent in Colfosco-Corvara. The mountains are spectacular, the ski terrain endless. The locals were welcoming and seemingly had much in common with Bavarians. Since I was traveling with Germans, I was assumed to be one—that is, until they heard me speak or saw my passport.

Signs of spring were everywhere; the days were sunny and warm, and corn snow was the norm. Ekke's father, Aquilin Trost, knew the area well and led us on some fine adventures. On one day, using a series of ski lifts, we completely circumnavigated the Grupo Sella massif, sixty miles of lifts and downhill skiing.

On another day we left at dawn to avoid avalanches, took early morning lift rides, and climbed the south flank of ten-thousand-foot Piz Boe. From there we crossed the top of the Sella Plateau and skied down a narrow canyon on the north side, a steep four-thousand-foot drop that brought us directly into Colfosco Village.

In the first week of April, I parted company with the Trost family. They returned to Allgau, and I headed west into Switzerland. We have never seen each other again, but memories of their kindness and congeniality have remained with me for a lifetime.

*   *   *

My destination was Zurich, Switzerland, where mail from home had been languishing at the American Express office. My first stop provided a day's skiing in St. Moritz, a crowded, expensive place, not to my liking. The next stop was one of those happenstances that good fortune has continued to provide throughout my life. It was late in the day, and I was tired from a long drive on icy mountain roads, when I saw a sign that read *Zimmer Frei* with an arrow pointing to a farmhouse. Unsure of lodging further on, and preferring to deal with German-speaking people rather than French, I decided to take a chance.

The farmer, Ludwig Wolfinger, and his wife and daughter were welcoming although clearly surprised to see an American in a Porsche with Belgian license plates. The house was partially heated by the warmth of farm animals that occupied stalls under the building. My second-floor room was cold and smelled like a barn, but the bed and blankets were clean and warm. The kitchen with its wood stove was the center of family life. I was invited there to drink warm milk before bed. Our communication was, as usual, difficult but enjoyable. The daughter, whom I judged to be about twelve years old, brought out her school English book so that I could review her homework and read a passage aloud. She informed me that I didn't sound like her British English teacher.

I stayed in that farmhouse for three nights, drinking fresh cows' milk, eating homemade bread, butter and cheese, while helping the young Swiss girl with her English studies, all for less than a dollar fifty a night. On the first day I made a quick trip to Zurich for the mail. It was not good news. The Vietnam War was intensifying, and my draft board was trying to verify that I was attending the Goethe Institute in Germany. I had previously applied for a draft exemption, based on my intention to study there, yet to this point I had never seen the place. In order to avoid being drafted, I now had to gain acceptance into some graduate program before the board discovered my dishonesty. Mom was working on that, having forged my signature and submitted several applications to law schools on my behalf.

On the next day I played tourist, visiting the national museum in Valduz, Liechtenstein. There I mailed letters home in response to the questions and application materials I had received from Mom. I covered each envelope with colorful stamps so that Dad could receive postmarked envelopes from Liechtenstein for his collection.

Upon departing the farmhouse amid goodbyes and well wishes, my next objective was Zermatt, where I hoped to fulfill my dream of skiing on the slopes of the Matterhorn. As I had done all along the way, I consulted my trusty Michelin map for the shortest route, one that led up the Rhine River Valley, past the city of Chur, and then up the valley of the Vorderrhine to the Oberalp Pass. It was a spectacular drive, with snow-covered mountains on all sides. The little Porsche sped along doing what Porsches do best, curvy mountain roads at high speed. I was having such fun driving that I didn't perceive the lack of traffic as anything but a chance for increased speed. After flying past an old man who was leading his horse and cart down the road, I happened to notice in the rear view mirror that he had stopped and was looking after me in an inquisitive manner. *Ha, he's never before seen a Porsche at high speed*, I thought.

Less than a minute later I rounded a blind curve. Directly in front of me, blocking the road, was a red and white striped steel bar with a circular, red stop-do-not-enter sign affixed to it. I slammed on the brakes. The Michelin tires squealed; the car slid ahead toward the barrier. I can still see that bar coming toward my head at eye level. The next thing I knew, I was covered in glass particles, as was the entire car interior. The bar had cleared the hood by half an inch and taken out the front window. It now rested just in front of my hands as they clutched the steering wheel. Thankfully, my dark glasses had provided eye protection.

I turned off the car and sat there for a long while in the cold silence of complete disbelief. The map had indicated nothing about the pass being closed during winter. There must have been warning signage along the way, but my ignorance of languages had rendered me oblivious to them. The lack of traffic had not set off any cautionary alarms in my mind because I was having too much fun playing Grand-Prix driver. Utter chagrin framed my state of mind as I climbed out of that car and used a whisk broom to clean glass particles off myself and the green leather seats. I was thankful there had been no observers of my folly, but the cold silent mountains were certainly laughing at me.

There was no choice but to bundle up and drive back down the road to seek assistance. It was a cold ride at slow speed. When I came to the old man with the horse and cart, he was still plodding down the road. As I slowly passed, he could see my state of affairs and just stood there shaking his head, a look of condescension on his face.

I found a garage and mechanic service in a village down the road. The owner directed me to a guest house, where I remained for two days, licking my psychological wounds. On the third day I was off again, driving more sedately, on a more certain route to Zermatt. A replacement windshield had been installed and the car thoroughly cleaned. The mechanics were excited to work on the Porsche, so I had them change the oil and clean the various filters. The entire cost of repairs and maintenance amounted to $107, US. In a letter to my parents, I told them that rocks had fallen from the roadside and broken my windshield. I don't believe that I ever subsequently owned up to the truth.

Upon arriving in the valley leading to Zermatt, I discovered that the only way to reach my goal and its famous Matterhorn Mountain was by rail train. No roads were open in the winter. I was loath to leave my car in an uncovered public parking lot, and lodging prices near the point of embarkation and in Zermatt proper were well beyond what I had become used to paying. So I chose to drive up a neighboring valley to the village of Saas Grund and its nearby ski resort, Saas-Fee, where the lodging and lift prices were more reasonable.

Even though it was late in the season, Saas-Fee had excellent skiing. On my first night it snowed, and the next day there was ten to twelve inches of fresh powder. I occupied the second gondola to leave the terminal station that morning. Standing by the window, I became enthralled with the surrounding mountain peaks and pristine, unmarked slopes below. Wrapped in my enthusiasm, I paid little attention to others in the gondola, but apparently one man was watching me.

After exiting at the upper terminal, I found an open flat space where I could strap my long-thong bindings tight around the Molotor boots. It was a sunny day, but cold. My breath was silver fog. The snow was fluffy-dry, impossible to make into snowballs. I checked the Saas-Fee map, choosing an intermediate run that stretched out to my right. Only two tracks led in that direction. They were enough to mark the way yet leave lots of unbroken snow. Gloves on, parka zipped, yellow-lensed goggles secured over my blue-tasseled beanie, a snug grasp on the Scott poles, with a couple of skating motions my skis moved into the fall line. The cold wind in my face enhanced the feeling of euphoric freedom that accompanied a rhythmic cadence of speed control in unbroken powder snow—extend float right, dig down, extend float left, dig down, again and again, over and over, like a dancer in a vast ballroom of shimmering crystal white. This was what I lived for.

I pulled up in a relatively flat area to catch my breath and reconnoiter. Looking back up the mountain, my dance was recorded in a winding track that led all the way to me. Then I was surprised to see another skier carving the exact rhythmic inverse of my track. The two tracks together formed a chain of hourglass patterns. As the skier came closer, I saw that it was a man wearing a green Bavarian felt hat.

"*Gruss Gott*," I said as he pulled up beside me.

"*Ah, ein mann aus Bayern*," he said with a big grin.

"*Nein, ein Bayer-Amerikanisch. Ich kein spreche Deutsch*."

"Well then, English it is. You ski like a Bayer. I've been wondering about your nationality. You have American Head skis, yet you don't look like a military. I heard you speak German when you purchased your lift tickets this morning, and you acted like a Bayer. When I saw you ski, I followed and redesigned your track. My name is Gunter."

"It's nice to meet you, Gunter. My name is Paul. I've been living and skiing with Bavarians for the past couple of months, so I guess I've picked up some of their habits."

"So *mein freund*, shall we make our mark on some of this snow before it gets too warm?"

"After you," I said. We skied together all that day and ate dinner together at a restaurant that evening. He said he was a lawyer from Munich and had come to ski in Zermatt. But he had arrived a day earlier than his reservations, so he came to Saas-Fee for one night.

The next day, Gunter showed me how to negotiate the train to Zermatt and pay for a three-day lift pass. He also brought me to the Schweizer Ski-Schule and helped me register for the Swiss Ski Federation's Gold Test and Certification. That involved skiing for an entire day with the lead instructor of the Zermatt Ski-Schule. I and two others, a Frenchman and an Italian, were run through trials that involved open slope skiing in a wide variety of terrains and snow conditions, everything from unbroken powder, to ice-covered mogul filled shoots, to slopes with heavy broken slush. In addition, we ran a preset slalom and downhill course. In every trial we were scored on skiing style and competence.

At day's end, I passed with twenty-two points out of a possible twenty-four. Based on the reception I subsequently received at the ski school, I suspect that the other two did not receive the necessary eighteen points required to pass. Aside from the congratulations of Schule personnel, my reward was a signed and stamped certificate with my picture on it, as well as a tiny gold triangular pin, stamped with the Swiss cross and the word TEST. I was told that Gold Test qualifiers were eligible for half-priced lift tickets throughout Switzerland. I was also told that Gold Test status qualified me to be hired by any Swiss ski school on a daily basis should they need an English-speaking instructor. Unfortunately, I never returned to ski in Switzerland, and thus never had the opportunity to make use of my gold status.

As the head of the Zermatt Ski-Schule shook my hand he said, "You should know that you are the only English-speaking person to pass the Gold Test this year in Zermatt or Saas Fee. Congratulations." At that moment I thought of Lutz Aynedter and my high school Red Hornet skiing days. Quietly I mused, *Thank you, Lutz, for giving me your style and a bit of your grace. Today it must have shown through.*

I skied only one more day in Zermatt, all the while marveling at that magnificent Matterhorn Mountain that dominates the valley skyline. Though I looked for him, I never saw Gunter again, and I have no memory of his last name, though I owe him thanks for helping me experience one of my life's great adventures.

*   *   *

I was anxious to get on my way to Geneva, where my mail was being sent to the home of my Uncle Jerry Cramer's friends, Hervey and Sally DeBivort. They had invited me to stay with them, and I was looking forward to the visit. The drive took me down the Vispa and Rhone River Valleys and around Lake Geneva. Spring was breaking out everywhere in these lowlands. The days were sunny and bright. Meadow greens and wildflower bouquets covered a landscape that rose up toward snowcapped peaks. The scenery was just as portrayed in *The Sound of Music*, a movie released that same month in America.

Hervey and Sally were most welcoming. Hervey was a Swiss citizen who worked for the United Nations in Geneva. Their son, Lawry, and daughter,

Carlyle, were away at school in America, so the DeBivorts seemed happy to have a young person around the house. When I told them that I had passed the Swiss Gold Test, they were awestruck. Their son had tried and failed.

I spent much of my time at their house reading, answering mail, and filling out graduate school application forms. Mom, a fervent anti-Vietnam War activist, was tirelessly trying to get me accepted into a law or business school. The draft board was trying to determine my whereabouts and whether or not I was attending the Goethe Institute. I was becoming increasingly concerned. The war situation seemed to be getting worse, and my only avenue to avoid being drafted was enrollment in graduate studies.

The DeBivorts informed me that at their request, Mom had sent a sports coat, slacks, tie and dress shoes, so that I might attend a formal occasion that had been planned during my three-day stay. It turned out that Hervey DeBivort was a friend of Dr. Raymond de Saussure, a noted Swiss psychoanalyst and the patriarch of an aristocratic Genevese family. Dr. Saussure and his American wife, Jamie Howenstine, and their daughter, Judy Ann, lived in Maison de Saussure, a multi-story chateau built in 1709. Judy Ann was planning to attend the University of Colorado in the fall. She and her parents were interested in talking with me about my experiences at C.U., and they were also interested in having Mom and my Aunt Janice write letters of recommendation to their respective sororities on the C.U. campus. Thus, Hervey, Sally, and I were invited to dinner at the Chateau.

The following is an excerpt form a subsequent letter to my parents:

> It's hard for me to describe the dinner. I felt so ill at ease that I remember little about it. Banks of candles lit the room, not an electric light in sight. Servants stood behind me watching my every move. The place settings had several forks, knives, spoons, plates, and three glasses. I was so afraid of doing something wrong that I couldn't enjoy myself. There were several courses of food that I did not understand. The main course was some kind of small bird covered in sauce. I can't remember the French name. The vintage French wine was tasty, but I could not pronounce the name. When the salad was offered by a servant, I managed to put it on the wrong plate. Judy Ann, who was seated opposite me, proceeded to do the same thing, so that I would not feel badly. I liked her. We had a good conversation. I was impressed with what

a lovely, down to earth American type girl she is … She'll do fine at Colorado, but I don't see how she can stand living in such a formal environment. There must be fifty rooms in the place. After dinner, Dr. Saussure, Hervey, and I retired to the Doctor's study, where he poured an after-dinner liquor. It must have been at least 150 proof. I was completely inhibited after that. Hope I didn't embarrass myself or anyone else.

Upon leaving the DeBivort home, I drove south into France, up the Valley of the Arve, over the pass at Combioux, and down the L'Ariy to Albertville, then finally up the Isere River to the exclusive, expensive resort of Val d'Isere. I was going there at the invitation of Christa and Gerhard, an invitation extended to me when we had skied together in Karanzegg in February. Since then, they had traveled and competed in several countries. I hoped they still remembered.

But the story of what follows actually began the previous year. Wilhelm "Willy" Bogner was the owner of a renowned German sportswear fashion company. Bogner stretch ski pants were sought after worldwide at the time. In 1964 Willy had gotten the idea of bringing together a cadre of world class skiers to make a colorful ski fashion movie, done entirely to music, kind of a ballet on skis that featured his company's clothing designs. He chose St. Moritz, Switzerland as a venue because it had good snow conditions late in the year, when the racing season was over and the best skiers were available.

He brought together some twenty-five of the world's top skiers, men and women from Austria, France, Germany, Italy and America. The lone American was Wallace Jerold "Buddy" Werner, who had represented the US in three Olympics. Since it was the end of the racing season, the participants were relaxed and ready for some unconstrained fun. After several days of movie making, the group was given a day off. Buddy Werner and his then fiancé, Barbi Hennenberger, a German Olympian and friend of Christa's, organized a small group for some fun skiing. Barbi asked Christa to accompany them. Werner wanted to take a slope that was marked for avalanche danger. Others felt uncomfortable, but Werner prevailed and off they went. The avalanche came. Christa was partly buried, as were several others, but Werner and Hennenberger were killed. That disaster ended the movie making for that year.

Now it was a year later and Willy Bogner had again brought together twenty-five world class skiers, this time in Val d'Isere, France, with the intention of finishing the movie he had now titled "Ski-Faszination." The four-star hotel in which Bogner had accommodated the participants was beyond my budget, so I found a less costly room nearby. Christa was happy to see me, and I think a bit surprised that I had come. Anyway, I got a greeting hug and we had dinner together at the Val d'Isere restaurant owned by one of France's famous skiers, Jean-Claude Killy.

Paul on the Litzum in Austria, 1965

Christa Prinzing and Troddle Hecker come to greet Paul
on the movie set in Val d'Isere, France, 1965

Christa introduced me to many in the cast and crew, including Herr Bogner. I became a regular fixture on the sets, helping to move equipment and assisting in any way I could. Excerpts from letters written to my parents from Val d'lsere capture my feelings at the time.

April 23rd 1965:

… I'm in Val d'lsere, France. It is a small mountain village south of the world-renowned Chamonix. I am sorry I cannot send you a map, but I have only one and need it to find my way between the many lifts and runs. The snow here is excellent and will be good far into May or even June. Christa and her brother, Gerhard, along with all the top German and French skiers and a few Italians and Austrians, live in a more exclusive hotel just around the block from me. The weather here has been bad—that is to say, it snows every day. However, all of us think that's great. Since overcast days are not good for movie making, we can relax and ski for fun. The 25 to 30 skiers here are famous names in their respective countries, but you might have heard of some like Sailer, Killy, and Mittermaier. The French skiers can't speak German or Italian, and the German and Austrian skiers don't speak French or Italian, so everyone ends up speaking a smattering of English, which is great for me.

The skiers are divided up into five groups. Each group wears exactly the same color and style of clothes, and each group has a particular musical rhythm that they must ski to in synchronization. All day today Christa and I worked on her particular rhythm. She has a slow one which, strangely enough, is much harder to master than a fast rhythm. When the movie is finally made (provided the sun ever comes out) it will be a ballet on skis.

Last night we watched the movie scenes that were shot last year. Several of the girls left the room crying when scenes of Buddy Werner came on the screen. Even Christa had a big tear roll down her face. Evidently everyone here thought much of Werner. They say he was always so happy and tried to cheer everyone up with comedy both before and after races. Christa told me that Werner came up to her and gave her a friendly kiss, then took off skiing down the hill. He had not gotten 40 yards when she heard the avalanche break away. She survived. He didn't. The whole episode has left an indelible impression in her mind and on the minds of everyone in the group of which I now find myself a part.

Well, I guess I don't have to tell you that I'm in seventh heaven. I can't figure out what it comes from, but my innate luck, easy going personality, and ability to ski well has put me in a place where I never would have dreamed when I was learning to ski at the Edelweiss years ago. Thank you, Mom and Dad, for giving me this opportunity ...

April 30th 1965:

... I'm still in Val d'Isere. It is a beautiful place and a wonderful ending to a fabulous ski season. I'll ski tomorrow and Sunday and then head back to Schliersee to pick up mail and see Hans and Hedi Stangle ... My face is black, and my hair is bleached almost white/blond from the sun. I am thin and in the best physical condition of my life; however, it is interesting to count all the aches and pains that I have collected in two-and-one-half months of continuous skiing. There are many! My feet are the most bothersome. I literally have the poor things held together with tape and pads. I notice though, that all the other skiers in the Bogner group have similar difficulties. Bogner himself has the worst case of chapped lips I have ever seen. He must eat everything through straws this week. Christa has a bad knee that has to be wrapped with tape every morning. Troddle Hecker (a wonderful young German skier) has feet problems with calcium deposits. She skis in pain every day. I don't think there is anyone in the group without something wrong after a hard year of training and racing. And to top that off, all these skiers must continue to train all summer long. They all go to nationally sponsored training camps on the various glaciers around Europe for the summer months. Christa and Troddle and Luki Leitner will go to Chile for the whole month of August. They all tell me that I'm so lucky because I can stop when I want. And I do feel it's time to stop ... Happy birthday Mom and Dad. I hope I can someday make it to 79, Dad ...

Sometime around the second or third of May I said goodbye to Christa and the others. We have never met again. I do believe there was some degree of attraction between us, more than just friendship. But the timing and circumstances weren't right. Christa's English was as bad as my German, so correspondence was difficult. Our worlds grew far apart, and the time of the internet had not yet arrived. I do know that Christa and Ekke married. I assume they had children and still live somewhere around the Karanzegg-Blaichach area of Bavaria. I hope their lives have been prosperous and satisfying. They certainly contributed to the quality of mine. Had it not been for the lurking prospects of the draft and the specter of the Vietnam War, I might well have stayed in Bavaria and actually attended the Goethe Institute. I liked the people, and they seemed to like me. That war influenced the direction of my life, as it did for so many others of my generation.

* * *

Spring is a time of fresh beginnings. My body had enough skiing, so I decided to return to Schliersee. There I planned to become a tourist, using the "Haus am Spiessbach" as my hub of operation. This time Hedi gave me a larger room with a lakeside view. I sold my Head skis for seventy-five dollars and gave my Scott poles to Hans. One of them was slightly bent, but he only needed one pole anyway. The rest of my winter gear I mailed home at the cheapest possible rate. After counting my remaining money and travelers checks, I determined that I had spent just over one thousand dollars, including the broken car window. It seemed I was on track to stay within my two-thousand-dollar budget for the entire trip, of course not counting the price of the Porsche.

Soon after arriving in Schiliersee, I met up with my fraternity brother's sister, Jori Wasem, at the Munich train station. We had been in telephone and mail contact since her brother Bob had suggest that we meet. However, we had never exchanged photographs or met in person. Since train schedules were unpredictable far in advance, our agreement was to meet on a certain day during a six-hour interval at the Hertz rental desk in the Munich train station. I was early, and so was she. We hit it off right away. She was an energetic brunette who was not afraid to take a risk or try something new. It was nice to be with an American again. I hadn't talked to one in three months.

That was the beginning of a five-week partnership and my first affair after the marriage debacle with Ann Frohberg. Being a bit naïve about sex, Jori's tender schooling served to enlighten my perspective. We were constantly together.

Hans took us sailing and trout fishing on Schliersee. We visited the famous Neuschwanstein castle and spent several days exploring the environs of Munich, from beer halls like the Hofbrauhaus to the Deutsches Museum and the Residnze. We overnighted in Salzburg and Kufstein Austria. We hiked the spring greenery and flower-filled meadows of Bavarian mountainsides. As young people do, we took everything one day at a time, paying little heed to what came next.

Toward the end of May, Jori and I said goodbye to Hans, Hedi, Susie and Sabine. I had the idea, and Jori agreed, that we should drive to Berlin and see the famous Berlin Wall. In those days of the Cold War, two young Americans in a Porsche with Belgian license plates driving across communist East Germany to West Berlin was not only naive, but it was arguably stupid, but we did it. And once in West Berlin, we drove through Checkpoint Charley into communist East Berlin for a day, just to see what it was like and what the Wall looked like from the other side.

At the Helmstedt border crossing into East Germany, our passports disappeared behind a one-way mirror while we sat in a room with no windows for over three hours. Eventually we were each ushered into a back room and separately interviewed as to our past, present, and future travel plans and reasons for going to Berlin. It must have been apparent to the German border guards that we were nothing but stupid American kids on a lark. They let us go onward after a serious lecture about the *Time* magazine that had been discovered under the Porsche's driver seat. "Bourgeoisie propaganda," they said. I had forgotten that it was there. It was never returned.

We stayed in West Berlin for three days. The coffee houses were a delight. Lots of people our age wanted to practice their English, and they introduced us to some fine clubs and restaurants. We walked along the Wall and saw the Brandenburg Gate from across a no-mans-land of barbed wire and machine gun towers. What we saw of life in East Germany and East Berlin was austere to say the least. The policemen carried machine guns, and the prices in restaurants were higher for us than for East Germans. Officially we could only use East German money and were forbidden to bring any of it out of the country. Twenty US dollars was the minimum exchange amount, and we had to spend it before leaving. There was a sense that we were being watched, especially when deviating from any main streets. Certainly all eyes were on the Porsche. No one drove such a car in their communist world. When exiting East Germany through Helmstedt, there was another long wait, during which I glimpsed the Porsche being raised up on a hydraulic lift, hood up, doors open, with a group of border guards peering underneath and spinning the wheels by hand.

We next stopped at Spangdahlem Air Base to visit Randy. When we arrived, he was on duty and not available, so Jori and I got a room in the village of Wittlich and spent two days driving along the Mosel River. I had a letter of introduction from Ernie Wente to a vintner in Lieser near Bernkastel. We stopped there but the person wasn't available, so we satisfied ourselves with wine tasting at several wineries. We were feeling no pain each night when we returned to Wittlich. In a couple of days, Randy was free, and we had a good visit. He helped ship my belongings home via military post. I kept only those essentials that fit in the Bergan backpack.

Leaving Randy, we drove to Brussels, where Jori and I parted company. She got on a train for, as she put it, "the sunny south," Spain and then Italy. After all these years I can still see her in my mind's eye waving goodbye in the train station. I then drove to Antwerp where the Porsche was loaded onto a freighter bound for a circuitous route to New York. Jori and I never met again, though I have corresponded with her and her brother, Bob Wasem, a pharmacist in southern California. Jori became a nurse and lives in that same area.

*　*　*

The next night I departed on a ship bound for Dover, England. After busing to London, I learned to use the Underground and found an address given to me by Katya Reidel, a girl I had met while skiing in Bavaria. She had told me that her sister was studying in London and would be happy to show me around when I got there. The sister, whose name I have forgotten, turned out to be a student at the London School of Economics. She lived with several students in a flat in one of London's suburbs. They welcomed me, saying I could sleep on their couch. That was fine with me.

Once I learned to navigate the bus and the Underground system, I found it easy to navigate London. I saw a parade of the Royal Guard in Hyde Park, the Changing of the Guard at Buckingham Palace, the interior of Westminster Abby, and the crown jewels in the Tower of London. I traveled to the village of Barham and saw the manor house that was the place of my grandfather Courtney Barham's roots. I attended a play, *Who's Afraid of Virginia Wolf*, and a concert by the London Festival Orchestra. Some of each day I spent on Trafalgar Square. In those days it was a place of gathering for young travelers like me. One night the students with whom I was living took me "out on the town." I have no idea where we went—bars, dance halls, Piccadilly Circus, I believe. In any case we stayed out after the Underground closing hour, and since no one was willing to pay for a cab, we walked home. It must have been five miles or more. By the time we arrived it was dawn's first light, and I was completely sober with aching feet and head.

After five days enjoying London, I took a train to northern England and a ship across the Irish Sea to Belfast. Once again trusting my Michelin maps, I hitchhiked to Castlederg with the intention of finding Irish relatives. My dad had advised against searching for relatives, saying that it was wise to "let sleeping dogs lie." Being young and inquisitive, I wasn't about to do that. I knew that Dad's father, Henry Callaghan, had immigrated from Ireland and married another Irish immigrant, Sarah Ann (McCrory) Rodgers, in San Francisco in 1878. At the time I knew nothing about the origin of Henry, but I did know that Sarah Ann had come from a place called Aghyaran (pronounced Ah-he-yarn) near Castlederg in County Tyrone, Northern Ireland.

Hoping for information, I approached the postman's window in the Castlederg post office. I told the clerk that I was an American named Callaghan and was looking for relatives named McCrory Rodgers who lived in a place called Aghyaran. Could he tell me how to get there? Of course, I had mutilated the pronunciation of Aghyaran.

Upon looking me over with a suspicious and questioning eye, he replied, "What's the name of the place? Here, write it down on this paper."

I did so, and a flash of recognition lit his face. "Oh, Ah-he-yarn! I'll draw ye a little map … here. Just stay on the street in front of this post office. When ye come to the fork, take the left." He glanced at my backpack and asked, "Do ye have transportation?"

"No," I said. "I'm walking."

"It's better than five miles, laddie. Ye sure ye don't want to be get'n a lift?"

"No, I'll walk," I said. I was so fit from skiing that five miles seemed of little import.

"All right, good luck to ye, laddie."

I hadn't gone half a mile when a noisy diesel lorry pulled up beside me. "Are ye the American who's go'n to Aghyaran?" asked the driver through the open window.

"Yes," I said.

"Jump in, laddie, I'm go'n that way." I threw my pack into the back and climbed into the cab. Off we went down the gravel road.

"I hear ye're look'n for the Rodgers place at Meenagrogan. Are they kin?"

"I don't know," I said. "All I know is that my grandmother was Sarah Ann McCrory Rodgers, and she came from Aghyaran."

"Well, I think I know where ye should be head'n. It's a bit this side Aghyaran. I'll drop ye off there. What's your name?"

"I'm Paul Callaghan," I replied.

"Hmm, don't know of any Callaghans in these parts, but that's a fine Irish name all right."

We eventually stopped on the road in front of a two-story, whitewashed building. Three chimneys protruded from the ridge of the tiled roof. It was separated from the road by a rock fence. The wide gate was open. There were no trees in the yard or anywhere around. The surrounding fields were plowed or green with grass, but somehow a sense of austerity pervaded everything. This was certainly not a wealthy farm.

"Good luck to ye, laddie," he said as I climbed down and fetched my pack.

In a moment I was standing there alone with no choice but to proceed through the gate and across the vacant yard to the front door. The woman who answered the door was in her thirties, with flour on her hands and arms as if she had been preparing baked goods for the oven. Her greeting reflected both surprise and caution. "Aye, good day tye," she said.

I explained who I was and that I had come to find relatives named McCrory Rodgers.

"Well, my husband is James McCrory. He's work'n in the fields right now, but he'll be back shortly. Ye come on in and wait ferum."

She ushered me into the kitchen, which seemed to be the only warm room. There, as I had suspected, she was kneading bread for baking in a coal fired stove. While we waited, she asked questions about life in America and my relatives there. Finally, James arrived. He was covered from head to foot in white dust. When he took off his paddy cap there was a ring around his head where the white stopped and the light skin and dark brown hair started. He glanced at me with a not too friendly expression.

"And who's this fella ye'v brought into our kitchen?" he said to his wife.

"He's been here only a few minutes. He says he's from America and look'n for his relatives named McCrory Rodgers. I told him to wait for you."

Without saying a word James went to the sink and washed his hands, arms and face. The quiet was a bit unnerving. He finally turned and said, "So what's your name?"

"I'm Paul Callaghan; my father is Henry Joseph Callaghan, and his mother, my grandmother, was Sarah McCrory Rodgers. All I know is that she came to America from Aghyaran."

He was silent for a few seconds and then said, "Well, it looks like your grandmother and my grandfather were brother and sister, so I guess that makes us cousins." We shook hands as he continued. "I'm James McCrory, and my grandfather was Dennis McCrory, your grandmother's older brother. He stayed here in Ireland on this land when all, save one sister, left for America. My Auntie Agnes will be happy to see ye. She's Grandfather Dennis's daughter, so a first cousin of your father … Oh, this is Mary, my wife, if ye haven't met already. I'm sorry I've got'a get back to the field. My brothers are wait'n for me. Mary'ul take care of ye till Auntie Agnes shows up. It's better that ye stay at Auntie's place. She's got an indoor toilet and hot water. I hope ye'l stay for a few days, cousin, so we can get together and sip a pint or two of Guinness."

In an hour or so Auntie Agnes and her husband James arrived by automobile to fetch me. It was unclear how the message of my arrival was communicated. There were no apparent telephones, yet news of my coming seemed to spread quickly.

I lived for four days with James and Agnes Moss of 86 Tullycar Road, Aghyaran. I learned that James McCrory was covered in white powered lime because it had to be applied when cultivating, in order to get things to grow in the poor soil. I found out that the family name was McCrory, or in Gaelic, MacRory, but when the British occupation came, they adopted the British-friendly and non-Catholic name of Rodgers. Nowadays they interchanged the two names depending on, as they put it, "the situation." They took me to the local Catholic church yard where five hundred years of McCrory relations are buried. They showed me land that had been McCrory land prior to the British invasion and was now owned by "wealthy Protestants." That land confiscation had happened eight hundred years prior, yet they still knew the boundaries of their ancestral roots. I could hear the hatred and sorrow in their voices when they told me how the British had burned four hundred years of baptismal and family records at the church yard.

On a couple of occasions James and his friends took me out drinking in and around Castlederg. I have no recollection of where we went, nor do I recall the names of Irishmen I met. I do remember the potent, black draft beer, served at room temperature and the general congeniality of all who had consumed a pint or two. It's likely that I interacted with members of the Irish Republican Army and certainly met many who were unsympathetic to British laws and regulations. On three sides, Aghyaran lies within two to six miles from the Irish border. I was given to understand that smuggling was a fairly common local enterprise.

Agnes Moss told me that her father, Dennis, had a sister named Mary. Mary, like Dennis, had not gone to America. She had married a man named Edward Callaghan from a family that, in those days, was living near Aghyaran. They eventually moved across the border to Killygordon in Donegal County. Agnes brought me to see the roofless, deteriorated, and overgrown walls of the house where Mary and Edward Callaghan had once lived. She said she thought they were both dead now, and she had no knowledge of their children, if any. I subsequently learned that the Callaghan clan originated in County Cork in the south of Ireland. Over several hundred years some members migrated north as far as Donegal County. The Edward Callaghan who once lived in Aghyaran with my great aunt, Mary, may have been related to my grandfather, Henry Callaghan. I'll never know, but my dad's older brother was named Edward.

During my stay I ate a lot of salt pork, potatoes, carrots, beets, milk, cheese and bread. After four days I thought it best to leave, since I was concerned about becoming a burden. Everyone I met was totally hospitable, but my presence was clearly a strain on their resources. James and Agnes Moss drove me the six miles to a border crossing at Toragh. A single border guard was on duty. He occupied a shelter about the size of a phone booth and seemed totally unconcerned about my passing. When I walked up, he nonchalantly reviewed and stamped my passport, saying, "Welcome to Ireland."

"How far is it to the paved road to Ballyshannon and Sligo?" I asked.

"About two miles, laddie. When ye come to a fork in the road, take the left and keep on walk'n."

Other than Agnes and James Moss, who were waving goodbye, there was no one else visible in that desolate place. I thought, *No wonder smuggling is prevalent around here. The South Ireland border guard doesn't seem interested, and the North Ireland guards are nowhere to be seen.* I waved goodbye to Agnes and James and walked on west. I've never seen them again, nor any of my Irish relatives. In the late 1990s I received word that Agnes Moss had passed away in a rest home in Belfast.

* * *

Upon reaching the paved road, it wasn't long before someone stopped to give me a ride. From there I hitchhiked along the west and southern coasts of Ireland. Everywhere I went from Sligo and Galway to Limerick, Killarney, Cork, Waterford, and Dublin, I was treated well by interesting and friendly people. I can't remember having a single problem. I slept in youth hostels for fifty cents a night and ate meagerly in the towns through which I passed. Several times I was invited to morning or afternoon tea by strangers. One lady was tending her garden when I ask directions. We talked over tea for an hour or more about my travels and life in America.

All along the way I found that people were interested in President Kennedy and how and why he had been assassinated. By luck or foresight, I had brought with me a roll of Kennedy fifty-cent coins. I passed them out to people who befriended and assisted me. Those coins were appreciated and were likely responsible for providing some unique experiences.

At one point on the road the traffic was sparse, so I was walked along thumbing a ride whenever a vehicle approached. A black limousine slowed as it passed and then stopped off to the side some distance ahead. As I hurried to catch up, the driver got out and stood waiting. He was a big man, clearly not a person to be crossed. When I reached him, he questioned me as to my nationality, purpose and destination. He then talked with someone in the back seat before saying, "My clients would have you ride with us, should you be agreeable."

"Yes, but no further than Cork," I replied.

"That's where we're stopping as well. Give me your pack. I'll put it behind." I kept my passport, traveler's checks and wallet on my person, so that if I were separated from my backpack, it wouldn't be a complete disaster.

He opened the door for me, and I climbed into a passenger seat that faced toward the rear. Across from me sat an elderly couple whom I judged to be in their seventies. Both were well dressed. He wore a coat and tie. Their accents reflected east coast America, perhaps New York or Massachusetts. They said that I reminded them of their grandson, who at that time was somewhere in Europe doing similar Euro-pass, youth-hostel traveling. They seemed to pay little attention to the passing countryside as they queried me about my journey, background and future plans. The time passed quickly, and we soon arrived at their hotel somewhere in central Cork. As their bags were being unloaded, I thanked them and was about to depart when the driver asked me to wait until he got them registered and situated.

Upon returning, he introduced himself as Michael. His accent and choice of words were Irish, but his speech reflected a bit more British sophistication than what I had so far experienced.

"Where are you going to sleep tonight?" he asked.

"At the Youth Hostel. I see on my map that it's not far away."

"Why don't you come with me. I know a place that has a comfortable room with private bath. The price won't be much. You look like you need a cleanup and shave."

I hadn't thought about my appearance in days, so I guessed he was right. "Great, thank you," I said as I tossed my pack into the open trunk. Upon climbing in beside him on the front seat, I noticed that the window to the passenger compartment was open. I guessed that he had heard everything that was said during my conversations with the old couple.

We drove away from the city center toward the outskirts of Cork and eventually pulled in to an electric gate. Michael had a card that made it open, and we drove up to a sizable mansion. I was becoming uneasy about this whole venture, but here I was. At this point there was no choice but to proceed.

Two or three cars were parked in front, but Michael drove our limousine around behind the building. Through a back door we entered a commercial-sized kitchen. A man was stirring some pots on the stove. Michael asked him, "Where's Orla?"

"Up front with customer relations," came the reply.

Michael told me to wait for him in the adjoining dining room. Upon entering I perceived a sense of severity that did little to calm my anxious state of mind. Illumination came from three tiers of flame-shaped lightbulbs in a black metal chandelier suspended from the room's ceiling beams. Fourteen carved wooden chairs surrounded the massive wooden table. Gold-framed oil landscape paintings hung on the dingy walls between black iron Tudor wall lamps. An elegant Persian rug with dominant blood-red designs covered most of the hardwood floor. Heavy, dark red velvet curtains, suspended from an iron rod with spear points at both ends, obscured all light from the single window. I took a chair near the table head and waited.

It wasn't long before Michael returned accompanied by a well-dressed, blonde woman named Orla, whom I judged to be in her forties. During introductions I could tell that she was scrutinizing me from head to toe.

"Come with me. I'll show you your room," she said.

I followed her into a service elevator and up to the second floor. The room seemed a bit small for the king bed that occupied it. The adjoining tiled bathroom had both a tub and a shower.

"After you've bathed, join us for dinner. Do you have a change of clothing in that pack of yours?" she said.

"Yes."

"Good. Wear them! And tonight, before you go to bed, put your dirty clothes in that basket over there. Place it outside the door in the hall. They will be washed and returned to you in the morning. Now, can you find your way back to the kitchen?"

"Yes, I think so."

"Good. Go directly there. Don't wander around. If you need assistance for any reason, push that button on the wall by the bed. We'll see you in an hour in the dining room for some food and drink."

"Thank you very much," I said as she departed. There was no response.

Dinner consisted of whiskey over ice, wine, stew, bread, and additional wine and whiskey over ice. Michael, Orla, and I sat at one end of the table. Orla was no different than others whom I had met along the way. She wanted to know about my life in America, why I was walking around Ireland, who had I met and where I had been. I became lightheaded as the night progressed, but I noticed that every so often two or three ladies entered the dining room with food from the kitchen. They sat at the far end eating and talking among themselves. It was clear that they paid deference to our end. If they showed interest in me, Orla informed them that I was a guest from America.

As the liquor began to get the best of me, I excused myself, saying that I really needed sleep.

"Can you make it to your room alone?" asked Orla

"I think so," I said as I tried to walk a straight line out of the room.

Michael interjected something about having to meet his clients at nine in the morning. I should be at breakfast before eight or someone would wake me. Orla asked a woman at the end of the table to accompany me. I don't remember her name, but she was a fine-looking brunette whom I judged to be five to ten years older than I. After opening my door, she asked if I needed further assistance. I said that I was fine, but before leaving, she turned down my bed and was about to place my basket of dirty clothes in the hall when she turned to me and said,

"Perhaps we should send those clothes you're wearing to the wash as well. Don't worry, they'll be ready for you by morning. Off with them."

While I disrobed down to my underwear, she continued to observe, as if that were the norm. "Those too," she said, pointing to my jockey shorts. When I hesitated, she rolled her eyes, bowed her head toward the floor, and said, "All right, I promise not to look." By the time I had kicked off the shorts and tossed them her way, she was once again in full observation mode. "Sorry, I sometimes lie. Nice package," she said as she turned to depart.

The next morning at the appropriate time, Mom's trusty travel clock rang. I didn't remember setting it. I was completely nude under the covers. Just inside the door the basket contained my ironed and folded clothes.

Orla never appeared at breakfast that morning. Michael and I ate and departed.

"Don't I have to pay something?" I asked as we left the house.

"No. That's not necessary, said Michael. Orla liked you.

"I wish I could have at least thanked her."

"Don't worry, Orla pays little heed to thanks."

Cleaner and more rested than I had been in weeks, Michael dropped me off on the main thoroughfare. "Well, Mr. Callaghan, where are you off to now?" he asked.

"I think I'll go the Blarney Castle and kiss the Blarney Stone," I said.

"Good idea. Every American Irishman should do that. It's not far. With luck you should be there before noon. And it's a pleasant, sunny day. Best of luck to ye, my lad. It's been nice know'n ye." He and the black limousine drove away, and I proceeded under the guidance of my Michelin map to the Blarney Castle. There I was held upside down by the legs from the castle turret so that I could kiss the famed stone, as all Irishmen should.

Upon reflection it seems clear that I had spent that night in an upscale brothel. As to who paid the bill, I suspect that the elderly couple may have given money to Michael, asking him to secure lodging for me. Or perhaps Michael had taken a liking to me and just wanted to get me the shower and cleanup that I so clearly needed. Or perhaps Orla was simply a generous lady. I'll never know.

In late June I flew from Dublin to London and on to New York. There I picked up the Porsche and drove across country to Colorado, where I visited Neil Dunbar, his wife, Barb, and their daughter, Hillary—my Goddaughter—before heading on to California.

Mom and Dad and I were together relaxing at the Chester cabin by mid-July of 1965. They listened patiently to my stories. The entire venture, air fares and all, had cost less than three thousand dollars, excluding the Porsche of course. Dad said nothing, but I could tell he was still upset about my extravagant purchase of that vehicle. When a year later I sold the Porsche for five hundred dollars more than I had paid for it, he quietly revised his opinion.

Because of Mom's hard work and persistence, that fall I was accepted into the San Jose State Graduate School of Business. Their admission requirements were less stringent than many schools. A student could be admitted on probation prior to taking the GMAT (Graduate Management Admissions Test), and to my relief, there was no foreign language requirement in the Master of Business Administration program. For the first time in my life, I felt psychologically ready for school and confident of success. I could only hope that academic status would protect me from the draft and military service in Vietnam.

Chapter 9

Peace Corps

Amid the interclass throng, I dipped and dodged my way across the San Jose State University campus. Near the student union I noticed a banner reading, "Peace Corps—Volunteer Here." *That's an idea*, I thought, *a possible alternative to the draft*. Last month I had been declared 1-A, fit for service. It was only a matter of time before a notice would appear in my mailbox, and I would be off to Vietnam to fight what I felt was an unjustified war.

Under the Peace Corps banner was a table covered with brochures, maps and pictures of volunteers doing good things around the world. Behind the table stood several energetic people, all about my age. One of them engaged me.

"Are you interested in joining the Peace Corps?" she said. It was impossible not to notice her enthusiasm, and she was good-looking too.

"Well, maybe," I said. "Can people in the Peace Corps still get drafted?"

"Technically yes," she replied, "but it almost never happens. Most draft boards don't draft volunteers while they're in Peace Corps service. But after your service is over, you're still draft eligible. Peace Corps service doesn't substitute for or negate your military obligation."

"If I join the Peace Corps, where would they send me?" I asked.

"You can pick any of twenty-eight countries where programs now exist. When an opening in that country becomes available, you'll be notified. You'll also be notified of potential assignments in other places as they become available. Right now, we're signing up volunteers for a program that will soon start in Micronesia."

I had no idea where Micronesia was, and didn't want to show my ignorance, so I asked, "Are you in the Peace Corps?"

"Well, I work for them now, but I was a volunteer. I spent two years as an English teacher in a small village on the Amazon River. It was a hard life, but I learned a lot and made some good friends. I'm hoping to go back for a visit next summer."

"Did you speak Portuguese before you went there?" I asked.

"Peace Corps gave us three months of intensive language and cultural training before we left the US. Believe me, when you get to a rural village where no one speaks anything but Portuguese and their indigenous language, you learn in a hurry. I'm pretty fluent in both languages now."

"Are all the assignments for two years?" I asked, as I thought, *I'm almost twenty-four. In two years, I'll be close to twenty-six, and they don't draft people who are over twenty-six.*

"Most assignments are for two years, and that includes your training period. If the circumstances warrant, and you agree, it's possible to extend your service for an additional year."

"What must I do to sign up?" I asked.

"You fill out this form." She handed me an eight-page document. "Return it to me along with Xerox copies of the required supporting materials—driver's license, birth certificate or passport, social security card, draft card. When I have everything in hand, I'll sign you up to take a short written exam. It takes only about a half hour. After that you just wait for the Peace Corps to notify you."

"How long does that take?" I asked.

"Well, an FBI background check is required. Sometimes that can take a month or two, but if you indicate on your application that you want to go into the Micronesian program, I'm pretty sure that the process will be expedited, so please give it a try. I can't promise you that Peace Corps service will be an easy experience, but I can promise you that it will change your life for the better. And at the same time, you'll be helping others less fortunate. We'll be here through Friday. My name is Cassie, Cassie Dorwin."

"Okay, Cassie, thank you. I'll try to get this stuff back to you tomorrow or the next day," I said as I turned toward the library.

"Remember," she said, "we're only here through Friday, and you have to take the test to be eligible for selection."

"Got it," I said over my shoulder.

The next day I had no classes, so I drove home to Livermore where I could confer with Mom about filling out the application. She was an expert in such things, and in addition, she had the necessary documents at her fingertips. I also brought along a load of laundry, just for efficiency's sake. Our family had only a wringer type washing machine and no dryer, so I expected the clothes would be ready on my next trip home. I told myself that Mom's washing was more sanitary than laundry done in my apartment's grimy public machines. I'm not sure Mom would have agreed, but like all good moms, she said nothing.

In a couple of days, I returned the completed application package to Cassie, and she scheduled me for the exam. To my surprise, the questions appeared to be almost entirely psychological in nature, with no apparent right or wrong answers. They were trying to determine how I might act in a variety of difficult situations. I simply answered honestly, according to my best judgment. Within a week or two my parents heard from neighbors and friends about being contacted by F.B.I and State Department officials. Before the month ended I received an invitation from Peace Corps Director Jack Vaughn, asking me if I wished to volunteer for service in Micronesia.

There was, however, one stipulation. My draft board had to agree to my Peace Corps service. With my anxiety in overload, I visited the Oakland, California Selective Service Office. Upon entering I took a number and waited. When it was called, I approached the counter, behind which stood a matronly woman of substantial heft. Her beady eyes looked down at me over the top of metal-rimmed reading glasses. Her brusque tone was disarming. "And what can I do for you today?"

"I have this letter of acceptance for Peace Corps service." I pushed it toward her. "Apparently, I must have my draft board's permission before I can join. What do I need to do to get that permission?

"Just a minute," she said as she marched across the room to a wall of filing cabinets, taking my acceptance letter with her. Upon extracting a file, she perused it for some time, then scribbled notations, made a copy of my acceptance letter, and marched back to the counter.

Still looking over the top of her spectacles, she said with considerable pomp and authority, "Well, sonny, it's your lucky day. We have filled our quota for this month and next. You can go into the Peace Corps, but you'll still be draft eligible 1-A when you get out."

Hearing those words provided one of the most euphoric moments of my life.

Because of heavy class loads, I hadn't bothered to find out where Micronesia was located, so with the help of *The World Book Encyclopedia* and the library's card catalogue, I set about informing myself. To my surprise Micronesia was composed of 2,900 islands scattered over 3 million square miles of Pacific Ocean southwest of Hawaii and east of the Philippines. Only 198 islands were inhabited by 73,000 Micronesians. Most of the islands were administered by the United States under a post WWII United Nations Trusteeship Agreement. *Interesting,* I thought, *that's only an average of 369 people per each inhabited island, white sandy beaches, palm trees, hula girls, pineapple rum coolers. Peace Corps service in Micronesia sounds much better than being shot at while wallowing in the muddy rice fields of Vietnam. Mr. Vaughn, I accept your invitation. It's a no brainer.*

But, as is often the case in life, worthwhile endeavors are seldom easy. Peace Corps was no walk in the park, or in this case, on the beach.

*   *   *

In late August of 1966, I was told to report to a building on the San Francisco State University campus. My parents dropped me off, along with one suitcase that contained the prescribed items of clothing and toiletries. Volunteers flew in from around the United States; some from the east coast were dressed formally in suits and sportscoats, others, like me, in pants and pullover. There were more than a hundred of us, mostly male, perhaps 20 percent female. For three days we were housed in a campus dormitory. During that time, both medical and psychiatric doctors probed, pushed and questioned. Our shoulders, thighs, and posteriors became pin cushions for enumerable inoculations, protection from tropical maladies unknown to me. The most obnoxious injections were syringes of gamma globulin, one in each buttock, to guard against hepatitis, they said. For days thereafter sedentary positions were uncomfortable.

Initially we were informed as to our pending assignments, should we successfully complete our training. I was to be assigned as a small business advisor in the Palau District of the US Trust Territory. I further learned that Palau was not a single island but a group of some 180 islands in the far western part of the Trust Territory, south of Japan and east of the Philippines. Only eight islands of the group were permanently inhabited by a total Palauan population of about ten thousand. Because I was a business advisor, it was likely that I would be stationed on the island of Koror, the capital and center of economic activity. Staff members said that I was lucky. Koror was a choice assignment.

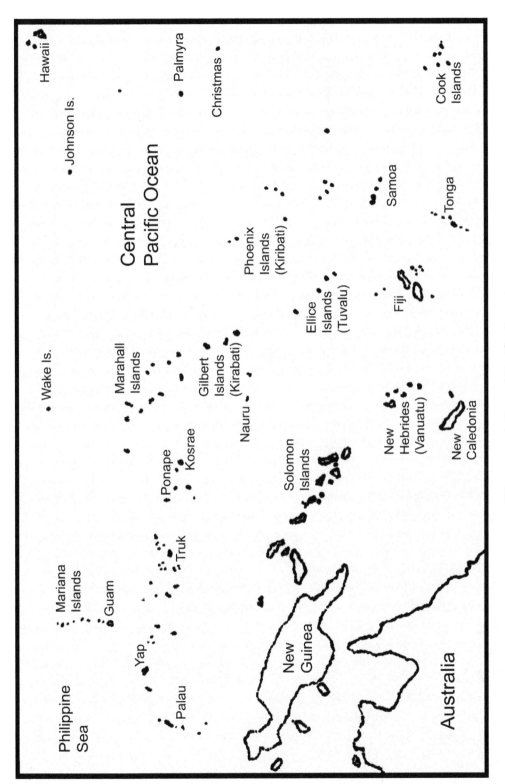

Western and Central Pacific Ocean

Each day we attended enumerable meetings and lectures dealing with the rules, regulations, and likely hardships of life in Micronesia. We would be living with local families and receiving a monthly living allowance of eighty dollars. When we returned home after completing our two-year commitment, we would receive a lump sum "readjustment allowance" of $1,800, $75 for each month of service. At every opportunity we were reminded that we were only trainees. If we wished to "deselect," we could leave at any time without negative consequences. All of us were required to continue wearing the same clothes in which we had arrived, save for underwear. By the third morning, those who had come in finer clothing were looking a bit disheveled. I just kept my head down and did as I was told.

In late afternoon of the third day, we were transported by bus to the San Francisco airport. There we boarded a chartered Boing 707 without being given any information as to our destination. It was my first time to fly in a jet aircraft. By luck I got a second-row seat by the window. Once airborne, I was quite sure we were heading west out over the Pacific because I could see the California coastal lights disappearing behind us as the plane clawed for altitude into the black, star-filled night.

When the seatbelt sign blinked out, the plane erupted into jovial socialization, as might be expected from a planeload of "flower children" in their early twenties. Some had brought guitars and other musical instruments, even a tambourine. Up and down the aisle groups played and sang 1960s folk and pop music. Lyrics and music not being my thing, I knelt in my chair and got to know some of those seated around me. From that position, I could see the entire length of the plane. In the back were some serious looking older folks. They appeared to be observing and perhaps taking notes.

Remembering people's names has always been difficult for me, and the years have further blurred my memory of that flight. The one person I do remember sat next to me. He was from New York, and his name was Howard (Howie) Lerner. He was a bit older than I and had previously served as a volunteer in Turkey. Now he was extending his service for an additional two years and would be going to the District of Ponape as a community development specialist. *This guy has already experienced what I'm about to go through*, I thought. *I'll stick close to him and watch what he does.*

When I asked Howie how to survive training, his advice went something like this: try to get along with everyone; be flexible; go with the flow; don't let things bother you; don't complain; don't be too out front, and don't be too reserved either; don't get involved in any group resistance movements; study the language, it's critical.

Before the plane began its descent, we were instructed to close our window shades and keep them closed during landing. We would have no visual clues as to our location. Perhaps it was the intent of our chaperones to teach calm in the face of uncertainty. There would be much uncertainty ahead for us. By my calculations the plane had been airborne for more than five hours. If we had headed west over the ocean as I suspected, we were most likely landing in Hawaii. I had never been anywhere west of San Francisco, so the thought of Hawaii was exciting. I judged that most of the others had paid little attention and had no idea where we were landing.

Because Howie and I were in the front, we were among the first people down the ramp and into the back seat of the waiting bus. The driver and another man counted us as we boarded. At some point the volunteers remaining on the tarmac were told to take the next bus, even though our bus wasn't full. I wondered why we were being separated into less than bus-sized lots, but said nothing.

The bus took us through the bowels of the airport, past enumerable taxiways and colored runway lights, eventually stopping beside an unmarked DC-3 airplane in front of an unmarked hanger building. Howie and I were last off the bus and up the stairs into the plane. An almost full moon lit the clear sky. A slight breeze fanned the warm and humid air. *This must be Hawaii*, I thought.

We squirmed into the last available seats in the front row of the darkened cabin. Again, I lucked out with a window seat. Howie sat beside me on the aisle. The man who had counted us onto the bus was standing near the opening to the pilot's cabin. I now understood that the less than full bus had to do with the DC-3's seating capacity.

Someone from much farther back yelled out, "Sir, what about our luggage?"

"You'll receive that in time," said the counting man. "Right now, buckle your seatbelts and keep the noise level down."

"Where are we, and where are we going?" yelled someone else from the shadows behind.

The counting man ignored the question, conferred for a moment with the pilot, and took the last empty seat across the aisle from Howie.

"We have a right to know where we're going," repeated the same voice.

The counting man rose from his seat, turned, and said in a clear voice, "If you don't stop asking questions, I am sure where you will be going, and that will be right straight home." He sat down again and all was quiet for an instant before the engines started. They were anything but quiet.

Howie whispered in my ear, "That's an example of what you should not do if you want to get through training. That guy won't last long unless he makes some big changes. When you're a guest in someone else's country, your American 'rights' do not exist."

We taxied for a few minutes, during which I could see little outside. Eventually the engine noise and vibration reached a crescendo as we bumped and rattled down the runway. Upon leaving the ground, I could see the moonlit ocean below. It was exciting, but I was exhausted and dozed off when the engines throttled back into their hypnotic drone. Sleep did not last long. Turbulence awakened me as the plane banked into a steep descent, flaps fully extended, engines at full throttle. "Where are we?" I asked Howie. "I've been asleep."

"Yes, I noticed," he replied. "God only knows where we are. We've been airborne for only a half hour or so. But remember, it doesn't make any difference where we are; just go with the flow."

It was a paved airstrip, but I could see only runway lights until we came to a stop in front of what appeared to be a small, closed and darkened terminal. The unlit sign on the building read, "Welcome to Molokai, the Friendly Isle." The word Molokai triggered my Catholic school memories of Father Damien and his leper colony. I said to Howie, "Look at that. We're on Molokai Island. I wonder if we're going to stay with the lepers?"

"You never can tell," Howie replied. "Just hang loose and go with the flow."

Once again, we followed the same drill: down the stairs and into a waiting bus. This time it was a smaller bus. There were twenty-four of us, not including the driver and the counting man who stood in the front watching us.

After about fifteen minutes on a two-lane paved road, the bus turned onto a dirt drive that led up a slight rise toward what appeared to be a derelict school. It stopped in front of a Quonset building that at one time had probably been a gymnasium. The counting man's voice pierced the greyness: "You are now at Kualapu'u School in Ho'olehua on the Island of Molokai. Some of you will be here for only a few hours. Others will remain here for your entire ten-week training program. Inside this building you will find bunk beds. Take any bed you wish, but team up with someone to make use of both the top and bottom bunks. More trainees will be arriving later, and they will require bunks as well. There are only two restrooms. You'll have to make do. Let's see how clean you can maintain them. Rest in your bed, but remain in your clothes. Many of you will be moving again in a few hours. For the good of all, it is best that you remove your shoes before entering. Carry them inside and place them under your bunk beds. Did everyone understand me? Are there any questions?"

A hand went up from a girl sitting just behind me. "Yes?" queried the counting man.

"Is there drinking water somewhere?"

"There are some drinking fountains inside. However, there are no glasses or cups, so use your hands as a cup. Any other questions?"

There was silence, so we began to disembark. I followed Howie.

When my shoes touched the ground, I realized why there had been a shoe removal instruction. The ground was composed of damp red clay that stuck like glue. By the time I reached the portico, the soles of my leather street shoes were caked. I followed Howie, shoes in hand, as he made straight for the restroom. "First things first," he said. After urination, he washed his hands and drank several gulps of water from the sink. I did the same. When we exited the restroom, a line of people waited to enter, and there was an equally long line at the drinking fountains.

I hung next to Howie as he chose a steel bunk in a back corner, as far away as possible from the entry way and the restrooms. After stowing our shoes, he took the bottom bunk and I the upper one. The mattresses were covered with a canvas-like material. At the foot of each bed lay a folded wool army blanket. There were no pillows. The building had only louvered windows, high up on the walls, so the circulation was poor.

"Howie, the air smells of mold."

"Welcome to the Peace Corps," he replied. "Go to sleep if you can. I expect we'll need the rest."

My watch read three in the morning San Francisco time. I used the army blanket as a pillow and fell asleep within minutes.

* * *

The next thing I knew, Howie was shaking the bed and saying, "Time to rise and shine. Actually, you don't have to shine, but you do have to rise. The buses are waiting for us."

The room was now full of commotion. All beds were occupied. I jumped down and followed Howie, shoes in hand, across the room, past bunks of confused and sleep-deprived volunteers. As we neared the door, the floor became increasingly muddy. Apparently not everyone had paid attention to the shoes off rule.

Emulating Howie, I urinated and drank several handfuls of water from the bathroom washstands. "Always try to think ahead," cautioned Howie as we slipped our muddy socked feet back into our shoes. "You never know what will come next."

A counting man at the door directed some trainees toward a building across the quadrangle, which he referred to as the cafeteria. We and others were told to board the waiting buses.

The last stars were visible in the blue-black sky as dawn crept onto the horizon. A gentle, warm breeze brought new, enticing smells. One star shone more brightly than the others. *The morning star*, I thought. At the time, I had no idea as to the roll its Palauan name would play in my future.

Before boarding, the bus driver made us scrape the bottoms of our shoes on an iron plate attached to the steps. When the bus was full, we were once again off into the unknown. All of us were more bedraggled and exhausted than we had been upon boarding in San Francisco. There was no banter or singing, just resolute silence. Those who had arrived dressed in coat and tie had long since discarded the formalities and now sported rumpled slacks and soiled dress shirts with rolled up sleeves.

Based on the sun's direction, I determined that the bus was proceeding east along the coast. After about an hour it turned onto a dirt road that ended in an open area about fifty yards from the ocean. The sound of breaking waves and the smell of salt air were immediately apparent.

A counting man stood by the driver and delivered the following instructions: "You have now arrived at the Peace Corps training facility on the east end of Molokai Island. More trainees will arrive shortly. Stand by the coconut tree with the white painted trunk and wait there. Do not wander off. After everyone has arrived you will receive further instructions." As each trainee disembarked, he checked off their name on his clipboard. When Howie and I reached the door, he said, "Lerner, Callaghan, you two come to see me after the food truck arrives."

"Where will we find you?" asked Howie.

"I'll be around," said the counting man.

"Do you have a name?" persisted Howie.

"John. If you don't see me, just ask for John."

As we stood waiting, I observed that the ground was sandy. No red clay, thank heavens. The surrounding vegetation was a tangled mass of gnarled scrub with a few coconut trees sprinkled in. The landscape looked parched. A humid, salty breeze blew inland from the ocean. The sound of crashing waves was rhythmic and unceasing. I thought, *It doesn't rain here much, and there's no drinking water. I'm thirsty. Howie was right. I wish I had drunk more this morning.*

A second and third school bus disgorged additional trainees, after which we gathered around a counting man with a megaphone who stood in a pickup bed. "Welcome to Peace Corps Training on the east end of Molokai Island. This will be your home for the next ten weeks. In case you wondered, it is twenty-eight miles to Kaunakakai, the nearest town. You won't be going there often. To your left you see six piles of US Army, six-man tents. Each pile has a sign on it indicating a Micronesian District. The signs read: Palau, Yap, Marianas, Truk, Ponape, Marshalls. You are to stand by the tent pile of the district to which you have been assigned. If you are assigned to Kusaie, stay with the Ponape group. Each group will then be responsible for erecting their tents in a designated location. A staff member will assist you in finding those locations, and language informants from each district will provide guidance. Beside each tent pile you will find some rope, trenching shovels, and machete knives. Use these as needed to accomplish your tasks. Note! Anyone who gets injured by one of those machetes will find themselves deselected and on their way home immediately.

"Some of you, no doubt, have questions like, where are water, food and restroom facilities. There is drinking water in that white fifty-gallon drum over there." He pointed. "There is a ladle hanging on the side. Do not drink directly from it. Everyone must use the same ladle. Food will arrive in a couple of hours. There is one toilet over there for emergencies." He pointed to a green porta-potty. "Use the shovels to dig a latrine for each district. Staff will provide assistance and advice in accomplishing that task. You will be health workers or teachers on islands far from district centers. There will be no amenities like sewer systems and running water. This is part of your training. If you have further questions, ask the staff members at your district encampment. Now go to your designated tent pile."

"Howie," I said, "that man just said we were health workers or teachers going to islands far from district centers, yet you and I are assigned to district centers, and we're not health workers or teachers. I'm a small business advisor and you're a community development specialist. Are we in the wrong place? This is confusing."

"Just go with the flow," he replied. "Maybe it has something to do with why we are supposed to check in with that John guy. Anyway, I'm headed to the Ponape group. Remember, look for John after the food truck comes."

No longer would Howie be my front-runner. I was on my own. Others standing by the Palau tent pile seemed to know much about Palau, so I stood by quietly and listened to their conversations. There were about twenty of us, only four women. Everyone except me seemed to be a health worker or teacher.

Soon a counting man arrived and took roll. My name was not on his list. "Are you assigned to Palau?" he asked.

"Yes, sir" I said. "They told me I'm supposed to be a small business advisor on Koror Island."

"Well, you're clearly in the wrong place, but stay with us until we get things straightened out. Now listen up, everyone. Follow me to the Palau site. Once you know where it is, you can bring these tents and set them up." The tents were constructed of heavy canvas and required several wooden tent poles. I judged it might take considerable effort to accomplish that task.

He led us down a path through the scrub to a clearing that was inland a bit from the ocean. Waiting there for us were some brown-skinned people of medium height who seemed a bit ill at ease. I assumed they must be our language informants. The counting man introduced them as Leo, Jonathan, Issac, Emil, Marjorie, Kazimoto and Lucas. They smiled and nodded politely. That is, all except Lucas, who was a bit sullen. "All right," said the counting man, "get those tents over here and set up. Place them where the Palauan informants direct you, and otherwise do as they say."

While we were hauling tents and equipment, I noticed two men, one with a full white beard, watching our activity from the edge of the clearing. They were taking notes. It was sweat-drenching work, complicated by the difficulty of coordination among strangers, many of whom had never previously set up a tent. After the first tent was erected, we were dripping wet and thirsty.

One girl in our group approached the language informants who were sitting together in the shade of several coconut trees. "May we please go get a drink of water?" she asked.

"Why do that?" replied Jonathan. "There are plenty of coconuts here." He pointed to a pile of green coconuts on the ground.

"How do I open one?" she asked.

"Emil will show you," replied Jonathan. "Get the others over here so they can learn."

When we were assembled, Emil held a green nut in the palm of his left hand, stem end down. With three swipes of his machete, he formed a pyramid on the top of the nut. With a fourth swipe he cut off the apex of the pyramid to expose a hole to the interior. A few more swipes cleaned up the edges to facilitate drinking. When Emil handed the opened nut to the girl, she immediately gulped it down nonstop, with the overflow running down her chin and neck.

"When we drink from a fresh coconut," said Jonathon from his sitting position among the informants, "we first offer it to others who are older and may also be thirsty."

The girl was clearly embarrassed, but by then Emil had whacked open two additional nuts, which he brought to Jonathon and the other informants before whittling more for us. We all shared until everyone was satisfied.

"Is anyone still thirsty?" asked Emil. There was silence as he and Leo exchanged words in Palauan. Then Emil said, "We don't waste food in Palau. Give me one of your empties and come over here."

Someone handed him their empty coconut as he walked to a nearby log. There he cut two chips from the side of the green nut and handed them to a trainee. He then lay the nut on the log and cut it in half, exposing the nest egg of soft, white meat inside. "Use the chip as a spoon, scrape the white meat out, and eat it. Share the other half with a companion; they may become a friend," said Emil with a smile.

When the remaining empty nuts were halved, we ate our fill. The white meat was a bit slimy, but sweet and satisfying. I hadn't realized how hungry I had become. We had not eaten since the airplane flight from San Francisco.

At that moment I began to comprehend how much there was to learn about this new world—not only language, but skills and a way of communal thinking. It was humbling and somewhat discomforting to realize that I would be learning much more than I could possibly repay. I joined the Peace Corps to help and teach others, yet here the "others" were helping and teaching me. I didn't know it at the time, but that mismatch would continue throughout my Peace Corps experience and on into forty-five years of Pacific Island life.

* * *

Food arrived in the main clearing just as we finished with a second tent. By the time I reached the food truck, a line had formed. Each person was handed a bowl and a package of disposable wooden chopsticks. Food was ladled from containers in the truck's trailer—one scoop of white rice covered with two sardines in tomato sauce. The man with the megaphone said, "Take your food to your district encampments and eat with your language informants. When you are done, wash your bowls in the ocean. Return them here. Throw your chopsticks in the fire at your encampment."

At the Palau site, we trainees sat together on the ground in front of the language informants, whom I noticed were eating different food that they had cooked on an open fire behind them. In silence, using their fingers, they ate what appeared to be barbequed fish and sliced purple potatoes. I later learned that the potatoes were called *kukau*, a variety of taro root.

In contrast, the trainees talked incessantly as they ate, mostly complaints about the food, the heat, the dirt, the lack of sleep, and the uncertainty of our situation. Some trainees had trouble using chopsticks but learned quickly by watching others. Most were hungry and ate everything.

One in our group who did not appreciate the cuisine threw his chopsticks into the smoldering fire and was proceeding to dump his half-eaten sardines there as well. Jonathan reacted, "Excuse me. Please don't do that. For one thing, someone else might be hungry for that *odoim* you are throwing away; for another thing, Palauans do not throw fish bones into the fire. Does anyone want this gentleman's *odoim*?"

Someone quickly volunteered, since it appeared from the conversation that *odoim* must refer to the leftover fish. I later learned that *odoim* is any meat or non-starchy food. Our language lessons had begun.

After eating we went to the ocean with Emil, who demonstrated how to use sand and salt water to scrape our bowls clean. After this we returned them to the food trailer, per our instructions.

While the others fetched a third tent, I looked for the staff member named John, whom I found not far away, talking with Howie. As I approached, John said, "Ah! Callaghan. I was just telling Lerner here that somehow this morning you two got into the wrong group. Everyone at this east-end encampment is a health worker or grade school teacher who will live in distant villages or on outer islands. You two will be living in a district center, so you need to be with the public works group at Ho'olehua. You can ride back on the food truck when it leaves in a few minutes. Go to the staff office at the school, and they'll get you squared away."

As per Howie's previous advice, I went with the flow. "Sure thing," I said. Despite this twist of events and uncertainty, I was pleased to be reunited with Howie and relieved to avoid further tent construction. We both sat on the truck bed and observed the goings-on around us. The only ones who seemed to have their act together were the language informants.

As we left the site, we passed an incoming truckload of army cots and a second truckload of suitcases. I hoped that mine was not among them.

*   *   *

At the Kualapu'u School in Ho'olehua, life was much easier than at the east-end training camp. We had electricity and running water (cold only), along with three hot meals a day and bunk beds in the gymnasium. The only real irritant was red clay dust from the adjacent pineapple fields that permeated everything and turned to mud when it rained. Six days a week our lives were programmed from five in the morning until eight at night. Other than an hour set aside for each meal, life was filled with language training, technical training, area and cultural studies, and oceanics. The later was my favorite—spear fishing, net throwing, snorkeling, and learning about tides, weather and navigation.

Oceanic training required that we be bussed to the ocean, usually to the docks in the town of Kaunakakai. These bus rides took us past a housing tract for employees of the California Packing Corporation, a firm that farmed pineapples in central Molokai. A row of almost identical white wooden buildings stood next to the road. All appeared well cared for, with lawns and gardens. However, one house caught Howie's attention.

"Look!" he said. "That house has a ham radio antenna. When I was in Turkey you could count on ham operators to help call home. This Sunday when we have free time, let's walk down here and see if that guy will help us call out."

The next Sunday we did just that, and "that guy" turned out to be a man named James (Jimi) Shimabakuro, a field foreman for the pineapple company. We became friends for the few weeks that I lived on Molokai. On Sundays, Jimi not only helped me to talk with Mom and Dad, but he and his friends also took me *tako* (octopus) fishing in their boat. That was my first experience spearfishing in the ocean. I learned how to spot the camouflaged octopus' holes, and how to spear them and kill them by biting between their eyes with my teeth. Back at Jimi's house, I learned to *lomi-lomi* them in a washtub full of salt brine and how to prepare them for the drying rack. Jimi's training proved very useful in later years. I still remember his kindness and welcoming nature, but after leaving Molokai, I never saw Jimi again and never had the chance to adequately thank him. My life is full of those moments when I should have been more attentive in acknowledging the kindness of others.

Initially there were fifteen of us in the Palau public works group at Ho'olehua—three small business advisors, three surveyors, four recreation specialists, one urban planner, two engineers, two architects. By the end of training only nine of us went to Palau. The others were deselected. For me the stresses of training were more mental than physical. Unlike others, I had been raised during the summers in a cabin without running water and electricity. I had slept on an army cot and used kerosene lamps and outdoor toilets. I had washed from buckets of water hauled from cold flowing streams and had dealt with mosquitoes and other vermin.

It was language learning that caused me apprehension. Language classes were held for two-hour intervals in open-air huts, each seating five to seven trainees along with an informant. I had feared learning language since my distressing experiences with Latin in high school and Spanish in college. Without doubt I was the worst language student in the Palau group. Other trainees seemed to hear a Palauan word or phrase and remember it almost immediately. I remembered nothing without a written visual image and frequent feedback. The Palauan language was not originally a written language, and its grammar didn't correspond to European linguistic rules. As time passed, I could tell that the language informants, especially Lucas, were becoming increasingly frustrated with me.

Periodically Lucas would approach me and say something directly to me in Palauan. When I was unable to respond, he exhibited exasperation and disgust, often simply walking away. In subsequent years I learned why he was so upset with my slow linguistic progress; however, at this point in time, I had no idea what was behind his attitude, so I tried to avoid him whenever possible. At times I forgot Howie's advice and spoke harshly of Lucas while not being attentive as to who might be listening. By so doing I may have caused irreparable damage to my relationship with Lucas and other informants. It took me quite a while to learn that one must internalize interpersonal difficulties when living in small island environments.

My linguistic incompetence became particularly disconcerting whenever Palauan visitors came to our language lessons "to see how we were doing." Some guests that I can recall were: Lazarus Salii (later a President of Palau); John Ngiraked (a politician who was involved in the assassination of Haruo Remeliik, the first President of Palau); Thomas Remengesau (later a Vice-President and President of Palau, whose son also became President); Joseph Tellei (a respected elder who had been the highest-ranking Palauan during the Japanese administration prior to WWII). I hated having these visitors arrive. "Who is the business advisor?" they would ask. The reason for their interest in me would become apparent later. At the time I had no idea why I was so frequently being singled out, and I dreaded having to deal with it.

At times the counting man with the white beard stopped by to observe our language classes. His name was Clayton Carlson (later a distinguished Emeritus Professor of Linguistics at the University of Guam). He had the authority to deselect any one of us, and his presence caused me such apprehension that I became incapable of demonstrating even my most merger linguistic abilities. It was somewhat comforting to know that the language informants also did not appreciate his presence. They created a Palauan nickname for him based on his long white beard: *kaming*, which means goat. Whenever a trainee spotted Clayton approaching, the trainee would quietly say, *kaming*, and we knew that the spy was at hand.

By the end of training, I was given a score of zero-plus on a scale of five for Palauan linguistic competence. That was probably generous. Everyone else received twos and threes. Someone even got a four. I should have been sent home. But in retrospect there were probably several reasons why I was retained. First, I had demonstrated an ability to cope with physical hardships, cultural diversity, and uncertainty. I assume that living conditions at the cabin, experiences as a fraternity pledge, and solo travels in Europe had provided skills that advantaged me over other volunteers, many of whom had come from orderly, comfortable and protected lives.

Second, I apparently got along well with everyone, even though I was not particularly gregarious and barely knew most names by the end of training. Each week we met individually with a psychologist, who asked us to list five fellow trainees whom we thought might make good roommates and good volunteers, as well as five trainees whom we felt would not make good roommates and volunteers. Initially my biggest problem was in remembering ten names to write down, so I made a list and memorized it before every session. I can only assume that these peer reviews went well for me, but they certainly did not serve to build trusting relationships among volunteers.

The third likely reason for my survival takes a bit more explanation. Early in our stay at Kualapu'u School, it became apparent that volunteers, informants and staff needed a convenient source for toiletries, laundry soap, snacks, drinks, and other sundries. Such items existed in Kaunakakai, but that was several miles away. Our only day off was Sunday, when stores in Kaunakakai were closed. I had been reading about co-operatives and how several large and successful ones currently operated in Micronesia. So I approached the other business advisors and the training staff with the idea of setting up a small co-operative store. The staff was skeptical but designated a space for my cooperative experiment and allowed me to proceed, so long as I kept them fully advised.

To make a long story short, we sold memberships for ten dollars and convinced a local store to deliver the requested items at wholesale prices. With the help of volunteer members, we business advisors staffed the store, stocked the inventory, and kept the books. At the end of training, we returned about twenty-five dollars to each co-op member. I was the person who received most credit for that success. However, in the interest of full disclosure, the 150 percent return on invested capital was largely due to deselected trainees departing without collecting their original contributions; thus, after liquidation, the remaining pot of money was divided among fewer participants than had originally contributed. I don't believe the Peace Corps staff completely grasped this nuance, but they, like everyone else, were happy to receive their twenty-five-dollar dividend.

The last, and likely most important, reason why the staff overlooked my dismal language skill was that they needed me. Only two business advisors remained at the end of training. The two paramount chiefs of Palau, the Ibedul and the Reklai, had both asked that a business advisor be placed in their households. Peace Corps desperately wanted to deliver on those requests. The goodwill of these two chiefs was crucial to the success of the Peace Corps mission in Palau.

I later came to understand that my probable assignment to one of these chiefly households had much to do with the interest shown in me by visiting Palauan guests; also, Lucas's frustration regarding my language skills resulted from his being married to Maria, an older daughter of the Ibedul. If I were assigned to live in Ibedul's household, my poor language skills would be viewed by the family as a negative reflection on Lucas, since he had been one of my teachers.

Anyway, for whatever reason, I was not deselected and became a full-fledged Peace Corps Volunteer sometime in November of 1966. My parents were sent an authorization that allowed them to ship seventy pounds of dry goods to me in Koror, despite Peace Corps providing no suggestion as to what items to include. We were the first Micronesian volunteers, and no one knew what to expect. I told Mom and Dad to send clothing and whatever they thought might be useful in a tropical environment where it rained 180 inches a year. They did their best, even though I never wore the raincoat or sweater and only a few socks, but the Zenith Transoceanic short-wave radio they buried amid the clothing ultimately proved priceless.

The weekend prior to our departure from Molokai, the Peace Corps provided a beach barbeque and picnic with beer, ribs, potato salad and the works. It was held at a public park on the west end of Molokai. Several hundred people attended, including staff, local dignitaries, all who had helped with training, and their families. It was an uproarious event, our first opportunity to relax in ten weeks. The entertainment that evening included a group of *mahu* (gay and cross-gender) people, all Indigenous residents of Molokai, well-known and accepted by the community. Their musical, comedy, and hula routines were hilarious, and we volunteers were introduced to a phenomenon that is common to all Polynesian and Micronesian societies—the complete social integration, acceptance, and respect of gay, lesbian and bisexual people.

* * *

Our subsequent week's furlough in Honolulu was a welcome break. We were grouped by island district into separate Waikiki hotels. I have never seen Howie again. I know that he went off to his assignment in Ponape (now called Pohnpei) and eventually married an island girl from there. At some point they departed Ponape for the US mainland, probably to the New York area, since that was where Howie hailed from, but I haven't been able to locate him.

The name of the Waikiki hotel where I was billeted escapes me, but it was located at the intersection of Kuhio Avenue and Lewers Street, somewhere behind the International Market Place. Due to major renovations, neither that hotel nor the International Market Place still exist.

Upon returning from Europe and entering graduate school at San Jose State, I had begun dating Carlyle DeBivort, the daughter of the couple I had visited in Geneva during my European trip. Carlyle was living not far from San Jose in the Palo Alto home of her uncle, Wilson Harwood. Her family and the Cramer family had always been close friends, so our steady relationship during the fall and spring of 1965–66 was looked upon favorably by our respective families. Once it was clear that I would have free time in Honolulu, Carlyle flew there to meet me. I think Mom probably paid for her plane fare. Mom liked Carlyle a lot, and so did I. Together, we enjoyed a beautiful few days, but my excitement about going to Palau probably overshadowed everything else. After that visit our lives drifted down different paths. Carlyle became an airline stewardess and now lives in Sun Valley, Idaho. I've seen her only once since our time in Honolulu. It was a few years ago when Jim Cramer and I visited Carlyle's mother, Sally, in a San Francisco rest home. Carlyle was also there at the time. She seemed to be the same happy person I so fondly remembered. It's interesting how events intervene to change our course. Had the Vietnam War not happened, much of what I have written here would not have occurred, and Carlyle and I might have continued our relationship.

Other than my happy time with Carlyle, only one memory remains from that furlough in Honolulu. After Carlyle's departure, I and Paul Berry, a fellow Palau volunteer, decided to rent a car and drive around Oahu, bringing with us our newly acquired snorkeling gear in case we spotted a place to swim. Initially we drove southeast past the entrance to Hanama Bay and the blow holes. I could see Molokai on the horizon just before we stopped at Sandy Beach. There the body surfers and boogieboarders rode the white foam of sizable waves. It looked like such fun that Paul and I decided to give it a try. Having no idea what we were doing, we donned a single fin and headed into the breakers, trying to emulate those around us. I caught some waves and rode them a bit before falling out the back side or being curled up and rolled over in the froth of the front side.

We were having great fun when a particularly large wave came along. As I started sliding down the face it curled over the top, spun me around several times, and slammed me, headfirst, into the sand. Luckily Paul was there to keep my unconscious body from washing back out to sea as the water receded. I quickly regained consciousness but had sand in my eyes and sinuses, and much skin was scraped off the right side of my face. I was a bloody mess.

There was no life guard or emergency assistance, so Paul drove us back to Honolulu, where we bought some peroxide, gauze and antibiotic ointment, in hopes of repairing my face as best we could. I was lucky not to have broken my neck or drowned. We kept that incident quiet for fear that Peace Corps officials might get wind of it. In light of our Molokai training experiences, we remained fearful of "deselection," despite having been pronounced full-fledged Peace Corps Volunteers.

As it turned out, the Palau and Yap volunteers were held back in Honolulu because of logistical difficulties. That delay gave me a bit more time to heal before having to encounter Peace Corps staff. We Palau and Yap volunteers finally boarded a chartered Boing 707 flight for Guam at one-thirty in the morning on Friday, November 18, 1966. My facial scars and black eye had begun to heal enough so that I could deflect most questions with joking responses. Furthermore, at that early hour no one seemed overly concerned about appearances.

Sitting on either side of me for that eight-hour flight to Guam were two Yap volunteers named Dennis Camblin and Thomas (Tom) Nance. We struck up a friendship that lasted for quite a few years but has faded over time. Tom was a hydraulic engineer who became well respected in Yap for his skill at drilling exceptionally productive village water wells. After Peace Corps service, Tom returned to Hawaii, where he still resides and is President of Thomas Nance Water Resources. Dennis became famous among Micronesian volunteers for marrying a Yapese girl, whose picture was on the cover of the May 1967 edition of *National Geographic* magazine. Peace Corps officials were less than happy about Dennis's marriage, since there were rules against marriage to Indigenous nationals during service. The marriage didn't last long. For several years after his Peace Corps service, Dennis operated a dry goods exporting firm based in Honolulu, with sales throughout Micronesia. Unfortunately, I've lost track of him.

We arrived in Guam around 9:30 a.m. on Saturday, November 19, having lost a day by crossing the international date line. The humidity and heat were noticeably greater than in Hawaii. The airport terminal building was a steel Quonset. *That place must be an oven by midafternoon*, I thought as we were bused to the Micronesian Hotel, another steel Quonset building that was at the time the only substantive civilian lodging on Guam. In the years after WWII, it had functioned as the US Trust Territory headquarters. Now that Trust responsibilities had shifted from the US Navy to the US Department of Interior, the administrative headquarters had moved to a decommissioned CIA installation on the island of Saipan. Only a liaison office remained in downtown Agana, Guam's capital.

Being young, energetic and excited, we spent the day exploring on foot. Most of us had little money left after our holiday in Honolulu, so we didn't rent cars or take taxis. On foot I did discover a store named South Seas Trading Company that had a Zenith Transoceanic 3000 radio for seventy dollars less than Dad had paid in San Francisco for the one in my Palau shipment. I also discovered the Whispering Palms Restaurant and Bar, with its female Palauan bartender, who seemed excited about my feeble Palauan linguistic capabilities. She said that few Americans ever bothered to learn Palauan, so we Peace Corps Volunteers were a refreshing change. Her excitement about us going to Palau provided a much-needed boost to my self-confidence.

*　　*　　*

On Sunday morning, November 20, 1966, we boarded a DC-4 bound for Yap and Palau. The aircraft was owned by the Trust Territory Government but operated and maintained by Pan American World Airways. There were two scheduled flights each week, on Tuesdays and Thursdays, but the Peace Corps had secured a special Sunday flight so that local people could be off work and able to attend our arrival ceremonies.

There were some fifty of us on that flight, including Peace Corps staff and Trust Territory officials. The lone Palauan steward occupied the galley beside the restrooms in the rear. For the entire flight he never moved from that location, serving water at his station only if requested. We were so anxious and excited that little conversation was audible above the drone of the engines. We flew above the billowing white clouds that stretched out over the dark blue water as far as one could see. Every so often we got a bumpy ride around the edge of larger cells. I maintained a fatalistic point of view. *What will happen in the next couple of years will happen*, I thought. I'll just keep trying to do my best and trust in Irish luck and God's will.

Two hours into the flight, my anxiety increased as the plane banked in a steep descent over wave-caped fringing reefs and then skimmed close over the water in an approach to Yap's World War II, Japanese built landing strip. The wing flaps were fully extended. Four engines growled at full power. The water suddenly ended and coconut trees whizzed by for an instant before the plane banged down onto the runway. Immediately the propellers reversed pitch and the brakes grabbed, pressing me forward against the seatbelt. We came to a stop in a cloud of dust at the runway's far end, just a few yards from the ocean. The pilot negotiated a U-turn and we taxied back toward the thatched roof terminal. On our way we passed several derelict World War II Japanese fighter planes, now ghostly hulks languishing beside the runway, the rising sun insignia still visible on their fuselage and wings.

We Palau volunteers weren't allowed to disembark, but I could see through the window that there were significant welcoming activities underway. Women young and old in grass skirts were nude from the waist up; men wore only colorful loincloths. Window seats on my side suddenly became coveted for a look at the topless girls. Yet a little over a year later, I would think nothing of it, as those in such topless garb accompanied me to the communion rail at Sunday Mass in Yap's capital, Colonia.

The Yap contingent having been left behind, we were soon airborne again, weaving our way between cumulus mountains of white clouds toward our new home in Palau. The nearer we got, the more certain it became that our real test was about to begin. Molokai had only been the prelude. The burden of responsibility, uncertainty and fear of failure weighed heavily as we approached.

The first land that came into view was Ngcheangel (Kayangel) Atoll, its four grey-green islands punctuating the eastern edge of a celadon, oval lagoon, a gemstone set all alone in a vast, deep blue ocean. Shortly thereafter, a vast expanse of coral reefs, known as Ngkesol, came into view, and then the green spine ridges of Ngerchelong at the north end of the massive high island called Babeldaob. We flew low over the airport at the southern end of Babeldaob so that the pilot could ensure that the dirt runway was clear of obstructions. We then passed low over Koror Island to announce our arrival, made a long, drawn-out turn over the Chelebacheb (Rock Islands), and circled back to another heart-stopping landing.

The airport had no terminal, only a graveled tiedown pad beside a thatched covering that provided shade for dignitaries. Cars and a bus were parked helter-skelter along the sides of the runway and around the tiedown pad. At the runway's end where our plane made its U-turn stood a firetruck with its red light flashing. Several months later, I learned that it was the only firetruck in Palau. The US Federal Aviation Administration required that a firetruck be on site at every landing and takeoff. For each twice-weekly commercial flight, that firetruck was driven from Koror to the airport in order to fulfill FAA regulations. The problem was that the firetruck had an unrepairable hole in its empty water tank and not nearly enough hose to reach the nearest source of water. Such was life in Palau and elsewhere in Micronesia in those days.

When that plane door opened my world changed forever. I can't tell you how many volunteers got off the plane with me that day, who they were, what they did, or how they acted. I only know that I survived the welcoming ceremonies, the torrent of unpronounceable titles and names, the countless greetings, the exhausting focus on a new language, the strange food and drink, and the insufferable heat and humidity.

Only a few things from that first day in Palau remain locked in my memory. One is the unique and unexpected smell. Salty sea air, damp volcanic soil, brackish swamps, and dense limestone forests combine to produce a rich, musty fragrance that entered my awareness immediately upon stepping from the plane. I'm sure that I could be taken blindfolded around the world and be absolutely certain when I arrive in Palau. To this day that smell anchors years of memories.

At the foot of the boarding stairs, we were greeted by J. Boyd MacKenzie, Palau's District Administrator, Thomas Remengesau, the Deputy Administrator, and Dirk Anthony Ballendorf, the Palau Peace Corps Director (in later years a friend and fellow faculty member at the University of Guam). It struck me that Remengesau had been a visitor at language training sessions on Molokai, and I hoped that he didn't remember me or my poor linguistic skills. But of course, he did, because everyone in Palau, except me, knew that I was to be the small business advisor who lived with the Ibedul.

From the airport we were transported by bus to a formal reception in downtown Koror on the grounds of the Royal Palauan Hotel, a corrugated tin building that provided the only substantial visitor accommodations. It took us some time to reach the Royal Palauan because we first had to cross Chongelungel, an ocean passage that separates Babeldaob Island from Koror Island. Our bus waited while officials, dignitaries, and the fire engine crossed ahead of us, ensuring that they reached Koror prior to our arrival.

Despite all its planning and preparation, Peace Corps had forgotten to provide drinking water in that oven of a bus. I sat drenched in sweat on the vinyl seat, watching through the open window as the WWII LCM ferry plowed back and forth, carrying four or five cars at a time. Its captain was a marvel of dexterity, deftly maneuvering the craft's rudders and powerful diesel engines to perfect landings, and then, despite turbulence, wind and current, holding the vessel's loading ramp firmly in place as vehicles disembarked and boarded. I noticed that those engines made an exceptional sucking sound when they were placed under stress. Later I learned that all Supercharged Grey Marine 6-71 T diesel engines produce that unique sound. Strangely, it still lingers in my mind, as I suspect it lingers in the minds of WWII veterans who made amphibious landings. The Palauans called that ferry the "M-Boat." Nowadays a bridge between Babeldaob and Koror has relegated the M-Boat, its captain, and its unique sound to the corridors of history.

Eventually we did arrive, dehydrated and sweat-drenched, at the Royal Palauan. There Dirk Ballendorf introduced me to the High Chief, Ibedul, who sat amid a semicircle of Palauan chiefs, government officials and dignitaries. The chiefs remained seated and stoic during introductions. The Ibedul was stone-faced when I knelt on one knee before him and said, *"Ungil chodochosong klou el rubak* (good mid-day to you, respected elder)." I had been told that it was improper to speak to the Ibedul from a position equal to or above him.

He showed no reaction to my words, looking straight through me as if I were not there. For a moment there was silence. Then Ballendorf, who was still standing, started to say something. The Ibedul waved him off with a flick of the wrist and said to me in English, "What do you think of Palau?"

My answer was something to the effect that I had not seen much of Palau yet, but the bit that I had seen was very beautiful. He replied again in English, "You will see more of Palau soon."

Then the man sitting next to him said, "The Ibedul wishes to welcome you, and he is looking forward to the Peace Corps' contribution to the Palau people."

Addressing the Ibedul, I replied *"Ke kmal mesulang, Rubak* (thank you, honorable elder). I will do my best." I had no idea how to say "I'll do my best" in Palauan. The man who had spoken for the Ibedul translated my words, and the chief acknowledged with a slight eyebrow movement. As Ballendorf hurried me away to more introductions, I blurted out, *"Ak moralung* (I'm going now)." There was no response from the Chief or his translator.

We slept that night in a hospital ward, just up the road from the Royal Palauan Hotel. Late in the evening Director Ballendorf informed me that I would be living with the Ibedul's family in that part of Koror known as Idid. He would personally take me there tomorrow. I didn't tell him that I already knew. Jonathan Emul, one of our Molokai language informants, had delivered the news earlier. I was honored and proud but uneasy, especially when Ballendorf said that it was my responsibility to set an example and not let Peace Corps down.

I slept fitfully between the clean but blood-stained sheets, amid my fellow volunteers, all of us having little idea as to the challenges ahead. At that point my goal was survival, one day at a time. I thought of Mom saying, "Just take things as they come. Do your best and listen to the little voice inside you. It is seldom wrong." I thought of Dad saying, "I'm proud of you, son. You'll do fine. Just say your prayers and 'keep your nose clean.'" That reminded me to thank God for helping me reach this point in life and to ask His help in tomorrow's adventure.

Perhaps at this point it's worth saying something about prayer. I find it strange that I continue to pray each night before I sleep, even though I no longer believe that there is a supernatural being who listens and answers prayers. It's just that I feel obliged to thank someone or something for the abundance of good that has befallen me. Additionally, prayer calms my spirit and strengthens my mind during difficult times. So I will continue to pray, just as I did that night in the Koror hospital ward.

* * *

A day later I awoke at dawn to the sound of roosters crowing and lay there, face up, between the damp sheets, observing the patterns of mold on the ceiling. Once painted a cream color, it had succumbed to the tropical humidity. Each macabre shape took my imagination into grotesque worlds that did nothing to calm my anxiety.

In a moment I would have to arise and face uncertainty. This was my first morning as a Peace Corps Volunteer in the house of Ibedul Torwal Noriyakl, Mayor of Koror Island and Paramount Chief of southern Palau. I had learned in training that he should be formally addressed as Ibedul, his chiefly title. During informal situations he could be addressed as *Rubak* (honored elder) or *Merreder* (leader/chief). If I wanted to sound American, I could call him Chief. Apparently, no one ever called him Mayor.

I threw off the top sheet and lapsed into a daydream about the previous day's events. All yesterday I had waited in the humid, hot hospital while Peace Corps staff escorted other volunteers to their host families. At midday a male nurse named Kladikm invited me to eat with the staff while I waited. Using our fingers as utensils, we shared rice, taro, fish, and sliced daikon radish while drinking coffee infused with condensed milk. The food was only a subterfuge that provided an opportunity for the hospital staff to interrogate the soon-to-be son of Ibedul.

In short order they assessed my Palauan language skills and determined that English was the most efficient means of communication. The questions continued unabated. How old was I? Who were my mother and father? Where did we live in America? Where did my parents' ancestors come from? What did my parents do for a living? Did I have brothers and sisters? Why had I joined the Peace Corps and come to Palau? Who were my language informants during training? What did I think of Palau? What did I think of Palauan food? Did I drink or smoke? What religion was I? Did I have a wife (girlfriend), children? They seemed genuinely interested in knowing everything about me, even though I'm sure they didn't fully grasp all my answers.

Upon returning to my hospital bed, I came to realize that the open-air maternity ward adjoined our sleeping area, yet throughout the night and day I hadn't heard any sound of women in labor and delivery. We had been told in training that stoicism in the face of difficulty was a valued Palauan trait, but I had no idea it was so engrained as to dampen expressions of pain and emotion during childbirth. Sometimes the newborns let out a squawk, but never the mothers.

Finally, that evening, Director Ballendorf delivered me, suitcase in hand, to the front door of Ibedul's house. The Chief was not home. Instead, I was greeted by a young man in his late teens or early twenties named Jones, who was apparently the Ibedul's son. He ushered me through the front door into a vestibule with tiled floor, hardwood paneling, and carved benches on which to sit while removing one's shoes. I slipped off my zorrie behind a line of flipflops neatly arranged from smallest to largest. The living room looked to be an upscale Western/Asian mix. The floors were ten-inch-wide planks of *dort*, an endemic hardwood, similar to Asian ironwood. Padded couches and chairs surrounded an intricately carved, mother of pearl inlayed coffee table. On one wall was a glass display case that exhibited a magnificent shell collection. Along another wall was a glass-encased Japanese samurai helmet and sword, beside which rested several honorary ribbons and medals. The far end of the room sported a bar with bar stools. Behind the bar was a full kitchen with electric stove, refrigerator, and stainless-steel sink.

Jones introduced me to the Chief's wife, Seruang, and to other family members who were waiting near the bar to greet me. Seruang spoke no English, so I did my best in Palauan. Jones then showed me around a bit before ushering me to my room, saying that the Chief would talk with me in the morning. During our brief tour it became clear that the entry way, living room, and bar with its electric kitchen were used mostly for show and the entertainment of foreign visitors. The daily family living was carried out more modestly and centered around an open air, wood-fired kitchen at the back of the house.

My living space was more luxurious and private than I had been led to expect. The room had a single bed, an armoire, and a table with chair. One light bulb with pull chain hung from the ceiling above the table. Unfortunately, the room had no cross ventilation. The single window faced a banana patch that blocked any potential breeze. Between the bananas and my room was an open pit, into which splashed the household wastewater. The stagnant air was permeated with musty dampness and the sounds of insects and amphibians.

Bathing facilities were housed in a shower/laundry room adjacent to the kitchen. A pipe emanating from the wall provided a stream of cold water for showering amid laundry tubs scattered about on the concrete floor. There was no hot water and no indoor toilet. Behind the house, beyond the cassava garden, next to the pig pen, was a pit toilet, replete with tissue torn from the pages of a Sears Roebuck catalogue. I was extremely thankful that I had not needed to relieve myself in the dark of this first night.

During training we had been taught to expect the anxiety of "culture shock." I knew I must overcome my apprehension. It was morning. I had to get up and face uncertainty and inevitable blunders. Just as I was about to force myself out of bed, there was a timid knock at the door. "Just a minute," I said as I climbed into shorts and a t-shirt. Upon opening the door, I saw that it was Dominica, a solemn, brown-eyed girl of about nine with perfectly trimmed afro style hair, whom I had met the previous evening.

After intense focus, she said, "Mr. Paul, come—eat—breakfast." Immediately after that she exploded into giggles and ran back down the hall toward a gaggle of children who were her support group in the daunting task of speaking English to an American. The lot of them beat a disorganized retreat around the corner as I said loudly, "Thank you, Dominica. I will be right there."

Before leaving the room, my eyes fell on my open suitcase, which lay on the table. I had started to unpack but had stopped because there were no shelves or drawers, and the few wire hangers that hung in the armoire would rust-stain any garment hung on them. *I'll deal with that later*, I thought as I closed the bedroom door behind me.

Breakfast awaited at one end of a ten-foot, dark red table that stood against the wall near the entrance to the open-air kitchen. Along the wall opposite the table, seated from oldest to youngest on the polished iron wood floor, were four little girls: Dominica, Miriam, Joann and Iris. They quietly watched my every move. When I said, "*Ungil tutau* (good morning)," Dominica immediately responded, *"Ungil tutau Mister Paul."* The others giggled. Not knowing enough Palauan to continue the conversation, I focused on the meal.

From training I knew that older men and guests eat before women and children. Unless I was joined by the Chief, I would likely eat alone. The food in front of me consisted of a mound of white rice with two sunny-side up fried eggs perched on top. A tablespoon lay beside the plate. A bottle of Kikkoman Soy and a glass of liquid that looked like lemonade rested near the spoon. I suspected that such fare was not the household's regular morning meal but likely the household's idea of what a newly arrived American guest might want for breakfast.

The egg yolks had an orange tinge and showed minute bloody signs of fertilization. They were cooked some time ago and were now cold, but I didn't care. I was hungry. After applying liberal amounts of soy sauce, and being mindful of values imparted from my Depression-era parents, I proceeded to clean my plate. All the while, four pairs of eyes were fixed upon me. The drink had a citrus flavor but was sickly sweet, sporting considerable undissolved sugar. With fortitude I downed it all.

As I shoveled the last rice into my mouth, the door to the porch opened. In strode the shirtless, barefooted Ibedul. I swallowed hard. He was imposing, his disposition stoic. This would be a test of my shabby Palauan language skills. I couldn't imagine why Peace Corps had placed me in the high chief's household, but here I was.

Petrified, I managed to say, *"Ungil tutau, Rubak* (good morning, respected elder).*"* Offering no reply, he took a chair opposite me. His dark, piercing eyes seemed to cross at times and were set in a permanent scowl. I noticed that Dominica and her cohorts had disappeared. There was an uncomfortable moment of silence before the Chief spoke in English. "How was your food? Do you want more?"

In Palauan I responded, "No, *Rubak*. The food was good. I'm full."

He replied, "In this house you should speak English. It is good that you learn Palauan, but you are here to teach me and my family English." He continued, "Today I will show you my *Chelebacheb* (Rock Islands south of Koror). They will come to take us soon. Be ready."

"Yes, *Rubak*," I said, not knowing exactly what it meant to "be ready."

He continued, "Some Palauans are calling you by the name Lebuu. I don't like that name for you. If anyone asks your Palauan name, tell them that you are my brother, not my son, and your name is Baul."

"Yes, *Rubak*," I replied. I had read enough Palauan history to know that in 1783, Captain Henry Wilson of the British East India Company had run his ship, the HMS *Antelope*, aground on a reef in Palau. The Ibedul in those times had helped the Englishmen until they were able to return to Macau. In gratitude for the Ibedul's hospitality, Captain Wilson had agreed to take the Ibedul's supposed son, Lebuu, with him back to London. I say "supposed" because there is some disagreement as to whether Lebuu was actually the son of Ibedul or just a close relative. In later years I have come to know that the name Lebuu has its origin in Yap, not Palau. In any case, Lebuu lived with Captain Wilson in Rotherhithe, England, and was known in British society as "The Black Prince Lee Boo." In 1884 Lebuu died of smallpox and is buried in the church yard of St. Mary the Virgin in Rotherhithe. I was relieved not to bear the responsibility of living up to the stature of Lebuu, and even more relieved to discover that fluent Palauan language was not expected of me.

Upon Ibedul's departure from the room, a young lady, about my age, appeared from the kitchen. Her movement was fluid and regal; her thin white t-shirt left little of her well-proportioned self to my imagination. "Did you like the food?" she asked in Palauan as she stood beside me reaching down for my empty plate. "Are you still hungry? Do you want more food?"

"No. I'm full. It was very good," I said as I struggled to focus on her face and not the t-shirt.

Her curt response, "Ungil (good)," carried a tone of annoyance as she whirled around and headed for the kitchen.

I called after her, *"Ng techang ngklem* (What's your name)?"

"Monica," I heard as she disappeared into the adjoining kitchen. Still reflecting on Monica's abrupt entry and exit, I grabbed some sunblock and a Molokai baseball cap from my room and joined Ibedul on the porch. There I waited, sitting on the top step at his feet, all the time remembering my training: "Don't ask questions. Learn by watching and listening."

Ibedul Ngoriyakl with Dominica, Miriam,
and Joann, Palau, 1967

Seruang, wife of Ibedul Ngoriyakl,
Palau, 1967

From my position on the steps, I could see across the yard to the dirt road that served as Koror Island's main street. Motor vehicles seldom passed, but the road was full of families walking to work, school, and other activities. They passed in single file—men first, then women, then children. The older children held hands and helped the younger ones. Some women and girls carried baskets on their heads. Group after group, they quietly filed by, heads bowed in respect for the Ibedul and this place of residence known as Idid. No one spoke or looked in our direction.

A pickup truck soon arrived. Ibedul sat in the cab with the driver. I held on in the back bed as we bounced along over the potholed dirt road to the place called M-Dock. Waiting for us was an open fiberglass boat with twin outboard engines. On board were a young man, my age, a middle-aged boat driver, and an older *rubak*. As per Palauan custom, there were no formal introductions, and it was apparent that everyone, save me, knew each other. They were welcoming but clearly taking my measure.

Upon boarding I was directed to a plank seat near the front—*the better to see*, I thought. The young man sat in the crotch of the bow facing me. In Palauan, I told him my name, Baul, and asked his. He warmly responded that his name was Kodeb. The *rubak* and Ibedul sat further toward the back, and the driver sat in the stern, where he controlled the twin engines, yoked together so that they functioned as one.

For the better part of an hour, we sped through maze-like waterways with narrow passages and sharp turns that wound among jungle-covered, limestone islands. Alarmed tropical birds scattered at our approach, and startled fish broke the placid surface as we passed. Multicolored shoals of coral rose and fell away as we sped over them. At times we exited the maze into magnificent open water vistas with green islands dotting the horizon in all directions.

These less protected passages were rough, but the boat didn't slow, and I learned that my seating position was not one of deference but rather a test of grit and endurance. The ocean's battering was transmitted through the hull to my seat and directly into my spinal column. Kodeb solved the problem by standing, feet apart, leaning back against a secure grip on the bow line. This allowed him to better feel the boat's motion while his legs absorbed the punishment. I stoically endured on my seat, not realizing that in time I would learn these waters well, spending hours and days of solitary exploration in this "Sea of Eden." Eventually we slowed to a crawl and passed through a narrow opening into a long grotto.

All around us limestone cliffs rose into jungle greenery. The caws and shrieks of startled birds echoed from their hidden roosts. The sand and sea grass bottom passed under us at least thirty feet below, yet tiny fish and snail trails in the sand were clearly visible through the crystal-clear water. As we crept along, it became apparent that the men were looking for something. I had no idea what, and I couldn't understand their conversation, so I marveled at my surroundings and waited.

After several minutes Ibedul pointed at a turtle that surfaced for air near the limestone wall. The driver hit the throttle. I tumbled backwards off my seat, but no one seemed to notice. By the time I made my embarrassed recovery, the boat had reached the turtle. Three others had joined it. They separated; we followed the largest one as it flapped along underwater like a swift oval-shaped bird. Each time it abruptly changed direction, the boat driver deftly stayed in pursuit. I held on.

The chase continued for a long minute or so. All the while Kodeb crouched in the bow, intently focused the turtle's flight. When it surfaced to breathe, Kodeb sprung from the fast-moving boat, landing on the turtle's back. Immediately the driver cut power as the turtle dove, taking Kodeb down with it, but skillfully the young man held on to the shell in a way that forced the turtle back to the surface. There followed shouts of advice and assistance from the elders, while I tried to stay out of the way and provide counterbalance to the listing boat. Shortly the three-foot-long turtle lay gasping, upside down in the bottom of our boat, and we were once again off at full speed toward an emerald green island that lay to the west over a wide stretch of open water.

My spinal discomfort had reached a severe state by the time we slowed in approach to the island's pristine, white sand beach. The boat driver said in English that this island was called Ulong. It belonged to Ibedul, and it was the place where the English Captain Wilson and his crew had lived after they were shipwrecked. At first it appeared to me that the beach didn't extend very far into the water, but as we came nearer, I realized that the white sand bottom was obscured by millions of sardines schooling along the shoreline.

"They're *mekebud*. It's the season," said Kodeb as the boat plowed through the whirling, flashing school and ran up on the sand. Kodeb and I pulled the boat farther up onto the beach and steadied it as Ibedul and the *rubak* clambered out and headed toward a tin-roofed shack that stood in the shade of a coconut grove.

The boat driver extracted a throw net from under his seat and flung it over the school of *mekebud*. The resulting catch was so large that he had to maneuver the bloated net around to the side of the boat. There Kodeb and I emptied the flailing fish into recycled five-gallon (Crab brand) biscuit tins, filling three to the brim.

Immediately Kodeb and the driver began popping the live, wiggling fish into their mouths as if they were candy. I noticed, however, that they did so in a guarded manner, out of direct view from the shack where Ibedul sat. I wondered if by custom the chief and *rubak* should eat first; however, it was also clear they were trying to test me. "Try one," said Kodeb.

I hesitated and then cautiously put one into my mouth. Two crunches and it was down, headfirst, scales, bones and all. The taste wasn't that bad. I tried a second. That pleased them greatly, not only because it showed that I had the gumption to eat what they ate, but also my joining them provided additional cover for their premature indulgence. "Now you're becoming a Palauan," said the boat driver. I asked his name, and he said it was Yoshiharu.

A machete in his teeth, the wiry Kodeb bounded up a coconut tree. Soon we were seated in the shade, each with our own neatly husked drinking coconut. Using old, chipped dishes from the shack, Yoshiharu prepared separate plates for Ibedul, the *rubak*, and me. Each plate contained a large pile of *mekebud*, a saucer of soy sauce, several slices of purplish swamp taro, and a beige, starchy substance neatly wrapped in a tight package of fibrous leaves. Yoshiharu and Kodeb ate from a communal bowl. Everyone used their fingers, and it was immediately clear that noisy slurping and sucking was an acceptable sign of satisfaction.

I watched how they unwrapped the bundle of starchy material and cleverly used the wrapping string to shear off mouth-sized bites of the gelatinous substance. I did the same. "What is this?" I asked Yoshiharu.

Kodeb responded, "It's *billum*. It's tapioca root that was grated and cooked before being wrapped and re-boiled."

At that point I recalled from training that Palauans seldom converse while eating. I said nothing more and tried to eat as they did. When my plate was empty, Ibedul asked if I wanted more. I said no, thinking what a struggle it had been to eat all those *mekebud*.

For the rest of the day, we motored our way back toward Koror, stopping at several places to view things that Ibedul felt were important. All the while I relied on Kodeb for clues as to proper behavior. Everything seemed to go well, but I had no clue as to what these men truly thought of me.

In the evening I found myself again seated alone at the red table. My muscles ached, and I was badly sunburned. Dominica, Miriam, Joann and Iris were again seated on the floor watching me. There was no sign of Monica. The food had been placed on the table prior to my arrival. This time the fare was much more mysterious and plentiful.

"Dominica," I said. "Come and tell me about these foods." I learned that the meaty broth was turtle soup, likely made from the one we had caught that morning. The glistening, soft, purplish mound was taro pounded in coconut oil. The crispy triangular shapes were fried fish heads. The two flattish fish with slices in their sides were fried *klsebuul* (rabbit fish). The squab-looking bird with head and feet peeking up through the broth was a *belochel* (wild pigeon).

Childhood admonitions came to my mind: eat what is put in front of you, clean your plate. I knew I could eat and perhaps enjoy these foods, but it was impossible to clean all these plates. There was just too much food. Nevertheless, I started with the pigeon breast. It was tender and tasty when combined with bites of taro. The fish heads were crunchy, a delicious complement to the taro as well.

The *klsebuul* was most delectable. I had completely stripped the white meat from one fish and had started on the other when Miriam, the second oldest of the four girls, approached the table. She was just tall enough to comfortably place her lower arms and chin on the table edge while continuing to watch me eat. I wondered what had provoked her action.

"Yes, Miriam? What can I do for you?" I said with a smile.

Initially she said nothing. Her big brown eyes looked at me from below her thick, curly afro. Her index finger tapped ever so slightly on the table top. There was a tinge of perplexed eight-year-old concern in her expression as she glanced at the food and then again at me. Finally, she said in an authoritative tone, "Mr. Paul, save—food—for—us. We—share."

Despite all that I had seen and learned that day, it turned out that the words of an eight-year-old girl provided a most profound learning experience. Sharing is caring in Palauan society. I never again cleaned my plate, and from then on, I ate sparingly, with the welfare of others in mind.

*   *   *

For several days I stayed around the house doing little, other than hanging out with Jones, his cousin Johnny Gibbons, their companion Thomas, and a Trukese guy named Willey, who was somehow attached to the household. Willey spoke only a little Palauan and no English, so our conversations were limited. He smiled a lot and jumped to attention whenever Ibedul appeared, as did we all. It wasn't until sometime later that I learned Ibedul and the Idid clan had historic ties through their Bilung (highest-ranking women) to the family of Chief Petrus Mailo of Moen (Weno), Truk Lagoon, some two thousand miles away. I suspect that Willey must have been a relative from Truk.

One morning a few days after my arrival, Ibedul informed me that some men were coming to ask that I work with them in the Trust Territory Economic Development Office. Two Palauans soon arrived and introduced themselves as Salvador Ongerung and Eusebio Rechucher, Cooperative and Credit Union Officers. We sat together on Ibedul's back porch, Salvador, Eusebio and I on the concrete deck, Ibedul occupying the only chair. Monica, braless in a modest muumuu, served iced lemonade from a kneeling position. Ignoring me, the two men conferred with Ibedul in Palauan. I understood enough to guess that they were asking Ibedul's permission for me to work in their office. Eventually, they asked me in English if I would be willing to accompany them on a trip to review the books of village credit unions on the island of Babeldaob. That seemed like a proper thing for a Small Business Adviser to do, so I agreed, subject to Ibedul's approval and my disclaimer that I had no previous experience working with credit union accounting.

"We might be gone for several days, so bring what you need," said Salvador. I had no idea what would be needed, but as they continued their conversation, I went to my room and filled a plastic bag with sunscreen, insect repellent, a change of underwear, a pair of shorts, a t-shirt, and a small flashlight. At the time I was wearing a short-sleeved cotton shirt, long cotton pants, zorrie, and a Molokai baseball cap. I would have preferred wearing shorts, but Palauan men wore long pants, so I did the same. As we departed Seruang provided a woven coconut frond satchel in which to carry my belongings.

We drove directly to T-Dock. Waiting for us there was a white-haired, older American gentleman, who introduced himself as Francis White, a Trust Territory contract employee and a specialist in credit unions. *Good*, I thought, *someone with expertise. I'm not carrying the weight of this venture alone.* Of course, this thought betrayed my total disregard for the potential expertise of Eusebio and Salvador. At the time I was completely unaware of my subconscious "White man superiority complex." Ethnocentrism is an insidious malady that must be guarded against if one is to be an effective agent of change. At the time I had a lot to learn in this regard. Subsequent lessons were painful but indelibly effective. I don't believe it's possible to completely avoid ethnocentrism in one's life, but awareness and vigilance are steps in the right direction.

In those days the Trust Territory Government recruited American employees on two-or-three-year contracts. In addition to a federal government salary, the contractees received a cost of living and hardship allowance, subsidized housing, shipment of household goods, and transportation to and from their point of hire for themselves and their dependents. In almost all cases these contract employees arrived in Micronesia without prior linguistic, cultural, or situational training. Most were woefully unprepared for the living conditions they faced. The Palauans referred to them as Statesiders. A few Statesiders flourished, but most just survived, staying to collect the high, tax-free salaries while counting the days until their return home.

Many Statesiders, especially contract teachers, worked side by side with Micronesians who were paid less than a dollar an hour for similar work. This disparity in pay and benefits provided for considerable friction and resentment. Furthermore, most Statesiders remained aloof from the Palauan community, hiring Palauan maids and nannies, but otherwise preferring to recreate and socialize only with Americans. Their subsidized housing compounds contributed to this isolation, and in Koror the Americans even maintained their own club building for social events, referred to locally as the American Club.

During Peace Corps training we had been encouraged not to associate with Statesiders. We were led to believe that contract employees were inept and uncaring, just out for the money, a relic of past colonialist policies. We were told that Peace Corps would usher in a fresh style of US trusteeship, one that would reduce the need for contract workers and lead Indigenous people to assume control of their own affairs. We were the vanguard of this change. Our association with Statesiders would not be helpful in gaining the trust of Micronesians and accomplishing the changes we had come to precipitate.

Because the American contract workers in Palau were aware of our Peace Corps indoctrination, many were initially distrustful of us, fearing that we might change Palauan attitudes and disrupt the status quo. Because of this Mr. White was polite but reserved and a bit uneasy in our initial encounter. I was mindful that he was a Statesider, and he appeared mindful that I was a potential agent of change, but one of as yet untested competency.

During the next four days we traveled along the coast, through the mangrove swamps, and up the rivers of Babeldaob Island. We stayed overnight in the municipalities of Aimeliik, Ngeremlengui, and Ngarchelong. My memory has faded as to which hamlets and villages we visited. But I do remember walking a quarter mile barefoot in the mud to reach the village of Ollei. There someone repaired my broken zorrie strap with rubber cut from an inner tube. I also remember seeing my first salt water crocodiles and a dugong, the seagoing relative of a manatee.

Each day and sometimes late into the night, under a Coleman gas light, we reviewed the records of small community-based credit unions, brought to us from surrounding villages. Without electricity, our most important piece of technology was Mr. White's paper tape, hand-cranked calculator. Eusebio and Salvador transported it with extreme care. Sometimes we were provided with chairs and a table. At other times we worked on the floor. Everything was damp. The documents smelled of mold. Staples and binders were rusted. But I was continually amazed at the exactness of record keeping and the low delinquency rates in every set of books. The organizations were tiny by American standards, most having between twenty-five and one hundred members, yet the record keeping was meticulous.

Some months later I gained insight into why there existed so many small, well-run credit unions in Palau. Apparently, the Japanese, during their twenty-five-year occupation, had introduced a system of rotating savings and credit associations known as *mujin-ko*. These proved to be compatible with the Palauan communal culture and were encouraged throughout the Japanese administration. With the arrival of the post-war American administration, the *mujin-ko* had simply been transformed by Palauans into an American credit union model.

I was also impressed with Mr. White's kind and gentle yet firm way of suggesting improvements. Furthermore, it was surprising that a man whom I judged to be in his late sixties or early seventies had the stamina to work productively for long hours in such a difficult environment. I found the heat and humidity excruciating, and I quickly learned not to sit under or near the Coleman light, not only because it radiated heat, but also because anything in its proximity was showered with burnt insects.

Eusebio, Salvador, and I slept on the floors of school houses or village *Bai* (meeting houses). Food was brought to us, and we were provided with a sheet or a blanket and a kapok filled pillow. I was glad that I had brought the bug spray, and I shared it with others. I also learned that long pants were a protection against mosquitoes and other insects. Mr. White, like most Americans, wore shorts that did not serve him nearly as well.

Each night when our work was done, Mr. White was spirited away to food and a real bed somewhere in the village. I was surprised at how respectfully he was treated by Palauans, even though he didn't speak their language. Once again, the importance of age and demonstrated competency became apparent. The status of age was also apparent during our travels by boat. I, being the youngest, sat in the roughest seat at the bow, whereas Mr. White was given more comfortable seating further astern.

One night near the end of our trip, I asked Mr. White why he had come to Micronesia. His reply changed my mind about him and taught me not to judge all Statesiders through the lens of our Peace Corps training indoctrination. "Well, you know," he said, "I had worked with credit unions for thirty-five years in several different states. It was time to retire, but I still felt competent and didn't want to just curl up on the couch and die, so my wife and I decided to have an adventure, and at the same time use my knowledge to do some good for others. Maybe that's part of the reason you joined the Peace Corps, isn't it? Anyway, we responded to a federal job announcement, and here we are in Koror. We're having an adventure. It's not everything we had hoped for, and we'll probably move on after our contract is over, but it's not been bad. And it's a hell of a lot better than curling up on the couch and dying."

Every so often I wonder what happened to Francis White after he and his wife left Palau. He was a decent person who taught me something about credit unions and did his best to help Palauans. It's another one of those situations in life where I failed to say thank you and farewell.

*   *   *

Upon returning to Koror, it was joyfully refreshing to stand under that cold shower pip and climb into fresh clothing. Monica, as she did for the rest of my stay, washed my dirty clothes by hand in tubs on the shower room floor, hung them to dry in the sun, and returned them folded to my room.

The next morning, I awoke with a headache and fever—102 degrees according to the standard issue Peace Corps thermometer. The Peace Corps doctor said I had the mumps, even though I told him that I had already had the mumps. After four miserable days, mostly spent in bed, things had not improved. That afternoon there was a knock on my bedroom door. A mustached Palauan man with Japanese features and twinkling, friendly eyes entered. He introduced himself as Dr. Ueki. "You're not feeling well, I hear," he said.

"Yes," I replied. "I've had a fever and mild headache for four days now. No energy. Dr. Blackburn thinks I have the mumps, but I've had the mumps before. Can you get the mumps twice?"

"American doctors don't know everything," he muttered. "Do you have diarrhea, or head or chest congestion or pain?"

"No," I replied. "Just the headache."

"Have you taken your temperature?"

"Yes."

"What is it?"

"It stays between 102 and 103."

After checking my pulse and heart rate, he took a container of large white pills out of his bag and put them on the table. "Take one of these antibiotic pills three times a day for ten days. Do not stop taking them, even though you might be feeling better. If after five days you've not noticed improvement, tell Seruang to let me know. Can you repeat what I just said?"

I did so, and he left the room with the admonition, "You don't have mumps, most likely an intestinal infection. I think you'll be getting well soon."

That was my first contact with Dr. Minoru Francisco Xavier Ueki, a giant of a man in my eyes. Our paths have crossed several times over the years. For a time, he was Palau's Ambassador to Japan. Though he recently passed away, Dr. Ueki was one of those people whom I have been most privileged to know during my lifetime.

Later I became aware that the Palauan community was concerned that volunteers might be unable to tolerate Palauan food and living conditions. No family wanted the stigma of having their resident Peace Corps Volunteer become sick. Apparently Seruang or Ibedul had asked Dr. Ueki to look in on me, despite the fact that I had access to a resident American Peace Corps doctor. For a short time after Dr. Ueki's visit, I detected an improved dietary pattern—frequent chicken soup, eggs, toast, and papaya at breakfast. As my health improved, the fare reverted to mostly fish and taro.

*   *   *

In a couple of days when I had started to feel better, Jones informed me that two men were waiting to talk with me in the front yard. When I asked who they were, Jones said they were the "Distad," short for District Administrator, and a man he referred to as Wilson. I should mention here that not just anyone could walk up to the Ibedul's residence and knock on the door. Palauan supplicants waited in the front yard or on the road, sending word as to their business via a ranking emissary. Few people were ever invited inside. I met with personal friends beside the road or elsewhere in Koror. Apparently, that protocol held as well for Boyd MacKenzie, the highest-ranking US Government official in Palau.

I found the two men standing beside their government pickup truck. MacKenzie was a dark-complected big fellow with short cut, curly black hair, part Hawaiian I judged. He introduced himself and his companion, Peter Wilson, Chief Fisheries Management Biologist—a husky, well-tanned bulldog of a man in his mid-thirties with glasses that hung on a string around his neck.

"We've come to ask for your help," said MacKenzie. "Peter here has organized a group of local boat builders into a co-operative called The Palau Boatbuilding and Drydock Association. They have constructed a boatyard and a marine railway on Malakal Island, and the Association is now in need of someone who can set up a bookkeeping system. We wondered if you'd be willing to assist in doing that. I'll let Peter explain things in more detail, but you should know that we've already talked with Director Ballendorf and the Ibedul about this. Ballendorf thinks it's a good idea, and Ibedul has granted his consent, provided you agree."

Wilson immediately jumped in with nonstop, overwhelming enthusiasm. "Almost all transportation in Palau happens by boat. There's a tremendous need for cheap, reliable, safe boats of all sizes. By bringing together the respected boat builders under one roof, we hope to improve quality and standardize production in a way that provides better, more affordable boats for Palauans. That will go a long way toward improving the economy and lifestyle of everyone around here. We've hired a respected Hawaiian boat builder to oversee operations. His name is Kiyoshi Matsumoto. Because he's Japanese, his advice is accepted and respected by the Palauans. During the last two years we have constructed boats ranging in size from fifteen to seventy-eight feet. The Association members and employees are happy with their pay and working conditions, but they'd also like to share the profits. The problem is, we don't have accounting records to show how profitable things are, and some TT Government officials question the long-term viability of this project. We need to answer their skepticism with numbers and facts. If you join our effort, you'll be doing exactly what Peace Corps sent you here to do. We sure hope you'll be willing to work with us."

As a small business advisor, I had far more leeway than did other volunteers. I could work for any private or public institution so long as my efforts were contributive and reflected positively on the Peace Corps image. My experience so far had led me to believe that it would be disruptive to help any private business at the expense of competitors, and it was inadvisable to assist any entity that countered the interests of Ibedul. Until now, the only seeming fit for my background and skills was the Economic Development Office under Salvador Ongerung, Eusebio Rechucher, and Francis White. Now there appeared to be a more interesting alternative, one that offered a clear-cut objective that might be accomplished during my time in Palau. I was intrigued.

However, it was clear that Wilson was an aggressive type, a contract Statesider who was quite used to having his way. I didn't want to be bulldozed into immediately doing his bidding, so I extended the conversation a bit. "What materials do you use to construct the boats? And what type of engines and propulsion systems?"

"Right now, we're using local hardwoods, mahogany from the Philippines and marine grade plywood. As time goes by, we hope to experiment with fiberglass laminate over wood. We hold the Mercury distributorship for Palau, so we're building some twenty footers for the Peace Corps and the government that have Mercruiser Inboard-Outboard Drives. We're also building some thirty-six footers for government use in other districts. These are powered by Yanmar diesels with straight shafts."

"Where would I be working?" I asked.

"Our Marine Resources office is located on Malakal, just across from the Fishermen's Co-op. It's a small space, but there's room for you to have your own desk. The Association secretary/treasurer, Ben Orrukem, works there and can help you. He knows the history of what has transpired from the beginning."

"How would I get to work?"

"I live on Topside," said Wilson, "and I pass this way every morning at seven-thirty. All you have to do is jump into the back of the pickup. If you want to come with me now, I'll show you around. You can see the operation and meet Ben Orrukem and some Association members. I'm sure you'll see that this is an exciting project with great potential benefit to Palau. When you see it, I'm sure you'll want to be part of it."

"All right," I said, "I'll go with you. Give me a minute to go inside and tell them where I'm going."

We dropped the Distad at his office in a pre-WWII Japanese building that housed most Trust Territory Government offices, as well as the US Post Office. The mail was distributed there after each twice-weekly flight from Guam.

We then proceeded along the potholed main road past the Japanese-built courthouse, the American Club, the Agriculture Station, and eventually over a causeway and bridge that joined the islands of Malakal and Koror. On the causeway, I marveled at the crystal-clear water beside the road. It was like driving past an aquarium filled with tropical coral and fish. At the bridge, youngsters were jumping and cavorting in a rush of incoming tide. All around, a dense green jungle blanketed steep limestone islands down to the water's edge. *What a miraculously beautiful place in which to grow up*, I thought.

Wilson interrupted my focus. "Must you tell those people where you're going every time you leave the house?" he asked.

"Yes, it seems like the courteous thing to do. I did that when I lived with my parents. The Ibedul's family is feeding and housing me. They treat me with respect and kindness. I think I should do the same for them."

"You consider those people your parents?" asked Wilson.

"Yes, for the time being," I replied.

His condescending tone caused me discomfort, but no more was said as we veered down a secondary road and came to a stop in front of a building that reminded me of a three-story, open air, tin-roofed hay barn, except that it was full of boats. Upon opening the pickup door, I was greeted by the whine of woodworking machines and the smell of freshly worked wood. Just inside the entrance, two large boats were under construction. I judged them to be the thirty-six footers that Wilson had mentioned. Their massive, straight, wooden keels lay beside each other in cradles, one on each side of a railway that led out the back into the waters of a sheltered cove The keels provided a foundation for low, wide transoms and ribs that terminated at a gunwale, which sheered upward to a long, straight bow stem. Men were clamping and screwing two-by-four mahogany planking onto the ribs and gluing dowel plugs into the recessed screw holes. Others were pounding waxed cotton caulking into the cracks between the planks.

Wilson said, "These are two of the thirty-six-foot 'Haole Sampans' we're building for the government. Matsumoto designed them in a style that's proved successful in Hawaii. They'll do ten to twelve knots and can be used for fishing or transport. We've assigned a different master Palauan boatbuilder to each boat. They each select their own workers. We put the two boats side by side in order to create a little competition between the crews, as well as to make it easy for Matsumoto to do some training and watch what's going on from his office loft up there." He pointed to a windowed room high above that overlooked the entire shipyard.

I was next introduced to Imeong, one of two lead Palauan boatbuilders and president of the Association. His young assistant was named Yukio. I also met two Association members, Esabe and Wong, who both worked in the machine shop. The lead Palauan builder for the other thirty-six-footer seemed to ignore our presence. I noticed that he maintained a short-handled adze hooked over his shoulder as he worked. Later I learned his name was Ngirrirenguul, from the village of Ngchesar, a fine carpenter but not given to socializing with Statesiders. In time I discovered that Wong, a man whom I judged to be in his mid-sixties, rode a black Harley motorcycle, the only one in Palau, other than one with a sidecar driven by Mr. White, the credit union accountant.

Behind the two thirty-six-footers, workers buzzed around a series of smaller plywood boats in various stages of construction. An Asian style boat with high bow and stern was hauled out on the marine railway. I judged it to be about seventy or eighty feet long. Workers were scraping, caulking, and painting below the waterline with maroon-colored copper paint.

"We've got a contract with Van Camp to drydock their fleet of Okinawan pole-and-line boats, so we work on them one at a time, trying to make the rounds of their whole fleet at least every six months. At the moment we have twenty-five full-time workers here, and the place is humming. It's almost too much for Matsumoto to stay on top of. There's always a problem with people not showing up because of Palauan custom obligations or too much drinking. Mondays and Tuesdays after a payday weekend can be particularly sparse. But Matsumoto's a tough boss and a good teacher. He can speak Japanese to the older workers and English to the younger ones. Things generally have been going pretty well."

Wilson and I walked down the marine railway to where the tracks entered the water. In front of me lay a sheltered cove enclosed by jungle-covered limestone islands, their green reflections captured on the placid water.

"This is certainly an impressive operation and a beautiful place to work," I said.

"Yes," said Wilson. "We built it from scratch. The Japanese had a vessel repair facility here before the war and a graving drydock down the road where the cove opens into the main channel. But the whole place was bombed to rubble during the war. We dug these railroad tracks from the jungle in northern Babeldaob, where the Japanese had a bauxite mine. We floated them here on bamboo rafts.

The sixty-foot trusses for this building's roof were salvaged from destroyed Japanese structures in Peleliu and carried here on a refurbished fuel barge. The roofing tin and most equipment came from scrap yards at the Naval Ship Repair Facility on Guam. It took us three years to build this place, and the hardest part was doing the underwater section of this railway. We had to place tons of rock fill hauled by truck and dumped from the M Boat. The concrete ties were poured on land and then hand-positioned underwater. We borrowed scuba gear from the Navy, but we had only one old compressor that could manage just 1800 psi. We crammed Kotex pads into it for air filtration. When it finally broke down, Palauan free-divers finished the job. Some of them can hold their breath for two or three minutes, but they were always afraid of fellows like that one over there."

He pointed to a bald limestone islet directly across the inlet from us. There, sunning itself, was a crocodile. "Wait here," said Wilson. "I'll get my gun from the car." He hurried back through the building and returned carrying a lever action rifle with open sights. Work in the boatyard came to a standstill as employees scrambled to various vantage points. Resting his gun on the adjacent retaining wall, Wilson squeezed off a round. It was a long shot, at least two hundred yards across the glassy, calm water, but the bullet must have hit the animal because it went flailing into the water sideways before disappearing.

The deafening noise reverberated throughout the cove, causing frightened birds to take wing throughout the surrounding jungle. The onlookers registered their surprise and enjoyment with a chorus of "oos" and "ahs" followed by much chatter. I realized that it was not the crocodile or its potential demise that they were excited about. It was the firing of a gun. Possession of any firearm except an air rifle was strictly prohibited in Palau. Wilson had a special government permit for his gun, and everyone wanted to see him shoot it.

Within a few minutes the sounds of drills, hammers and saws resumed, and we drove the quarter mile to the Fisheries Office. It was a single-room, concrete bunker that was part of a renovated Japanese freezer plant. It was air-conditioned, a luxury in Palau at the time. The place had just enough space for a few filing cabinets, four desks, and a table that I assumed might be allocated to me, should I agree to join this effort.

I was introduced to the two secretaries, Mieko and Naomi. Their last names are now hidden in the neuro chaos of my aging mind, but lest I forget to mention it elsewhere, Mieko and her husband eventually moved to Honolulu, where with love and care they raised disabled twin boys into manhood. At various times over the years, I have encountered their family, and Mieko will always have my utmost respect for the cheerful and caring way that she dealt with those boys.

Benjamin (Ben) Orrukem was also at his desk in the office. He was the Association's secretary/treasurer, a rotund, outwardly jovial fellow, whom I judged to be in his late thirties or early forties. His spoken English was good, and he seemed genuinely interested in having me work with him to create a bookkeeping/accounting system. Little did he know that I had never done this before and would be learning right along with him, hopefully a step ahead.

It became clear to me that Wilson's loud, direct, forceful manner was more than a bit disconcerting to Palauans, but it was also clear that they respected his accomplishments, and at least on the surface, they paid deference to his wishes. His Hawaiian upbringing and knowledge of Japanese language allowed him to fit in a bit better than other Statesiders, but he was a colonialist who found it difficult to tolerate the slow pace of progress in Palauan affairs. He needed to make things happen. He was a man in a hurry, with ideas well ahead of his time. As an example, in the 1960s, no one listened to his idea of attracting tuna by making bamboo rafts that mimicked natural floating ocean debris. Thirty years later, such Fish Aggregation Devices (FADs) have become a mainstay of tuna harvesting technology throughout the Pacific. Behind this man's gruff exterior, I detected a person of fairness and kindness who genuinely desired to make Palau a better place. I thought, *I can work with this guy.*

"So what do you think of our operation?" he asked. "Are you willing to help us out?"

"Yes, I'll give it a try," I said. "You've built quite an enterprise here, Peter, under tough conditions. I'd like to contribute what I can." From then on, I called him Peter to his face, but when speaking with others, he was usually referred to as Wilson. To this day I feel a sense of gratitude for his contribution to the richness of my life.

"That's wonderful. We certainly need you. I'll pick you up tomorrow morning in front of your house at seven-thirty sharp."

"I'll be there," I said. "But before you take me back, can I buy some fish at the co-op? I'd like to bring some home to Seruang." The Palau Fishermen's Co-operative stood on the dock in front of the Fisheries Office, just across the unpaved street.

"Sure. Come with me. You need to meet the co-op manager anyway. You'll probably be working with him at times."

When Wilson introduced me to the manager, he and I smiled at each other. It was the same Yoshiharu who had been the boat driver that first day when Ibedul had taken me to see the southern islands.

"Are you taking fish home to Idid?" Yoshiharu asked in Palauan.

"Yes," I said.

"Come, I show you the good ones for your family."

He took me to a huge eight-foot-long ice chest filled with different varieties of reef fish packed in flake ice. Pawing through the contents, he picked out six nondescript, grey-colored fish, each about ten inches long. "These *klsebuul,* but you take other." From a different ice chest, he extracted a large green fish with a bump on its head. I was sure it must weigh at least fifteen pounds.

"That's probably more than we need," I said.

"Never mind," said Yoshiharu, "It is *maml,* for Ibedul. His fish. Tell him you got from Yoshiharu."

"All right," I said. "How much do I owe you?"

Yoshiharu glanced at Wilson, who had been hovering in the background. Looking back at me, he said, "No money now. Thank you for come to Palau and help us. Next time you pay." He was right about that. I subsequently learned that obligations in Palau can extend for years. Payment may take many forms, and in the end, the price is sometimes much higher than was anticipated.

"Thank you, Yoshiharu. I'll tell Ibedul," I said in Palauan.

I sensed that Wilson was a bit uncomfortable at my use of Palauan language and slightly annoyed that Yoshiharu would given away the co-op's fish to the chief's family because of Palauan custom.

As we left the co-op, a green government pickup drove up, and a large-framed, well-built islander, with a high forehead and short, curly hair, climbed out. Walking toward us, his thick features did not look Palauan or Micronesian. He spoke directly to Wilson. "Boss, two problems. Kinney doesn't want to go out tonight because Teruci and Tabulak didn't show. Also, Mr. Owen at Entomology wants his boat tomorrow morning. They need to take some visitor to Peleliu."

"I'll talk to Owen on the phone," said Wilson. "He thinks the world revolves around him. Is Kinney on the boat?"

"Yes, Boss."

"I'll go talk to him as soon as I bring Paul here back to Ibedul's place. Can you go find Teruci and Tabulak and bring them to the boat?"

"Teruci's drunk in the Blue Gardenia, Boss, and Tabulak's wife says he has some custom in Angaur."

"You go get Teruci and bring him to the boat. He can sober-up there. Maybe the crew can pound some sense into him. Oh, Tosh, this is Paul, our new Peace Corps helper. He's agreed to work with us full-time. Paul, this is Toshiro Paulis, my right-hand and chief of all things fisheries."

"Hello," I said as we shook hands. His hand was rough and much larger than mine, but it conveyed a welcoming and gentle sense of power and confidence.

"You stay in the house of Ibedul?" he questioned.

"Yes," I said.

He didn't reply, but his dark brown eyes penetrated my soul as his eyebrows rose in acknowledgement. I had felt a similar piercing gaze from Ibedul at the Royal Palauan Hotel on my first day in Palau.

Turning back to Wilson, Toshiro said, "Okay, Boss, I'll bring him, but he's not going to be happy."

"Screw him," said Wilson. "We've bent over backwards to help that kid. He's damn lucky to have the opportunity he's got. Let's try and save him from himself."

"Okay, Boss. I'm on my way."

As he drove off, I had no inkling as to the richness that would be brought into my life by Toshiro (Tosh) Paulis, the eldest son of a paramount Chief from a faraway Polynesian island called Kapingamarangi.

For the next year and a half, I worked in the Fisheries Office and at the boatyard on a number of activities and projects that involved ordering, scheduling, correspondence, and implementation of an accounting system. In addition, I assisted Yoshiharu with record keeping at the Fishermen's Co-op and maintained catch, effort, and payroll records for the MV *Emeraech*. The latter being one of Wilson's pet projects, and probably worth some further elaboration at this point.

Boatyard crew on newly constructed vessel. PCVs Paul Callaghan
and Dale Baisch seated on upper deck, 1967

Chapter 10

Peace Corps, Continued

Two years before my arrival in Koror, Wilson had acquired the plans for an eighty-five-foot Hawaiian style pole-and-line tuna boat (referred to in Hawaii as an *aku boat*). Matsumoto had overseen its construction at the yard, but he was forced to reduce the vessel's length when keel timbers, shipped from Rabaul in New Guinea, proved too short. When finished, seventy-eight-foot MV *Emeraech* (*Morning Star*, in Palauan) proved quite an accomplishment for the boatyard and the Palauan carpenters who worked on her. Dignitaries, including the High Commissioner of the Trust Territory, came to the launching. The *Emeraech* sported a Caterpillar diesel main engine and twin twenty-kilowatt Gray Marine generators, with circulating pumps and six wells to transport live bait and fish. The plan was to operate the *Emeraech* with a Micronesian crew in order to demonstrate that Micronesians could profitably engage in large-scale commercial fishing. Also, Wilson hoped to demonstrate the superiority of Hawaiian style vessels and techniques over the Okinawan methods being used by Van Camp to stock its Palau freezing facility.

From its inception, the *Emeraech* project was beset by both cultural and technical difficulties. Maintenance and repair of the sophisticated mechanical and electrical systems presented difficulty for the marginally literate work force. Wilson contracted a well-known Hawaiian fishing captain named Richard Kinney to operate the vessel and train the crew. Richard was a loud-mouthed Portuguese-Hawaiian whose demanding style was not well suited to dealing with a crew from diverse parts of Micronesia. They were all accomplished seamen and fishermen, but they spoke different languages and were unfamiliar with the Hawaiian methods of fishing and the operation of a large power vessel. All communication had to be done in English or Japanese, but none of the crew spoke either language well enough to understand technical matters. There was much on-the-job learning and considerable friction in the process. To make a long story short, the *Emeraech* project did not meet Wilson's original expectations. The vessel caught fish and had some successful trips, but it never produced enough profit to warrant crew shares that exceeded the wages available on shore, in much less arduous employment.

I spent many a day and night at sea on the *Emeraech* and got to know Captain Kinney and the crew quite well. A typical trip began in the late afternoon as we anchored in the calm waters among the Rock Islands, where we hoped to catch bait for the next day's fishing. At dark, a powerful light was lowered some twenty feet into the water and held away from the boat by a bamboo pole. If everything went well, by midnight the attracted school of anchovy bait (called *nehu* in Hawaiian) grew large enough to blot out the light. At that point, a triangular net was loaded onto a skiff and spread vertically around the perimeter of the lighted area. Gradually the light was raised toward the surface, moved toward the boat, and dimmed in order to further concentrate the school of bait fish. When Kinney gave the word, crew members hauled lines that brought the net up under the school, trapping the anchovies alongside the *Emeraech*.

Bucket after bucket of live *nehu* bait fish were then gently scooped into the *Emeraech's* four baitwells. Circulating pumps kept the sea water oxygenated, and dim underwater lighting allowed the fragile creatures to see each other and maintain their natural schooling patterns. A good night's baiting could yield sixty or seventy buckets and sometimes even a hundred or more, with the excess being released. Not all nights were productive, however. Sometimes the light had to be redeployed a second or third time, and even so, there might not be sufficient bait to warrant a fishing trip.

While waiting for bait to collect around the light, some crew members slept while others used handlines to fish for predators—jacks, barracuda, and the like. These carnivores circled in the eerie green grayness at the edge of the lighted area, hoping for a meal of anchovy. Some of them ended up as a meal for the crew, along with rice, shoyu and lemon.

If baiting succeeded early enough, the crew got a few hours' sleep before *Emeraech* headed out sea. The western route over the reef required negotiating

Ulong Channel, an unmarked, narrow, sand-filled passage near Ulong Island. Although it allowed quick access to the open ocean, it was dangerous in the dark and impossible at low tide or during bad weather. Sometimes Captain Kinney decided to use the northern or eastern passages. Although these were safer, they required longer running times to reach open sea.

Once *Emeraech* was outside the reef in the open sea, our visual search for tuna began. Amaram and Dison were usually on the bridge. Kinney was grooming them to take over as captain someday. Like Toshiro, they came from the islands of Kapingamarangi and Nukuoro, the only culturally Polynesian islands within the geographic boundaries of Micronesia. Amaram was a bit older than Dison, but they both had been raised on the ocean. Their eyes could see beyond the horizon. Amaram spotted birds flying over schools of tuna at such distances that it took ten minutes of motoring in their direction before my eyes could detect anything other than ocean and sky.

Later in the 1990s, Amaram, then a white-haired old man assisted by a younger relative, visited me at my home on Guam. We talked about old times, and he told me how he had left the *Emeraech* and gone to Hawaii, where he had crewed on Kinney's boat the *Sooty Turn* (later renamed *Lehua*). He saved his money and worked to acquire his merchant marine papers. After shipping out around the world for several years, he eventually bought a coconut plantation in Pohnpei. There he lived quietly near the ocean, content with life. I don't know what happened to Dison, but I'm sure that he has caught many a fish since last I saw him.

Upon approaching a tuna school, Kinney slowed the *Emeraech* to a crawl, and dipnets of *nehu* were thrown overboard. If things went according to plan, the tuna began a feeding frenzy, and the *nehu* sought protection along the sides of *Emeraech*, thus drawing the excited tuna closer to the vessel. Salt water spray from nozzles located along the stern and the aft gunwales provided a mist that further excited the tuna and disrupted their view of fishermen above.

Every crew member, me included, grabbed one of the long bamboo poles that were stored in a rack below the bridge. Each pole had a line tied to its tip. The line was slightly longer than the pole and had a feather-covered, barbless hook affixed to its end. While balancing on the slippery, narrow walkway that ran around the aft gunwales and stern, crew members cast the lures into the frenzied fish under the spray. There were no hand-holds or bodily supports. Balance was critical. Falling overboard might well prove deadly, as sharks often came to the fray.

When a tuna grabbed the lure, the crew member leaned back and pulled with all his might. The fish couldn't be allowed to turn downward or it would win the tug of war. With the right pressure and technique, the tuna could be lifted from the water, fly past the fisherman, and land on the deck behind. When the line was relaxed, the barbless hook usually fell from the fish's mouth, ready to be recast into the milling school.

The scene on deck was one of chaotic action—fish flew through the air, scales, blood, and turmoil, Kinney yelling at crewmen, crew yelling at each other, more bait, less bait, to port, to starboard, faster, slower, watch out! Tuna tails banged the deck like hammers as the flopping, bloody mass of fish grew larger. All scupper holes around the deck-sides were plugged so that blood didn't run into the sea, drawing sharks and disrupting the feeding tuna. Using balance alone, crewmembers poled fish from the pitching walkways while at the same time remaining attentive to the safety of their mates. Fish came flying onboard from all directions. Lines got tangled. Fishermen were struck by their own fish and those of neighboring crewmates. My first attempts at poling resulted in skipjack tuna flying completely across the deck and back into the ocean on the other side of the boat. Sometimes a large yellowfin might win the tug of war, turn downward and break the line, or worse, pull the pole (hopefully not the fisherman) overboard. If the fish were large, the crew resorted to two-man rigs, two poles attached to one line, giving twice the lifting power.

Eventually the "bite" would subside with the tuna retreating to their deep, dark world. Sometimes there might be as much as five tons of fish thrashing on the blood-filled deck. The exhausted crew then hammered out the scupper plugs and washed the lake of fish blood, slime and scales into the sea. The sharks arrived too late for the big party but in time for a few scraps. The tuna fish were then slid into the two aft holding wells between layers of flake-ice. In celebration, crew members reached through the gills into the chest cavity of a skipjack, pulling out its still-beating heart. This they popped into their mouth, crunched, and swallowed. "For strength and continued good luck," they said. To their delight, I sometimes joined them. It slipped down quite easily.

So long as the light of day persisted and bait remained in the wells, we continued our search for tuna schools. Only with a full load of ten tons or at dusk did we head for the lighthouse at Malakal Channel and the VanCamp Dock to unload. Depending on Captain Kinney's mood, we might then return directly to the baiting grounds or stand down until the next evening.

Blame for difficulties that befell *Emeraech* can be attributed widely. There were vessel design issues, electrical and electrolysis problems, mechanical maintenance complications, as well as crew compatibility and communication difficulties. But in my opinion, Captain Kinney bears considerable responsibility. He was hired by Wilson on a government contract that contained no productivity incentives. When operating conditions were not perfect, Kinney chose to remain in port rather than go fishing. As was common practice in the industry, the crew's pay was based on a share system. They received 60 percent of the catch's value after expenses. So for them, not fishing meant no pay. On the other hand, Captain Kinney lived in government-supplied housing while collecting biweekly government paychecks.

Because the crew came from diverse Micronesian islands with different languages and customs, they lacked the leadership and unified discipline to police themselves and to challenge Kinney. Wilson never seemed to recognize this.

*   *   *

As long as I'm on the subject of Richard Kinney, I'll take this opportunity to tell a little-known story. Richard initially came to Palau alone, leaving behind in Honolulu his wife, Emma, a respected Hawaiian lady from the island of Molokai. In Palau, Richard lived in government-supplied housing in the village of Ngerbeched, across from what was then the hospital. He hired a housekeeper with whom he fathered a baby girl. Shortly after the child's birth, Richard's wife, Emma, arrived in Palau. The community knew that the housekeeper's child was Richard's daughter, but I have no idea if Emma knew. To my knowledge, no one ever said a word. Eventually Richard and Emma returned to Honolulu where they both lived out their lives, Richard eventually retiring from fishing on his aku-boat, the *Lehua*.

The baby girl was raised in Palau by her mother and named Kaelani Kinney after her father. She grew into a good-looking young lady with a bit of a wild streak, often frequenting local bars and clubs. In one of these taverns, I'm guessing perhaps the Cave Inn, she met a man named Larry Lee Hillbroom. Larry was a California-educated attorney and founder of DHL Worldwide courier service. As an eccentric multi-millionaire, he was a frequent visitor to Palau. I was once sitting next to him in a booth at that same Cave Inn bar. We had just met and were having a conversation when he was called away by Joshua Koshiba,

President of the Palauan Senate. As Larry left, he handed me an envelope. "For safe-keeping," he said, "until I get done talking with these people." After a few minutes and several sips of my Scotch on ice, I couldn't resist looking inside the envelope. It contained a stock certificate for shares of Continental Air Micronesia. The certificate was endorsed on the back by Larry, so ownership could be transferred into the name of anyone who held it. I've often wondered who was to receive that certificate—a mystery never revealed.

Anyway, one of Larry's eccentricities was that he preferred sex with young girls. Kaelani was a young lady who fit his style. She got pregnant and delivered a baby boy whom she named Junior Larry Hillbroom. Larry disappeared from the child's life, ultimately becoming a resident of Saipan, where he became a Supreme Court Justice for the Commonwealth of the Northern Marianas Islands. Saipan was a place where Larry could shield his world-wide income from US tax law while continuing to pursue his idiosyncratic behaviors. Kaelani continued her life of nightclubs and fun in Palau, while Junior Larry was raised by his grandmother in Palau's Ngerbeched hamlet.

During the 1994–95 academic year, my wife, Nina, and I took sabbatical leaves to work in Palau. We and our son, Oldak, who was then five, lived near Nina's family in Bkul-a-Tiul, an extension of Ngerbeched Village. Sometimes, Junior Larry (his Palauan name is Imeong) could be found wandering the street in front of our house. We and other neighbors fed him and saw to it that he got home safely to his grandmother's care.

Around that same time, Larry Hillbroom was killed along with a friend when his aged Cessna aircraft went down in the ocean north of Saipan. Shark-eaten body parts and debris were reported by fishermen but not recovered.

Soon afterward, potential heirs started popping up elsewhere around the Asian-Pacific rim. Genetic testing and a long court battle resulted in Richard Kinney's grandson, Junior Larry Hillbroom, at the age of fifteen, inheriting somewhere in the neighborhood of 90 million dollars. Other heirs also got a share of Larry's money, but it's likely that numerous potential heirs were unaware of their opportunity. It's said that during his Pacific escapades, Larry Hillbroom had sexual relations with many young girls.

Subsequently, the story of Junior Larry's life has become sordid, unhappy, and wasted. His story and that of his mother, grandmother, and grandfather are tales that involve unscrupulous, greedy individuals—tales that I know only in bits and pieces and will not relate in these pages, except to note that Junior is apparently now suing his attorneys and trustees for breach of fiduciary responsibility and other matters. Based on what I've seen and heard, Junior is more than justified in doing so, but I'm afraid at this point any success will be but a pyrrhic victory.

*　　*　　*

After I had been working at the Fisheries Office for a month or so, Wilson, Matsumoto, and the Association decided that I should have my own boat. Boat ownership was a symbol of Palauan male status, and the "son of Ibedul," who was providing free assistance to the Association, should certainly be accorded such respect. Within a week, carpenters had constructed a fifteen-foot, marine plywood runabout powered by a twenty horsepower Mercury outboard. The bow covering, gunwales, and seat boards were painted high visibility orange. The remaining interior and exterior to the waterline was a light grey. Several coats of maroon copper paint protected the hull below the waterline.

It was agreed that I would pay the Association fifteen dollars out of my ninety-dollar monthly Peace Corps subsistence allowance. When I left Palau, the boat would remain at the boatyard. That way I was technically renting the boat from the Association, thereby circumventing Peace Corps rules against volunteers owning motorized vehicles. I was ecstatic and had the name *Orakiruu* (Full Moon in Palauan) painted on both sides of the bow.

Paul in *Orakiruu*, Malakal Harbor, Palau, 1967

At the time I knew almost nothing about boat maintenance or operation, and I knew even less about weather and sea conditions or reefs and passages in Palau. On the first Sunday after acquiring the boat, I and Paul Berry took *Orakiruu* to Ulong Island for some fishing, snorkeling and relaxation. It was a clear, calm morning when we started out. We had with us an ice chest with food, beer, and water, as well as two five-gallon cans of premixed outboard fuel. In addition, we had one spinning rod with ten-pound test line and some Castmaster lures that belonged to Paul. After rounding the headland of Malakal harbor, Ulong could be seen on the horizon and was a clear straight course to the south. *Orakiruu* sped along on plane, and in less than an hour, having used three-quarters of a tank of gas, we arrived at the beach on the island's southern side. I was surprised that there were no *mekebud*, as there had been a few weeks earlier when I visited that place with Ibedul.

At that point we discovered that anchors and mooring lines are an important part of boating gear. Having neither, we could only beach the boat and periodically move it higher as the tide came in. When the tide retreated, it took considerable effort to move the boat back down the beach and into the water. As the day passed, we snorkeled, drank beer, rested in the shade of dense tropical overgrowth, and marveled at our good fortune to be in this place while others our age were slogging through the rice paddies of Vietnam. Late that afternoon, sporting sunburns, we started for home.

Upon rounding the island's east end, we discovered that the north wind and waves had increased markedly. Nothing but whitecapped rough seas lay between us and our destination. We could only creep along, slamming up and down, the wind constantly in our face, the bow spray drenching us. We had nothing but a couple of paper cups and our hands with which to bail. Had we known, we could have taken an easier route into the lee of the Rock Islands. But we had no idea, and continued to grit our teeth during three long hours of slow and uncomfortable progress toward our goal, the headland at the harbor mouth.

It was almost dark when we arrived at the boatyard dock—tired, cold and wet, with less than a quarter tank of fuel to spare. Tosh was waiting there, standing beside the Fisheries' green Datsun pickup. The day before I had informed him about our planned trip to Ulong. "Why do you come so late?" he asked. "Are you all right?"

"Yes," I said. "We're okay. It was rough on the way back."

Tosh said nothing but walked over to the edge of the dock for a closer look at us and *Orakiruu*. Satisfying himself, he got into the pickup and drove away, leaving us to our own devices. We drank the last two beers before setting out, snorkel gear and fishing rod in hand, on the two-mile trek to Idid. Paul was temporally sleeping in the Peace Corps office that was located along the way. He had been assigned to the island of Sonsorol in the far southern part of Palau. The field trip ship that was to deliver him there had not yet departed, so the Peace Corps office was his temporary home.

Both of us were tired and a bit shaken by our experience, so we trudged along quietly. Soon it began to rain. We were drenched and shivering by the time a car sped by, plastering us with pothole mud. It then slid to a stop, made a U-turn and pulled up beside us.

"You look like you could use a ride," said the Palauan man behind the wheel.

The red Datsun had a "Taxi" sign on its side. "Yes, I think we could," I said.

"Are you going to Idid?" he asked. I wondered how he knew that.

"Yes, but we need to stop at the Peace Corps office on the way."

"That's easy. Get in."

I climbed into the front seat, Paul into the back, with his fishing rod sticking out my window.

"My name is Hatsuich, said the driver. Are you the Peace Corps who lives with Ibedul?"

"Yes," I said. "My name's Baul."

"Why are you guys out walking on this dark, rainy night?"

"We went to Ulong Island and got back late," I said.

"I see you have a fishing pole. Where's the fish?" said Hatsuich with a smile.

"We were relaxing and sightseeing, not really fishing," I replied.

As our conversation continued, I suspected that Tosh had sent this cab to make sure we got home safely. And that we did, with Hatsuich talking and asking questions the entire time.

At Idid, Ibedul was sitting on the porch. Hatsuich dropped me off in the street, refused to take any money and sped away.

"You went fishing?" Ibedul asked as I walked up the steps.

"No, *Rubak*," I replied. "We just went to Ulong to snorkel and have some fun."

"I was told that you took fishing gear. Where are the fish? Palauans don't waste gas without bringing home fish. Next time first you catch fish, then you make fun. If no fish, you stop at the Co-op store. They have fish."

I realized that I was being chastised for playing on a weekend and not supporting the family's food needs. "Yes, *Rubak*," I said, lowering my head. "Next time I will bring fish."

That night I thought it best not to eat the food that had been left for me on the table. I showered and went straight to bed. The cold shower water washed off the salt and dirt while cooling the sunburn. I slept well despite a tumultuous rain storm.

The next morning Wilson picked me up as usual, and we drove to the boatyard. The minute Matsumoto saw me he said, "Hey you, haole boy, come here."

When I walked over to him, he motioned toward the dock and said, "I make you boat. Your job, take care of boat. You go look. Then you fix."

I discovered that *Orakiruu* was half-full of water but still afloat, with the ice chest and gas cans bobbing around on the inside. The engine was dangerously low in the water. Using a long-handled aluminum pot from the employee coffee room, I gingerly pulled the boat next to the dock and began to bail. After a while I was able to safely climb inside and continue. Eventually I scooped out the last bit of water, washed off the gas cans and ice chest in fresh water, and started the engine. Happily, it ran well.

The workers didn't look at me or say anything as I passed back through the building. They had seen that Matsumoto's harsh criticism was not just reserved for them, but if warranted, could even be dispensed to the Peace Corps of Ibedul. Although I was upset and embarrassed, the incident provided another valuable learning experience.

As we drove to the Fisheries Office, Wilson said, "When you think it might rain at night, run your boat up on the mats that we've placed on the sides of the ramp at the yard. Make sure it's above the high tide mark and pull out the transom plug. That way it can self-drain. And don't mind Matsumoto. He finds it difficult to deal with what he considers stupid, irresponsible behavior. He'll have forgotten about it tomorrow. But Tosh is a different story. He called me yesterday evening, wanting to take my boat and look for you. He was quite worried. I told him that it was no use trying to find you in the dark. If you didn't come back, we'd look for you in the morning. When you see him, you had better apologize. He was pretty upset."

Later that day I did apologize to Tosh, saying that I had no idea that the trip back from Ulong would be so difficult. "You'll learn," he said, seeming to put the matter to rest.

On the next Friday, Tosh approached me. "Can we take the *Orakiruu* fishing tomorrow?" he asked.

"Sure," I said. "Where do we meet?"

"Stop by my house after work today. We'll make some fishing gear."

Around five-thirty that afternoon, Wilson dropped me off at the American Club. Tosh lived in a Quonset nearby. Upon walking into their yard, I met his Palauan wife, Bertha, and their son, Dannyboy. Bertha was collecting the laundry, pillows and blankets that had been aired in the sun. "Go on in," she said. "He's waiting for you."

Slipping off my zorrie on the front stoop, I pulled open the screen door while voicing the usual arrival announcement. *Alii. Alii, Alii* Tosh?"

Tosh appeared from the back room dressed only in a red lavalava. The tin Quonset was sweltering hot.

"You might want to wear one of these," he said. "They're a lot cooler."

"Sure," I said.

He produced another red cloth and showed me how to wrap it properly so that things didn't fall apart at embarrassing moments. We sat on the painted plywood floor, drank beer and ate fried cuttlefish while Tosh worked on his fishing lures. He explained nothing. It was my job to watch and learn, but that was difficult because Bertha, who had joined us to nibble on the cuttlefish, kept interrupting with questions. She, like other Palauans, was interested in finding out about this American Peace Corps who lived with Ibedul and worked with her husband at Fisheries.

I tried to answer her queries about my parents, my age, my girlfriends, my religion, my reasons for coming to Palau, etc., while at the same time watching Tosh build his trolling lures. Using long-nose pliers and his strong fingers, he attached one end of a single strand, stainless-steel wire to a four-inch-long, rusted steel hook, which he then meticulously sharpened with a rattail file. Next, he passed the wire's free end through the center hole of a lead casting that resembled a fish head with imbedded red glass eyes. Using fine nylon thread, he secured all manner of plastic and cellophane streamers around the lead fish head so that they would obscure the hook when it was dragged through the water. Finally, using the pliers, he constructed a triangular-shaped attachment eye on the free end of the wire. This, I assumed, was where one would attach a swivel that connected to a fishing line.

Around nine in the evening the air had cooled a bit. Tosh had finished three lures, and several empty beer bottles were grouped together under the coffee table. I noted that the room was full of government-issued western style furniture:

couches, chairs, a coffee table. All were used as armrests or backrests for those sitting on the floor. *This facet of cultural variation must result from it being cooler on the floor*, I thought. Just then, Bertha placed in front of me a tray on which rested a bowl of turtle soup, some chopsticks, and a plate of sliced purple taro.

"Eat!" said Tosh. "When we're done Bertha wants to play *hanafuda*. Do you know how?

"No," I said.

"It's a Japanese card game. We'll teach you."

It was after midnight when Tosh dropped me in front of Ibedul's house. "I'll pick you up at eight in the morning. High tide is not until one. Make sure you're standing outside where I can see you. Wear a hat, otherwise you'll look like a cooked mangrove crab (bright red)."

The next morning at around eight-fifteen Tosh showed up in the green Fisheries pickup. Ibedul was sitting on the porch in his underwear. I was surprised that Tosh got out and addressed him directly. They conversed for several minutes in a mix of English, Japanese, and Palauan, and their demeanors seemed mutually cordial, although I understood little of what was said. Apparently the two of them were comfortable interacting with each other. That was not usually the case when others came to fetch me. Before climbing into the cab, I acknowledged my departure: "*Rubak. Ak moralung.*" Ibedul responded with an almost indiscernible upward eyebrow motion.

Tosh dropped me off at the boatyard and then drove to the Fisheries Co-op, where he waited for me to ferry *Orakiruu* around the end of Malakal Island. When I arrived beside the dock, Tosh handed down three cans of premixed fuel and a plastic laundry basket containing a coil of long-line cord attached to five feet of chain that was in turn connected to a piston assembly from a large engine. "I got you some equipments for your boat," he said. "You need an anchor." Also in the basket were a one-gallon bottle of drinking water, some plastic tubing for siphoning gas, two pair of gloves, and a piece of folded canvas. "Stow the basket up front under the bow cover," he said.

Next he handed me a long bamboo pole, "for poling in shallow water," he said, "and it's a swimming partner if you have a long way to go." Finally, before getting into the boat, he passed down several additional items: a glass ball with rope eye and netting woven around it, a four-foot-long, razor-sharp gaff hook with woven lanyard handle, a two-foot piece of iron pipe, a small plastic bucket with a short rope attached to the handle, and a box containing his fishing lures and two parachute cord handlines, each with built-in rubber tubing shock absorbers.

"You drive," I said as he got into the boat.

"Your boat. You drive. You learn. Go out the channel to the lighthouse. Keep red marks on your left."

Orakiruu was so heavily-laden that she barely made it up on plane, but we soon skimmed past the lighthouse on a turbulent river of incoming tide.

"See that white sand island with the single coconut tree on it?" said Tosh.

"Yes," I said. It was just barely visible on the eastern horizon. The tree looked as if it were growing out of the water.

"Head for that. Watch for birds."

It was a clear day with almost no wind. We sped along towards the coconut tree, *Orakiruu* ascending and then descending the rhythmic ocean swells that were generated by some faraway storm. At the sand island we slowed our speed and put out both handlines, one short and one long, on either side of Orakiruu. Tosh passed the lines around the oarlocks, holding on to one and passing the other to me. "That's your line, and this one's mine," he said. "So we know who catch the fish. Better wear these." He handed me a pair of leather work gloves.

"Do you see birds?" he said, nodding to the north, without apparently paying any attention himself. It was impossible not to see them. They were everywhere in the water and the sky—swooping, diving, crying out with excitement. Within seconds, in two different places, about fifty yards apart, the ocean erupted into a boiling frenzy of white foam and yellow dorsal fins.

"Go there, between the schools," he said while motioning with an outstretched arm and clenched fist. Within a minute we were between the frothing schools, and they began to close in around us. Big yellowfin splashed on all sides of *Orakiruu*. If I had dared, I could have reached out and touch one. "Get ready! Hold on. Don't wrap that line around your hand," he yelled, just as the rubber shock absorbers on his line snapped to their maximum length and the line buzzed through his gloved hand and out around the oarlock post. "Keep the boat going straight," he yelled." Pick a faraway cloud and aim for it."

Within a second or two my line did the same thing. With the outboard tiller under my arm, I struggled to keep the boat going straight while trying to arrest the outflow of line. The heat of friction was discernable though the gloves.

After several minutes Tosh was able to gaff and board his big yellowfin, whacking it on the head with the iron pipe. He then took over the fight for my fish, saying, "Don't move your feet. Keep them on the deck where they are." *An odd thing to say*, I thought, but I did as I was told while steering toward a distant cloud.

By the time Tosh boarded the second fish, everything inside *Orakiruu* was a blood-splattered slimy mass of confused lines, gear and fish. "Keep the school in sight, and don't move your feet around. Pull out the drain plug in the transom, keep it in your hand, and try to remember to put it back before we slow down," he commanded.

While I steered toward the birds that had moved some distance away, Tosh cut the gills of both fish, filling the bilge with even more blood. He then washed everything down with bucket after bucket of seawater, all of which drained out the transom hole as we moved along. By the time we again reached the birds he had organized everything, spread the wet canvas over the fish to protect them from the sun, gotten both handlines back into the water, and was in the process of taking in and wrapping up one of them. "This time we use only one line. Big fish!" he said.

I now understood the part about not moving my feet. It was important that the confused piles of handlines not be disturbed, that way they played out smoothly, exactly as they had been laid down, and furthermore, there was less chance of feet becoming entangled when a big fish made a run.

"Is that one line mine or yours?" I asked.

"Yours and mine," he replied with a smile.

We soon hooked and, not so soon, boarded a third yellowfin, after which he said, "Enough, we go home. Where is home?" he asked without looking up from his cleaning and organizing efforts.

I quickly surveyed the horizon. "Over there," I said, pointing toward some knobs of land on the western horizon that looked no bigger than my two fists extended at arm's length.

"Good. Always know where is home. Do you have enough gas to get there?"

"I've got about a tank and a half," I said.

"Is that enough?" he asked, again without looking from his work.

"I don't know."

"I guess we'll find out. Go!"

It helped a lot that both the wind and swells were at our back on the way home. Tosh, of course, had thought about that. I hadn't realized that *Orakiruu* was so fully loaded that she could only plane going down the face of swells as they pushed us from astern. With Tosh's guidance I learned to steer so that the boat remained on the wave face as long as possible. We made it to the lighthouse and up the channel to the Co-op dock by late afternoon with a half tank of gas to spare.

The three fish together weighed in at 170 pounds. Yoshiharu paid us fifteen cents a pound. That settled our fuel debt, with six dollars left over. I chipped in another four dollars, and we purchased reef fish for Tosh to take home and for me to bring to Seruang. Palauans ate pelagic fish—tuna, mahi-mahi, and the like—only as a last resort, preferring the smaller, tastier reef fish. In addition, I soon learned that Palauans also didn't covet lobsters, laughing at Statesiders who paid twenty-five cents a pound for them.

That day with Toshiro Paulis was my first adventure on the open ocean in a small boat, far from land. The awesome vastness of nature had provoked profound feelings of personal insignificance and vulnerability, yet there had also been a sense of cohesion with nature, and the exhilaration of executing a successful hunt. I had previously experienced similar feelings in a duck blind at dawn on a frosty morning and when watching the starry infinity from my sleeping bag at twelve thousand feet. Here those feelings appeared again in an entirely different setting. I now understood why it was that some men are drawn to the sea as a lifetime livelihood. On that day, I also gained an inkling as to the magnitude of knowledge stored in the mind of Toshiro Paulis. I knew I had much to learn and was determined to do so.

Bertha and Toshiro Paulis in the Rock Islands, Palau, 1967

From then on, I became a regular guest in the Paulis household. For reasons unknown to me, Ibedul seemed not to disapprove. On weekends we often went to the Rock Islands. I snorkeled with Bertha while she collected seashells. She was a devotee of shell collecting and knew the Palauan names and habits of hundreds of different mollusks. I fished with Tosh, each time learning a little more about a tropical sea and the creatures that live there. We played *hanafuda* into the late-night hours and drank more than a few beers. From Tosh and Bertha, I learned how to catch and cook several kinds of crabs, how to build a thatched roof of coconut leaves, how to cook fish on an open fire without metal grates or utensils, how to harvest and eat megapode and turtle eggs, how to collect edible seaweed and clam meat, how to drive a boat over and around coral reefs, how to harvest and eat coconuts at various stages of life, and much, much more. They taught me about island life: how to relax and be part of my surroundings, how to make do with what is available, how to enjoy the good times in life while quietly enduring the bad, how to learn by watching and doing, how to hold valuable knowledge closely, sharing it only with those most deserving. I was honored to be one with whom they shared.

In 1970 Tosh was one of five best men at my wedding in Guam. Sometime in the 1980s, Bertha died of chickenpox, a deadly disease for islanders. Tosh remarried and became closely involved with the Lutheran Church, where he sang in the choir. I once met his second wife but never knew her well. The last time I saw Tosh, he was a white-haired old man walking with the aid of a staff near the hospital in Meyungs Municipality. We talked and reminisced a bit, but the fire was gone out of him by then. He died in 2009 and is buried in Pohnpei, probably alongside his ancestors from Kapingamarangi. He and Bertha were major contributors to the fabric and breadth of my life.

Pacific Islanders are not given to oral expressions of thanks. Gratitude is shown in other ways, through life-long giving and sharing. In retrospect, I may have failed to balance the scales with Tosh and Bertha. For that I am sorry.

*   *   *

For the first few months in Palau my daily ritual remained unchanged. I arose around six, ate whatever was presented to me by Monica, and caught a ride to Fisheries with Peter Wilson. Working there all day, I frequently ate lunch with the office girls or at Tosh's house, or sometimes at Peter Wilson's house. He took a siesta after lunch. I liked that.

Usually about six in the evening, Peter or Tosh dropped me off in Idid. There I took a cold shower, ate a portion of whatever food was left on the table for me, and proceeded to the living room, where I helped Dominica and Miriam with their homework. Both girls were attending the Seventh Day Adventist School in Koror.

Those nightly homework sessions helped me to understand what was going on in the household and the neighborhood. The girls were not always happy about having to attend, but their father had laid down the law, so we were together for an hour or two every weekday evening. I checked their homework and we talked in English about many things. It was a happy, friendly time. At times other children ventured into our sessions, always girls, never boys. One such visitor was a teenage girl named Gloria who said she wanted to practice her English. Apparently a bit shy, she stayed in the background while Dominica and Miriam dominated activities.

After these homework sessions were over, I usually retired to my room, exhausted from the day's stress and the oppressive heat, happy for time alone to write a letter, read, or just sleep. Unbeknownst to me, some in the family were concerned about my being alone too much, as well as my apparent lack of interest in nighttime entertainment and female companionship. Palauans equate solitude with loneliness, and in Palau, most social activity occurs in the late, cooler hours of night. I was alone in my room when other Koror based volunteers were frequenting the bars, restaurants and nightclubs. In those days, a beer or a shot of whiskey both cost twenty-five cents.

Since I acted differently than other volunteers and Statesiders, the family thought I might be unhappy, or perhaps gay. Being gay is not necessarily viewed as a bad thing, but if I were gay, the family would have to adjust its expectations and accommodations. Direct inquiry is always avoided, so Jones and his cousin, Johnny Gibbons, attempted to ascertain my sexual preferences through incessant questioning. Often they asked if I fancied any particular Palauan girls, and why did I not attend the Boom-Boom Room or the Texas Saloon in the evenings like other volunteers. "There must be some Palauan girls that light your fire," they would say. "Maybe you like only the white kind!"

Over and over this happened until one day Jones asked again if there was any Palauan girl that I liked. I really didn't know a name to give him, but I desperately wanted to stop his nagging, so I said, "You know that girl named Gloria who comes to our homework sessions in the evenings? She's really good-looking. I like her. His response was stoic, except for a little swallowing motion in his throat. *Good*, I thought. *That finally shut him up.*

I didn't know at the time that my response was a huge blunder. Gloria Gibbons by birth status was to become the highest-ranking woman in Palau; her title would be Bilung, her son destined to be Ibedul. I was considered a family member. It was thought most unacceptable to express an interpersonal attraction for a relative of the opposite sex. Jones never questioned me again, but of course he spread the word, and Gloria never again attended my evening homework sessions. She later attended college in Texas, became Bilung at the death of her grandmother, and has always been friendly and kind to me. In 2006 when I visited Palau with my teenage son, Bilung Gloria held a most gracious welcoming party for us at one of Koror's finest restaurants. Several family members attended, including Dominica and Miriam. In 2010 Bilung's son, James Littler, fished with me in Guam on my boat *Kergirs*. At that time, he was an airplane pilot flying cargo routes. It appeared to me that he would be a caring and wise leader should he eventually become Ibedul.

On the Friday night after my blunder with Jones, I decided to venture out to the Boom-Boom Room, just to see what went on there. It was located about a quarter mile up the road from Idid, at the entrance to Ngerkesoaol hamlet. I hadn't walked a hundred yards when two Palauan girls in a blue Karmann Ghia convertible, the only sports car in Palau at the time, pulled up beside me. The driver said, "Where are you going, Peace Corps? You want to ride with us?"

"Sure!" I said. "But there's not much room."

"Just sit on the top in back. There's room for your feet behind our seats. Where are you going?" asked the driver a second time.

"The Boom-Boom," I replied. "Where are you going?"

She didn't answer but tromped on the gas. I almost rolled off the back as we whizzed up the hill past Mindszenty School and came to a dust-cloud stop in front of the Boom-Boom Room. The air vibrated with rock and country music that streamed through the screened windows. The three of us settled into a booth near the door. Peering around the smoke-filled room, I saw no one I knew. All were Palauan, except for some boisterous White guys at the bar. My companions said the loud guys were "coastguards." The waiter delivered, and I paid for three Budweisers, just as a "coastguard" came to ask one of my companions to dance. She smilingly complied, and they worked closely together on a Hank Williams ballad, after which he left her on the dance floor to find her own way back to our table.

Gradually I became aware that all booths except ours were occupied by either all women or all men. No couples were sitting together. Some were dancing together, but when the music ended, everyone returned to his or her unisex table.

It was impossible to determine who might be connected with whom. That didn't seem to bother the "coastguards." They just focused on the girls in whom they were interested, buying them drinks and dancing with them during slow dances.

Even though dancing has never been my forte, as the clock approached midnight, I was on my third beer and had danced once or twice with each of my companions. I discovered that the name of our driver was Moded, a nurse at the hospital. She was a beautiful and aggressive lady. Dancing closely with Moded left one with a complete understanding of what might be possible. I long since have forgotten her companion's name. It might have been Metbob, or something close to that.

Anyway, as the night passed, the "coastguards" became noisier and increasingly disruptive. A little before midnight, Moded said something in Palauan. Her demeanor reflected serious concern. I got the last part of it: "… we go. Quickly now!"

Up and out the door we went, leaving behind unfinished drinks and my one-dollar can of salted peanuts. On the outside there was a throng of Palauan men. They were mostly drunk and not happy campers. Words were exchanged between my companions and some of them. It was clear that I was being identified as a "Peace Corps" and not a "coastguard." Someone referred to me as Lebuu. I thought it not an appropriate time to disabuse him of that name. We boarded the car as we had come, me sitting in back on the canvas top. As we drove away, I thought those "coastguards" are probably headed into some rough waters.

Down the road we passed my house and continued to a house somewhere in Ngerbeched hamlet. There we were joined by two Palauan men, apparently the girls' partners, but even then, I couldn't discern exactly who was paired with whom, or whether either man had previously been at the Boom-Boom. The five of us drank, chewed betel nut, smoked, talked and laughed until the early morning hours. Their questions were similar to those I received everywhere I went—my parents, my religion, my girlfriends, my age, my food preferences, my feelings about Palau, etc., etc.

I was dropped off at my house just after dawn. Ibedul was sitting on the porch. "Where have you been?" he asked in a tone that meant business.

"I'm not sure, *Rubak*," I said. "I was picked up on the road by two girls driving a blue convertible sports car. One was named Moded. We went to the Boom-Boom for a while and then to a house in Ngerbeched."

"Those people are 'u-drive,' not good for you," he said. "You should keep away from them."

"Yes, *Rubak*, I will," I said as I beat a hasty retreat to my room.

Later I learned that the term "u-drive" was the local designation for a rental car, but it also was used to refer to promiscuous women who frequented the bars and had relations with visitors.

*   *   *

The next Friday night two girls showed up about the time our homework session ended. As was common in Palau, neither introduced themselves, but the taller of the two exuded a warmth and reserved poise that caught my attention. The shorter one acted as spokesperson and asked in Palauan if I might like to accompany them to eat *udon*. I accepted, not knowing exactly what she meant.

We walked a short distance to a place on the lower road called the Blue Gardenia. Its owner and hostess greeted us warmly, me in particular, as Ibedul's Peace Corps. The place was small and not crowded. Unlike the Boom-Boom, it was relatively quiet, and some couples were actually sitting together. I had a beer along with my *udon*, which I discovered was soup with thick noodles in it. The girls drank orange soda. The jukebox played music of the owner's choosing, unless a patron deposited money to select something else. We didn't dance, although a few couples did.

After eating, the talkative girl introduced her friend as Anastasia. Our eyes met in friendly acknowledgement, but she remained silent while her companion subjected me to the standard battery of questions to which I had become accustomed. My interrogator was clearly interested in ascertaining the state of my wellbeing. She knew I had been sick after arriving and wanted to know if I was now feeling better. She knew I ate lunch at the Fisheries and wondered why. Was the food at home causing me any problem? She knew I spent time in my room alone and wanted to know if I was lonely or homesick.

All the while Anastasia listened attentively. She was dark-complected, a little above average height for a Palauan woman, with a long neck, high cheekbones, and beautiful almond-shaped brown eyes. Those eyes, I can still see them, exuded just a hint of sadness. Her pearl post earrings barely showed at the bottom of thick, wavy black hair that was formed into a flat bun on the back of her head. She wore a short-sleeved, ballet neck white blouse that was tucked under a beltless, straight, black skirt that had a silver embroidered hem. On her left wrist was a pounded coin-silver bracelet. Anastasia exuded a humble self-confidence that could only come from being completely at ease with her position and status. I wanted to know more about her.

On our walk home she obliged. "Would you like to meet me tomorrow night at Santos Bar? It's the one just up the hill from George Theater on the same side of the street. I live near there."

Being unfamiliar with Palauan custom, this initiative on her part was unexpected but welcome. "Sure. What time?" I asked.

"Nine-thirty is a good time for Palauans. Is it too late for you?"

"No, that's fine."

"I'll be standing beside the building, where the trail leaves the road and goes down the hill," she said.

"Oh, we don't meet inside?"

"No, outside where the trail starts down the hill. I'll be there at nine-thirty. Can you bring some orange soda?"

"Sure, I'll meet Anastasia beside Santos Bar at nine-thirty with a six-pack of orange soda," I said.

She smiled. "People call me Tasia. It's easier."

"Tasia it is," I replied.

The two girls walked me home and disappeared into the night. I'm not sure I ever knew the name of Tasia's spokesperson.

At nine-thirty the next evening we met at the appointed place, and Tasia took me down the hill to her bedroom that had an exterior entrance. We drank warm orange soda and enjoyed the most beautiful sexual freedom I had known until that point in my life.

Our relationship lasted the entire time that I was a volunteer. Tasia stayed by my side as advisor, defender, teacher, lover and friend. No one could ever ask more of a partner than was given to me by Anastasia Brel.

I now believe that Ibedul or his wife, Seruang, requested that Tasia take care of me. Tasia's mother, Klouldil (big/important woman), and Seruang were sisters from the hamlet of Ngerkesoaol. Tasia held membership in a prestigious Koror women's group known as Maibrel (my friend). Its roots go back centuries. In 1783 when the British Captain Henry Wilson wrecked his ship, *Antelope*, on Palau's reef, he and his crew spent months stranded on the island of Ulong. At the Ibedul's request, the women of Maibrel provided accompaniment and assistance to the wrecked sailors. The members of Maibrel have traditionally performed highly regarded services for the Ibedul and for Koror.

Needless to say, Tasia and I became very close. We attended all social functions together. At Palauan events, men and women usually separated into unisex groupings. Tasia's advice helped me to hold my own among the men, but I was never at ease and often found myself unable to grasp the full meaning of their nuanced discussions. At these events, Tasia, like all Palauan wives, selected and served my food to wherever I was sitting. She timed her arrival appropriately, so as not to serve me before men of higher rank. My standing as a member of Ibedul's household somewhat compensated for my young age, and Tasia could judge that balance well. She was a master of Palauan custom and etiquette. Her advice to me was given in a reserved, almost humble way, always in the third person. "Paul, Palauans don't speak their mind without being sure how others around them feel. Out of respect, Palauans *melengmes* act in a humble manner, saying what they believe others want to hear. Palauans never talk harshly of anyone in public unless it is done through humor or in some indirect way. Palauans show the utmost respect for those of older age, never directly contradicting them. Paul, Palauans will be more relaxed around you if you chew betel nut." Although Tasia herself seldom chewed betel nut, she taught me the procedures and protocols for its preparation and use in various social situations. I grew to appreciate the nut's relaxing effects. With Tasia's help I slowly learned the nuances of behavior that signaled whether the spoken word "yes" meant yes, or maybe, or no, or some combination thereof.

Monica Ngoriakl and Anastacia (Tasia) Brel, Koror, Palau, 1968

I don't believe that Tasia had more than a grammar-school education. She worked as a switchboard operator at the government-run telephone exchange. In those days each call had to be connected by hand. Although it was considered inappropriate, the operator could, if she wished, hear conversations. Tasia knew much of what was going on in Koror, a handy attribute. But I never heard her mention a word about anyone's personal affairs. I suspect that she was given that position because of her integrity and fealty to Ibedul's family.

Tasia's father had died before I came to Palau. She said he had come from some islands in New Guinea and had worked at the power generation station in Koror. Tasia lived with her mother in a household full of children, at least two or three of whom were hers. Their names, save one, have long since departed my mind. Tasia's young son, Brian, had a heart valve condition that concerned her. I asked Mom to send party favors, balloons, and the like, and I ordered a birthday cake and ice cream so that he could have an "American" birthday party with the neighborhood kids. He eventually was able to go to Hawaii for heart surgery, but I don't know the final outcome. From Tasia's bedroom window, I watched those kids in the street below, excitedly running in the chemical fog behind the government mosquito abatement truck as it plied the streets of Koror on its nightly spray of DDT insecticide. I wonder how that innocent play affected the rest of their lives.

Sometimes on weekends Tasia and I used *Orakiruu* to ferry the children of our households to picnics on beaches near Koror. At other times, the two of us accompanied Tosh and Bertha for a weekend in the Rock Islands—snorkeling for clam meat, catching coconut crabs, cooking over an open fire, sleeping on a bed of palm fronds. They showed me a star that remains directly over Palau. Navigators could use it to find home. I've forgotten its name and can no longer find it.

Tasia and I had a beautiful relationship and a happy time together, but there was always that unspoken understanding of the sorrow that would ultimately befall us. I would leave, and she would be left behind. In those days, being young and self-centered, I was able to live for the moment, and a beautiful moment it was. I'm not sure that Tasia was able to do the same. Her relationship with me may have started out as an assignment, but in the end, it clearly became more than that for us both.

*   *   *

During 1967, additional fisheries assigned Peace Corps volunteers arrived in Palau. Their story is beautifully described in P.G.(Patrick) Bryan's book, *The Fish and Rice Chronicles: My Extraordinary Adventures in Palau and Micronesia.* These arrivals assumed some of my responsibilities and freed me to focus on the boatyard, the Ibedul, and my Idid family life. Patrick Bryan took over duties at the Palau Fishermen's Co-op. He would later become a fisheries officer in Saipan, Majuro and American Samoa, as well as a best man at my wedding and a lifelong friend. Norman Vas helped with the *Emeraech* project. He would later become a commercial fisherman on the island of Kauai, marry there, and raise a family. Gene Helfman took on several biological research projects, such as capturing baby Hawksbill turtles just as they hatched and raising them for release into the wild. He is now Emeritus Professor of Ecology at the University of Georgia.

Tasia and I sometimes double dated with Steve Murray, now a retired professor of anthropology at U.C. Santa Barbara, and his Palauan girlfriend, Tokiko Tkel, Toki for short. The four of us occasionally took *Orakiruu* to nearby beaches for a day of relaxation or together attended bars and nightclubs in Koror. On one such occasion, at about eleven-thirty on the night of March 1, 1967, we four sat together at a table in Santos Olikong's bar, listening to the jukebox, sipping our drinks, and munching on fried spring rolls. It had been raining throughout the day, but that was not abnormal during rainy season. We had become used to sloshing through the water and mud in zorrie using banana leaves as umbrellas. I did notice that the wind and rain had increased since our arrival, but the jukebox drowned out most ambient noise, so I paid little attention; *just a passing squall,* I thought.

Then suddenly there was a wrenching sound of grinding metal directly above us. An explosion of noise and wind hit us as water came pouring through the ceiling. For an instant we were frozen in place as the waitress came running from the kitchen yelling, "You better get out of here! The roof has blown off."

She's right about that, I thought. The floor was filling with water, and the power was still on. The jukebox was still playing, although I could no longer hear it above the noise.

When Steve opened the door a torrent of wind-whipped rain drenched us. The wind was so strong and the floor so slippery that he and I together couldn't get the door closed again. We left it banging on its hinges and followed the girls through the kitchen and out the back door on the leeward side. Tasia yelled, "My house! This way!" Throwing our bodies into the gale, we slipped and slid down the steep path, which was by then a gushing stream of muddy debris. Just inside Tasia's back door, we huddled on the floor, drenched and shivering as we tried to understand what had happened. The wind and rain outside were so loud that we could only yell at each other. Luckily, the hill provided some protection from the wind's direct impact, but still torrents of rain streamed sideways, working their way through every crack and crevice. Soon we were sitting in water.

Then abruptly the storm diminished. Within a few minutes, the wind and rain had completely stopped. We opened the door and stepped out into an eerie stillness, just a few wisps of air and complete silence. Stars were visible overhead.

"I'd better go home and see if everyone is all right," I said.

"Yes, go now," said Tasia. "I'll stay here with my mother and the kids. Hurry and be careful. I think the wind will come again soon."

Toki enforced Tasia's advice. "Yes, it won't be long. Go as fast as you can. We'll stay here."

Water was still gushing down the trail as I made my way up past the demolished bar and onto the main road. The quarter mile to Idid was littered with downed trees, limbs and power lines. The damaged buildings were dark and quiet. Nothing moved. Even the normally barking watchdogs were silent. I had only starlight to guide me around obstructions. When I entered the yard at Idid, I saw that the roofing tin on the front of our house was gone. Family members were huddled in the five-foot-high space underneath the building. Ibedul, Seruang, Dominica, Miriam, Joann and Iris were there, along with Jones and Johnny and several others, among them two old ladies, the Bilung and her neighbor, Metauii. I joined them, sitting on a sheet of plywood in the mud.

"Typhoon," said Ibedul. "It will come back." No sooner had he spoken than the wind began to increase. Soon the terrible noise and pounding rain were upon us again, but this time they came from the opposite direction. Pieces of tin, plywood, and tree branches cartwheeled past in the dark. The house was substantial and would not likely blow off its foundation, but it shook with the gusts, and water dripped on our heads through joints in the *dort* floorboards. There was nothing to do but wait, shiver and pray. Despite discomfort and fear, stoicism prevailed, even among the youngest children. Everyone endured. There was no crying or complaining. The only ones shown special consideration were the two old ladies, who were seated in the driest locations with blankets and plastic tarps.

That night and in the days after Typhoon Sally's onslaught, I learned much about Palauan tenacity and resilience. It was impressive. Of the 935 homes that existed on Koror Island prior to the storm, only 162 remained livable. Almost all commercial buildings were destroyed or severely damaged. The Caroline Fishing Company's fleet of nine tuna boats was sunk. Ibedul was a partner in that venture. Electric power and municipal water were not restored for months, yet as the sun rose that first day, people began to gather their possessions and rebuild. They cleared the roads with machetes and shared food and assistance. They cooked and ate and laughed together in lean-tos made of scrap and rubble, drinking water from catchments and coconuts. I never saw a person show remorse or lament their losses.

Initially there was an overabundance of food because the fallen bananas, papayas, and breadfruit would spoil if not eaten quickly. Some taro swamps had been inundated and tapioca uprooted, so women spent much of each day over open fires, cooking and preserving breadfruit, cassava and taro. Luckily for us the roofing tin from our house had been painted a maroon-red. Much of it was returned, even though some pieces had blown a mile away. Within three or four days we once again had a roof over our heads, but everything inside our house had been soaked. All my books, papers, pictures and slides went into the burn pile, as did the unsalvageable belongings of others. My prized Zenith Transoceanic 3000 radio was waterlogged and of no use.

While I worked helping to clean up at the boatyard, which fortunately had suffered minimal damage, Monica dried my clothes, sheets and salvageable belongings in the sun. The mattress took many days and it was never the same. I slept on the hardwood floor along with everyone else. Adversity strengthened the bonds of our extended family and my place in it. I was no longer just a guest.

The aftermath of Typhoon Sally helped me understand why it is that islanders are slow to relinquish traditional ways, have little regard for individualism and material possessions, and place such importance on the maintenance of tranquil personal relationships. It is people who provide aid and assistance in times of need. Material possessions can be destroyed by nature, rendered useless, and relegated to burn piles. During difficult times in a horticultural-hunting-gathering society, it is human capital with its associated industry and knowledge that is of most value. There is danger in becoming too dependent on electricity, sewers, potable piped water, and roofing tin. Across the road from Ibedul lived a titled *rubak,* Eychaderemai Sumong. His home had a traditional palm leaf thatched roof. During the storm's extreme atmospheric pressure fluctuations, the thatch provided structural ventilation. Not a piece of his roof blew away. On the morning after the storm, with just a little smoothing, Sumong's roof and home were back intact. The rest of us were searching in all directions for roofing materials. The old ways are not always inferior to the new.

As the days and weeks rolled by, aid from outside Palau arrived. It was referred to as *haikiu*—donated food—probably a word of Japanese origin. Clothing donations were appreciated and quickly absorbed into the community. Guam sent thousands of donated shoes. These were less appreciated, since Palauans seldom wore shoes, other than to church on Sundays. The US Department of Agriculture sent tins of meat that tasted like spam. These tins were sought-after delicacies and carefully stored away. Years later, some Palauans were still consuming tins of Typhoon Sally *haikiu* spam. Probably the most appreciated *haikiu* came from the islands of Yap—a shipload of betel nut, lime and pepper leaves—the salvation of devoted Palauan chewers.

*   *   *

My life in Idid was continually stressful, requiring constant attention. Communication was always circuitous, never direct. My standing with Ibedul seemed to ebb and flow from day to day, depending on his momentary disposition. He never confronted me about any concerns but frequently vented his discontent during meetings with Peace Corps staff. The Director, Dirk Ballendorf, would then remind me once again how much Peace Corps depended on my success in Koror's highest-ranking household.

Not infrequently, Ibedul returned home inebriated in the darkness of early morning. He then sometimes grumbled loudly to Seruang about matters that were actually meant for my ears. His words easily passed through the thin walls of my room, but because of my language inadequacy, I couldn't always understand the precise reason for his unhappiness. It was often difficult to discern whether his irritation rested with Peace Corps in general or me in particular. I knew that he was unhappy about my spending so much time at the boatyard working with Peter Wilson, whom he considered a loud, uncouth *chad ra ngebard* (foreigner). It also bothered him that I was helping Ben Orrukem, a member of a rival Koror clan, who worked as a kind of manager at the boatyard. In general, he was perturbed that I was living in his house yet helping others more than I was helping him.

Each morning I awoke thinking that the previous night's tirade had certainly signaled the end of my stay in Idid. But that never happened. Each new day seemed to bring with it a reprieve. I was never expelled, and as time passed, our relationship grew closer. So what was it that allowed me to weather the storms? I can't say for sure, but it was likely Tasia's influence. She was related as a niece to Seruang and must at times have interceded for me. To put it bluntly, in Palau men make the noise while women call many of the shots behind the scenes.

There were other reasons as well for my continued tenure in Idid. I wasn't rowdy, and didn't frequent bars, parties, and nightclubs, as some volunteers did. In fact, I associated little with non-Palauans. Under Tasia's guidance, I tried to behave in ways that brought no discredit to Ibedul or Idid. I tutored the girls every night. Their English improved and so did their school grades. I supported and served Ibedul in public, often acting as his designated driver, chauffeuring him to bars and restaurants. The Blue Gardenia was one of his favorite nighttime stops.

All clubs and bars in those days were required by law to close at midnight, but that didn't happen if Ibedul was a patron and wished the establishment to remain open. I sometimes waited until one or two in the morning while he finished the last of his Scotch and milk. The police often arrived to determine why the bar hadn't closed. Upon seeing the Chief's white Nissan, license plate #1, they usually continued on their patrol without stopping. Sometimes an officer of high clan lineage might venture inside. After respectfully acknowledging Ibedul, the officer would harangue the bartender or owner about the legality of required midnight closing. The bartender would apologize and indicate that he would immediately comply. The policeman would leave, having done his job, and the bar would remain open until Ibedul departed.

As his trust in my loyalty grew, Ibedul sometimes asked for my explanation and opinion of legislation and other documents written in English. When guests visited, I often acted as bartender, mixing and serving drinks. It pleased Ibedul to show off his Peace Corps houseboy, and because of that, I was privy to meetings that would normally be inaccessible to outsiders. When English-speaking visitors approached Ibedul for assistance, he sometimes pretended not to understand and spoke through an interpreter. After the supplicants departed, he would ask me to confirm his understanding of what had been said.

One of these get-togethers is worth mentioning. Chief Petrus Mailo of Moen, Truk (now called Weno, Chuuk) visited our house with a sizable entourage. During that evening there was considerable back and forth translation between Palauan, Trukese, and English, much of which I didn't understand. However, as

I stood behind the bar, one thing was clear to me. Chief Petrus had come to Idid to pay his respects to Ibedul, but he also was there to greet the Bilung, whom he referred to as "his sister." Unbeknownst to most Westerners and probably many Palauans, these two families are connected over two thousand miles of Pacific Ocean. This was especially surprising to me, since it's commonly understood that Palauans and Trukese do not mix well together. It would be interesting to know the full story of how that family relationship came about.

I lived in Ibedul Ngoriyakl's house for the entirety of my Peace Corps service. By the time I departed Palau, he and I had built a comfortable relationship. In 1969 when I was completing my M.B.A. at San Jose State, Ibedul visited my parents' home in Livermore. During weekdays while I attended classes, they took him on trips to Yosemite National Park, Miur Woods, the Napa wine country and Hurst's Carlsbad estate. On days when I had no classes, he and I traveled to points of interest around the Bay Area.

One evening in San Francisco, Ibedul wanted Japanese food. I knew of only one Japanese restaurant. It was located on California Street, just above the financial district. We parked in the California Street Garage and walked into the restaurant. Having no reservations, we were unceremoniously seated at a regular American-style table, with knife and fork service near the kitchen door. Once seated, Ibedul asked to use my pen. To my alarm he began writing in Japanese on the menu. When the waitress arrived to take our order, he spoke in Japanese and handed her the menu with the writing on it. She immediately went into the kitchen. Within a minute or two, the head chef, the manager, and his assistant were standing at our table, bowing profusely. In short order we were transferred to a room enclosed behind shoji panels. It had a low Japanese-style table with a pit under one side for *gaijin* like me to hang our legs. For the rest of the night, we were served like kings. I have no idea what Ibedul wrote on that menu, but the restaurant manager commented to me that my associate wrote stylish kanji and spoke fluent old-style Japanese. We stayed for several hours and drank considerable sake. I paid the two-hundred-dollar-plus bill and somehow drove us back to Livermore.

In 1972 Ibedul passed away in Japan from metastasized stomach cancer, self-destruction from years of high living on Scotch and milk. I didn't attend his funeral, as I had just started my doctoral studies in Hawaii and couldn't spare the week it would take to travel to and from Palau. However, I did write the following note that was published in the Palau newspaper, *Tia Belau*:

Thoughts about a Chief—What kind of man was this?

Born in a German World;

Raised in a Japanese world;

Yoked with leadership in an American world.

A man who taught himself to speak and read three languages.

A politician's politician, being always in the middle, yet never on the spot.

A man of tradition who accepted the new, growing younger in heart as he grew older in years.

A man who few knew well and many misunderstood, having little empathy for the burden of his position.

Occasionally abrupt and forceful of temperament;

Often reserved and quiet, almost shy.

A man who few loved, some respected, and many feared.

A leader, a symbol, a politician, a father, a fisherman, a traveler, most of all Ibedul of Palau.

A man I once had the good fortune to know and love, while a guest in his world.

I will never forget Ibedul Torwal Ngoriyakl. From him I learned much about self-composure under stress, the power of silence, and the strength of indirect discourse. I also learned how power and privilege must be judiciously balanced with the weight and responsibility of leadership, in a way that avoids arrogance and maintains empathy for those in need. This is a hard balance to maintain, and Ibedul was a masterful practitioner.

*   *   *

Despite my success at living in Ibedul's household, I wasn't always a perfect volunteer or a paragon of moral character. I made some major blunders and some foolish mistakes. However, with Irish luck and the help of others, I did avoid disaster and learned from my mistakes. Two interrelated examples follow.

There was a young carpenter at the boatyard named Yuki. He was particularly skilled and a fast learner. Matsumoto spoke highly of his dedication and reliability, so with Wilson's approval, I decided to reward Yuki with a substantial pay raise. Subsequently, Yuki stopped coming to work. At first we thought he must be sick, but eventually Tosh located him. The following conversation was directed at Peter Wilson but intended for my indirect consumption as well.

"Boss, I found Yuki in the Texas Saloon. They said he's been drunk straight through for three days now. All he would say to me is that he's not coming back to work. Boss, did you give that kid a pay raise without raising the pay of Imeong and Ngirrirenguul?"

"Sure I did. He deserves it. Why should I raise the pay of those two old farts? They are twice as slow as Yuki."

"Boss, you put that kid in a real bind. There's no way he can come back and face those two old men. If you want him back, you've got to give Imeong and Ngirrirenguul a similar raise, and even then, I'm not sure we can get him back."

"That's bullshit," said Wilson. "I'm not gonna do that."

"Then Yuki's not cumin back, Boss. And Matsumoto will be plenty upset."

"Shit, Tosh, do whatever it takes to get that kid back to work. I can't be bothered with this stupid Palauan custom crap." Peter Wilson's colonialist attitude was sometimes his own worst enemy.

After considerable cajoling and a pay raise for his elders, Yuki did return, but preferred to work on projects separated from the two older carpenters. Once again, I learned about the importance of age and the communal nature of Palauan society. From then on, increases in compensation were based on the Association's overall productivity and shared by all employees, with deference paid to age and experience.

A couple of months later, Yuki and I stopped at the Texas Saloon for a beer after work. As time passed it was nine o'clock, and the one beer had transformed into several, along with sashimi and various other appetizers. A woman had joined us, apparently a friend or relative of Yuki. For the sake of anonymity, I will refer to her by the alias, Tildi Berock. Her statuesque beauty grabbed my complete attention. Yuki might as well have disappeared. I could only see Tilda. When we danced to the jukebox music, her chin fit comfortably on my shoulder beside my neck, and her hair provided a welcoming pillow. Our bodies rubbed together in all the right places, leaving little doubt as to the impact she was having on me. When the music stopped, I was thankful for the relative darkness and stayed close behind her as we walked back to our table, lest someone notice the conspicuous bulge in my crotch.

A half hour before the midnight closing, I walked with Tildi well in the lead, down the street to a small house that was nestled, almost out of sight, in the surrounding foliage. There we spent a glorious couple of hours enjoying each other from as many positions as one might imagine.

Suddenly, without warning, Tildi said, "Get dressed. You must go. Now! Hurry!"

"What's wrong? Did I do something wrong?

"No, just go. Quickly!

I rushed into my clothes and headed out the door, leaving her sprawled in the nude on the pandanus mat floor. There had been no light in the house, so my eyes were completely adjusted to the darkness. When I stepped outside, I was confronted by four Palauan men. They were clearly not happy, but they parted to let me pass between them. Three turned to face me while the other went into the house. Within a minute the shrieking and yelling began. Tildi was being beaten. I stood in the starlight beside a huge tree trunk while the three men made it clear with their body language that I should leave and not interfere. By then Tildi's cries had become frightened whimpering sobs, but the male anger had not subsided. At any moment he could come out of that house and start after me. The only thing I could do was leave and walk the short distance home to Idid in sober reflection. Probably the only reason I wasn't harmed that night was because I was the Peace Corps who lived with Ibedul.

But that was not the end of the story. Three days later I began to experience a burning sensation upon urination. By the next day, white puss exuded from the end of my penis. *It must be gonorrhea*, I thought. We had been taught about that in training and warned of its prevalence in Micronesia. So off I went to the emergency room at the hospital. There were no doctors' offices in Palau in those days. Everyone who was sick went to the hospital for whatever ailed them. The doctors were not American certified physicians but medical officers trained at the Fiji School of Medicine in the University of the South Pacific. All residents had a hospital number, the key to their records. Mine was and still is 14087. When I arrived at the emergency entrance, I wrote that number on a clipboard that hung near the nursing stand.

All those in waiting sat outdoors under a tent roof. When your number was called, you spoke with the triage nurse who assessed your need and assigned your order in the queue. No one had any idea where in the queue they had been placed or how long it might take to be called. Time was irrelevant except in emergencies. I told the nurse that I thought I had gonorrhea. She replied with an upward flick of her eyebrows that meant "yes" or "all right" or "okay, I heard you." With an otherwise expressionless face, she said that I should take a seat. My name would be called. The discourse around me had mostly to do with the actual and suspected illness of those in waiting, as well as the maladies of various Palauans throughout the community. There were few if any medical secrets under this tent or within the community. Word traveled fast. But what was this *chad re a ngebard* (Westerner) doing here? Was he not the Ibedul's Peace Corps? They must not be feeding him well. Why was he sick? He looks healthy. What could possibly be the matter? Don't be so loud. He understands Palauan.

After a forty-five-minute wait, I was ushered into a small laboratory. Sitting at the lab-counter on a stool was an attractive Palauan woman in her thirties.

"Hello," she said, "my name is Dr. Ulai Otobed. Are you Paul?"

"Yes."

"What seems to be the problem?"

"I think I have gonorrhea," I said.

"What makes you think that?"

"My penis hurts when I urinate. It's red at the tip, and it drips some white stuff that sticks to my underwear."

"Let's have a look. Take off your pants and underwear and have a seat on that lab stool."

I complied while she donned a pair of rubber gloves. My testicles hung over the stool's edge. Taking my penis between her fingers, she examined it before lighting a Bunsen burner on the counter behind her. From a drawer she extracted a six-inch glass shaft, from one end of which protruded a two-inch stainless wire with a loop on the end. This she thrust into the burner flame until the wire was white hot. When she removed it from the flame it slowly changed from white to red to pink to its original stainless color.

Thereupon she said, "This may hurt a bit. Hold on to the seat."

Before I could react, she pushed the wire up my penis, gave it a twist and pulled it out. The action was over before the pain registered. But it certainly registered. I flinched and groaned.

She paid no attention as she rubbed mucus from the looped end onto a glass slide which she then popped into a nearby microscope. Upon viewing the slide for what seemed to be a long while, she said, "It looks like your self-diagnosis is correct. From whom did you acquire this problem?" I stammered a bit, so she interjected. "Let me put it this way. Who have you had sex with lately other than Tasia?

Going With The Flow

I was aghast that she apparently knew about my relationship with Tasia, but I should not have been surprised. Everyone knew everything about everyone in Palau, Peace Corps especially.

"I had sex with Tildi Berock about a week ago."

For the first time Doctor Otobed's expression reflected a telltale smidgeon of surprise. "And have you had sex with Tasia since then?"

"Yes, once."

"All right, I'm going to give you two prescriptions for antibiotics. Pick them up at the pharmacy window on your way out. One is for you, and one is for Tasia. Tell her I said that you both should take them. You do know not to stop until you have completed the full course, don't you?"

"Yes, Doctor. I know that."

"Then make sure that Tasia does not stop either."

"Yes, Doctor. I will."

As she filled out the prescription orders, she said, "Now I'm going to give you some advice, Mr. Paul. Stay at home with Tasia. Stop fooling around. You Peace Corps can cause a lot of trouble for people without realizing it. There are things you don't know. That girl was severely beaten probably because of you. If you care about her, stay away from her, or the consequences might be worse next time. And I don't want to see you in here again with the clap. Tasia is a good person. Don't make her sick again."

"Yes, Doctor," I said, my eyes sheepishly downcast as she handed me the two prescriptions.

I never saw Tilda again. If my information is correct about the man who beat her, he went on to become President of Palau. Tasia dutifully took the antibiotics and never questioned me about how I had acquired my malady.

*   *   *

When one is an outsider living in an unfamiliar culture, some unexpected situations can arise. The following is an example of machinations that can occur when a twenty-five-year-old male with raging hormones is transplanted from his lifelong patriarchal environment into a matrilineal society. Once again, Irish luck and perhaps the intervention of others saved me from the unknown.

For some time, I had been enamored by a young lady who lived across the street and down the hill from Ibedul's house. I can no longer remember her name, so for this writing, I'll call her Niomi. It was common knowledge that Niomi's mother, in a fit of rage, had killed her husband with a machete. It never entered my consciousness that such a temperament might be an ongoing inherited family characteristic that could possibly impact me.

As was often done by Palauan young men, I decided to call to her in the night or tap on her window in the hope of arranging a meeting. One night when Tasia was on duty at the switchboard, I sat concealed in an island of bushes near the road watching Niomi's house. Despite having maintained watch for some time, I hadn't seen her arrive or depart, nor had I detected any activity around the house. I could have worked up the courage to tap on her window, but alas, I had no idea which window that might be, and somewhere beneath my testosterone rush there was this dim vision of a machete-wielding mama charging in my direction.

Around eleven o'clock I had lapsed into deep thought, so I didn't notice a car that had stopped on the road behind my thicket. I was jolted into reality when a male voice said, "*Alii*, Paul, are you there?"

"Yes. Who's there?" I replied.

"I need to talk with you."

I didn't recognize the voice nor the vehicle as I moved toward the road and the stranger. How did he know that I was sitting in this thick foliage? Who was this person? He turned out to be a young man, my age or a little younger, but shorter in stature. Most Palauans were. His other features were blurred in the darkness.

"Yes," I said again when I got closer.

"Someone wants to meet with you. She sent me to bring you."

"Who is this someone?" I asked, my mind rushing to the thought that perhaps Niomi had noticed my observation post and was proposing a rendezvous at some safe location by sending a cousin to bring me there. That would not be an uncommon event in the Palauan way of things. On the other hand, perhaps her mother was waiting for me with a machete. My hormones demanded that I disregard the latter possibility.

"You'll find out when we get there. Get in the car." He opened the door for me. It was one of those Asian imports with the steering wheel on the wrong side for American roads. They were fairly common in Palau at the time, due to their relatively low import costs.

"Where are we going?" I asked, as I hesitated to get in.

"Ngerchemai," was the response.

That was a hamlet in the northeast corner of Koror Island, a place where I had never been, and to my knowledge, knew no one. However, in the hope of meeting Niomi, I piled into the front seat and off we went. We turned off the main road at a point near the Catholic Mission. Street lights were nonexistent. The road was narrow and partly graveled. Eventually we stopped in front of a darkened building that I took to be a community or clan *bai* (meeting house).

My driver said, "Go inside. She's waiting for you."

I walked up a couple of rock stairs and onto the hardwood floor of a vast room. The building was open on two sides, so moonlight partially lit the interior space.

"Take off your zorrie before you come in," said a woman's voice from the darkness. I did so, leaving them on the steps and then moving in the direction from whence the voice had come. My excitement and anticipation of a tryst with Niomi had my heart pounding.

In a dark, back corner stood a Palauan woman barefoot on a pandanus mat, dressed in a muumuu. It was not Niomi. "Come here," she said. I walked to the edge of the mat and hesitated. She grabbed my hand, pulling me toward her. "Come over here. I won't bite." She stood at arm's length in front of me. I recognized her as Reako, the wife of an acquaintance. She and Tasia were both telephone switchboard operators and friends, I thought. Tasia had told me that Reako was a high clan woman from Ngerchemai. That explained her presence in this place, and being privy to Tasia's work schedule, allowed her to know my unaccompanied schedule. But why?

In one synchronous movement Reako pulled the muumuu over her head, threw it aside, and stood before me completely naked in the grayness of ambient moonlight. She grabbed my crotch and began uncinching my belt. Soon I was as nude as she. In less than a half hour, every bit of my available sperm had been thrust deeply into her body. At that point she seemed satisfied in a completely detached way. It was as though she had completed the task she set out to do and viewed it as having been a successful undertaking.

"You'd better get your clothes on. Someone might be coming," she said. "The Palauan boy will give you a ride home. He's waiting by the door."

When I emerged, he was sitting on the steps beside my zorrie. He dropped me off at the same place where he had picked me up. I never saw him, or the car, or Reako again, and for some reason, the pursuit of Niomi became less interesting as the days passed.

There are several possible reasons for what happened that night. It's unlikely that Reako cared for me. Her love making was mechanical, and she made no effort to arrange a return meeting. She may have simply wanted to get pregnant with Peace Corps sperm, not an uncommon desire among Palauan women in those times. She may have wanted to make a point in regard to Ibedul's Idid clan. She may have been upset with her husband or someone else. However, it seems likely to me that Reako was jealous of Tasia, or Tasia had offended or shamed Reako in some manner. Having her way with me provided Reako with ego inflation or payback or both. On the other hand, it may have been some combination of all the above. Or it's possible that Reako and Tasia collaborated in order to distract me from Niomi. It's even possible that Niomi and Reako were related, and the whole episode was arranged as a reflection of Niomi's unhappiness about my pursuit. I will never know. But you can be sure that young men are but pawns in a matrilineal society. It helps to be a wise and knowledgeable pawn. I was not always such.

*   *   *

In mid-September of 1967 I was riding home from work with Peter Wilson in the Fisheries pickup. Midway through Koror, he asked, "Paul, why don't you come on home with me and have dinner with us? Ann is cooking roast beef, and Father Hoar will be there along with Van Schoote. He just came in today on the Guam flight."

"I don't know, Pete. I really should go home. Seruang has probably already cooked my food, and I should do homework with the kids."

"Never mind that," said Peter. "You can miss their homework just this once. There's some *klsebuul* (rabbitfish) in the back. Yoshiharu just gave them to me. Take those into your house and tell them that you have to go somewhere with me. That should get you off the hook."

It was hard to pass up free, high-quality fish for our household, as well as a roast beef dinner and a chance to talk with Father Hoar and Dr. Van Schoote. Furthermore, it was useless to resist. Peter never took no for an answer. I did as he suggested while he waited for me on the street. Inside all went well. Seruang was happy to get the fish, and the kids were happy to eat my food and take a break from homework lessons.

As Peter and I drove toward his house on Topside, my thoughts drifted to that day in early September when a white, thirty-five-foot long, jib-rigged ketch had sailed into Malakal Harbor and dropped its anchor at the boatyard.

The Wilson Family: Peter, Ann, Ramsay, Buik, and Lebuu, Palau, 1967

She was named *Kate* and was captained by one Alphonse M. Van Schoote, a Flemish-Belgian M.D., board certified in pathology, who had studied at Duke and Columbia Universities. A couple of years prior, Van Schoote had arrived in Truk Lagoon, having sailed *Kate* from Saipan, where he had purchased her from an Australian who had sailed her around the world from her birthplace in Hong Kong.

While in Truk, Van Schoote had endeared himself to the paramount Chief, Petrus Mailo, and was subsequently employed by the Trust Territory Government as Chief Medical Officer for Truk District. Working out of *Kate*, Dr. Van Schoote provided medical services to Micronesians in the far-flung islands west of Truk Lagoon and east of Yap, an area geographically known as the Eastern Caroline Islands. His stature among these islanders had grown immensely since he had begun building dispensaries and training midwives in places where there had previously been no medical services. In order to facilitate this work, he had established a non-profit entity named Health Education Life Project (HELP) to solicit funding from European and American donors.

Upon his arrival in Palau, Van Schoote had arranged to drydock *Kate* at the boatyard for hull maintenance and engine repair. Shortly thereafter he had departed on a fund-raising tour through Europe and America. Now, almost six months later, he had returned. I was anxious to hear about his travels.

When we arrived at Peter's house, Father Hoar, Dr. Van Schoote, and Peter's wife, Ann, were having cocktails on the front deck. Peter immediately went to join them. I tarried in the kitchen where Satski Yobech was washing dishes. Satski was a Palauan girl of about nineteen who worked for the Wilsons as a housekeeper and au pair for their three boys, Ramsay, Buik, and Lebuu. She greeted me in Palauan. "*Ungil kebsengei rubak.* You haven't stopped by lately. I thought you might have forgotten this house and me. Both *Rubak* and *Mechas* will be out late tomorrow night."

Her indirect invitation was not unexpected. I had stopped by a couple of times in the past, and after the boys had been put to bed, the interaction between Satski and me had been quite enjoyable. However, I knew that if such activity were continued, it would soon reach Tasia's ear, and that might not be good for Satski.

I changed the subject. "I'm too young to be called a *rubak*, Satski. Just Paul will do."

"Well, Mr. Paul, you live in that high clan place with those high clan people, so I thought you would be a *rubak* by now. Life in Idid must be so good that you have forgotten about us regular people."

There was no salvation from a perturbed and persistent Palauan woman who wanted attention, so I said, "We can talk later, Satski; right now I've got to have a drink with those people on the veranda."

As I departed, Satski mouthed under her breath one of those standard Palauan swear words, a derogatory reference to my mother.

Two footnotes are worth mentioning here. First, Satski Yobech became Palau's Postmistress, a position she held for many years. Because of her assistance, my stamp collecting hobby benefited greatly. Second, Peter and Ann Wilson's decision to name their oldest son Libuu was not looked upon favorably by Ibedul. The name Libuu originated in Yap and had long been held closely within the Idid clan. Wilson's use of that name without asking permission created an unspoken rift between the two men, a rift that Peter probably never realized.

On the porch I settled into a teak captain's chair and sipped the cold Budweiser I had removed from the refrigerator as I departed the kitchen. Van Schoote was holding forth about his travels while Peter, Ann, and Padre Hoar listened.

Dr. Van Schoote was a big fellow, muscular, handsome, tanned, dirty-blond with a fluid French accent. As was his habit, he was attired in white shorts with a white short-sleeved shirt, unbuttoned so as to show off a donut shaped pendant that hung on his chest. The pendant was given to him by Chief Petrus Mailo of Truk as a symbol of his appreciation for Van Schoote's medical work. Apparently mesmerized by him, Ann Wilson was paying little attention to what Van Schoote was saying as her eyes wandered intently over his physical aspects.

Ann, like Peter, had been born and raised in Honolulu. She had a model's figure and was not averse to showing it off. Amid much controversy and subsequent gossip, she had been the first woman ever to wear a bikini into the Koror public market. Palauan rumors had her sleeping with both Van Schoote and Father Hoar, as well as the District Administrator and others. I can substantiate none of that, other than to confirm that the Palauan grapevine gossip regarding all four individuals was littered with suggestive tales.

Because of the rumors, I was concerned about how the evening might unfold between Peter, Van Schoote, and Padre Hoar, especially after they consumed more alcohol. Van Schoote was known to despise missionaries, despite his having worked alongside his brother, a Jesuit Bishop in the Belgian Congo. He often disparaged Trust Territory Government employees as incompetent, especially anthropologists and health care administrators. And he regularly demeaned Peace Corps staff and volunteers as useless do-gooders. I suspected that he perceived these groups as threatening to his recently acquired primacy within the outer island communities of Truk, and it was true that each of these groups, for differing reasons, had been critical of him and his lifestyle. If rumors were true, Ann Wilson's presence provided an additional catalyst for potential friction among these three men. I didn't want to be dragged into any such clash.

I digress to mention that Father Richard (Dick) Hoar, S.J. was one of four Jesuit priests who at that time served Palau's Catholic Mission. He was a tall, handsome, grey-haired Irishman from Buffalo, New York. During my time in Palau, I came to understand that Jesuits, the Society of Jesus, are truly the Jedi Knights of the Catholic Church. They set an exceptional standard of selfless humanitarian service, and their aptitude in matters spiritual is further enhanced by their capacity in matters secular. Though their personalities and backgrounds differed, each of these four men always conveyed a calm, non-judgmental dedication to God and the betterment of humanity. The kitchen at the Catholic rectory was always open to Peace Corps volunteers. A visitor could count on conversation, food, and a cerebral uplift from whomever was present. A bottle of Scotch whisky and ice cubes were usually available in the refrigerator.

Father Hoar was an electrical engineer, ham radio operator, and builder in charge of construction and maintenance for Catholic schools and churches. Father Juan Bizkarra S.J. spoke only his native Basque, Japanese, and Palauan. Having traveled to Japan in 1938, he was marooned there during the war. Upon returning to Palau, he served the people of Angaur and Peleliu until his death, and is buried at the church he built with them. Father Edwin G. McManus S.J., a bearded traditionalist, arrived in Palau in 1948 and was responsible for compiling the first Palauan-English and English-Palauan dictionary. Father Tom Flavin S.J., a young man with a guitar and a Master's Degree in Sociology, rescued many a young person from the nightclubs of Palau, myself included. If one wanted guidance late at night after the bars had closed, the trick was to make sure that pebbles thrown on the rectory's tin roof did not fall over the bedroom of Father McManus. He was not a fan of late-night activities. Fathers Hoar and Flavin never seemed to mind being summoned in such a manner. During one such episode, about a dozen of us who needed sobering-up were loaded into two Mission pickups and driven to Renrak causeway, where we went skinny dipping under the full moon—boys on one side, girls on the other—the two priests ensuring against any cross migration.

Getting back to the dinner at the Wilson's house, we had just seated ourselves at the table when there was a commotion at the back door. Out from the kitchen strode one, Jack Adams, a tall, lanky Australian in his late fifties, not the most mannerly of men. "I heard there was some good cook'n and a wee-bit-a grog in this household," he bellowed in his vernacular. "Ah, I see there is. Where's my chair? Room should always be made at the table for the less fortunate. The Bible says so. Right, Padre?"

"I'm not sure there is such an exact translation, Jack, but you've got the general idea," replied Father Hoar. "The difficulty in this case arises from one's interpretation of the term 'less-fortunate.'"

"Jack, get that chair by the wall," said Peter. "There's room beside Paul. You're always welcome in this house. Satski, bring Jack some utensils, a plate, and a wine glass!"

Jack pushed in next to me. He smelled like a blend of several open liquor bottles. Not wanting to leave the doctor without at least one insult, Jack continued. "I see that you're drinking some Frog cab sav. I've got some better Aussie Merlot in the pickup for a follow-up after this bloody fermentation's been laid to rest."

Jack was one of those Pacific Island characters who one remembers for a lifetime. It would be generous to characterize Jack as a "diamond in the rough."

His arrival only added to my concerns about how the evening might unfold among the guests sitting at this table. Jack had been a machinist and engineer on an Australian cargo ship that ran aground on a reef off Ponape Island in the late 1940s. After the wreck, Jack jumped ship and remained in Ponape. There he managed to marry Yvette Eischarts, the only child of the largest European land owner, Carlos Eischarts. Since then, while working for the Trust Territory Government, Jack had overseen several large construction projects, among them the causeway to the Ponape airport and the harbor at Tinian Island. Jack was temporarily in Palau dismantling some unused radio towers, so Peter had asked him to moonlight at the boatyard machining parts for Van Schoote's ketch, *Kate*.

"How are the gears coming along for Alphonse's boat?" asked Peter.

"Fuck me dead, I've been flat out work'n on'm, but I know it's absolutely not going to work," said Jack. "The gear ratio that ya specified is not nearly enough to move that hefty rudder while under sail. I've made what ya wanted, but that fucker won't work unless ya put a big wheel on it, and such a wheel is too big to fit under the mizzen boom. The whole idea is a dog that won't hunt."

"So does that mean I have to leave next week using my old tiller handle?" asked Van Schoote.

"Well mate, yu'd be a fucken drango to use that rig that I'm make'n for Pete. There's just no room in that cockpit for a proper sized wheel," replied Jack.

"No matter what, I must leave by next Wednesday. The season is late. Once the trades pick up there's no way to sail against them. I'll be stuck here for another six months."

"Don't worry, Doc. We'll have you ready to go by next Wednesday," said Peter. "But if Jack is right, you may have to stick with your tiller."

"Yu bet your ars I'm right," commented Jack.

"We can deal with this later," said Peter. "Right now, let's enjoy this roast beef. By the way, Doc, do you have crew or are you going solo?"

"I have one fellow from the Hall Islands who's working at Van Camp and wants to go home, but right now there are only two of us," replied Van Schoote.

Out of the blue without thinking about it, I asked, "Can a person like me go along?"

Van Schoote looked at me seriously and asked, "Do you get seasick?"

"No," I replied. That was a lie.

"Have you ever sailed before?"

"No."

"You do realize that this is no easy trip? It'll be nothing but hard work. Those fools in TT headquarters think I lead a glorious, romantic life, sailing around. There is no glory out there. If you fall overboard, you're dead. That's it! Lots of bad things can happen. You had better be sure you really want to go. And you had better be absolutely ready to do exactly as I say, no matter how you hurt and no matter how your body and mind wants to do otherwise."

"I understand," I said. "I want to go and I'll do whatever you tell me to do."

"Boy, you'd better put some restrictions on that," muttered Jack under his breath.

"Well then," said Van Schoote, "You can come along, that is if Peter okays it. You seem like one of the more level-headed Peace Corps that I've met. Most of them are, what do you say, 'flower children.' And if you go, you're going to learn there's nothing glorious about long distance sailing. It's just a lot of uncomfortable hard work, and the ocean is relentlessly trying to kill you."

"And sometimes it does," interjected Jack.

"He's level-headed and reliable," said Peter, "and it's fine with me if he goes. I think you'd learn a lot on such a trip, Paul. But what about Peace Corps? They might not approve. It is somewhat dangerous, you know."

"Could we just not tell them?" I asked.

"I don't want the responsibility of you being on board against Peace Corps wishes," said Van Schoote. "They already hate me. You go talk to them and see what they say. And let me know right away. I've got to plan the food and supplies."

"How many days will it take?" I asked.

"Twelve to twenty days, depending on the wind and sea conditions," replied Van Schoote. "Any faster than that would be a miracle. *Kate* is a cruiser, not built for speed, and we're late in the season, so the wind might not cooperate."

"I'll check with Peace Corps tomorrow and let you know," I said. That was the serendipitous beginning of a great adventure.

Around 10:00 p.m. when the after-dinner cognac started to flow, I gave my thanks to Ann and Peter, avoided Satski, and walked home. I have no idea as to how the rest of that night transpired, but the elements for incendiary conflict were primed and in place.

The next day I went to the Peace Corps office and requested the standard one-month vacation allowed to all volunteers. According to the rules, I could spend that month anywhere in Micronesia excluding Guam, and Peace Corps covered the air fares. I requested vacation to Truk. The Palau Peace Corps Director, Dirk Ballendorf, approved my round-trip travel, without knowing the truth about how I would be getting to Truk. He never found out until I told him the true story years later after he had gotten his Doctorate at Harvard and become a professor of Micronesian history at the University of Guam.

On the morning of September 20, 1967, we departed Malakal Harbor with the outgoing tide—a Hall Islander named Ipuan, Van Schoote, and me. Our objective was Moen, an island in Truk Lagoon, some 1,400 miles to the east-northeast. The sea was calm and windless, so we motored eastward at a steady five knots. By noon Palau had disappeared from the western horizon and we became a lone speck in a vast ocean that met the sky in all directions.

In the afternoon Ipuan spotted a floating log, so we motored around it with trolling lines out. Three times around resulted in us boarding eight mahi-mahis. Ipuan filleted one of them for Van Schoote to use in our fish soup dinner. The other seven fish Ipuan cleaned in salt water and hung from the mainmast spar. For the next sixteen days, he periodically climbed that mast and ate some of that sun-dried fish. There are no flies and few contaminants in the open ocean. At night the phosphorescence in the blood of the stomach cavities glowed as the carcasses dangled in the wind, an earie sight from below.

That evening the sails finally caught wind. Unfortunately, it blew out of the northeast, necessitating a close-hauled tack that allowed only slow, torturous eastward progress. Day after day we beat into the wind and waves. Spray continuously blew over the port bow. We were lucky to make two or three knots an hour. At the end of my four-hour watches, I slid below deck into one of two bunks at the bow, my clothes damp, my eyebrows white with dried salt, every muscle aching. With a life preserver as a pillow, exhaustion brought sleep on the unpadded bunk that pitched and yawed in continuous rhythm to the sound of water against the hull. Any change in that sound and rhythm was an alarm bell that signaled a variation in speed or direction, warranting a trip above deck to ensure that all was well.

Thus we continued, two awake, one asleep. Van Schoote planned to stay well south of the main Caroline Islands, because encountering a reef under sail at night is most dangerous. *Kate* had no electronic navigation equipment or radar. GPS had not yet been invented. Our location estimates were determined by sextant—sun for latitude, stars for longitude. On some days clouds prevented these measurements, but we knew that our extended close-hauled tack had forced us somewhat south of east. Unless wind conditions changed, at some point we would have to tack back north to regain latitude.

To further complicate things, the engine stopped working. That meant we were without emergency propulsion and unable to charge the batteries that powered our running lights and radio, the only means of line-of-sight communication with other vessels or islands. Boatyard repairs on the engine had apparently been inadequate. Van Schoote vented his frustration about this to whomever happened to be with him on deck. "If you die out here, you can blame Peter Wilson and that *merde* boatyard of his. I'll never go back there again."

In the morning on the seventh day, after calculating our position, Van Schoote thought that we should be nearing our first landmark, Eauripik Atol. If we were on course the island should pass north of us at some point during the day.

"Ipuan, you radar. Climb the mast and look for land. We should see island today."

"No need climb, *sencho*," replied Ipuan. "Island is over there." He pointed to the northeast horizon. Neither Van Schoote nor I could see anything but ocean and sky in that direction.

"Go up there anyway," said Van Schoote. "I want to make sure it's Eauripik and not Ifaluk or Woleai."

Ipuan grudgingly ascended. Standing on the main mast spar atop his dangling mahi-mahi, he pointed in the same direction that he had previously pointed. "There," he yelled. "It's atoll. Two, maybe three islands. Got people. We stop?"

"No stopping. No time. We need to keep going. Are the islands far apart on the reef or close together?" yelled Van Schoote.

"Two or three islands, far apart," was the reply.

Then Van Schoote turned to me. "Sounds like Eauripik. I don't want to run the passage into that lagoon without an engine. We're not stopping."

It took another hour before I could see the green of land passing to the north. Eauripik was the most southern island in this part of the Carolines, so we were apparently on course. For the rest of our passage Van Schoote referred to Ipuan as Radar because of his spectacular eyesight and sense of the sea.

On the eighth day, the wind shifted further to the north. We held an easterly course with ease. But as the wind swung, it picked up intensity, and we soon had to reef the main and mizzen sales while taking some pretty big quartering swells.

I was at the tiller when Van Schoote emerged from below. "Radar says there's a typhoon to the northeast of us. If he's right, we can expect things to get smokey and rough as the wind works its way to the north and then to the northwest. Hold that compass heading at 80 degrees. We may be in for quite a ride. Keep your eyes open. I'm going to get some sleep before the shit arrives." I noticed that Radar was already asleep on the windward deck, his body propped against the exterior cabin wall.

For the next six hours I held to 80 degrees, and it seemed we were making good easterly progress, but the swells were increasing as the wind shifted further north. Even with reefed sails, *Kate* was heeling over at about 30 degrees, so I decided to ease the main and mizzen sheets just a little. My experiment seemed to work. We heeled over a bit less, the telltales streamed better, and *Kate* seemed to pick up speed. I was congratulating myself when Van Schoote, having felt the change, stuck his head out from the cabin. "What did you do?" he growled.

"I let out the main and mizzen sheets. The wind is moving more to the north," I said.

"Well, I guess not all Peace Corps are stupid. Looks like you're learning something. Loosen the jib a little too. That should help with the steering. Here." He handed me a bowl of rice with a hunk of canned mackerel on top and a bottle of water. "Make sure you eat this. It's going to be a long night. Call me if anything seems wrong and wake me in two hours if I'm not up. Are you holding 80 degrees?"

"Yes, sir," I replied. "Eighty degrees." He disappeared below. Ipuan was still on the foredeck against the cabin wall. It was impossible to determine whether he was sleeping or awake. He had not moved in hours.

The blueness of sky and sea had turned to grey as an ominous haze obscured the sun. I ate the rice and mackerel with my fingers while reflecting on the vastness of ocean around me. We were but an insignificant chip of wood at the mercy of powerful and indifferent natural forces that cared not whether we lived or died, succeeded or failed. *Kate*'s wake provided the only sign that we had traveled this way, and it vanished in less than a minute after our passing. Should we disappear below these waves, there would be no remaining sign of our existence and purpose. It struck me that our position on Kate was analogous to that of humanity on Earth as it passes through the cosmos. I asked that God protect us on our trip and all of humanity on theirs.

By late afternoon, the three of us were on deck, I having had the least sleep. Ipuan was downing a chunk of odiferous mahi-mahi protein, which he had ripped from his larder on the mainmast spar. Van Schoote had finished installing the storm jib and was stuffing the larger working jib below deck through the forehatch. I was still at the tiller, where I'd been all day. The sunset was an ominous blood-red color. The wind was now almost due north, and because of that, I'd been forced to steer a more northerly course at 60 degrees. Van Schoote said that was okay because we would eventually be forced to run south with the big waves when they came. I wondered how much bigger they could get. They seemed pretty big already. I had no idea what was yet to come.

The dim, garnet sunset had morphed into blackness, I was sent below to sleep and advised to keep my flashlight at the ready. We didn't use deck lighting or running lights in order to conserve our battery power for emergencies. Even the tiny compass light was used sparingly. Exhausted, I immediately dropped into a deep sleep.

The next thing I knew, Van Schoote was yelling down the passage way. "Paul, on deck now!" At that same moment, *Kate* heeled over to port so that I was thrown out of the bunk into a standing position. As I struggled through the galley toward the aft ladder, my bare feet felt dampness, and I could hear the sound of sloshing bilgewater. Once on deck I was greeted by blackness and torrents of wind-driven rain mixed with salt spray. One could tell the two apart because the ocean spray was decidedly warmer. Ipuan was in the cockpit at the tiller, his drenched ghostly form illuminated by the compass light. Van Schoote, a flashlight in his teeth, was lashing down the most extreme reef points on the mainsail. I worked my way toward him, thankful for the teak handholds along the cabin roof. The deck was awash and movement required coordination of all fours. *Kate* was tossing like a cork in a millstream. There were no safety harnesses and we wore no lifejackets. Early on in our voyage, Van Schoote had said, "If you go overboard at night, you're dead. Wearing a life jacket just means you will die more slowly."

When we finished tying off the last reefpoint and hoisted the abridged mainsail, Van Schoote could finally extract the flashlight from his mouth. That unleashed a torrent of French that I didn't understand, other than to note a high frequency of the words *merde*, *putain*, and *connard*, the general sense of which I had learned while skiing in Europe.

He next yelled at me in English. "Go to the aft cabin and pump that bilge pump as if your life depends on it, because it does. Didn't you see that water in the bilge when you came through the galley? That fuckin Peter Wilson and his god-damn boatyard are going to kill us. They couldn't be bothered to seriously caulk anything above the waterline, the lazy bastards." As I made my way on all fours toward the aft hatch that lay astern of the cockpit, I heard Van Schoote scream into the night, "Fuck you, Peter Wilson!" followed by a stream of French or Flemish that I judged to convey similar sentiments.

Dropping down through the hatch into the blackness of the aft cabin, I found my feet in water up to my ankles. With the flashlight hung from a deck beam, I wrestled the hatch cover back into place and found the bilge pump. Its wooden handle moved back and forth over a 160-degree arc—one direction for suction, the other for discharge. Sitting on a step stool, I began to pump—left-right, left-right. To save batteries I extinguished the light and pumped in darkness, the water sloshing around my feet as it rushed back and forth with *Kate*'s violent motion. There was no ventilation, no window, no way of knowing what was happening on deck. I was protected from the wind and rain and warmer than those on deck, but I was isolated and alone, unable to see my fate yet certain that it wasn't far away.

The hull's every creak and groan and unexpected motion brought added anxiety. Would *Kate*'s three-inch teak planking and her oak ribs hold up under this pounding? The musty, dank air reeked of diesel fumes. I vomited until there was nothing left in my stomach to vomit. I kept pumping, changing positions when necessary to rest one arm or the other. At times I fought to maintain balance on the stool, wondering if *Kate* would roll completely over and that would be the end for me. It was the first time in my life that I had ever seriously reflected on the possibility of death. I prayed several times, thanking God for the many benefits that had come my way in life and asking that He (She or It) see fit to extend my time on this earth beyond this present predicament.

After two or three hours, I sensed that I was making some headway. The bilge water was now only covering my toes. That hopeful realization lightened my spirit as I doggedly pumped onward. Despite my inability to see above deck, I knew we were running fast in a following sea, because the propeller shaft ran directly beneath me. The gear box had been set to neutral, so the propeller and shaft could rotate freely. Whenever *Kate* descended the face of a wave, the propeller spun just like a windmill. That caused the shaft bearings to make a whining sound under my stool. The intensity and length of each whine signaled the relative height and steepness of the wave face we were descending. By this measure the waves were getting bigger. I kept pumping. The adrenalin-fed rhythm of sound and motion overcame time and conscious thought.

At some point the hatch cover opened. Van Schoote peered down from above. "Here's something to eat." He handed me a water bottle and a package of crab cracker sea biscuits. "How are you doing? Apparently you're making progress. We haven't yet sunk."

"I'm okay. The water's down below the floorboards now. When I started pumping it was around my ankles." Without stopping I drank the whole bottle of water.

"I didn't realize I was so thirsty."

"You've been down there for six hours. I don't need dehydrated, hypoglycemic crew members. We've got enough problems as it is, but things are looking up. Radar thinks we're past the worst of it. We'll have these big following seas all day, so we've got no choice but to run with them. We're making good progress to the east-southeast. Tomorrow we can steer further north and make up the latitude. Take a break? Come up on deck. Fill your water bottle in the galley and drink it all. There's some chocolate and an open jar of peanut butter in the sink. They're not bad together, and they'll keep your energy up. Then get back to pumping. I want that bilge completely dry before dark."

I was so stiff and cramped that I could barely crawl to a seat in the cockpit. There I remained for a few minutes eating the crackers, inhaling the fresh air, and watching the giant, whitecapped walls of water building behind us and on all sides. Ipuan didn't acknowledge my presence. He appeared to be in a trance, wholly one with the sea around us. Throughout the night he had been at the tiller, guiding *Kate* safely down the face of each wave as it passed. He remained at his post throughout this day and into evening. I can still see those bloodshot eyes, that salt encrusted face, that unshakable focus on the job at hand. *Kate* was a thirty-five-ton surfboard. He was the master surfer. We were along for the ride. The waves came in sets, each just a bit different. If *Kate* broached on the face of a wave, we would capsize. Without Ipuan's tenacious excellence in seamanship, I most likely wouldn't be writing this memoir. Whenever I hear Westerners criticize Micronesians as lethargic, lazy, unfocused, or unskilled, I think of Radar, a simple fisherman from the Hall Islands who undoubtedly saved my life and who most certainly left an indelible mark of respect in my mind.

After a bit I summoned the energy to climb down into the galley and eat a hunk of dark chocolate slathered in peanut butter. It tasted wonderful. Ipuan would have none of it. He wanted his fish from the mainmast, but neither Van Schoote nor I were willing to climb there, so he settled for an open can of sardines in tomato sauce. I returned to pumping, this time with the hatch cover ajar for better air and light. By day's end the swells were somewhat reduced and the wind was coming from the west-northwest. We were making excellent time running east-northeast, our compass back to a steady 80 degrees. In early evening, Van Schoote took over the tiller while Ipuan slept on the foredeck. He didn't like going below where he was out of touch with nature. I slept below until midnight when Van Schoote woke me to take over at the tiller. "Just hold 80 degrees," he said as he went below. It wasn't long before I noticed a star-lit figure sitting cross-legged on the foredeck. It was Ipuan keeping a watchful eye on me and our surroundings.

The next days were bright and sunny with moderate seas and winds from the west. *Kate* ran as fast as her cruising hull allowed, eight or nine knots, under genoa and spinnaker. Long after Radar announced its arrival, Van Schoote and I sighted the island of Pulusuk, our marker for holding an east-northeast course on the last leg to Truk Lagoon. Lest the reader think that my reference to the "arrival" of an island is inappropriate, it's important to understand that traditional Micronesian navigation techniques require that the navigator conceive of himself and his vessel as being stationary while all physical objects (wind, waves, clouds, fish, birds, sun, stars, islands) pass over and around him. In the mind of an islander like Ipuan, islands arrive and depart. The vessel and its contents remain stationary.

The weather held, and sixteen days after leaving Malakal Harbor in Palau, the 1,463-foot tip of Mount Winipot arrived on the northeastern horizon. The mountain's base, Tol Island, lay inside Truk Lagoon. Our destination was in sight. However, there was a problem: the wind had stopped. We were becalmed. Without a working engine, there was no choice but to wait. The ocean was mirror-glass calm. Our sails remained up in hopes of catching even the slightest whiff of air, but their only immediate service was to provide shade from the blistering tropical sun. We put a rope ladder overboard and the three of us swam and took salt water baths in the 85-degree ocean. That evening we dined on a fine meal of canned mackerel over rice with lemon juice and soy sauce. Ipuan had already consumed the last of his pungent mahi-mahi. Sleep that night was difficult due to the incessant flopping of windless sails as *Kate* rocked from side to side.

The next morning, Mount Winipot was nowhere to be seen. During the night ocean currents had pushed us away from Truk in a direction known only to Ipuan, who said he still knew the lagoon's position. Van Schoote's sextant and some laborious calculations proved Ipuan right, of course. Toward evening a light wind filled our sails, but Van Schoote didn't want to attempt entering the lagoon after dark without an engine, so we hove-to and lowered the sails for the night. At dawn we set out to rediscover Mt. Winipot. It soon appeared a little north of where we had expected.

"You can never tell in what direction the currents will push you," said Van Schoote. "Sometimes they run three or four knots, and when they hit a big stationary mass like Truk Lagoon, they create unpredictable gyres."

"How far are we from the lagoon?" I asked.

"When you and I can see the top of that peak, we're forty to fifty miles out from the south pass. Radar can probably find it at sixty or seventy miles, but he's looking for signs of the mountain, not the mountain itself. I suppose he can detect changes in atmospheric conditions, lighting, clouds, colors that surround the mountain and indicate its location well before it can actually be seen. Anyway, if this wind holds, we'll be through the pass by early afternoon and tied up at Moen dock before dark. There should be enough battery left so that once we're inside the lagoon, I can radio Public Works to expect us."

As we sailed closer, islands popped up all over the horizon. Truk Lagoon is one of the world's largest. Its fringing reefs are 140 miles in circumference. Sixty-nine islands exist along its edges and within its 820-square-mile lagoon. The task of finding and navigating the south pass seemed mindboggling to me. My untrained eye couldn't judge the size and proximity of islands on the horizon. When approaching a pass under sail, knowledge of tidal conditions is extremely important. A lagoon the size of Truk contains immense volumes of water that must flow in and out twice daily. Passes can become fast-flowing rivers in a matter of minutes. Experienced judgment was required to determine, on the move, whether reefs were sufficiently submerged to accommodate *Kate's* draft. Luckily, Ipuan and Van Schoote knew these waters well, and by noon we were sailing through the south pass and headed north on a steady east wind. Our objective was Moen Island, the center of Truk District economy and governance.

For three hours or so we sailed north up the center of the lagoon, avoiding reef shallows and islands as we went. When we approached Moen Island, a government launch met us, threw a line, and towed us to a dock near the town center. We had arrived. It was the late afternoon of October 9, 1967. In celebration Van Schoote opened a bottle of warm Champagne. Ipuan didn't think much of it, but drank a little in order to be polite. Van Schoote and I happily drank the rest of his share.

Alphonse M. Van Schoote, Ipuan, Paul Callaghan on board *Kate* in Truk Lagoon, 1967

"So you've made your first ocean voyage under sail," said Van Schoote. "Now you're a sailor, and I hope you'll tell all those Trust Territory officials how glorious and romantic it is to sail with Alphonse Van Schoote. They think I'm just playing around out here, wasting public money. Those bureaucrats don't give a damn about the sick people on Namonuito, Pulap, Puluwat, or Pulusuk. If people on those islands get sick, they should just wait for the doctor on the field trip ship, which stops for a day or two twice a year, that is if the weather's not too bad. I go there at least four times a year and stay until I've done all I can do. It's not glorious and it's not romantic. It's just a lot of fuck'n work. None of those TT officials would do it. They should pay me triple time."

"Thank you for taking me along with you," I said. "I'm not really a sailor now. I've just begun to understand how much I don't know."

"You held up well out there. You can sail with me any time. Why don't you tell Peace Corps that you want to transfer to our Project HELP and sail with me full-time? Oh, but then they might think you were nothing but a glory seeking romantic. You better go back to Peter Wilson. He needs someone to clean up after him. Maybe you can improve that boatyard, but for sure I'll never take *Kate* back to that place."

"Thank you for your offer," I said, "but I can't leave the house of Ibedul, or Peace Corps would have a fit."

"Well, you're welcome to sleep at my house if you're tired of *Kate*. Radar will stay onboard tonight and keep an eye on things."

"I think I'd like to stay aboard tonight too," I said. "It feels really funny walking on land. The ground feels like it's moving, especially after this Champagne. Tomorrow I'll come to your place, if that's all right?"

"That's fine. It's always hard to walk on land once you've gotten your sea legs. It'll take about a day on land to get settled again. You're welcome to stay at my house or on the boat for as long as you're here on Moen."

"Thanks," I said. "I'll come to your house tomorrow night. I just want one more night on *Kate*."

"Watch out, if sailing gets into your blood, it might change your life," he said with a smile as he stepped onto the pier to talk with some government officials.

That evening several of Ipuan's relatives or friends stopped by. They sat on the dock drinking beer, talking, and listening to taped Trukese music on a well-used, battery-operated cassette player. I bought a six-pack of Budweiser at a nearby store and joined them for a while. Not understanding a word of Hall Island language, it was hard to be fully included, but they were friendly and shared some of their food. I drank a couple of beers and headed off to bed on the hard wood of my favorite forward bunk. It seemed a little less comfortable than it had during my exhausted sleeps at sea.

The next morning, I awoke shortly after dawn to the sound of an outboard motor and a small boat bumping up against *Kate*'s hull. Once on deck I could see that it was Ipuan in a boat that looked to be about sixteen feet long with a 25-hp. outboard. Visible in the boat were a fifty-gallon drum of gasoline, two cases of motor oil, and a gallon bottle of water. He had just cast off and was organizing some provisions when I called down to him.

"Ipuan, where are you going?"

"I go Nomwin, Mr. Paul. See wife and son. You good sailor and good peacecorps. *Kinisou chapur, kene nom* (thank you, goodbye)."

Nomwin is one of two atolls in the Hall Islands, approximately ninety miles north of Truk Lagoon. Much of his trip would be in the open ocean, and I was quite sure he carried no safety equipment or compass.

Ipuan waved as he turned into the channel. I waved back. I have never seen him again, but I value his compliment: "You good sailor and a good peacecorps," as much as any I have ever received. I am remiss that I don't even know his full name nor the proper spelling of Ipuan.

That same day I moved into Van Schoote's government-supplied Quonset housing. There I slept on the living room floor for five nights before flying back to Palau via Guam. By chance, there was a female Peace Corps volunteer sharing that same living room floor with me. Her name was Shirley Holland. At the time, she was helping with a Peace Corps training program on the nearby island of Udot. During her days off she sometimes hitched a boat ride to Moen and made use of free lodging on Van Schoote's living room floor.

Shirley was a top-notch executive secretary. Her services were in demand throughout Micronesia, so she was one of those volunteers who moved around a lot, working at times for Peace Corps administrators in various locations, the Congress of Micronesia in Saipan, and even a short time for Peter Wilson in Palau. Throughout our Peace Corps days and in our subsequent lives, Shirley and I have crossed paths numerous times, as reflected in succeeding chapters of this memoir.

While on Moen, I flirted with the idea of flying to Ponape Island. A fourteen-passenger Grumman Albatross SA-16 seaplane made that run twice weekly. I had heard that Ponape was quite beautiful, but my only personal contact there was Jack Adams, and he was still in Palau. I also knew that Toshiro Paulis had several relatives living on Ponape Island, but I had neglected to secure Tosh's introduction to them. In the end I decided against visiting Ponape because if for some reason the plane had mechanical problems, and it often did, I could get stuck there and miss my return booking to Palau.

However, those five days on Moen were not wasted. I contacted a Trukese fisheries conservation officer named Town Paul, whom I had gotten to know while he was training in Palau. For years Town Paul had been a well-known Trukese poacher, an egregious user of reef destroying explosive and chemical fishing techniques. Peter Wilson had decided to make Town Paul a paid conservation officer in hopes that a regular paycheck might redirect his knowledge of Truk Lagoon into a force for good. The jury was still out on whether Peter's experiment had born fruit. However, Town used the government conservation boat on three separate days to transport me on visits to the islands of Dublon, Fefan, and Parem. Of the three, Dublon was especially interesting because it had been the headquarters of the Japanese military administration prior to and during WWII. The remaining underground bunkers and war relics were fascinating.

I also visited the office of Chief Petrus Mailo. Ibedul had given me an envelope to deliver to Petrus. When I accomplished that task, the Chief invited me to lunch at the Truk Trading Company. The two of us sat together for a couple of hours talking about the work of Peace Corps, Van Schoote's Project HELP, and my recent passage from Palau. I believe that few other Westerners have had such an opportunity to interact personally with one of the most respected traditional Micronesian leaders of his time.

The flight back to Palau was uneventful, with the exception of a chocolate-covered Dairy Queen cone during transit in Guam.

But that is not the end of this story. Two years later in late July or early August of 1969, I had arrived in Guam after finishing my M.B.A. at San Jose State and was temporarily living with friends near the Micronesian Hotel. One morning I decided to eat breakfast in the hotel's restaurant. Upon entering the lobby, I encountered Alphonse Van Schoote. He greeted me warmly.

"Hello, Paul. It's good to see you. What have you been doing? Are you still with the Peace Corps?"

"No, since leaving the Peace Corps I've been studying in California. I just arrived here the day before yesterday from Honolulu. I'm on my way to Palau because Peter said he would like to hire me to manage the boatyard."

"So you are free without employment?" he asked.

"I don't have a job yet, if that's what you mean," I said, "but I've got some offers here on Guam. The thing is, I'd rather work at the boatyard. There's a lot of potential there."

"You know what I think of that fucking boatyard," said Van Schoote. "That's why I am here. We're on our way to Kobe, where serious professionals can give *Kate* a thorough going over. Why don't you come along? There are only two of us. A third crew person to share the load makes things much easier. We'll drop you off on the way back in Guam or Palau, or wherever you like. Or, you could come to work with me in Truk at Project HELP."

"When are you leaving?" I asked.

"Tomorrow morning."

"How long will it take in Japan?"

"Two to three months I suspect. Hopefully quicker."

"I'm sorry, Alphonse. I just can't go with you this time. I promised Peter and others that I'd come to Palau in the next few days," I said.

"I'll miss your company. Good luck with that fucken boatyard. Maybe you can make it into something better than it is now. But you've got your work cut out for you. *Au revoir,*" he said as he turned down the hall toward his room.

"Have a safe passage," I yelled after him.

The next morning, forty-three-year-old Alphonse Van Schoote and one Trukese named Amanto sailed north out of Guam's Apra Harbor. They were due to arrive in Kobe, Japan, on August 19, 1969. They never arrived. The ketch *Kate* and her crew of two have never been seen or heard from again. *Kate* could have hit some floating object causing her to spring a severe leak. They might have been run down in the dark by a passing freighter. They could have caught on fire. No one will ever know.

So what kind of man was Dr. Alphonse M. Van Schoote: a dedicated humanitarian doctor or a narcissistic adventurer? I really don't know for sure, perhaps some combination of both. He was certainly an individualist. I only know that during a brief time on land and during eighteen fairly stressful days at sea, I never heard him say anything complimentary about any individual or organization, other than telling me that I "held up well." He continually demonstrated ethnocentric, colonialist, demeaning views of Micronesians, the very people he professed to help. He couldn't bother to address Ipuan by his proper name, despite the fact that this Trukese man was a team player and contributed much to our successful voyage. In my mind Van Schoote was like many foreigners who lived in Micronesia at the time: running away from something. That something may have been his perception of himself or others in his past life. In any case, he contributed to the richness of my life, and for that I am thankful.

*   *   *

I was at work the morning after my return from Truk. Only a few people knew about my sailing adventure. Peace Corps staff said nothing. If they knew anything, they probably decided to leave well enough alone. The Ibedul had not voiced any objection. I had delivered his message to Chief Petrus. I had returned safely and on time. Wilson was happy with my performance. All was well that ended well.

During the next eight months I settled into the rhythm of Palau Island life. On weekdays I normally awoke at 6:00 a.m., caught a ride to the Fisheries Office at 7:00 a.m., took a lunch break around noon, got a ride home before 6:00 p.m., showered, ate dinner, and held a homework session with the girls. After that, I might go directly to bed, or depending on Tasia's work schedule, I might walk down the road to her house, sometimes returning in the early morning hours.

My normal route home from Tasia's took me past the Koror Police Station, where a rotund, boisterous, jovial policeman habitually sat in the portico near the station door. As I passed, he invariably yelled in Palauan, "Where are you going? Where have you been?"

I always responded in the same way: "I'm going home; I've been fishing."

He would then laugh and say something like, "Same fish as last night?" or "You must be a good fisherman." We would both laugh as I proceeded on my way. Of course, he knew exactly where I had been and where I was going. I wish I could remember his name. He seldom let me pass without a bit of friendly harassment.

At every opportunity, I took *Orakiruu* south into the Rock Islands, sometimes alone, but often with Tasia or Toshiro and Bertha. They taught me much about the land and sea. I learned to navigate the labyrinth of islands between Koror and Peleliu, and to find the best locations for overnight living and fishing under various tidal and weather conditions. I learned how to spear, handline, and net fish, how to cook over an open fire, how to catch coconut crabs, harvest clams and seaweed, how to be comfortable in uncomfortable situations. Mostly I learned to appreciate the depth of my ignorance when it came to living in this unique tropical ocean world, so I determined to learn as much as I could in the time that remained to me. When not at home in Idid, I could be found at the boatyard, at the fisheries dock, or somewhere in or on the water.

I learned how to scuba dive and became quite comfortable working underwater. Using the Fisheries Department equipment, I accompanied Toshiro as he checked for leaks in the undersea water lines that ran between Babeldaob and Koror Islands. At one point I kept sharks at bay with a bang stick while Toshiro made nighttime underwater repairs to the *Emeraech*. We salvaged lost anchors, harvested giant clams, and speared innumerable fish. By the time I left Palau, I was a competent scuba diver and a passable spear fisherman.

As time passed, I became more Micronesian and less American. My attitudes and expectations changed to reflect the realities of my environment. I was forced to question and reevaluate many norms I had brought with me from America—the importance of time and punctuality, the worth of individualism, the benefit of planning, the wisdom of candor, the value of wealth and personal property, the meaning and purpose of love and marriage. I gained appreciation for the value of consensus as opposed to majority rule, for the power of extended family loyalty, for the importance of indirect discourse, patience, and sharing in the maintenance of personal relationships, for the dominance of nature over the efforts of man, for the skill of observation, and the importance of experience.

In early December of 1967 my parents sent supplies, party favors, and decorations for a children's Christmas party. Such events were seldom if ever undertaken in Palau, but with Tasia's help, we held a party for the children of Idid and Ngarkeswaol. A letter to my parents contains the following report:

Dear Mom and Dad … The Christmas party was thrown for about 20 kids from various parts of Koror. All the party items you sent proved a great success. You would have laughed at the setting—an old unoccupied house with no windows and many holes in the floor, commandeered from someone. The table was a 4x8 sheet of ¾ inch plywood from the boatyard, with an old steel bed frame stuck underneath for legs. Your table cloth did wonders for it. The kids had a great time pasting together the bells and decorating the Christmas tree. The meal consisted of gallons of watered-down Tang, 40 pounds of raw and fried tuna, handmade donuts with little black specks in them, that were not sesame seeds, a cake made from Bisquick, which had to have the worm larvae extracted first, candy coated tapioca, a green papaya salad, rice wrapped in seaweed, and tons more rice and shoyu sauce. It was all prepared by Anastasia and her brother, John, on a wood fire and single-burner kerosene stove … We had balloons for everyone, used the games you sent, plus decks of cards (both Japanese and American). Everything was a great success. You have made your Christmas mark in Palau.

On January 15, 1968, I wrote in a letter to my parents:

Everything going well here. Same old grind. I really enjoy my work more than anything I have ever done in my life. It's frustrating at times, but I am beginning to get a feel for the people. This place, its people, its beauty, its way of life, have become a part of me. You will really notice a change in this kid when I finally make it home … Both Peter Wilson and his assistant, Toshiro Paulis, have left for a conference in Manila. That leaves me as the acting Fisheries Management Biologist for the Trust Territory. I'll tell you, there are plenty of headaches on my shoulders for the next three weeks … I've got to run a boatyard and a fisheries program, and on top of that, the movie actor Lee Marvin will soon arrive with a cargo ship full of equipment to make a war movie on beaches near Koror—I've got my hands full."

The movie was titled *Hell in the Pacific*, starring Lee Marvin and Toshiro Mifune, a well-known Japanese samurai actor. A 539-foot ship was chartered to transport equipment and personnel to Palau. During filming, it remained in Koror harbor to provide accommodations for the film crew and actors. For several months Lee and his girlfriend, Michelle Triola, became quite the dignitaries around Koror town. It soon became clear to everyone that Lee was an infrequently sober alcoholic. It was Michelle who kept him going and got him to the sets on time. Luckily for Lee, there were few lines of dialogue in that movie script.

Several years later, Michelle sued Lee Marvin in a landmark California palimony suit. She, rightfully in my opinion, won the case and went on to live some thirty years with the actor Dick Van Dyke. Lee commissioned the building of a forty-six-foot sports fishing boat at the Palau boatyard. He named it *Ngerengchol* after the beach on which the movie was made. For several years thereafter he fished Palau's waters in an unsuccessful quest to catch a world record marlin. Later he moved the boat to Guam, where my friend Patrick Bryan operated it as a charter boat. The movie *Hell in the Pacific* may have had artistic qualities, but it was never acclaimed, and unlikely a financial success.

*   *   *

Those last few months of Peace Corps service passed quickly. As the end approached, I grew increasingly apprehensive about returning home. I knew that reentry into American society would be difficult. But I felt I must leave Palau in order to gain perspective before making a decision to return. My plan was to complete my MBA at San Jose State. That effort would take two semesters plus a summer school, during which time I intended to live alone and slowly unwind from being a Palauan.

When I departed Palau on July 16, 1968, I paid Tasia's fare so that she could accompany me as far as Hawaii. She had never before been outside Palau, and I delighted in seeing her react to the newness of things. Our trip took three weeks, as we spent time in Yap, Guam, Truk, Ponape, Kwajalein, and Majuro before reaching Hawaii. Along the way we encountered people that I knew or relatives and friends of Tasia. Pacific Islanders are interconnected in countless ways over many generations and long distances.

In Honolulu we stayed in Waikiki at the same hotel where I had stayed after Molokai training. Tasia was entranced by the elevators and escalators and bright, colorful lights. We bought an ice chest and filled it with things of value for her to carry home. We drove around Oahu, visited museums, went to movies, ate in restaurants. When I finally put her on that Continental Air Micronesia flight for Guam and Palau, she gave me a final lesson in Palauan stoicism. In those days one could accompany passengers to the boarding gate. There with head held high, she touched my face with her fingers, as if to make sure she could remember every facet. Then she turned and walked away down the boarding ramp without looking back. I didn't see her again for twenty-five years.

I returned to our hotel room and sobbed my heart out. The hardest part of my Peace Corps experience proved to be the leaving, not the arriving nor the day-to-day living. I knew at the time that I could, if I wished, remain in Palau. There was a place for me. I could fit in. Other volunteers had chosen to stay. It would be a simple lifestyle close to nature, something I had always wanted. But I also knew that if I chose to stay, it would be for my lifetime. Within a few years I would no longer be able to compete in the outside world. My thinking would become insular and my life island-paced. Deep inside I knew that I wanted more than that. I needed to finish my MBA and see what else the world had to offer. Tasia couldn't accompany me on my journey. She had not the skills to sustain herself in a fast-paced American world. She wouldn't feel at ease unless she was constantly by my side. I wasn't ready to accept that responsibility. Yet Tasia had stood beside me when I was ill-equipped to handle the intricacies of her world, and now I was not willing to do the same for her. Despite the pain and guilt, I chose to leave. To this day the thought of that parting remains one of extreme emotion. Tasia seemed to know from the beginning. Having been left behind before, she was better prepared. Whereas I, being young and egocentric, had lived for the present and denied the inevitable until the end, when reality came crashing down on me. Incidentally, all those Peace Corps who decided to remain in Palau are still living there today.

Several years after leaving Palau, I was happy to hear that Tasia had married a man named Baskasio Oiterong, a mathematics teacher at Palau High School and later at Palau Community College. I had occasion to meet him several times over the years. He impressed me as a quiet, thoughtful, kind person, exactly the partner Tasia deserved.

Evidence of Baskasio's character arose in 1995 when I and my Palauan wife, Nina, were attending an Education Ministry function on one of Palau's Rock Island beaches. My son Oldak, then five years old, was playing in the water between two moored boats. It was a dangerous place to play because the boats could drift together and smash the child between them. I hadn't noticed, but Baskasio did, and made a special effort to remove Oldak from harm's way. Later he gently admonished me in the Palauan way: "You know, Mr. Paul, we must pay attention to our small children. It's dangerous for them to play in the water between moored boats."

Later that same year, Nina and I were attending a function at a nightclub in Koror. At some point during the evening, Nina said, "Tasia is sitting with some people in a booth across the dance floor. Do you want to say hello?"

"Yes, okay," I said, with some trepidation. It had been more than twenty-five years. What could I say to her?

When we approached the dimly-lit booth, I saw perhaps six people sitting around a circular table. Tasia sat facing us, her face emotionless, but our eyes met in recognition. Her husband, Baskasio, sat beside her. For several minutes, Nina and I made small talk in Palauan with those at the table. At some point Tasia put out her hand as if to touch my face, as she had done in the airport years before. Without thinking, in front of everyone, I grasped her fingers, bent over, and kissed the back of her hand before touching it to my forehead, a sign of fealty and respect among Chamorros in the Mariana Islands, and known as such by Palauans as well. Nothing was said between us. I never saw her again. She has now passed away. I hope we can meet in the afterlife, should there be such a place.

As for the boatyard, my Accounting Report of Operations showed that although the net revenue was positive, it was insufficient to cover the essential government-subsidized salaries of Peter Wilson, Kiyoshi Matsumoto, and Toshiro Paulis. Unfortunately, my report played into the hands of some of Wilson's superiors, who felt that subsidized economic development was unwise. However, with the support of Van Camp Sea Food and Wilson's advocacy, the yard continued to function for several more years, providing employment, training, and a sense of pride to those who worked there. It is no longer in existence.

Chapter 11

University of Guam

Dad picked me up at the San Francisco airport in mid-August of 1968. After a day or two in Livermore, he and I drove to the Chester cabin, where we spent a week with Mom. I went fly fishing. Dad and I sawed and split wood. The three of us walked and talked together, each day swimming in the cold river. Despite having no basis upon which to understand my experiences, Mom and Dad listened attentively and empathized as best they could, asking questions that provoked answers of little meaning to them. However, that was exactly what I needed to begin reentry—an opportunity to vent and reconnect with my roots.

Within a couple of weeks, I had found an apartment in San Jose, off Winchester Boulevard, near the Winchester Mystery House. My draft board in Oakland appeared to have lost interest in me, and I made no effort to contact them. In a few months I would be twenty-six years old and no longer eligible for the draft. Classes began in early September, and I dove into my studies with abandon. The work provided an escape from the melancholy that I felt for Palau and for those I had left behind. At night I studied on the coffee table while sitting and sleeping on the floor. I ate rice, canned sardines, and lots of freeze-dried ramen noodle soup. I found taro at the Asian stores, but it didn't taste like the *kukau* in Palau. Sometimes I cried myself to sleep over the loss of Tasia and my Palauan world. It was little use talking to others about where I'd been. They couldn't relate to my experiences, and to a large extent, I had lost interest in theirs.

Other than essential academic contacts on campus, I stayed to myself, until one Sunday afternoon in late September. I was sunning myself after having swum several laps in the apartment's common area pool. My eyes were closed as I lay on my stomach in a poolside chase lounge. I heard a similar deck lounge being rolled up nearby but didn't bother opening my eyes until a woman's voice said, "Do you mind if I join you? This corner has the best sun."

Rolling onto my side, I said, "Sure. Have at it. I'm happy to share my sun." She was a woman of medium height, maybe two or three years older than I, with shoulder length black hair. She wore a one-piece black swimsuit, black sandals, dark glasses, and had no jewelry or wedding ring.

"Thank you," she said as she deposited her towel and dark glasses on the lounge chair, slipped out of her sandals and dove into the pool, just in front of a sign that said no diving.

When she returned a few minutes later, and had gotten her pleasing form situated on the lounge chair, I asked, "Do you swim here often?"

"No, just sometimes on weekends or holidays when it's a nice day. It's usually too cold by the time I get home from work."

"And what do you do?" I asked.

"I'm a nursing instructor at San Jose City College. I saw you leaving with some books under your arm. Are you a student?"

"Yes, I'm working on my M.B.A. at San Jose State," I replied. "My name's Paul, Paul Callaghan."

"I'm Rose," she said.

"Roses are beautiful. You do justice to your name," I said with a grin. I seldom said stupid things like that, but for some reason the words just flowed out of my mouth.

Her retort was immediate, "And I believe that's called Irish blarney. Callaghan is an Irish name, is it not?"

"Okay, you got me on that one," I said. "So do you have a last name?"

"It's Fadel-Idriss. Rose Fadel-Idriss."

"For sure that's not an Irish name. What is it?"

"I'm Armenian. Do you know where Armenia is?"

"I honestly don't. Some place in Eastern Europe?"

"Yes, what's left of Armenia exists in Eastern Europe, but it has been absorbed into other countries. Millions of Armenians have been slaughtered or scattered to the wind, and here I am. My homeland is now part of Turkey."

"The Irish were scattered to the wind too, by the potato famine, and here I am."

"Yes," she replied, "but the Irish still have a country to return home to, should they wish to do so."

Over the next few months, Rose and I were frequently together. I found her to be both sensual and intriguing. Her lightning-fast mind operated under a cloak of modesty and concern for others. Every minute with her was stimulating, both mentally and physically. Although neither of us could relate to the other's past, we had something in common. She was an immigrant, and I was at that moment in my life, a pseudo-immigrant. Neither of us felt that we fit comfortably into the fabric of American society. Being together provided and escape for us both.

Rose's parents had fled to Syria during the Armenian genocide in Turkey. She was born and raised to a young age in Syria. At some point she and her mother, I never heard mention of a father, immigrated to America as refugees. Rose had graduated with honors from Stanford, with a Master's Degree in Psychiatric Nursing. Her mind was exceptional in many respects, but she was particularly amazing when it came to card games. She was a master duplicate bridge player, apparently quite well known in Palo Alto and South Bay bridge circles.

Sometimes Rose would, in her words, "exercise my mind and sharpen my focus." This was done by fanning out, face up on the table, a well shuffled deck of cards. After a minute or two of concentration, she then had me close the deck and peel off the cards, one at a time from the top. She could name each card before she saw it, all the way through the deck, and at any point tell me what cards of each value and suit remained in the deck.

We once went skiing together at Heavenly Valley near Lake Tahoe. After dinner at a Harrah's Casino in Stateline, Rose asked, "Would you mind if I played a little blackjack."

"No," I replied. "But I don't like to gamble. I always lose."

"That's okay. It's better if you don't come with me anyway. Maybe you can have some dessert in that coffee shop. I'll only be a half hour or so."

In about thirty minutes, she appeared at my table with two men in suits, one on each side or her. "Paul, we have to leave. These gentlemen are escorting me out, and they were kind enough to allow me to let you know. We must go now."

Once outside I asked, "What was that all about?"

"They don't like card counters at their tables. Let's try that casino down the street. I'd like to play a little more. Do you mind?"

"Sure, let's go," I said. "Anything to get inside and out of this snow storm." Big flakes were beginning to cover us as we hurried along, arm in arm, in the quiet of falling white. *Tomorrow will bring some powder skiing*, I thought as the lights of our destination grew closer.

Upon entering the doors and shaking off the snow from our clothing, we were met by men in suits who suggested that "card counters" were not welcome at their establishment, and we should move on.

Returning in the direction we had come, Rose said, "I'm sorry. Apparently word travels fast around here. I guess that's it for tonight. Here, you take these chips and cash them in at Harrah's when we pass by. I'll wait for you at the car."

I did as she said, and that handful of chips resulted in proceeds of $520. Enough to pay for our weekend trip, after refunding Rose's initial one-hundred-dollar stake.

Among her many facets, Rose was an opera enthusiast. For several seasons she had worked as a volunteer usher at the San Francisco Opera House. Once the curtain lifts and the doors close, ushers are allowed to sit in empty seats or on the steps of aisles. As Rose put it, "a way to see the opera for free."

Since she was a regular and knew on a first-name basis those in charge of ticket sales and security, Rose had me approved as a volunteer usher. On opera nights, Rose and I, in semiformal dress, drove to San Francisco early enough to eat a light meal at one of her favorite Greek or Armenian restaurants. She made sure that I knew the story and history of the opera we were about to see. We ushered in the highest balcony section because of a little-known and well-kept secret. When the doors closed, we found empty seats in the last and highest row. Somehow the sound from the orchestra and stage wrapped around the domed roof and showered that back row with amazing acoustical clarity. Despite an immense distance to the stage, every word of dialogue and every note of music rang clear in those seats. With Rose's opera glass, the experience was far superior to other seats in the house.

After the opera ended, we often sought out one of San Francisco's bagel shops. Rose knew the best ones. Or we visited a Middle Eastern bar or restaurant that provided belly dance entertainment. Rose was, as she put it, "a student of the art of belly dance." The one time that she performed for me in traditional attire at her apartment, I thought that she surely must be a reincarnated Queen of Sheba or Cleopatra herself. I did my best to perform as I envisioned Mark Anthony might have done. It was a memorable evening.

Our relationship ended in a most unexpected way. Sometime in early 1969, I had gone skiing for the weekend. Upon returning to my studio apartment, skis and poles in hand, late on Sunday night, I realized that the door was unlocked. Had I departed without locking it? Upon entering I saw the lights were on. At that instant two female voices yelled in unison, "Surprise! Welcome home!" It took me a moment to recognize their faces—Jean Waring and Shirley Holland. Both were ex-volunteers from Palau. Jean had served in the village of Ngchesar on the island of Babeldaob. Shirley, as previously mentioned, had served at various posts in Micronesia.

Dumbfounded, I blurted out, "What are you guys doing here? How did you get in?"

Shirley spoke, "We convinced the manager to let us in. It wasn't hard. If it's all right, we're going to hang out with you until we can find our own place. It shouldn't take us long."

"It's great to see you guys. Why are you in San Jose?" I asked.

"We just thought it'd be a nice place to hang out for a while. My brother just moved here from Washington and got a job with IBM, so we'll hang out with him a bit too. Are you hungry? I made some chicken adobo and rice. Jean made a green papaya salad. Come, let's eat."

"It does smell good. Looks like I've got cooks living with me now."

"Yes, and don't worry, we'll clean and organize too. This studio is a bit small for three of us, but all you have to do is go to school and study. We'll do the rest."

"Okay, but my contract specifies one occupant, so please keep a low profile. I don't want to get kicked out. No swimming, and you'll have to park on the street."

"Don't worry, we'll be invisible. Now put those skis down and let's eat."

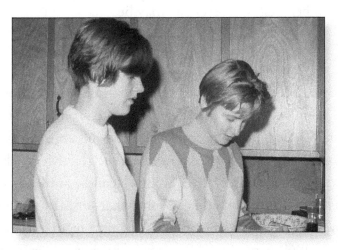

Jean Waring Boal and Shirley Holland, San Jose, California, 1969

For the next two or three weeks, Shirley and Jean slept on the couch that opened into a bed, and I slept on the floor using the couch cushions. Each day I left early and returned late, doing most work at the library. The girls hunted for jobs and an apartment. All three of us were struggling with reentry into American society. Much around us felt uncomfortable, but when we got together each evening, our common experience allowed for mutual support and empathy. We played tapes of Palauan music, ate Pacific foods and relived our Micronesian experiences. On weekends we attended Palauan gatherings as far away as Fort Ord on Monterey Bay. I was actually sorry to see Shirley and Jean leave when they moved into a neighboring apartment building. Jean got a teaching job at a nearby elementary school, and Shirley got a secretarial job with the San Jose State University R.O.T.C. Program.

At the same time that Shirley and Jean arrived in my life, Ibedul also arrived on one of his visits. Although he lived with my parents in Livermore, and they did a lot to chauffeur him around, on weekends he was my responsibility. Shirley and Jean helped entertain him, but his presence, along with school requirements, left me little time for anything else. Without proper explanation, I cut off communications with Rose. All she knew was that two women had moved in with me, and I had stopped calling. I now realize that my lack of honest communication with Rose was immature, unjustified and shameful. I very much regret that thoughtless inaction. I have lost track of Rose. Internet searches remain obscure, likely because of last name changes associated with marriage. In any case, I write of Rose in these pages because our short time together broadened my horizons and enriched my life. I remember her fondly, am sorry I treated her poorly, and wish her well, wherever she may be.

*   *   *

Two Japanese American girls lived in an apartment next door to Shirley and Jean. Darlene Tomiko Kawano and her roommate, Tommi Aoki, were teachers at the same school where Jean was employed. They became friends with Jean and Shirley and soon became incorporated into all our social activities. Although Darlene came from a traditional, conservative, Shinto Japanese family, her upbringing in the agricultural area of Fresno had been somewhat similar to mine in Livermore. We hit it off well together and were soon dating on a regular basis.

On June 13, 1969, I received a Master of Business Administration (MBA) degree from San Jose State. I attended commencement ceremonies, something I hadn't done as an undergraduate, because it gave Mom and Dad a chance to be proud of their son in a cap and gown. Their support and confidence in me had made it all possible.

After the ceremony, we gathered at Shirley's and Jean's apartment—my parents, as well as cousin Jim Cramer, Darlene and Tommi, Darlene's brother, and others I can no longer remember. Although I didn't recognize it at the time, that day was a milestone in my life. Until then, I had little self-confidence when it came to academics. School work, especially reading, was always difficult. Undergraduate studies at Colorado had been trying and unrewarding. The imminent threat of a Vietnam draft had forced me into graduate school. The resulting degree opened possibilities far beyond anything I could imagine at the time.

Shirley and I desperately wanted to return to Micronesia. Jean, however, had fallen in love with Jeff Boal, another Palau volunteer who was then living and working in Venice, California. So shortly after my graduation Jean left for southern California to be with Jeff. They were subsequently married and for a time lived and taught in Japan. Jean eventually received her Master of Divinity degree from The San Francisco Theological Seminary. For several years she was minister of the Trinity Congregational Church in Weaverville—the gateway to California's Trinity Alps. Jean and Jeff are now retired and live in Sebastapol, California.

Most of my fellow MBA graduates took jobs in Silicon Valley corporate settings. I bought a one-way plane ticket to Guam. In late June of 1969, Shirley, Darlene, and I departed from San Francisco on Pan American World Airways. Upon arriving in Guam, we stayed with Larry and Sue Johnsrud, who lived a short distance from the airport on the grounds of the Micronesian Hotel. The Johnsruds were friends of Peter Wilson. Shirley and I had previously stayed with them when we traveled through Guam as Peace Corps volunteers. They had two daughters: Cyndi, thirteen, and Camilla, ten. Both girls viewed our arrival as an exciting change of pace. Their father, Larry, an architect, had converted a surplus Navy Quonset building into quite a palatial and comfortable, air-conditioned home.

I should explain that throughout Micronesia, households routinely accommodated the arrival of friends who dropped in unannounced whenever the aircraft landed. This custom was handed down from earlier times when canoe travelers arrived unannounced, from great distances, having spent weeks at sea. Inter-island travel in those days was so difficult and dangerous that contact between relatives and friends might occur only once or twice in a lifetime. Failure to provide hospitable welcome and care would be unthinkable. This norm of reciprocal hospitality became a desired trait throughout Micronesia. Since commercial lodging was unavailable in many Pacific Islands, American residents practiced an open-door policy as well. The Johnsruds were no exception. They welcomed us warmly, knowing that the debt would be repaid whenever the occasion arose in the future.

Darlene applied for a teaching job in Guam's public school system. In those days, accredited teachers were in short supply, so she was quickly hired, and her employment included government-subsidized housing. Shirley flew off to Trust Territory Headquarters on Saipan Island, 130 miles to the north of Guam. There she was soon hired as a staff stenographer with the Congress of Micronesia. While in Saipan, Shirley lived in the home of Ray Ulechong, the Director of Public Affairs for the Trust Territory Government and a member of her adopted Palauan family. As an interesting but sad footnote, Ray was later electrocuted and died while flying a kite with his children on Capitol Hill in Saipan.

I had three employment possibilities. The University of Guam had responded positively to my teaching application. They offered me $7,800 a year plus benefits, and housing for $55 a month, beginning in September. Peter Wilson had offered me a job managing the Palau boatyard, but that had yet to be confirmed by the Trust Territory Headquarters in Saipan. Finally, Larry Johnsrud had offered me a job as office manager for Johnsrud and Associates, his forty-employee architectural firm.

As a first step, I decided to fly to Saipan to check on the details and likelihood of the boatyard job. There I lived, along with Shirley, as a guest of the Ulechong family. Besides negotiating my employment with the Office of Economic Development, I also spent time with Shirley in and around the Congress of Micronesia. It had been created in 1964 by Trust Territory officials in an attempt to unify the diverse island groups and at the same time introduce Micronesians to an American-style democracy. The twelve-member Senate consisted of two members from each of the six Trust districts: Marshall Islands, Truk, Ponape, Northern Marianas, Yap, and Palau. The House was composed of twenty-one seats distributed among the six districts by population. Bills passed by both houses were signed or vetoed by the High Commissioner, who was appointed by the President of the United States.

Because of our previous Peace Corps relationships, Shirley and I were well-known by Palauans in the government and the Congress. There were three

Palauan delegates to the House: Roman Tmetuchl, who at the time was married to Ibedul's sister, Dr. Minoru Ueki, who had cared for me as a sick volunteer, and Polycarp Basilius, who was a ranking member of Shirley's adopted Palauan family. One Palauan Senator, David Ramarui, was the uncle of Emil Ramarui, who had been my language informant in the Molokai training program. The other Palauan Senator, Lazarus Salii, later became President of Palau. It was a time of hope and learning. A fledgling island nation was being formed, and we were excited to be a small part of it, both as observers and occasional advisors.

Before my return to Guam, the Economic Development Office offered me a one-year contract to manage the boatyard at a GS pay level of $14,680 a year, plus housing, medical care, and transportation to and from Palau, but there was no certainty that the contract would be renewed for additional years.

Within a few days, I flew to Palau to assess the situation at the boatyard. Upon landing, I found that the *Emeraech* was about to embark on a medical rescue mission to Sonsorol Island, some three hundred miles to the south. At Peter Wilson's invitation, I jumped on board. The crew members were mostly the same fellows I had fished with during my Peace Corps service. We had a happy reunion, playing *hanafuda* late into the night. After motoring for twenty-four hours, we arrived at Sonsorol and its northerly neighbor, Fanna. Of course, eagle-eye Amaram was the first to spot land on the horizon. The two islands appeared as green nobs popping out of a calm, blue equatorial sea. They lay just five degrees north of the equator. The seas were glass calm, but there was no anchorage or docking facility at Sonsorol, so the *Emeraech* remained under power while cargo and passengers were ferried ashore in the bait tender. Dison and I jumped overboard and swam to shore.

The island was less than one square mile of densely forested coconuts and hardwoods. The highest spot was perhaps eight feet above sea level. About forty people, mostly old and young, lived in a single village. Most middle-aged inhabitants had left for employment and better lives in Koror. One Peace Corps volunteer teacher was assigned to the island. He was overjoyed to see visitors and happy to receive his mail for the first time in three months. I thought of my friend Peter Black, who served his entire Peace Corp term one hundred miles further south on the island of Tobi, population twenty-two. These were beautiful but isolated and lonely places, requiring a special reverence for solitude. I felt lucky to have been assigned to the relative luxury of Koror, rather than to one of these outer islands. Peter W. Black completed his assignment with distinction and became a respected Ph.D. anthropologist. Retired from George Mason University in Virginia, he now lives near Hilo, Hawaii, and remains likely the world's only nonnative speaker of Tobian language.

The patient we came to extract had passed away prior to our arrival, so we unloaded a ton or so of mail and supplies and started for home in late afternoon. I would have liked to venture further south to Pulo Anna, Tobi, and Helen's Reef, but no one wanted to risk a change in weather, being so far from a safe anchorage. Perhaps in my next lifetime I will see those places. A friend and fellow volunteer, Patrick Bryan, did visit them and published a note entitled "The Rape of Helen Reef." It's worth a read if you can find it.

For the next month I lived in Ibedul's home in Koror, renewed friendships, rested and observed work at the boatyard. I also spent considerable time with Father Hoar and other Jesuits at the Catholic Mission. They assured me that if my job opportunities didn't work out, I was welcome to live and work with them at the Mission. That was a tempting offer. To this day I greatly respect the Jesuits' contribution to humanity, and over the years I have contributed financially to their efforts. Had my mother allowed my enrollment in the Jesuit-run Bellarmine College Preparatory High School, I likely would have become one of them.

While in Palau, I didn't make contact with Tasia, nor did she with me. When Ibedul had visited us in California, Darlene's Japanese cooking had impressed him, and he had, no doubt, returned to Palau with stories of my relationship with Darlene, Shirley, and Jean. Perhaps Tasia felt that her duties toward me were completed, and she didn't wish to revive a painful relationship unless I took the imitative. For much the same reasons I too chose to let matters between us remain as they were.

At the end of August, I returned to Guam. The paperwork for my contract at the boatyard was still mired in Trust Territory Headquarters bureaucracy. The University of Guam contract had been approved by the Governor's office and was awaiting my signature. After two days of anguished procrastination, my mother's oft-repeated maxim carried the day: "A bird in the hand is worth two in the bush." I signed the documents that officially made me an instructor in the Department of Business Administration. Given my lifelong reading difficulties and general distaste for things academic, no one was more surprised by such an outcome than I. At twenty-seven years old, I was the youngest full-time faculty member. In order to differentiate myself from students I wore a short-sleeved dress shirt, slacks, and tie, one of only a few faculty members to do so.

Paul Callaghan at University of Guam, 1969

With employment came government housing, thus allowing me to extract myself from the Johnsrud household and more easily avoid any obligation to work for Larry. He, Sue, and baby Cyndi had arrived on Guam eleven years earlier. In that time Larry had built a sizable architectural firm as well as owning a majority interest in the Island's only upscale clothing store, The Playboy Shop. He also held minority interests in other Island enterprises, including a strip club. The problem was that the financial underpinnings of his burgeoning empire were tenuous. I wrote home in an August 1969 letter to my parents:

> He (Larry) operates on a shoestring. He is a hell of a good mover in that he somehow makes payroll and keeps one step ahead of the bill collectors. (If I work for him) I will be handling his books and signing the checks, so I should be able to keep myself paid, but I don't trust him. He has arrived at a point where he can really go someplace, or he can crash into bankruptcy.

Within a year or two Larry did manage to lose everything. His businesses collapsed, he left Sue and his girls, ran off with a beautiful Palauan woman named Antonia Joseph, and eventually moved to Palau. There he ran a construction supply store that eventually ended in failure. Sue and the girls left Guam and moved to Florida. I have kept in contact with them, and they tell me that after thirty-five years living in various places around Micronesia, Larry finally moved to Florida to be near his ex-wife and daughters. There are many interesting Pacific stories that will never be written.

*   *   *

My government housing turned out to be a one-bedroom, tin-roofed, concrete duplex in Yigo Village, about twenty minutes north of the university. It was located in the jungle, along a potholed dirt road, out of sight from the surrounding Chamorro and Filipino neighbors. My first significant purchases were a window air conditioner and a white Datsun station wagon. It cost $2,200. The monthly payments were $102. Whenever I drove in or out of my neighborhood, I passed Takano's store, a ramshackle mom-and-pop operation where the village's unemployed truants hung out. Twice during my first weeks of residency I came home to find the house ransacked. Access had been gained by pushing the air conditioner inward, onto the floor. I didn't own much of value in those days, so nothing was missing other than a few beers and some food from the refrigerator. After replacing the air conditioner for the second time, a friend from the university provided a sign written in Chamorro that said in effect, "Please, brothers, don't push in this air conditioner. The front door is open, and there's beer in the refrigerator." I never again had a break-in problem or any missing beer.

In those days the government-operated telephone system was an inadequate, overloaded postwar relic. Most homes had no phone service, and those that did were subject to party lines and poor service. The only way to make long distance calls was to drive to the Western Union office in Agana and pay by the minute to sit in a booth. When it rained, and it did that a lot, Island-wide phone service became a static-filled hit or miss proposition. Neither my university office nor my Yigo apartment had a working telephone. Guam Telephone Authority did not entertain any new customers or install any new lines, especially when it came to young American newcomers like me.

One day while in the Dean's office, I was bemoaning my lack of a working home telephone. A Chamorro student worker named Julie Guerrero pulled me aside. "Professor Callaghan, my father works for Guam Telephone Authority. If you go to the GTA main office in Tamuning and ask for him, he may be able to help you. I'll tell him to expect you."

I did as she suggested and was ushered into a gigantic air-conditioned office with an ornately-carved wooden conference table. Clearly Mr. Guerrero, a rotund man in his sixties, didn't just work for GTA. He was the Executive Director. As I approached his desk, he stood and greeted me with a smile and a handshake. "*Hafa adai*, my daughter tells me that you are a recently-arrived professor at UOG. Welcome to Guam. We need young people like you to help improve our Island. Julie says you need a phone. Where do you live?"

"I live in Yigo, sir, near the Takano Store. There appears to be a phone line into the building and one of those little connection boxes on the wall in the kitchen, but there's no phone."

"All right, just a minute," he said as he went outside through a back-entrance door that remained open. I could see him rummaging in the cab of a GTA pickup. Soon he returned with a black rotary dial telephone, its lead wire coiled around the instrument.

"You look like a smart young man," he said as he handed me the phone. "Connect the green wire to the green wire on the wall. Connect the red wire to the red wire on the wall, and do the same with the black wire. If that doesn't work, move the colored wires around until you get a dial tone. If you can't make it work tell Julie, and I'll send someone out there."

"Thank you very much, sir," I said. "Isn't there some paperwork I should fill out?"

"Never mind. Welcome to Guam. Make sure to let Julie know if it doesn't work."

"I will, sir. And thank you again."

That evening I was able to connect the phone and call out, but there was no way of knowing my phone number for those who might wish to call me. Thankfully, it wasn't too long before the phone rang. It was a wrong number, but the man on the other end was able to tell me the number he had dialed. From that point on I had a working phone that could call and receive; also, I never paid a phone bill while living in Yigo Village.

My teaching load at the university was twelve credit hours: two sections of Management, one of Marketing, and one of Money and Banking. I taught until nine at night three days a week. There was little time in my life for anything else besides preparation, teaching and office hours. Shirley had returned to Guam after the Congressional session in Saipan and now worked for the Guam Community Action Agency. She and Darlene lived together on the far western side of Guam in the village of Santa Rita, where Darlene taught at the elementary school. They had no telephone, so our busy lives grew apart and our paths seldom crossed.

My free time, what there was of it, became filled with activities. On weekends I began scuba diving and spear fishing with new found friends, Dale Beagley, a physical education teacher at the university, and Bill Williams, a local attorney. As the semester progressed, four Palauan students—Yoichi Rengiil, Mobo Morei, Yuriko Adachi, and Nina Tewid—asked me to be on their bowling team in the Friday afternoon Royal Lanes Students League. Jose (Joe) Paulino, who chaired the Physical Education Department at the university, enlisted my participation in his afternoon tennis program. All three courts were filled with students from various Micronesian islands, as well as some university staff and faculty. Unless it rained, we played until dark. The courts had no lighting.

Most mornings before classes I drank coffee in the dilapidated, tin-roofed Student Center. There I often sat with Beagley, Paulino, and other university staff. Their conversations provided an opportunity to keep abreast of institutional goings-on. Sometimes I joined Palauans, usually those from the bowling team. Like other Micronesians, Palauans were most comfortable grouped by themselves. I was one of the few outsiders to join their tables. They were kindly tolerant of my less than auspicious Palauan linguistic skills, and our conversations allowed me to keep up with news from Palau as well as student campus gossip. Dale Beagley was another teacher who could frequently be found associating with the Palauan students. He was by nature a gregarious, friendly fellow who never forgot a name. As a wordplay on his last name the Palauans referred to him as "Big Alii." *Alii* is the Palauan greeting word similar to hello in English.

In mid-December of 1969, Mom and Dad and our family friend, Catherine (Kit) Carson, made the long trip to Guam. They stayed at the Sleepy Lagoon Hotel while I finished fall semester exams and grading. We then went to Palau for the holiday season as guests of Ibedul. Shirley and Darlene were also in Palau for the holidays. There were memorable adventures and wonderful times in the Rock Islands and villages of Babeldaob. In my mind's image I can still see Ibedul dancing with Kit Carson at the American Club in Koror on New Year's Eve. To my knowledge, he had never before danced with any American, and only once before had he set foot in the American Club, a place he viewed as a bastion of American colonialism. For my parents, the trip provided a better understanding and appreciation of my Pacific world and my reasons for wanting to build a life there. After that visit they never questioned my decision to remain.

Mom and Dad and Kit had returned to California, and my spring semester had begun when Shirley announced that she was leaving for Nairobi, Kenya, to be with my cousin, Jim Cramer. They had dated some during our time in San Jose, but I had no idea that their relationship was serious enough to warrant Shirley's travel to Kenya, where Jim was teaching under a Rhodes Fellowship at the University of Nairobi. In any case, we had a noisy, well-attended, all-night party that ended around six in the morning the day we put Shirley on the airplane. She and Jim were subsequently married, but then some years later divorced. Shirley now lives in Washington State with a long-time partner named Don. Darlene taught for another year or so in Santa Rita Village and then returned to California, where she taught elementary school for almost forty years. She now lives in Clovis, California. Though we have traveled different roads, Shirley, Jean, Darlene, and I are still in contact with each other.

*   *   *

An excerpt from my 1969 Christmas letter to family and friends expressed my feelings about living and working on Guam:

> Most of you probably never envisioned me in an academic role, and I must admit that I am as surprised as you are. But I am enjoying every minute of it. The students in my classes are of every race, nationality, and creed. There are Christians, Buddhists, Muslims and Sikhs, Filipinos, Japanese, Koreans and Chinese, Tongans, Hawaiians, Samoans and Saipanese, Chamorros, Palauans, Ponapeans and Trukese, Yapese, Taiwanese, stateside Americans and many combinations thereof. It is most rewarding and challenging to teach in a way that is meaningful to the a wide variety of cultures, backgrounds and languages sitting in front of me each day.
>
> The Western Pacific is one of the few frontiers left, and Guam is the hub of regional activity ... There is still room out here for a guy to make his individual mark and not be a cog in the wheel of some

large corporation. Living on the frontier has its little inconveniences, like 125 inches of rain a year, constant 80-degree temperatures with 80 percent humidity, shortages and high prices, typhoons and tidal waves, but I wouldn't trade under any circumstances for a life of smog, traffic congestion, and hectic competition.

As my second semester began, the Governor had appointed me to the Juvenile Justice Advisory Board. I was a member of several university committees. Life was full of social activities. I wrote again to my parents:

> I am going to be the Master of Ceremonies for the Miss University of Guam (Miss Chamorrita) contest next month. Every Saturday we practice—WOW! Those girls! Man, do I love being a young, unmarried college professor.

Amidst all this, a new important person entered my life—a nursing student named Nina Tewid. She was a member of our Friday afternoon bowling team and also one of Joe Paulino's favorite tennis players. Nina, her Palauan name was Kilad, also worked as a student helper for Dr. O. Randall Brayman, a psychology professor whose office was just down the hall from the office I shared with two other faculty members. My student helper, Jennifer, was Palauan, so the two girls frequently gossiped in the hallway, seemingly oblivious to the possibility that I might understand what they were saying. At any rate, as the spring semester progressed, Nina and I became increasingly friendly. She lived with sponsors on the naval air base in Maite, so I often provided transportation to and from our bowling and tennis activities. In a letter to my parents dated March 21, 1970, I wrote:

> Dear Mom and Dad, I am going with the most beautiful Palauan girl you have ever seen. I'll send you a picture once I get them developed. She has lived on Guam for about 8 years and is a student in the School of Nursing here at the University. Her name is Nina Tewid, and she was at the party at my house when you were here.

By May, Nina and I were pretty much a regular pair during non-school hours. Some faculty and staff were uneasy about our relationship. Their legitimate concerns about the propriety of teacher-student relationships became entwined with their subconscious socio-cultural prejudice and jealousy. Nina was not a student in the Business School, so it was difficult to allege any conflict of interest or favoritism on my part. However, I suspect that some stateside faculty were opposed to interracial relationships in general, and it's likely that the Chamorro faculty and staff wondered why a professor would choose to be with a Palauan student when many eligible and beautiful Chamorro women were available.

Guam was, and still is, predominately a Chamorro society, the university predominately a Chamorro institution. In those times local families looked favorably on their daughters marrying an American. During my first year at the university, I was continuously being matched with local women—among others there was May Cruz, a stunningly beautiful English professor who shed me for an American lawyer, thank God; and there was Rosa Roberto, the Registrar, who ultimately married a fellow professor, Lee Carter. Rosa later became university president.

For Nina and I, it was enough that our close friends and the Palauan community were supportive of our relationship. Moreover, as the semester came to an end, two incidences served to enhance my professional standing and draw attention away from our private lives. First, I was awarded runner-up for the honored title Professor of the Year. The winner was psychology professor O. Randall Brayman, Nina's employer. Since his office was just down the hall from mine, he and I often chatted between classes. During these sessions, we sometimes played what we called "the ethno-culture game." From our position on the second floor of Building A, we could see students walking across campus toward us. The challenge was to guess which Micronesian district or Asian country the students hailed from, based solely on their appearance and the way they carried themselves. When the student in question reached our location, we inquired as to their origin in order to determine if our presumptions had been correct. Over the course of that year, we became pretty accurate. Randy was a fine mentor and role model for me. We two were the only teachers to regularly wear short-sleeved dress shirt, slacks and tie. It was an honor to be ranked with him. In a May 18, 1970, letter to my parents I wrote:

> The other day we had a University Awards and Honors Ceremony. I was surprised to be selected first-runner-up for Professor of the Year. I guess I was very close to winning the title because people told me that in past years there had never been a runner-up award. Not bad for the first year here.

The second incident happened on a Friday afternoon late in May. A student messenger stuck his head in my office door and said, "Professor Callaghan, Dr. Yamashita wants to see you."

"Right now?" I asked. I was momentarily planning to pick up Yoichi and Nina for our bowling league at Royal Lanes.

"Yes, sir, as soon as you can."

"All right. Tell him I am on my way."

Dr. Yamashita was the university president, not a man to be kept waiting. On the way to his office, I mulled over what it was that I might have done wrong. Was it something I had said in the classroom? Had someone complained about my teaching or grading, or my personal life? Nina had been sponsored by the Yamashita family and for a time lived in their household. They knew her well and still considered her part of their family.

My guard was up as I entered the President's office. Dr. Yamashita was sitting behind his desk in conversation with Jack Dumond, a professor from the College of Education. Their reaction was immediate.

"Come on in, Paul. Have a seat," said the President. Jack pushed a chair around so that we both sat facing the President.

"Congratulations on almost becoming Professor of the Year. I hear it was close. Clearly you are well liked by the students, and my daughter confirms that you are a fine teacher."

I knew that there was a Yamashita in my Principles of Economics section, but I had no idea she was the president's daughter.

"Thank you, sir. I'm trying my best," I said.

"Do you intend to teach summer school and return to us next year?" he asked.

"Well sir, I had hoped to teach summer school, but the Trust Territory Government has offered me a contract to manage the Palau boatyard, so I haven't decided about fall semester yet."

The boatyard management contract had finally been approved by Saipan T.T. Headquarters. Both Wilson and Toshiro were now after me to fly to Saipan and sign the documents.

Jack Dumond spoke up. "You don't want to take that job and live in Palau, do you? Aren't you enjoying your time here? You're certainly well respected, and you're becoming a valued member of the university community. I think you should give serious thought to not changing horses in the middle of the stream."

Wow, I thought, *that idiom would leave most students totally baffled.*

"They're offering me almost fifteen thousand dollars plus housing and transportation," I replied.

"So how long is the contract?" asked Dumond.

"One year," I replied.

"And then what? Suppose it's not renewed? And if it is, you'll end up in Palau or somewhere else in Micronesia for the rest of your life. Is that what you really want?"

Yamashita spoke, "Suppose I offer you a two-year contract as Assistant Professor, beginning next year. That will pay you around thirteen thousand if you teach summer school, plus the same housing and health benefits you're currently receiving. Remember, Guam has an excellent retirement fund that's not available when you're working for the Trust Territory. What would you say to returning next year under those conditions?"

"I'd say that I'd be happy to stay at U.O.G. under those conditions, sir."

"Good," said Yamashita. "Now let's celebrate your promotion to Assistant Professor."

He took a bottle of whiskey and three glasses from the bottom drawer of his desk. Dumond extracted ice cubes from the office refrigerator. That bottle was half-full when we started and empty when we finished. If Dr. Carey, Dean of the Business School, was ever consulted, I never knew about it. My first promotion was accomplished over Scotch on the rocks, late on a Friday afternoon, without application, documentation or peer review.

As it turned out I was lucky not to have taken that boatyard management position. Much of what Jack Dumond suggested would likely have taken place. When Kioshi Matsumoto and Peter Wilson departed Palau in the early 1970s, the boatyard administration was ceded to Toshiro Paulis, Ben Orrukem and the Association elders. They lacked the necessary business and administrative skills to oversee the yard's survival, and it gradually withered into an empty hulk of a building. Lesson learned: sustainable long-term economic development cannot be built on a foundation of government-subsidized expatriate leadership, vision, and expertise. After Wilson's departure, Toshiro and Ben simply could not carry on. Toshiro was disappointed by my decision to remain with the university, and I felt some guilt for letting him down. But in the end, I don't believe that my involvement would have resulted in any different outcome for the boatyard.

*   *   *

By the time I arrived at the Royal Lanes, Nina and Yoichi had found alternate transportation, but our team had forfeited one game. My tardiness was not appreciated but in the Micronesian way, went unacknowledged.

That summer Nina and I and Joe Paulino lived together at his home in the Village of Inarajan on the southeast coast of Guam. Joe's wife and children had gone to Hawaii for the summer to be with her parents. The Paulino Clan owned almost the entire perimeter of Agfayan Bay, where a river of that same name entered the sea. Joe lived at the mouth of the bay, where it opened out into the ocean. His house was near the water, surrounded by ancient, monolithic Latte stones and other signs of prehistoric human occupation. Behind the house rose a cliff and a towering natural rock formation that resembled the shape of a bear on its haunches; thus, Joe's property was known as Bear Rock.

Nina (Kilad) Tewid and Paul Callaghan at Bear Rock, Guam, 1970

Many Chamorros were fearful of going near Bear Rock, saying it was a home for *Taotao Mona*, ancient spirits, protectors of the land. Joe was the youngest brother in his family, so he had inherited the land that others didn't want. But Joe made Bear Rock into a magical, sacred place. His house was built on a stonework foundation, a building designed to be one with its surroundings, invisible from the main road to all but the most discerning eye. We slept each night and awoke each morning to the sound, sights and smells of the sea. The calming presence of ancient spirits hung in the air and resided in all plants, rocks and crevices. On moonlit nights a cacophony of insects and amphibians sang of their presence. The tides, ocean and weather conditions became part of our lives. We fished with spear, net, pole and line. We snorkeled, rafted and swam. We hunted for crabs and turtle eggs. Coconuts, bananas and papayas were available for the taking. The forty-minute drive to and from the university campus was so beautiful that I hardly noticed the time. Those months at Bear Rock were some of the best days of my life. I wrote to my parents in June of 1970:

> Nina and I are spending the summer with our friend, Joe Paulino, a Guamanian teacher at the University. He lives on a beautiful bay called Agfayan in the southern part of the Island. We are the only people who live on the bay and every day I can go fishing. We eat lots of fish. There is no telephone, and it reminds me of the good old days in Palau. Joe's wife went to Hawaii with the kids for the summer so Joe, I, and Nina hold down the fort until their return. I wish you could experience this place.

*   *   *

After leaving Joe's house at the end of summer, Nina and I moved into my Yigo apartment. Shortly thereafter I asked her to marry me. Her reply went something like this: "Why would we want to ruin our wonderful relationship by getting married? We are living together. We are in love and enjoying each other's company. We don't need to be married."

When I continued to press for an answer, she said, "I was raised Palauan. I am Palauan. I do not want to become American, and I do not want to live far from Palau. I am the oldest among my brothers and sisters. When my brothers build a house or when there is a family funeral or emergency, you, as my husband, are required to contribute big money. If you were Palauan, you could get most of that money from your sisters and their husbands. But you have no sisters, and if you did, I'm sure they would not contribute. You have little understanding of what it means to be the husband of a Palauan women. Our customs are not easy for outsiders to bear. If I am your wife, my family always comes before our relationship and our personal life. That's hard for Americans to accept. I don't think you understand the implications of marriage in Palau. If we are just living together, we can avoid most Palauan custom issues. Marriage only makes our life together more difficult."

I persisted, saying that I was willing to accept those customary obligations, so over the next couple of weeks Nina conferred with aunties on Guam, and then flew to Palau to consult with her parents and relatives. Much to my delight, upon returning she said that our marriage could go ahead. So on the morning of November 28, 1970, we were married in a Catholic service at St. Anthony Church in Tamuning Village. I was twenty-eight and she was twenty-two. Joe Paulino acted as a best man. His son Andre was the ring bearer. Patrick Bryan stood on the altar with us. Toshiro Paulis walked Nina down the aisle in place of her father, who at that time was fishing for tuna on Richard Kinney's boat in Hawaii.

As we turned to descend from the altar, it was gratifying to see so many in attendance. There were university students from Micronesia, some accompanied by their sponsoring families. Nina's classmates and teachers from the Nursing School were there, as well as teachers and students from the Business School. There were several of Nina's relatives and their families and friends. The Paulinos and Quans, the Crains and Yamashitas, the Clays and Quinatas were all there along with friends and acquaintances from throughout the Island. In the south transept stood three Jesuit priests from Palau: Fathers Bizkarra, Hoar, and Condon. They were transiting Guam on their way to Palau and heard about our wedding. Their attendance was a grand honor.

Joe Paulino announced from the pulpit that all attendees and their families and friends were invited to a reception beginning at six o'clock that evening, on the grounds of Bear Rock. As the Palauan students sang "Climb Every Mountain," Nina and I began our long walk down the aisle and into forty-three years of married life. During those years we did climb many mountains and ford many streams together. It brings me frequent heartache that she is no longer by my side.

Several hundred people attended the reception at Bear Rock. Joe had enlisted help from his own and several closely-related Chamorro families. Nina's aunties had assigned cooking and food preparation responsibilities to Palauans living throughout Guam.

Jose E. Paulino at Bear Rock, Guam, 1971

Toshiro had recruited people from Ponape and Kapingamarangi to help with thatching, basket weaving, and the cooking of two pigs underground in the island way. The logistics and food preparation took several days and nights. Parking lots had to be cleared, sound systems installed, firewood delivered. As is often the way in Guam, off-duty utility workers installed power and water lines that bypassed meters. The Palauan Student Association provided an elaborate four-tiered wedding cake.

Under Joe's direction, everything came together by seven o'clock that evening, including a blessing of the table by Fathers Hoar and Bizkarra, a five-piece band, and traditional Palauan dances by torchlight. Some guests stayed until dawn. Nina and I departed around two in the morning, totally exhausted and well aware that the reciprocal costs of this celebration would be borne by us for the rest of our lives.

In December we flew to California to introduce Nina to my parents, who had not made the trip to Guam for the wedding. Nina had never before been beyond Palau, Yap, and Guam. It was an exciting adventure for us both. In Livermore, Mom and Dad held a cocktail reception in our honor. Many of Livermore's elite attended, along with Dad's nephews, Art and Richard Deck, and the Cramer family. Some Palauans that Nina and I knew from around the

Bay Area were also invited. Much to my happiness, Kit, Maurine, Estelle, and Jackie attended, providing their usual hugs and effervescent emotional support. It was quite an eclectic gathering, a mixture of people who otherwise would never have associated.

I overheard one conversation that sticks in my mind. It went something like this:

"Hello, I'm Steve. Try the turkey and green olives on the crackers. They're the best."

"I'm glad to meet you, Steve. I'll do that on my next trip to the table. I'm Carl. I see you prefer beer over Manhattans and martinis. That's probably a smart choice. Are you from the Livermore area?"

"No, my wife Maria and I live in Hayward. Maria is related to Kilad. Oh, I mean Nina, the new Mrs. Callaghan. We call her Kilad. That's her Palauan name. Are you from Livermore?"

"I was born and raised here, but I live in San Francisco now."

"What do you do?"

"Oh, I've been in banking in various positions over the years. How about you?"

"I'm in transportation. Got to keep the wheels of progress moving, you know."

Steve Reynolds was a bus driver in Oakland. Carl Wente was the President and Chief Executive Officer of Bank of America.

A detailed description of our wedding, as well as our life together before and after marriage, can be found in Nina's biography, *Flight of the Dudek: A Story of One Person's Journey by Paul Callaghan*.

*   *   *

For the next year-and-a-half after returning from California, our pattern of life flowed between our Yigo Village apartment and the university. Elsie Tutii, one of Nina's cousins, came to live with us for a semester until she gained access to the university dormitories. In addition to her nursing courses, Nina worked part time at the university bookstore. I taught a full load of four classes and on some days didn't finish until after nine at night. The three of us drove to school early in the mornings, ate our meals in and around the campus, and drove home again late in the evenings.

As a footnote, Elsie still lives in Guam, having retired from a thirty-year career in sales with Duty Free Shoppers. Her son, Joey Taitano, lives in San Diego, where he worked for some years as a buyer for Nordstrom and more recently Ives St. Laurent.

On weekends, Nina and I spent time diving, spearfishing, picnicking and partying. My spearfishing kept our freezer stocked while providing enough to share with friends and relatives. Our favorite nightclub was the Fishermen's Tavern, a Palauan hangout owned by Nina's auntie, Michiko. She was married to a Japanese/Saipanese man named Joe Imamura. Joe claimed to be the son of the prewar Japanese military commander of the Mariana Islands. He could spend hours over a beer and maps, telling me about his various legal battles to reclaim his "stolen" inheritance of Saipan and Tinian lands. He never seemed to win any of these court cases, but his chatter was tolerated and his friendship appreciated.

The Fishermen's Tavern, Fish for short, had a rough reputation. It had Palauan music and dancing with no cover charge, and because of our relationship with Michiko and Joe Imamura, Nina and I felt comfortable there. The secret of survival at Fish was to leave the premises before closing, when the fights usually broke out, sometimes with flying beer bottles, rocks and tire-irons. When Fish got rowdy, even the Guam police were reticent to enter.

I was enjoying my work in academia, to the point that I had abandoned the idea of managing the boatyard, and the Saipan authorities had finally stopped contacting me about the job. During the 1970–71 academic year, I was asked to be faculty advisor for the Palau Student Organization and was again awarded Professor of the Year honors. This time there was no runner-up. During that year I also spoke at two off-island economic development conferences. One was held at Saipan's newly built Royal Taga Hotel, sponsored by the Saipan Chamber of Commerce, and the other was on Ponape, sponsored by the Trust Territory Government.

At midterm break, Nina and I joined some faculty members on a month-long, whirlwind South Pacific excursion that took us from Guam to the tiny island of Nauru, from there to Nadi and Suva in Fiji, and to Auckland, Melbourne, and Sydney, then on to Noumea in New Caledonia, Port Vila in the New Hebrides, and Honiara in the Solomon Islands. We returned home the day that spring classes commenced. Along the way I visited fisheries and aquaculture instillations, while Nina worked her charming personal magic, finding relationships and making friends at almost every stop. She played tennis for two days with a Fijian girl whom she met on the grass courts near the Grand Pacific Hotel in Suva. The girl said her father was a member of Fiji's Parliament. Everywhere we found people who knew or were related to our friends or relations. Pacific Islanders are in many respects one huge family.

In August of 1971, I was appointed Acting Associate Dean of the Business School—an appointment of some controversy, since I didn't hold a Doctorate degree. It was intended as an interim appointment until a suitable permanent Dean could be recruited. That took almost a full year, during which time I initiated a Master of Business Administration program, handled class scheduling, budgeting, and planning, as well as faculty-student public affairs. Thankfully I was able to do so in a way that convinced most faculty that a young guy with a lowly Master's degree could be a decent administrator. That is not to say that I always pleased my peers. At one point I became upset with the lack of empathy and cultural understanding among our "Stateside" contract faculty. With the intension of stimulating their awareness, I walked the halls, eavesdropping on classes while making a list of idioms used by faculty during their lectures. The list included such phrases as: "it's a piece of cake," "you've hit the nail on the head," "it's a no brainer," "tit for tat," "think outside the box," and many more. I then read the list in faculty meeting and suggested that everyone consider the difficulty that these idioms present to those who have English as a second or third language. The response was less than heartwarming and the results of my effort much less than I had hoped.

In Guam's 1970 general election, the incumbent Democratic Party was defeated and the newly-elected Republican Governor, Carlos Camacho, appointed a new university president to replace Dr. Yamashita. The new president's name was Pedro Cruz "Doc" Sanchez. He impressed me as being a visionary who understood that Guam was part of Micronesia, and in turn part of a much larger Pacific world. Unlike his predecessor, who had been insular in focus, this man was worldly and experienced with high standards and high expectations for faculty performance. He held a Master's degree from Columbia and a Ph.D. from Stanford. He had worked for the Peace Corps under Sargent Shriver, been Director of Education for the Virgin Islands, and held several Federal Government posts in Panama and elsewhere. On top of that, he was married to a Samoan lady and had co-authored *A Complete History of Guam*, a frequently used and cited chronicle of Guam's past. I was excited about his arrival and looked forward to being a contributing member of his administration.

So when he called me into his office "for a chat," I was nervous but excited about meeting such a respected and accomplished Chamorro. The gist of our conversation went something like this:

"Hello, Mr. Callaghan, it's nice to finally meet you. I've heard good things about you and your teaching. Also, congratulations on your recent marriage. Joe Paulino invited us to your reception. I wouldn't expect you to remember.

You were otherwise occupied. But my wife and I attended and enjoyed the food and Palauan dancing. There certainly were lots of people there. Thankfully Joe reserved a parking place for us, otherwise we would have had to walk a quarter mile from the Inarajan cemetery."

"Thank you, Dr. Sanchez. It's nice to finally meet you when I'm in a more mindful condition. Also, congratulations on your appointment as President. We needed a change of leadership."

"I certainly intend to change some things that likely won't make everyone happy, but we'll take it slowly. My son Simon tells me that you are well thought of by the students, and that last year they voted you Professor of the Year. His friends tell him you're a good instructor, and according to my staff, your work as Acting Dean has been exemplary. Thank you for your service and commitment."

"Thank you, sir. I'm enjoying my work as Acting Dean. I've learned a lot, and I've found I like teaching too."

"Well, we should have a permanent Dean recruited by the end of spring semester, so you'll then be able to concentrate on other things. In that regard, I called you in today to give you timely notice that I will not be renewing your contract after August. You are clearly an excellent teacher and apparently a competent administrator, but you need a terminal degree in order to go anywhere in this profession. If I don't force you to get a Doctorate, you'll take the easy road and stay here as an Assistant Professor for the rest of your life. That won't be good for you, and it won't improve this university. Our institutional moto is "Excelsior," and I intend that we work our way toward that goal. Go get your Doctorate, son, and come back here. We need people like you, but only after you've gotten the proper academic credentials."

I was dumbfounded and unable to muster a reply other than, "Okay, sir."

He continued, "You get going and apply to graduate programs. Keep me informed, and I'll support you in any way I can with letters of recommendation or whatever. My sources tell me that you have financial resources sufficient to afford off-island schooling, but if that's not true, let me know and I'll see what we can do to help. We'll put you on educational leave without pay until you return, but return with that Doctorate. I'm betting that because you're married to a Micronesian, you'll return and contribute to this region, even if it's not at the University of Guam."

"Yes, sir. I hope so, sir."

"Now get going on those applications. My door is open to you at any time. As you know, there's a Deans' meeting at three this afternoon. I'll see you there."

"Yes, sir. I'll be there. We're going to review the Business School's proposal for an M.B.A. program. I hope you'll support it."

"I'll support it if I can be sure that you'll be able to recruit and hold the requisite terminal degreed faculty for such a program. 'Excelsior' means quality. There will be no diploma-mill credentials handed out by U.O.G. under my watch."

That meeting with Dr. Sanchez proved to be an important fork in the road of my life. He was right. Without being prodded, I would have likely spent many years at the University of Guam teaching introductory courses while having fun diving, sailing, fishing and traveling in the summers. Perhaps that pattern of life might have been simpler, but it would not have been as diverse and exciting as that which has transpired. I never knew Doc Sanchez well, but he made a positive contribution to the course of my life, and I am grateful to him.

Without delay I started applying to graduate schools that offered marine resource economics programs. There were only three of consequence in the United States: University of Hawaii, University of Washington, and University of Rhode Island. I quickly dismissed Rhode Island, feeling that it would pose too much of a cultural and climatic leap for Nina, and likely for me as well. Hawaii was my preferred choice since it was located in an island environment similar to Guam.

My immediate boss, Dr. Edwin Carey, hand-carried my application to the University of Hawaii Economics Department and spoke with the Department Chair about my situation. The application contained letters of recommendation from President Sanchez and Peter Wilson, among others. A subsequent communication from Dr. Salvatore (Sal) Comitini, an associate professor of economics at the University of Hawaii, read in part:

> "With regard to your letter of January 11, 1972, I have checked on your application and can inform you that you have been admitted to the Ph.D. program in economics. If you have not been officially informed by the Graduate Division, you will be shortly … I have informed the Sea Grant Director, Jack Davidson, of your interest, and I can say there is a good chance that you could become involved in my skipjack tuna project upon beginning your doctoral studies.

After receiving this assurance, I withdrew my application to the University of Washington, feeling that life in Honolulu would provide a more comfortable fit for both Nina and me. That decision was further confirmed when Nina received acceptance to the University of Hawaii's School of Nursing. We could both attend school at the same time. The question was how to pay for it. I had only Comitini's unconfirmed possibility of a research assistantship and no idea as to what benefits or salary that assistantship might entail.

As has consistently been the case in my life, Irish luck came to the rescue. During my first year on Guam, I had joined a group of investors in two limited partnerships. Both involved the purchase of remote, largely inaccessible, jungle-covered land in the mountains of central Guam. There was no particular plan other than to hold the land and eventually resell it for a profit as Guam's economy grew. The partnerships were legally titled Tenechong and Billy Bay Development Companies. I had put ten thousand dollars into each as a gamble on the future of Guam's economic growth. However, as luck would have it, on January 24, 1972, Sargent Shoichi Yokoi, the last Japanese military straggler from WWII, was captured in his cave-hideout in the dense jungle of our Tenechong property. Within a few months, tourism companies from Japan were vying to purchase our land. My ten-thousand-dollar investment turned into sixty thousand dollars overnight, enough to pay for both Nina's and my Hawaii educations.

In late May I flew to Honolulu. There I met with Sal Comitini and Jack Davidson, Director of the Sea Grant Program. They were supportive but couldn't guarantee financial assistance until later in the summer. One-bedroom housing within walking distance of the University was priced at around $220 a month. Before returning to Guam, I put a deposit on a one-bedroom unit, with parking stall and central laundry facilities. It was near Punahou School, about a ten-minute walk from campus, and the rent was $195 a month.

Mom and Dad visited us in Guam for two weeks in August of 1972. The four of us spent several days together on Saipan Island. There I was able to show them the jungle-covered Isley Field, from which American B-29s had bombed Tokyo. We walked through the last Japanese command post on the north end of the island, and we stood on the edges of Banzai and Suicide Cliffs, where hundreds of civilians and Japanese soldiers had jumped to their deaths rather than be captured by Americans. Back on Guam we snorkeled and swam and picnicked. I cajoled Dad, who was then in his eighties, into wearing a snorkel and mask while lying face-down on an air mattress, his face hanging over the edge. For an hour I pushed him along the reef complex in Billy Bay so that he could enjoy the colorful corals and fish. He had a great time, even though his bald head became a bit sunburned.

*　*　*

Soon after Mom and Dad returned home, Nina and I departed for Honolulu, where for three grueling years we lived, studied, worked and played. Day after day, rain or shine, we walked back and forth to the University of Hawaii campus, attended classes, ate in the East-West Center cafeteria, studied together in one of the libraries, and walked home to sleep each night. Our second-story apartment on Clark Street became our personal oasis, a place where we could relax with a little television before bed. I was watching the Olympic Games as the Israeli team became the object of a terrorist attack, but news such as Watergate, the oil crises, the Vietnam War, became only background noise to our academic immersion.

Interestingly, our apartment on Clark Street was a block away from an apartment building where a young man named Barack Obama lived with his grandparents and attended Punahou School. Frequently Nina and I jogged on the Punahou School track. It's possible that I came close to bumping elbows with a future President of the United States. I'll never know, but I enjoy imagining so.

The East-West Center cafeteria was located in the basement of Jefferson Hall. There we ate with a cadre of regulars, some of whom I still remember. Palmyri S.B. Murthy was a graduate electrical engineering student, always upbeat with a daily tidbit of humor. At times he helped me overcome rough spots in integral calculus and differential equations. I assume life led Palmyri back to India. I know nothing of his subsequent life, but I fondly remember his kindness and upbeat spirit.

Dale Jackson, a towheaded electrical engineer turned agricultural economics student, wore bleached and tattered Levi's and blue canvas low-top shoes. Like me, he'd been a Peace Corps volunteer in Micronesia. We were sometimes classmates and spent one summer together designing computer programs that performed stepwise linear regressions and linear programing solutions. After graduation, Dale taught at several institutions on Oahu, but I've lost track of his whereabouts and can find no trace of him on the internet.

Victor Yano from Koror, Palau was another regular at our cafeteria table. Victor, at age nineteen, was finishing his biochemistry degree and had been accepted into the University's John A. Burns School of Medicine. He ultimately graduated first in his class with national test scores in the top 5 percent. After interning on an Indian reservation, he returned home to Palau, where to this day he continues to practice family medicine in his private clinic.

One frequent attendee at mealtime was Long Huy Pham. He was a year ahead of me in the economics program and knew all about courses and professors and department intrigue. When the Tet Offensive overran Saigon, I sponsored some of Long's family members as immigrants to America. Today he and his family live in the Washington, D.C. area, but I haven't contacted him in years. Long's brother-in-law, Dr. Luan Nguyen, a fine tennis player and friend, directed the University of Guam's Office of Information Technology for many years.

On the University of Hawaii Manoa campus, I was known as the husband of that Palauan girl who carries school books stacked on her head. Nina was, in her own way, a campus celebrity. She walked everywhere with books balanced on her head, a skill she had mastered from childhood in Palau. As a nursing student, she took biochemistry and anatomy classes with the medical students and got to know some of them. One such student was a returned Peace Corps volunteer from Palau named Greg Dever. Like me, he was married to a Palauan woman named Martha. We sometimes double dated. Greg continues to practice pediatric medicine in Palau and is an adjunct faculty member at the John A. Burns School of Medicine while also directing the Area Health Education Center, a nonprofit entity that provides health training throughout the Micronesian island area. Nowadays whenever Greg and I get together, it's our custom to absorb some quantity of Jameson Irish Whiskey while we, to use the Hawaiian vernacular, "talk-story."

When not in class, I worked thirty hours a week for Dr. Comitini at the University Economic Research Center. There I met a programmer named Imogene Kikuchi Estores. She assisted several professors at the Research Center with statistical analyses on the IBM mainframe. I often helped her carry reams of computer cards to the computing center. In return she showed me how to use SPSS and SAS statistical programs on the mainframe. With her help I became quite skilled at performing stepwise and multiple linear regressions, factor analyses, and matrix algebra operations. But more importantly, I gained insight into the underlying mathematical processes of those statistical operations, how to interpret outcomes and guard against misleading results. It wasn't long before some professors started asking me to process their computer runs. Thanks partly to Imogene, when it came time to do my dissertation, I could process and interpret my own computations.

As an aside, for a short time I was the token *haole* on Imogene's Thursday night bowling team, which included her husband-to-be, Leonard Estores.

During my second and third year in graduate school, I had an officemate and classmate from Taiwan named Tupai Yu. I'm unsure as to the correct spelling of her name and have lost track of her whereabouts, but Tupai was math competent and English challenged. I, on the other hand, was math challenged and somewhat English competent. We sometimes worked together on reading assignments. She helped me, and I helped her. That collaboration worked out well; however, I owe her thanks for more than just her mathematical and theoretical insights. She set an impressive example about how to maintain fortitude and dogged perseverance in the face of horrendous obstacles and setbacks. She never gave up when others, including some faculty, told her that she should. She never let defeat deter her from her objective. Her entire being was focused on the attainment of that degree, to the exclusion of everything else. I believe it took her five or six years, but I heard that she eventually made it. I will always hold much respect and admiration for Tupai Yu.

In early January of 1974, Dad died. I flew home for three days to attend his funeral. Livermore's old guard were in attendance, but at age eighty-seven, most of Dad's friends and all his siblings had already passed on. Just a week or two prior, during Christmas break, Dad and I had talked about my life on Guam, and I sensed that he was proud of what I was trying to accomplish. We both knew that he didn't have long to live, so we talked openly about the ramifications of his death. He expressed his wish that I "not linger over his casket" and "get on with my life." That made his passing a bit easier for me, but I was still heartbroken. He had always been there when I needed him. If he thought that my plans were a bit foolish, in most cases he let me figure that out for myself.

Mom was left with the work of closing the estate, selling the Livermore house, and moving to Chester. That took her more than a year, but she handled it with methodic German organization. Knowing Mom's intention to move to Chester, Dad had requested that he be buried there rather than in the Callaghan family plot at Livermore's Saint Michael's Cemetery. Mom handled that as well—not an easy task, because the ground in Chester was frozen at that time of year.

Returning to school was difficult. I was filled with sorrow for Dad and guilt for not helping Mom; however, with Nina's help and Tupai's example, I plodded onward, trying to focus on the work at hand, something I knew Dad would want me to do. At the same time, our lives in Honolulu became more complex. Ibedul's daughter, Dominica, came from Palau to live with us. She attended nearby

Washington Middle School, and for a couple of years we became temporary parents of a teenager. Nina handled most parenting chores in addition to her own studies. I helped out when I could, and the three of us lived quite happily together in the Clark Street apartment.

In May of 1975, Dominica graduated from middle school, and Nina graduated from U.H. with her B.S. in Nursing. By mid-June I had passed my qualifying exams and received Committee approval of my dissertation topic. That meant I had attained the august status of A.B.D. (all but dissertation).

We sent Dominica off to Palau with a diploma, accolades, and plethora of flower lai. For the first time in a while, Nina and I could relax and have some fun at beach gatherings and parties with friends in the Palauan community. Greg Dever and I downed more than a bit of Jameson together. He was grinding away in medical school. I worked on computer runs and library research for my dissertation, while Nina got a temporary nursing job at Queen's Hospital before flying home to Palau for a couple of weeks in late August.

By the first week in September 1975, we were both back in Guam, living in university housing on Dean's Circle, a short walk from campus. When Nina arrived from Palau, she brought with her the daughter of a cousin, our new teenage foster-charge, Tessie Faustino. Within a month Tessie became a social and academic success at nearby George Washington High School. It wasn't long before the boys came knocking at our door and I came to understand the difficulties of parenting a beautiful young lady cheerleader, pom-poms and all. The experience convinced me that parenting might prove easier with boys rather than girls. In spite of our busy schedules, Nina and I did our foster parental best. Tessie ultimately graduated and went on to attend Chico State University in California. She married a California boy and is now living in Poway, California, so I hope we did reasonably well at keeping her on the right path.

Nina found immediate employment at Guam Memorial Hospital. Each day I taught my four-course load, maintained office hours, and walked home to work on my dissertation, sometimes continuing late into the night. Save for a Christmas trip to Palau and some weekend socializing, this ritual continued into the spring of 1976.

* * *

Then on Friday, May 21, 1976, our world changed. We had known that She was coming. Classes had been canceled. We had stocked drinking water and extra provisions, but we were not ready for Her ferocity. Tessie, I, and Auntie Donina stayed at home for Her arrival. Nina was holding down a twelve-hour shift as charge nurse on the critical care ward of Guam Memorial Hospital. Thankfully our house walls and roof were concrete. By noon Typhoon Pamela's sustained winds had reached 140 miles per hour with gusts to 180. The following quote from a long-saved publication does some justice to the feeling of being in a Super Typhoon.

> The ripping tin, the roar of the wind, the grinding of metal, the cracking of trees amid the horizontal deluge, all combine to make a din unlike anything you've ever heard … The typhoon sounds as if nature is out to get you, to finally challenge man, head-on, in his tin and cement houses. It crashes against your walls and slams pieces of wood at you, trying to break down your house and your spirit. You feel that the typhoon is a living, breathing thing, a monster trying desperately to get at you to rip off your head and stuff it in your ear. (Awake! 1976, 9/8 pp.13-15)

I liken our experience, hunkered down in that house, to lying prostrate between two railroad tracks while the world's longest freight train passes overhead at high speed, all the time wondering if an oncoming freight car might have a low-hanging appendage.

Our house held together, but rain water blew with such force through the cracks in the wooden louvered windows that spray struck walls on the opposite sides of rooms. All our possessions were soaked, mattresses and pillows waterlogged, picture albums and favorite books ruined beyond salvage. I saved my computer and dissertation materials by wrapping them in garbage bags. Around 10:00 a.m. the power went off and never returned for almost four months. By 11:00 a.m. the water stopped running and never returned for two months. At some point the telephone service stopped and never returned for years. Cell phones had not yet been invented.

At about 3:00 p.m. the typhoon's eye began to pass over Guam. We went outside into calm and sunshine. Flocks of ocean birds were soaring in the blue sky, trapped there by the surrounding walls of wind. It was eerily quiet. Not a blade of grass remained, nor a leaf on any bush or tree. The windward surfaces of buildings were plastered with a grey-green mulch that had once been vegetation. The crowns of coconut trees were blown away, leaving only their trunks as topless stalks. Power poles were scattered like sticks, tangled and broken wires lay all around. In our front yard a flame tree with a three-foot diameter trunk had been stripped of its leaves and tipped on its side, its severed roots reaching for the sky. Our yard was filled with wood, tin roofing, and random debris that had blown from God knows where. Luckily, nothing except water and pureed greenery had penetrated into our house.

By 6:00 p.m., the winds returned with the same terrifying ferocity, this time blowing in the opposite direction. As the hours passed, we huddled together on the wet sofa in damp blankets. After midnight the winds gradually lessened. At dawn we were greeted by a haze-filled sunrise and almost no wind. Upon venturing outside, we discovered that the flame tree in the front yard had been blown back upright and now stood, denuded, but in its original position.

We hauled out furniture, mattresses, blankets and clothing to dry in the sun. Donina and Tessie cleaned up around the house and yard as best they could without water. I siphoned some gas for the chainsaw, grabbed one of our machetes, and started for the hospital in my four-wheel-drive pickup. On the way I drove in, around, over and through the worst devastation imaginable. Downed power poles and a maze of tangled wire littered the roadways. Cars, truck trailers, boats, and shipping containers were scattered like toys in a kid's sandbox. Only foundations remained where buildings had once stood. Tin roofing and siding lay everywhere. In one place I saw an eight-foot sheet of one-inch plywood that had been driven into a telephone pole with such force that the pole was now acting as the center pedestal for an almost perfectly level eight-foot table.

When I reached the hospital, I found Nina with other nurses and ICU patients in the basement boiler room, intravenous bottles hung from overhead pipes. The windows and one wall of their third-floor intensive care unit had blown out early in the storm. The staff had secured the flapping stairwell doors with fire hoses and managed to get twelve patients and the necessary equipment into the basement, where emergency power was still viable and the boilers provided warmth. No patients were lost that night.

Back at home we made a water catchment out of a fifty-gallon drum that had blown into our yard and began boiling and barbequing over an open fire whatever food we could salvage from the refrigerator and freezer. Everyone on Guam was doing the same, so for several days after the storm there was an abundance of food and much neighborly sharing. Soon our life settled down to open fire cooking, FEMA supplied disaster relief rations, kerosene lit evenings, saltwater baths, and laundries at the Marine Laboratory.

Unlike other faculty families living on Dean's Circle, our FEMA supplies were supplemented thanks to Donina's and Nina's knowledge and ingenuity. We had coconuts for drinking, fresh fish, coconut crabs, taro, seaweed salads, and an ever-dwindling supply of bananas and papayas that had been blown down by the wind. I couldn't tolerate the boiled fruit bat, but Donina, Nina, and Tessie seemed to enjoy that cuisine. It wasn't long before air shipments of food and critically needed betel nuts began arriving directly from relatives in Palau.

Nina continued her job at the hospital, and the four of us got along quite well, but there was little to be done other than wait for utilities to return, but that wasn't likely to be soon. The university wouldn't open until fall, and there was no way that I could work on my dissertation without power, so in early June we agreed that I should return to Honolulu and try to finish it there.

Greg Dever's wife, Martha, and his son, David, were spending the summer in Palau, so Greg offered me a couch, food, drink and affable company at his house on Clement Street in Manoa, a short walk from campus. Both of us were busy graduate students, but on some weekends, there was time to blow off steam together. A few of Greg's fellow medical students could only be described as incorrigible mischief makers. For example, at one point they had grown displeased with the university's cafeteria contractor—high prices, poor quality food, inconvenient hours, etc. So one day in the dark early morning hours, they arrived at Greg's house distributing a load of frozen food they had just purloined from the cafeteria contractor's freezer. We ate steak and eggs that morning and had some fine cuts of meat throughout the month, as did a cadre of medical students and their friends.

My dissertation Committee was a multi-ethnic collection of egocentric individuals who weren't always on the best terms with each other. Salvatore (Sal) Comitini, a marine resource Ph.D. from the University of Washington, was my advisor and Committee Chairman. He was also the principal investigator for the Sea Grant project that for three years funded my tuition and monthly stipend. During that time, I had grown to distrust him. He held the rank of Associate Professor, yet it seemed that he was somewhat insecure regarding his position. At times he displayed demeaning behavior toward me while appearing to be more accommodative and supportive of other graduate students. At his request I had spent months in the National Marine Fisheries Service library creating an annotated card file of all references having to do with Hawaii skipjack tuna history, science, industry and institutions. That exercise gave me an excellent grasp of pelagic fishery literature; however, at the time I was upset because Comitini let that card file sit on his desk for two years. During that time another researcher published an annotated bibliography containing most of the same citations and references. I felt that Comitini's lethargy had cost us a publication. In retrospect, I understand that even if he didn't benefit from my work, I certainly did, and perhaps that's all he planned in the first place.

The remainder of my Committee consisted of Yung C. Shang, a well-known Chinese agro-economist who specialized in Asian aquaculture; Moheb "Mo" A. Ghali, an Egyptian econometrician with considerable background in production function modeling, similar to that used in my dissertation; Youngil Lim, a Korean specialist in international trade; and James E.T. Moncur, an American specialist in Asian-Pacific water rights and practices. During the summer these people were off-island involved in research or consulting activities, but by late June 1976, I had gotten a draft into their hands, and by early August I had managed to incorporate responses to their sometimes conflicting concerns. An oral presentation/defense was scheduled by the Graduate Division for the first week in September, when by that time they were all scheduled to be back on campus.

Just when my future seemed in order, Dr. Comitini called me to his office and informed me that he was leaving for Jakarta, where he would be working with the Indonesian Government on a fisheries project for the next ten months.

"Unfortunately," he said, "I won't be able to attend your dissertation defense until next summer."

I replied, "You mean we can't have the defense as planned in September? I've made all the changes you and others suggested. I'll have the latest draft to you in a week or two. I'm as ready as I can be."

"I'm afraid not, but this'll give us nine months or so to get everything nailed down and tidy. You know, you're never as ready as you can be. You have your job in Guam. They're not going to fire you, are they? We can communicate by mail, and we'll be more ready when I get back."

My mind was a blur. I had been working, adrenalin-charged, for the last three years. I had patiently listened to his ramblings. I had taken care of his irritating requests. Now, at the last minute, Comitini had pulled the rug out from under me. It felt like every ounce of energy had been ripped out of my body. I couldn't say anything. I just walked out of his office.

Two doors down the hallway was Dr. Ghali's office. His door happened to be open. Without thinking I walked in, my eyes full of water. He looked up from his desk.

"Callaghan, what's wrong? Close the door. Sit down. What's the problem?"

When I explained to him my reason for being upset, he rolled his eyes in disgust and said, "Yes, I heard he was leaving, but that shouldn't prove an insurmountable problem. Based on my reading of your last draft, you appeared to be progressing quite well. Did you do as I said and check for heteroskedasticity in those regressions?"

"Yes, sir, I did. I printed out a graph of all 363 residuals and could see no visible sign of heteroskedasticity. Then I ran a White's Test that turned out insignificant at the 95 percent confidence level. So I'm pretty sure there's no heteroskedasticity."

"You're not 'pretty sure,' Callaghan. You are 95 percent confident," he chided. "You know, you've been extremely lucky, ending up with an R-squared of 79. Using monthly averages instead of thousands of individual observations may have contributed to that high R squared. At your defense you had better be ready to explain the how and why of that."

"I will, sir," I said. "I'll be ready."

Looking at his calendar he said, "Your defense, as I understand it, is scheduled for Friday, September 3. Is that right?"

"Yes, but now Dr. Comitini has postponed it until sometime next summer."

"Callaghan, listen to me. You just focus on being ready to defend on this upcoming September 3, at 9:00 a.m. I'll talk with Dr. Comitini and the others. Your job is to be ready. I'll take care of the rest. Now get out of here and go to work."

I have no idea what transpired among my Committee members, but I did successfully defend my dissertation on September 3, 1976. Dr. Comitini did not attend, but the rest of the Committee did, along with several economists and faculty members from other disciplines, the Sea Grant Program Director, and Dr. Roy Tsuda from the University of Guam Marine Laboratory. I heard later that Dr. Comitini was sent the Committee's signature page and told by the Department Chair to sign it.

I didn't attend the December formal graduation. Neither Mom nor Nina and I wanted to travel that far just for the sake of marching in a cap and gown. If Dad had been alive and wanted to attend, I would have done so. I wish he could have lived long enough to see me finish the race. I'm sure that no one in my family, me included, ever expected that I'd be a successful doctoral candidate.

Many people contributed to that success, but two stand out: Dr. Pedro Sanchez, who pushed me down the road in the first place, and Dr. Moheb Ghali, a superb teacher of econometrics and my advocate during the last turbulent stages of the effort. Doc Sanchez passed away in 1987. His son Simon continues the family name and public service legacy on Guam. Mo Ghali is now Professor Emeritus and Dean of the Graduate School at Western Washington University. He has published three books and more than fifty academic journal articles. Sal Comitini is nowhere to be found in any of my internet searches.

Other than some satisfaction in learning, I didn't enjoy those years of drudgery at U.H. Most of my fellow graduate students were quite brilliant and completely fascinated with economic theory. They thought and talked about little else and seemed to have no life other than economics. The few American students in the Department were all younger than I. They had come to graduate school directly from undergraduate institutions, having had little real-world experience other than part time employment.

The foreign students, mostly Asians, were closer to my age and had come from bureaucratic government backgrounds. They would return home to compete against their country's elite, those who had attended Oxford, Harvard, and the like. Therefore, the Asian students were manic about theoretical detail and classroom performance. No grade less than an A was acceptable. Their competitive drive and intellectual capability were immense, but their insight into practical applications of economic theory to common everyday problems seemed, in many cases, totally lacking. When their classwork was completed and their written exams passed, usually with flying colors, they often had little idea how to find and undertake a practical dissertation topic.

My perspective was different than the other students, and I kept that perspective hidden, especially from faculty. My goal was to get out of there with a degree as fast as possible, doing whatever it took. I viewed every course and every requirement as a hurdle in a race to the finish line. I didn't want to be a famous, well-published academic. I didn't care to spend a life on the cutting edge of economic theory. Learning for the sake of learning was not my bag. My thoughts were focused on practical applications for what I was learning. How might I construct and test an acceptable dissertation hypothesis?

Without letting anyone know, I operated backwards. Normally scientists find a question that needs answering. Then they formulate an expected answer or hypothesis, after which they collect and analyze data in a way that will allow them to reject or not reject that hypothesis. I, on the other hand, had sole access to a data set of six thousand fishing trips undertaken by pole-and-line tuna fishing vessels operating from the Van Camp Corporation's facilities in Palau. In the field of fisheries economics, that was an exceptional and rare data set. All I had to do was find an acceptable theoretical question that could be hypothesized in such a way as to allow the use of this data to test the assertion. If I could do that, then I would have a dissertation to drag across the finish line.

My approach worked. I finished in four years, at that time the second shortest doctoral completion in the department's history. The dissertation was titled, *Employment and Factor Productivity in the Palau Skipjack Tuna Fishery: A Production Function Analysis*. During those four years I gained respect for the awesome intellect of some human beings, and I learned much about economics and about myself, the most important being a realization of how little I knew.

*   *   *

By September of 1976, much of Guam's typhoon damage had been repaired. Power and water had returned to our Dean's Circle home. Tessie had officially graduated from high school and was living in Palau with her mother, preparing to attend Chico State College in California. I was back to teaching in the Business School, and Nina had been hired as an instructor in the School of Nursing, so we both now worked within walking distance of home.

Two biweekly paychecks lead to a much more relaxed and carefree lifestyle. Within a couple of months, we had purchased an old rundown bungalow on the ocean in the southern village of Merizo. Joe Paulino and his son Mark helped me clean up the grounds and refurbish the seawall. I hired the father of a friend and fellow faculty member, Anthony "Tony" Quan, to renovate the two-bedroom house. The whole undertaking, purchase price and renovation, came to around $22,000. Within a few weeks it was rented for $200 a month. Initially, we had intended to live there. Merizo was a quiet, traditional seaside village, with a lifestyle similar to Palau. In the end it was the one-hour drive to campus that forced us to face practical reality. With differing teaching schedules, we would need two cars and would each spend inordinate time on the road. Eventually we sold the Merizo house for a tidy profit.

In late November my friend and fishing-diving companion, Bill Williams, told me of a duplex being sold by a client of his law firm. It was located on a ridge overlooking the sea in Yona Village, only a ten-minute drive south from the university. The owner was an architectural firm, Mackinlay, Winnacker & Associates. Mieko Winnacker, the wife of a partner, was handling the sale. She was heavily into astrology and associated beliefs. There were several interested buyers, but she wanted someone with exactly the proper birthday as well as other characteristics known only to her. I knew Mieko lived in Honolulu, and since I hadn't heard anything after submitting my offer, I gave her a call while attending a workshop there. She immediately invited me to dinner the next night at her home—a home that turned out to be a mansion at the top of Wilhelmina Rise, one of Honolulu's most exclusive mountaintop neighborhoods. There I was treated to an extraordinary, Japanese-style dinner. Mieko, her older sister, and I sat at a round table that sported a gold and ivory inlaid lazy Susan. I did my best with the jade chopsticks while being subjected to an inquisition by both ladies. They wanted to know everything about me: my age, my upbringing, my lifestyle, my education, my wife's background, and so on. Despite an evening of conversation, I found out little about Mieko, other than she was a U.C. Berkeley architecture graduate and likely a dominant force within her husband's architectural firm.

Upon my return to Guam, Bill Williams informed me that Mieko had decided I could buy the duplex, provided that I agreed to sign the closing documents on a specific calendar date of her choosing. I took out my first ever mortgage from Citibank, at $72,000. We completed the closing documents on the appointed day, buying the duplex subject to completion of bank required typhoon repairs. On the night of January 24, 1977, Nina and I slept there on futons in the dining room. By month's end, we had moved our belongings from Dean's Circle housing. Each weekend I painted interior rooms while Nina worked in the yard planting bananas, papayas, and various useful plants and herbs, as well as a breadfruit tree transplanted from Joe Paulino's Bear Rock. That Yona residence, with its 180-degree ocean view, subsequently underwent two renovations and additions as it housed us and our children, foster children, relatives and friends for the next thirty-five years. Nina still lives there.

* * *

During spring break of 1976–77, we accompanied my office mate, Tony Quan, and his family to Manila. Tony was the second eldest son of a well-respected Chamorro family. He held a Master's Degree in Economics from Marquette University, and we had become fast friends while teaching together. Tony's wife, Risa Garcia Quan, invited us to stay in her family home, located just across Roxas Boulevard from the shores of Manila Bay. The five-story house and servant's quarters were situated in a compound entirely enclosed by a ten-foot-high concrete wall, topped with barbed wire and steel spikes. For both Nina and I it was shocking to experience such poverty immediately adjacent to such wealth. The Garcia household had a staff of at least seven full-time helpers. When I asked a gardener how much he was paid, his answer in pesos amounted to five US dollars a month. In fairness though, I don't know what in-kind benefits he received. Most of the help appeared to sleep and eat on the premises.

Anthony H. (Tony) Quan with daughter Amanda, *yaya* (au-pair) with daughter Ailene, and Clarisa (Risa) Garcia Quan, Manila, 1977

Every day fishermen beached their *bangkas* just across the street and sold fresh fish directly from their boats to crowds of buyers who competed with one another, haggling and bargaining over prices, quality and weight. This was fascinating to a fisheries economist, so early each morning I asked to be let out of the compound to observe the fish marketing activities. When the grizzled old chauffeur opened the iron gate, he habitually cautioned, "Sir, remember, don't give the beggars anything, no matter what they say to you, and don't forget to keep your wallet in your front pocket. Watch out for your camera. Please come back soon. Don't stay long or Mrs. Esther will worry."

Esther Garcia was the family matriarch and mother of Tony's wife, Risa. Her husband, a prominent lawyer, had died sometime after WWII. Esther now managed the family affairs while grooming her two sons to eventually take over what appeared to be an assortment of real estate holdings.

If I spent too long by the boats or in the adjacent fish market, a servant would be sent to fetch me. It was relatively easy to find a White American in that crowd of brown humanity. After a couple of days, I began taking one of the household servants along with me. Doing so helped with translation and interpretation of my questions. Soon it became clear to me that price differentials were heavily influenced by personal relationships and custom. A complete understanding of these fish market transactions would require a blend of economics and other social science thinking. Such interdisciplinary research was a novel idea in those days, less so today. In any case, the more I learned at the market the more enthusiastic I became and the longer I stayed, necessitating that Esther send a second servant to fetch both me and the first servant.

The minute that iron gate closed behind me each morning, I departed from one world and entered another. Squatters occupied derelict buildings, doorways and public spaces. Children appeared from all directions, dancing around, hands outstretched, chanting, "Americano, Americano. We hungry. Just twenty centavos. Please. Please. Americano." It was unnerving to ignore them. Everywhere around me I sensed a strange combination of poverty, resignation, and pollution, but also hope, diligence, and ingenuity. Despite the sewer smells and exhaust pollution, people went about their daily lives doing what needed doing, buying, selling, and transporting, on scooters, bicycles, and tricycles, in jeepneys, buses, trucks and cars. Their activity filled my senses with a cacophony of sights, sounds, smells and vibrations. For me it was a microeconomic textbook come to life in front of my eyes. I wanted to understand every minute detail of what I was seeing. Given the opportunity, I would have happily spent weeks in and around that fish market on Roxas Boulevard.

Inside the gated compound our lives remained quiet, serene and luxurious. Our dirty clothes from the prior day appeared washed, ironed and folded on our bed each evening. Our sheets were changed every other day. Meals were served in the dining room with its hand-carved table, chairs and wall panels. Some meals were more formal than others. Neither Nina nor I saw the inside of the kitchen or the other several floors of the household. The Quans and Esther Garcia and her sons seemed to appear at the appropriate times, from various directions. Whenever we went out, we were chauffeur-driven. Mrs. Garcia took charge of shopping trips, negotiating on our behalf at jewelry wholesalers and Manila's top rattan furniture factories. Nina bought hand-crafted pearl and gold jewelry at exceptional prices. We also purchased rattan living room furniture and had it shipped to Guam. Esther took us on a chauffeur-driven four-day trip to her summer home in the mountain town of Baguio City. There we walked in pine forests and ate Tony Quan's favorite strawberry pie, baked by nuns in a nearby convent. On the way back to Manila we stopped to tour Taal Volcano Lagoon.

At one point I said to Esther Garcia, "You're lucky to have so much household help. They have certainly made our stay comfortable."

She replied, "Mr. Callaghan, it's not all that it appears to be. Tell me, do you have an electric washing machine and dryer at your house in Guam?"

"Yes," I replied.

"And perhaps you have automatic yard sprinklers, a food processor, and various cooking appliances?"

"Yes," I replied again.

"Keep in mind, Mr. Callaghan, that those machines and equipment don't ever get sick or pregnant, or have social problems, or have hungry children who need food, education and health care. These people stay with me because their lives are much better under my roof than they otherwise would be. But the cost of their services is not trivial."

That exchange has stuck in my mind over the years. I still wrestle with the validity of her implied socio-economic balance.

Two events during that spring holiday in Manila have remained in my memory. The first occurred on Good Friday, the supposed day of Jesus's crucifixion. The Garcia household staff was not required to work that day, so I went alone through the iron gate into the outside world. Upon entering Roxas Boulevard, I was engulfed by a sea of humanity, part of a religious procession. Whatever was in the lead had already passed, but I followed along with the crowd, all the while trying to keep my bearings for eventual return. Shortly the procession turned up a side street and massed in front of a church, the front door of which presented a bottleneck. At that point I became a bit more relaxed, knowing I wasn't far from the Garcia compound and could find my way back. So I remained in the crowd to see what lay ahead. As the only American White guy around, I was paid some slight deference, and in short order squeezed through the door and down the center aisle of a magnificent interior. The church I later learned was called Malate, or Our Lady of Remedies. I know little of architecture, but it seemed to me that both Muslim and Christian influences were present. Atop the main altar was a statue of the Virgin Mary, clearly the crowd's objective.

Having seen enough, I retreated out a side door, only to be confronted by a grotesque display of penitential self-flagellation. Men with blood dripping down their faces wore crowns of real thorns and beat themselves with whips that contained hooks, nails, and barbed wire. A huge wooden cross lay on the ground, and a man wearing a crown of thorns was being lashed to it in preparation for having his hands nailed. I wanted to take pictures but didn't dare. There were no cameras in sight, and I was the only apparent foreigner around. I just stood back and watched as the nails were pounded through the man's hands, and the cross, with him on it, was tilted aloft. Those images still remain in my mind. I certainly hope God forgave his trespasses, whatever they were.

The second event occurred on Holy Saturday night, the night before Easter Sunday. Dressed in semiformal attire, Esther Garcia, Tony, Risa, Nina and I were dropped off by our chauffer in front of the Metropolitan Cathedral in old town Manila. The crowd had already gathered for Easter Vigil High Mass, and there appeared to be only standing room on the grounds outside the building. Paying no deference to anyone, Esther marched us through the crowd, up the front steps, and into the vestibule.

"Unfortunately, we're late," she whispered. "We'll have to sit separately. Paul, you come with me. The rest of you, wait here. I'll be right back."

After blessing ourselves at a marble holy-water font, Esther led the way down the center aisle of the Gothic cathedral. I felt the gaze of a thousand eyes piercing my back as we approached the sanctuary. Four rows from the altar rail, Esther stopped at a pew with a vacant aisle seat. She genuflected, turned to me and said, "Paul, you sit here." As I genuflected and slid into the pew, Esther nodded a greeting to some surrounding faces. She then marched back up the aisle, leaving me to my fate, surrounded by Manila's aristocracy. The brass plate on the end of my pew carried the title "Senator." The last name was Santos. I had no idea what I would do if he arrived to claim his seat, and I had no idea what dignitaries were sitting in those first few rows. I did know that every eye was upon me, wondering who is this American sitting in the Senator's pew.

The High Mass and homily were delivered in Tagalog. I understood nothing, but thanks to my Catholic upbringing, I knew the ritual and could recall some Latin responses. When it came time for communion, I went to the altar rail along with everyone else, even though I hadn't been to confession or communion since my marriage. I wasn't about to be the only White boy sitting in that pew alone while everyone else passed by me to the communion rail. At the end of Mass, those seated in the first ten or so pews exited down the center aisle, while other participants waited in place. Once again, I felt eyes staring at me.

It was a relief to see Esther and the others waiting for me on the steps. "Where did you guys sit?" I asked.

"We were in the choir loft," said Nina. "It was a great view and beautiful singing."

"Did you enjoy the service? The choir was magnificent, wasn't it?" asked Esther.

I had been so anxious that I hardly remembered hearing the choir. "Yes," I said. "The High Mass was beautiful and the choir was outstanding."

"Did you talk to the man sitting next to you? He is Supreme Court Justice (the name long since forgotten). He's quite a conversant and friendly person."

"No," I said, wishing that I had been less timid. He had smiled at me a couple of times.

More about Tony Quan in a succeeding chapter.

* * *

In the summer of 1977, Nina worked part-time at the hospital while I taught summer school classes. In August Mom visited. After Dad's death, she had moved from Livermore to Chester, where she was settling into a small two-bedroom house on a meadow at the edge of town. The long flight via Honolulu to Guam was hard on her, and Guam's heat and humidity proved a difficult adjustment from the cold, dry air of Chester. But Mom was a good sport, and the three of us had fun swimming, snorkeling, sightseeing and shopping together. We visited Guam's historic places such as Two Lovers Leap, the Spanish Fort of Agana, and Umatac Bay, where Magellan had landed in 1521. Mom bought some jewelry that she valued greatly and wore for the rest of her life. The Paulino clan threw a party for her at Bear Rock in Inarajan. I know Mom had a good time, but tropical weather was not something she enjoyed. It was her last trip into the Pacific, but she left with an understanding of our lifestyle and a visual image of our home with its magnificent ocean view.

About the time Mom departed, Nina's two brothers, Saba and Nino, came from Palau to live with us. At the same time, Joe Paulino asked that his son Mark stay at our house. Joe thought it would be beneficial for Mark to experience living in a non-Chamorro household that was part-Micronesian and part-American. All three boys attended George Washington High School near the university. They got along well together, and for the better part of the next three years we became a family of five. Tennis was our main afterschool activity. In those days Nina was on the university tennis team, and the three boys played in several all-Guam tournaments. On some weekends the boys and I went spearfishing together in my Boston Whaler boat. Saba was the best fisherman and the best tennis player. Nino was the best student, and Mark kept the peace. Raising three teenagers was no easy task, but I was rewarded by their company and contribution to the richness of my life.

Nino and Saba Tewid, Guam, 1977

In the fall of 1979, our family went through a major transition. We leased our Yona house, furniture and all, to a visiting medical doctor from Montana. Nino and Saba moved into their own Callaghan-subsidized apartment within walking distance of both the university and George Washington High School. Saba worked while Nino finished his last year of high school. Mark returned to his family in Inarajan. Nina moved to Honolulu to work on a Master's Degree in Nursing, and I moved in with my diving and fishing buddy, Bill Williams, whose wife, Jane, also left Guam for Hawaii to work on her Doctorate in Anthropology.

Bill and I lived together in his Nimitz Hill home for two-and-a-half years while our wives struggled in graduate school. I continued teaching while Bill managed his law practice, but in our spare time the two of us had much fun sailing, diving and fishing together. Our friendship was forever cemented that day when he backed from his garage directly into the side of my brand-new pickup truck, and further confirmed on a night during the Guam to Rota Yacht Race, when Bill arrived on deck to find me sailing in the wrong direction. We arrived at Rota Harbor in last place, an unacceptable result for Bill's competitive personality. When Jane finally arrived back home from Hawaii, she was aghast to find dusty dishes in the cupboards. Bill and I had managed to each use only one knife, fork, spoon, bowl, cup and glass, as well as one communal sauce and frying pan, during the two-and-a-half years that we lived together—the better to reduce dishwashing requirements, we thought.

Paul Callaghan with Jane and Bill Williams, Guam, 1986

In retrospect, that separation from Nina was probably not a good thing for our marriage; however, it was something Nina felt she had to do, and I wanted to support her, being always proud of her accomplishments. The two of us did get together quite often, as I had frequent fisheries-related meetings and conferences that brought me to Honolulu. She lived in a ninth-floor apartment at 845 University Avenue with a broad *mauka* view of Manoa Valley. During holiday and summer breaks we traveled to visit Mom in California and Nina's family in Palau. On May 16, 1982, I was a proud, camera-carrying husband when Nina graduated with two degrees on the same day: a Master of Science in Nursing and a Master of Public Health. As she put it in a letter to my mom, "I've finally reached the light at the end of the tunnel." In a way, we both had.

By September of 1982, we were back in Guam, living in our Yona house once again, both deeply involved with our teaching and community affairs schedules. During our almost three-year separation, we had each become our own individual, accustomed to doing things how and when we wished. Hawaii life had Americanized Nina to some extent, but her Palauan nature still dominated. Living with Bill had caused me to regain some of my American cultural focus. For both of us, the readjustment to married life wasn't easy.

With Nino living in the university dormitories and Saba living with his wife-to-be and working at Continental Airlines, Nina and I found ourselves residing together alone. For the first time in several years, we had only each other to consider, along with our respective event-filled professional lives. We settled into a rhythmic but busy routine. The days and years rolled on, interspersed with relaxing summers in Chester and holidays in Palau. During those years, I was offered employment opportunities by the Trust Territory Government, the Government of New Guinea, the South Pacific Commission, and the United Nations Economic and Social Commission for Asia and the Pacific. All these positions came with enticing salary, tax and benefit packages, but required relocating to various Pacific sites. In every case Nina and I chose to reject the offers and remain in Guam. It was easy for us to envision a comfortable academic life in Guam that lasted into our old age. Unfortunately, that would not turn out to be the case.

As to the ultimate disposition of our three teenaged charges, Saba was not much of a student, but he possessed a kind-hearted, jovial personality that netted him many friends. After graduation from high school, he worked at a noodle house and as a baggage handler for Continental Airlines, before moving back to Palau. He was living there, married with two sons, when he drowned while spear fishing at night. I don't know the full story of Saba's passing, and perhaps no one does. After high school, Mark moved to Honolulu along with his mother, Pauline, and brother, Andre. He has lived there ever since, working in the nursery and garden supply industry. Nino graduated from the University of Guam with a degree in accounting. He now lives in Palau and is married with three grown children. For many years he has held the position of Public Auditor for the Republic of Palau, a respected leader and *Rubak*. He remains a reliable contact and anchor to my Palauan past.

Chapter 12

The Council

It was January of 1978. I had just deposited my paycheck and was walking across the Bank of Hawaii lobby in Guam's Julale Shopping Center. A voice behind me said, "Dr. Callaghan, can we have a word with you?"

Only academics referred to me as Dr. Callaghan, so I turned expecting to see someone from the university. That was not the case. Two young Chamorro men stood there, both dressed in slacks and short-sleeved white shirts with ties. One I didn't recognize. The other I knew to be Benjamin J. Cruz. People called him "B.J." He had recently returned to Guam from law school at Santa Clara University and now worked for Governor Bordallo.

B.J. shook my hand and said, "Do you mind if I call you Paul?"

"No, not at all. Paul's fine," I said. "I really don't like titles, but at the university they won't let those things go."

"Great, Paul it is," he said. "People call me B.J." He made no effort to introduce his associate.

"Yes, I know," I replied. "I was at your house in Talofofo a few months ago. It was a Saturday afternoon."

"Oh, yes, I was flying high that day," said B.J. "There were lots of people. I'm a bit foggy as to who all came and went. I hope you had a good time."

"I did," I said. "The view over Talofofo Bay from your place is spectacular."

"Well, I hope you enjoyed more than just the view," he said with a twinkle in his eye.

His aside was perceptive, since at the time my naiveite had been shaken by the cornucopia of liquor, food, entertainment and other distractions that had been available that Saturday afternoon.

"You're always welcome to stop by on the weekends. There's usually something interesting going on," he said. "Anyway, the reason we've chased you down is that Governor Bordallo would like to know if you'd be willing to serve, along with his brother Paul, as Guam's representative on the Western Pacific Fisheries Management Council. The Council meets periodically in Honolulu and elsewhere in the region. It's responsible for regulating the fishing activities in US waters around the Marianas, Samoa, Hawaii, and other US Pacific Islands. They pay a daily stipend, and you'll get to travel on federal money. It's a great opportunity. We understand you have a degree in fisheries economics. That's true, isn't it?"

"Yes," I said. "Marine Resource Economics."

"Good, so if you're willing, the Governor will submit your name to the US Secretary of Commerce for consideration."

"Sure," I said. "I'm willing."

"Fine, so can you bring your resume to me at the Governor's office by four o'clock today?"

"Yes, sure. I can do that," I said.

"Good. See you this afternoon."

"Thank the Governor for considering me," I said as the two of them hurried away across the lobby, apparently late for some engagement.

Upon returning to the university, I set about updating my resume and informing myself as to what this Western Pacific Regional Fishery Management Council was all about. From the Federal Register and other sources, I discovered that the Council had been established by Congress in 1976 under Public Law 94-265, *The Magnuson Fishery Conservation and Management Act.* That Act initially did two things. It created a two-hundred-nautical-mile band of exclusive ocean jurisdiction off the coasts of the United States, its territories and possessions. The first three miles from shore remained under the jurisdiction of each individual state and territory. The remainder out to two-hundred miles is referred to as the US Exclusive Economic Zone, or EEZ.

The law also established eight regional councils to oversee the fishery resources within the EEZ. Voting membership on these councils included state and territorial fishery management officials, regional directors of the National

Marine Fisheries Service (NMFS), and knowledgeable appointees representing industry, recreational, and conservation interests. Nonvoting representatives from the Department of State, US Coast Guard, and US Fish and Wildlife Service also sat in council meetings. These councils were given the responsibility of creating conservation and management plans for the fishery resources within their respective zones. The NMFS and Coast Guard were responsible for regulatory enforcement of these plans.

The Western Pacific Regional Council, headquartered in Honolulu, had twelve members and held jurisdiction over an EEZ that was larger in area than the continental United States. It included waters that surrounded the State of Hawaii, Commonwealth of the Northern Mariana Islands, Territory of Guam, Territory of Samoa, and all the US Pacific possessions: Wake Island, Jarvis Island, Howard Island, Baker Island, Johnston Atoll, Kingman Reef, and Palmyra Atoll.

After several weeks of waiting, the Secretary of Commerce approved my appointment on October 22, 1978. I was soon off to Hawaii aboard Pan Am Flight 002, to attend the thirteenth council meeting at the Kona Hilton Hotel in Kailua-Kona. My expenses were paid by the council, including a daily salary at the rate of GS-15. For the first time I felt thankful that I had spent those trying years acquiring a Ph.D. in Marine Resource Economics. That degree was probably the thing that set my council nomination apart from those proffered by other Pacific Island governors, and it made possible many subsequent years of enjoyable work in Pacific fisheries management.

My flight from Guam crossed the International Date Line, so I arrived at the Kona Airport before I had left Guam and the day before the meeting started. I was met and transported to the hotel by the council's Executive Director, Wilvan G. Van Campen, and his secretary, Kitty Simonds. As we drove into Kona town, Kitty briefed me on two items for the next day's meeting—the Billfish PMP and the Spiny Lobster FMP. I had read the binder of briefing documents, but it was helpful to receive additional clarity and be reminded of acronyms such as FMP, Fishery Management Plan, and PMP, Preliminary Management Plan. At the time I had no idea as to the myriad of fishery management acronyms that would become commonplace vocabulary in the years to come.

My hotel suite had its own bar and a balcony that overlooked the breaking waves along the shoreline. I was so impressed with the bathroom telephone that I called Nina in Guam and Mom in Chester while sitting on the toilet, just to tell them that I had "arrived," in more ways than one.

Kitty Rose Simonds, Homer, Alaska, 1982

That evening Kitty invited me to dinner with, as she put it, "a few council family members." It was an eye-opening adventure as our vanload of participants moved from club to club. Large amounts of sushi and sashimi accompanied a profusion of alcoholic beverages, all paid for by agents of Japanese and Korean fishing firms who felt they needed council approval to fish in US waters. Most everyone became increasingly inebriated as the night progressed.

When we finally returned to our hotel, the Hilton's disco refused to allow Kitty to enter because she was wearing shorts and flipflops, whereupon Kitty and Henry Sesapasara, from American Samoa, entered the women's restroom together. When they emerged, Kitty was wearing Henry's pants and loafers, while Henry wore Kitty's shorts and flipflops. We were all then allowed into the disco, with no one apparently caring about Henry's attire.

It's worth mentioning here that Henry was the Director of the Office of Marine Resources in American Samoa at the time. We were about the same age and have remained friends ever since. Over the years Henry has held many responsible positions in the Government of American Samoa, both elected and appointed. He is now a titled community elder—Va'amua Henry Sesapasara. At the time of this writing, he once again represents American Samoa on the council, heads the Department of Marine and Wildlife Resources, and is active in fishery-management matters throughout the Pacific. The oil painting of sharks in my house was done by Henry's friend, Saoud, and given to me as a gift, along with a lengthy Samoan chant, the import and translation of which have long since been lost.

At two in the morning when the disco closed, some of our group, mostly those from Washington, D.C. and elsewhere in the mainland, decided to take a moonlight ocean swim in front of the hotel. With considerable antics, they splashed their way into the dark tidal pools adjacent to the barrier reef. Most knew little of ocean reefs and didn't perceive the rising tide nor the growing swells. Phosphorescence and shimmering white foam drew them ever closer to the breaking waves. Kitty and I and a few others watched from the balcony, hoping that common sense might prevail over euphoria, and that no one would be hurt.

In the end, only one person suffered measurable damage. Doyle Gates, head of the Western Pacific Program Office of NMFS, had for much of the evening been shepherding a shapely secretary from the NOAA administrator's office. She had never before swum in a tropical ocean at night, so Doyle was anxious to show her some secluded parts of the reef. When the two of them reappeared on land, Doyle was in considerable pain with several black sea urchin spines firmly imbedded in his buttock. With the aid of some deftly used scissors and a pair of pliers, he regained a semblance of decorum before retiring to his room, unaccompanied.

It was well past three in the morning before I flopped into bed. The wakeup call came at six. After a shower, several glasses of water and an aspirin or two, I ventured down to breakfast on the hotel veranda that overlooked the ocean. At one table Kitty and several others were in deep conversation with the NOAA administrator, Terry Leitzell. *Kitty surely has stamina*, I thought. *My head feels completely disjointed, yet at this early morning hour, she's apparently operating in high gear. Quite a lady.*

I cruised the buffet for a plateful of scrambled eggs, bacon, and toast. The coffee that I desperately needed was missing. I assumed it would be served by the waiter when I was seated. My attention had shifted to locating an empty table when a voice beside me said, "Dr. Callaghan, would you like to join us?"

Three men were sitting there. The one who spoke arose in a welcoming fashion. He was Japanese, small in stature, with twinkling eyes and a mustache that joined a full goatee. "My name is Kenji Ego. This is Frank Goto and Buzzy Agard. We're council members from Hawaii, and we understand you're the new council member from Guam. Please sit with us." He motioned to the empty chair at their table.

"Thanks," I said as I put down my plate and slid into the chair, hoping that my coffee cup might soon be filled. I noticed that all three men were surreptitiously eying the pony tail I had been growing for a couple of years in the hope of better relating to my students.

Kenji continued, "Welcome to the council. Your fellow member from Guam, Paul Bordallo, speaks highly of you. He says you are a university professor who specializes in fisheries economics. Is that right?"

"Well," I said, "I have a degree in Marine Resource Economics, and I do some fishing whenever I can."

"And what kind'a fishing is that?" asked Buzzy. Although his question was direct, his demeanor exuded thoughtful kindness. He was a tall, gaunt man, with intense brown eyes set in a weather-beaten face—Hawaiian with some European blood, I judged. He wore sunglasses perched above his forehead with a string from earpiece to earpiece so they couldn't fall below his chest.

"I've got a small boat, twenty-one feet, and a Zodiac. I do some spearfishing and a little trolling around Guam," I said. "During the season I do some night handlining for Akule, and whenever it's calm, and that's not often on Guam, I do some deep bottom-fishing for Onaga, Opaka, and the occasional Lehi. I'm married to a Palauan, and that means no matter what else I do, I must put fish on the table, as well as on the tables of in-laws."

"Have you had any commercial experience?" asked Kenji.

"Only tangentially," I said. "I was a Peace Corp volunteer in Palau, assigned to the Trust Territory Government Marine Resources Division. At the time, Van Camp maintained a freezer transshipment facility in Palau and stocked it with a small fleet of Okinawan crewed pole-and-line vessels. I've spent some time on those Okinawan boats, as well as a couple of week-long trips on small Japanese longliners that transshipped in Palau. I also worked with the finance and bookkeeping side of a fishermen's co-operative and a small boatyard in

Palau. The chief boatbuilder was from Hawaii. Maybe you know him, Kiyoshi Matsumoto."

Kenji reacted immediately. "When it comes to boatbuilding, he's one of the top old school sampan carpenters. I just saw him last week. He's building boats on Oahu now. How and when did he go to Palau?"

"When I was there in the mid-1960s, Matsumoto had been contracted by the Trust Territory Government to teach boatbuilding. A guy from Hawaii named Peter Wilson was chief of the T.T. Marine Resources Division at the time, so he knew Matsumoto and brought him to Palau."

"Yea," said Buzzy, "I knew that guy Wilson. He's a *haole kamaaina* from Oahu who was into shark fishing here and did a documentary on sharks. I think it was called *Sharks Are My Business*. Anyway, he was a real talker and promoter. Where is he now?"

"His father was a doctor. They lived in Kahala," muttered Frank Goto, a somber Japanese gentleman, who to this point had remained silent and expressionless.

"I think he's in Saudi Arabia doing something with fisheries development," I replied as I shoveled some eggs into my mouth and downed the coffee that had finally been poured by the waiter.

They seemed interested, so I continued. "Matsumoto and Wilson got government funding to build a seventy-five-foot Hawaiian sampan pole-and-line boat as a demonstration project. They named it the *Emeraech* and contracted a captain from Honolulu to run the boat and teach locals how to bait and fish for tuna, Hawaiian style. His name was Richard Kinney. In Palau I sometimes went out with him on the *Emeraech*. Now that he's back in Hawaii, I've made a couple of trips with him out of Kewalo Basin on his boat the *Sooty Turn*. Do you guys know Richard?"

"Kinney is a hard one to miss," said Buzzy. "I heard that he went to work in the Trust Territory for a while. As I remember, when he came back, he told everyone how bad the place was and how lazy the locals were."

I said nothing, but thought, *Kinney had an affair with one of those locals, his housekeeper, so in some ways the locals must not have been all that bad.*

The waiter filled my coffee cup. It was lukewarm, so I drank it down in gulps as he served the others. Before leaving he filled mine a second time. My head continued to remind me of the previous night's activities, but I realized that these three guys were learning about me, and I knew nothing about them, so I asked, "What do you folks do that got you appointed to this council?"

"I'm director of the Hawaii Fish and Game, under the Department of Land and Natural Resources," said Kenji, "And this maverick Hawaiian buzzard has fished the Kingdom's waters from Pearl and Hermes to South Point. He's always on the front end of every innovative idea for catching more fish, or crabs, or lobsters, and lately, deep-water shrimp. Most times he's using new techniques before anyone else learns about them, and before the State can pass regulations to rein him in."

"Don't believe everything that comes from Kenji's mouth," said Buzzy. "I've harvested a few ocean resources in my time, and I might have figured out some new ways of making a living at it, but I don't break the law, and lately I've become much more of a conservationist."

"Yes," quipped Kenji, "I'll give you that, but only after you killed most of them did you decide that you had better try and save the rest."

"As for Frank here," continued Kenji, "he's the godfather of the United Fishing Agency auction, the largest fresh fish auction in the US, second only to Tokyo's Tsukiji."

Frank remained silent, appearing a bit sullen, his demeanor yielding no acknowledgement of Kenji's words or hint of welcome to me.

In later years I learned that Buzzy had been the first to use aerial spotting to locate schools of Akule and tuna. He not only spotted for his own boats but sold his services to others. Rumor had it that the reason he crashed his plane on the runway at Honolulu Airport and lost his pilot's license was because his attention was distracted by a woman passenger while landing the aircraft. I don't know if that's true, but he wasn't flying anymore by the time I met him.

I also learned that Frank Kunio Goto's stern, withdrawn attitude was only a cover for a man with a kind heart who had risen through the school of hard knocks. Like others of Hawaii's Japanese elite, he had served in the 442nd Infantry Regiment during World War II. At times during 1950s and 1960s, strong arm tactics were required to encourage fishermen to sell their catches through his United Fishing Agency auction, rather than selling them directly to wholesalers, restaurants and markets. Frank's heavy-handed approach resulted in United Fishing Agency securing a near monopoly on fish sales in Hawaii, a monopoly that continues to this day under the watchful eye of Frank's grandson.

I had pretty much inhaled everything on my plate and was on a fourth cup of coffee when Buzzy asked, "How is the bottom fishing around Guam?"

"Well, I'm a calm weather bottom fisherman," I said. "If it's rough I stay home, and in Guam, the trade winds make it rough most of the year. The leeward banks are pretty well fished out, but in May through September, you can get some calm days. Then the windward banks are pretty productive. I only fish to feed our household and my wife's extended family, but once in a while when I have a good day, I'll sell some at the co-op to pay expenses. There are just a few full-time fishermen on Guam. Most all of them use multiple gears, depending on the season. I think it's pretty tough to make a living as a full-time small boat fisherman. Most high-liners hold second jobs. Some people over the years have tried to scale up to larger vessels, but the costs increase exponentially and the local market can't absorb a seasonally erratic supply. A friend of mine, Kuni Sakamoto, came from Hawaii to try commercial bottom fishing in Guam. Now he works as a technician for the University of Guam Marine Lab. He says the regular pay there beats long hours at sea in a small boat and the uncertain prices at the Coop."

"So you know Kuni!" said Kenji. "He was a top-line bottom fishermen on Oahu. Then he just disappeared. I wondered where he went."

"Well, he's in Guam," I said. "He taught me how to set up my bottom rigs and tie proper knots. He helped me build a sea anchor out of a parachute and install my Furuno paper recorder. But his advice never included the where-to-fish part. That was up to me."

I could see across the veranda that Kitty had left her table with the NOAA administrator and was moving toward the ballroom. "Shouldn't we be getting to the meeting?" I asked. "I see Kitty is headed that way."

"No need rush," said Kenji. "Kitty's a stickler for venue organization. She wants to make sure that the council staff has the table placement and seating arranged to her satisfaction, and she wants to make sure that the sound system, podium, and everything else is in proper order for Wads. He relies on her a lot."

I knew that Wadsworth (Wads) Y. H. Yee, a State Senator from Hawaii, was Council Chair, but I had not yet met him.

"How about Dr. Van Campen?" I asked. "Isn't he the Executive Director?"

Kenji glanced at Buzzy, who rolled his eyes and said, "Van Campen has the credentials, but Kitty runs the show around here. That's something you best learn straightaway."

"Now that I think about it, she did kind of take charge when they picked me up at the airport yesterday," I said. "What's her position? Isn't she Van Campen's secretary?"

"Yes," said Buzzy, "but she was on US Senator Hiram Fong's staff in Washington, D.C., and Wads Yee is the Senator's nephew. She's close to Senator

Inouye too and friends with people on his staff. Her husband, John, is editor of the *Honolulu Star Bulletin*. If you want something around here, you're generally better off asking Kitty before you mention it to Van Campen."

"Kitty's da boss," said Frank dryly.

"Thanks for the advice," I said. "I'll try to keep my head down and follow Paul Bordallo's lead."

"That's a good approach," said Kenji. "Where is Paul? I haven't seen him yet."

"He won't be here," I said. "Apparently he and Rufo Lujan were taking a flight via Tokyo and it was canceled. I don't think he's coming at all now."

"Well in that case," said Kenji, "there's one thing you should know about how council management decisions have traditionally worked. If an issue impacts only Guam, then the Hawaii and Samoa members will support whatever the Guam members want to do. We expect that you'll do the same for issues that impact only us. In other words, we try not to mess around with management issues in the other guy's fisheries."

"How about issues that impact all our fisheries?" I asked.

"Then you vote how you think is best for your island," said Buzzy. "The hard one is when the representatives from one place don't agree among themselves as to what should be done. And that happens sometimes here in Hawaii."

Kenji muttered under his breath, "The State is always right." Buzzy didn't respond.

Frank muttered, "Except when they're wrong."

Kenji pushed back from the table, saying, "I've got to get the meeting binder from my room. See you gentlemen in the meeting. I believe it's in the Alii Surf Room at the end of that covered walkway." He nodded in the direction that Kitty had previously taken.

"Me too," said Buzzy as he and Frank shoved away from the table.

"Guess I'd better do that too," I said, getting to my feet.

As we four waited for the elevator, a tall, dapperly dressed, blondish *haole* gentleman approached us. "Aloha on this fine Hawaiian morning," he said. "Are we ready to insist that this Billfish PMP protect the rights of Hawaii's sports fishing community that generates millions of dollars for the State's economy every year?"

"Peter, we understand the concerns of your constituency, but there must be an equitable balance between sports and commercial fishing. Don't worry, I think we're on the way to getting there," said Kenji.

"I truly hope that 'getting there' means keeping those longliners far away from our billfish grounds," replied Peter.

"Dr. Callaghan, I'd like you to meet Peter Fithian, the fourth member of our Hawaiian contingent. Among his tourist related activities, he runs the Hawaii International Billfish Association (HIBA) that sponsors the world-famous tournament here in Kona every year. You can expect him to be an intense proponent of sports fishing interests. Peter, Dr. Callaghan is the new council member from Guam."

"Well, welcome to the council," said Peter as he shook my hand. "We at HIBA do fund research on billfish. If you have time in the next few days, stop by our office. Our chief scientist, Charles Daxboeck, will give you a rundown on our research efforts. I trust that you will follow the lead of Paul Bordallo. He's been a reliable sports fishing advocate over the years."

"I'll do my best to represent Guam's interests," I replied.

As the elevator door closed behind us, I thought, *Of course Paul Bordallo is a sports fishing proponent; he owns the largest boating and ocean related sporting goods store in Guam.*

As the elevator ascended, I noticed that all their rooms were on floors higher than mine. Frank's was uppermost. I wondered if Kitty oversaw room arrangements with the same acuity that she did seating and meeting arrangements. The answer, of course, was yes, and over the coming years, my room got higher and higher, but only a few times was it at the top.

The meeting book was an inch-and-a-half thick, and I wasn't sure I fully grasped its contents. But I felt that I had allayed concerns among the Hawaii contingent that I might be a babe in the woods political appointee without practical experience.

* * *

Upon calling the meeting to order, Chairman Yee initially introduced me as Dr. Culligan from Guam. Throughout the day, he referred to me by several different Irish names, until he finally settled on Calahan.

Around the U-shaped table were representatives of the State of Hawaii, the Territories of Guam and American Samoa, the Commonwealth of the Northern Marianas, the US Fish and Wildlife Service, the Coast Guard, the National Marine Fisheries Service, the State Department, and NOAA General Council. The absence of Guam's other two representatives left me without guidance and a bit intimidated as I endeavored to understand the agenda's various nuanced issues.

The Western Pacific Council was in the early stages of its efforts to manage precious corals, spiny lobster, and deep-water bottom stocks. On this day, however, discussion centered on the Billfish Preliminary Management Plan (PMP) that was being prepared by the National Marine Fisheries service. This Billfish-PMP was intended to be a stop-gap measure, remaining in place only until the council completed a permanent Billfish Fishery Management Plan (Billfish-FMP). Progress toward the permanent plan had been slow. Initially the council had tried to develop a Billfish-FMP in conjunction with the Oregon based Pacific Council, which represented the interests of California, Oregon, and Washington. Some contentious issues had derailed those joint efforts, and now our council was about to vote to go-it-alone and develop a Billfish-FMP unique to the Pacific Island region. A major issue of contention between the two councils centered on the fact that the continental states did not allow commercial sale of some billfish species (marlin, sailfish, and the like), whereas Hawaii and the island territories had a long tradition of encouraging the sale, marketing, and consumption of billfish.

Both the preliminary and the permanent billfish plans covered high seas species such as marlin, swordfish, sailfish and sharks, as well as mahi-mahi and wahoo, but neither plan included any tuna species. That exclusion seemed inappropriate to me because tunas were of primary economic and social importance throughout the entire Pacific region.

What I soon learned was that the Magnuson Act exempted "highly migratory species" from its purview. Lobbyists for industrial fishing interests, such as Hunt Foods, VanCamp, Star-Kist, Bumble Bee, and the American Tuna Boat Owners Association, had influenced both Congress and the National Marine Fisheries Service to label thirteen species of tuna as "highly migratory species," thus removing them from the Act's provisions and the council's jurisdiction. By extension, this policy also meant that the United States didn't recognize the right of any country to manage or regulate tuna fishing in their exclusive economic zones.

At the time, US tuna purse seine vessels fished with impunity in the national waters of several Pacific Island countries, the justification being that tunas are a "highly migratory species," and thus can only be effectively managed by international agreement. There were few such agreements in existence at that time, so the US further asserted that since it didn't regulate tuna fishing in US waters, it didn't recognize the right of other nations to do so in their waters.

For many years this United States tuna policy led to chaotic, unregulated, multinational competition for access to Pacific tuna stocks, and it frustrated the council's effort to gain Commerce and State Department approval for its Billfish FMP.

Objections to the proposed Billfish FMP centered around the fact that fishing gear used to catch tuna also caught billfish. Any management measures restricting the harvest of billfish in US waters also affected the harvest of tuna. Management measures contained in the proposed Billfish FMP, such as observer requirements, reporting requirements, and area closures, would make it more difficult for foreign and domestic vessels to fish for tuna in US waters, thus setting a precedent that might encourage other nations to similarly restrict US tuna fishing vessels.

Despite America's position, some countries began to include tuna in their claims of exclusive jurisdiction. During the late 1970s and 1980s, American fishing vessels were increasingly detained and fined for illegally fishing in the waters of Pacific countries. So in 1978, Congress came to the rescue with an amendment to the Fishermen's Protective Act [22 USC 1971–78 (1988)]. That amendment created a fund to pay fines and compensate American fishermen for losses sustained when apprehended in violation of foreign laws. In essence, this law provided a US Government subsidy that encouraged US fishermen to fish with impunity wherever they wished.

There were domestic ramifications from US tuna policy as well. For example, the council's drafting of its Billfish FMP was hindered by a lack of data. Prior to the *Magnuson Act*, only a few states required fishermen to report catches. There was no national reporting requirement, and databases on billfish and tuna catches were few and incomplete. The American Tuna Boat Owners Association did maintain purse seine catch records by species and vessel. But despite repeated requests, the Association refused to share such "private data" with government agencies and councils. After passage of the *Magnuson Act*, councils could require catch reporting and observer coverage, but not for tuna fishing vessels. The most useful billfish catch and effort data was supplied by Japan and the South Pacific Commission. Ironically, our US fisheries management plans were being based on foreign supplied information.

It wasn't until 1987, nine years after work had begun, that the council was able to gain regulatory implementation of its Pelagic Fisheries of the Western

Pacific Region FMP. The plan covered six species of billfish, mahi-mahi, wahoo and several species of oceanic sharks, but not tuna.

This three-decade long "tuna free for all" and its resulting domestic and international turmoil came to an end in 2000, when Congress finally included tuna under the *Magnuson Act*, thus authorizing domestic jurisdiction over all tuna and billfish species in American waters. International progress followed in 2004 with the signing of the Western and Central Pacific Fishery Convention, a treaty that established a commission composed of twenty-six Pacific nations and seven Pacific territories for the purpose of managing highly migratory fish stocks, including tuna and billfish.

International treaty law supersedes domestic law, so councils cannot now recommend management measures for pelagic species that are less stringent or in conflict with those promulgated by the international commission. However, councils can implement requirements for domestic vessels that are more stringent than commission management measures. Examples of such measures are council regulations that contribute to the protection of sea birds, turtles, sharks, and marine mammals.

As I sat in my first council meeting that day in Kona, trying to understand the complex issues and the views of people sitting around that U-shaped table, I had no idea that I would spend the next thirty-five years of my life deeply involved in efforts to conserve and manage Pacific fisheries resources. For thirty of those years, I chaired the council's Scientific and Statistical Committee. For ten years I served on US delegations to a series of Multilateral High-Level Conferences, negotiations that led twenty-six nations to adopt the Western and Central Pacific Fishery Convention along with its administrative Commission (WCPFC). I'm proud to say that I originated a few words and some ideas that are contained in that convention, as well as an idea or two that were not included but in retrospect should have been. After the convention's signing in Honolulu in 2004, I represented Guam, or the Commonwealth of the Marianas, at thirteen annual commission meetings, and for four years chaired the commission's Standing Committee for Finance and Administration.

At my first council meeting, I had no idea that I would someday have the honor of chairing the first national meeting of Scientific and Statistical Committee Chairs from all eight councils across the United States. I had no idea I would serve for ten years on the Steering Committee of the University of Hawaii's Pelagic Fisheries Research Program (PFRP), responsible for dispensing millions of dollars in federal fishery research funding. Sometimes I am reminded by friends that at one PFRP gathering I coined the term "fish flow," which is now used throughout the social science literature to signify the market and non-market distribution channels through which fish pass between fishermen and ultimate consumers.

On that day in 1978 at the Alii Surf Room of the Kona Hilton Hotel, a door opened that changed the rest of my life. Like many such door openings, at the time I didn't recognize its significance. I had not the slightest inkling that fishery management issues would cause me to travel across the United States and to destinations around the Pacific rim, and to numerous island nations in between. At the time it was inconceivable that I would dine with chiefs, directors, secretaries, and ministers, shake the hand of a king, address delegates from twenty-eight nations, and that these experiences would result in lasting personal friendships throughout the Pacific.

*   *   *

When sitting in that first council meeting in Kona, I also had no suspicion that the vivacious council secretary, Kitty Simonds, would become a life-long friend, ally, and confidant, the godmother of my son, and a valued comrade in my old age.

In December of 1978, Wilvan G. Van Campen resigned as the council's Executive Director. By mid-1979 a new Executive Director, Jack C. Marr, was hired, and Kitty was given the added title of Press Officer. In July she was promoted to Assistant to the Executive Director. Then in April of 1980, Jack Marr resigned. A search committee was formed consisting of me; Kenji Ego; Buzzy Agard; Doyle Gates; Peter Reed, a business man and hereditary chief from American Samoa; and Jay Puffinburger, the manager of Honolulu's Bumble Bee Seafoods cannery. Our group sifted through some twenty applications before selecting Svein Fougner, who took leave from his NMFS position in Long Beach to assume the Executive Directorship in October of 1980. After serving two years, Svein returned to NMFS, and Kitty was named Acting Executive Director. She was confirmed as permanent Executive Director in July of 1983.

At the time I thought, *This woman runs the show behind the scenes; we might as well make her the official boss. She'll either be gone in a year or two, or she'll last longer and do better than any others before her.* At this writing, almost forty years later, Rose Benjamin "Kitty" Simonds continues as Executive Director of the

Western Pacific Regional Fishery Management Council. Her staff now includes twenty permanent and contractual employees. Over those years, Kitty has fought for and prevailed on countless issues that have enhanced the sustainable use of fish stocks and bettered the lives of Pacific Island people.

I was privileged to be present and contribute a bit as Kitty's council made history. Its Precious Coral, Bottomfish, and Seamount Groundfish Plans banned bottom trawling and other destructive harvest techniques over 1.5 million square miles of Pacific Ocean, established permit and reporting requirements, no-take zones, quotas, minimum size limits, and observer coverage. The council's Pelagic Plan banned drift gillnets, limited the number of commercial vessels in the Hawaiian and American Samoa fisheries, mandated statistically viable observer coverage, created a first-in-the-Pacific satellite vessel monitoring and reporting system, pioneered fishing techniques that reduced interaction with protected species, and mandated the immediate closure of fisheries whenever protected species interactions exceed prescribed limits. At this writing, the council has established Annual Catch Limits (ACLs) for all the most commercially viable species, and maintains a close watch on hundreds of other species that are regularly caught in the Western Pacific Region.

Kitty's council has spearheaded Congressional revisions of the *Magnuson Act* that have incorporated tuna, recognized the indigenous fishing rights of Native peoples, and set aside money from foreign and domestic fines and forfeitures for use in marine-related community development, training, and demonstration projects in America's insular possessions. Over the years, Kitty's council has funded the travel of world experts to council-sponsored workshops. These workshops have explored cutting-edge thinking on the biology and population dynamics of pelagic fish, sharks, turtles, oceanic birds, whales, and marine mammals. Workshops have also delved into statistical issues related to data collection and the socio-economic impacts of fishery management actions on insular human populations. As Chair of the Science and Statistical Committee, I was frequently involved with these undertakings.

As an example, let me describe my involvement in one council project that had international ramifications and absorbed my energy for several months. The 1982 U.N. Law of the Sea Convention led to a worldwide proliferation of regional fishery and ocean resource related agreements among nations. Most of these agreements contain what are referred to as Disproportionate Burden (DB) clauses that protect the rights of small developing nations. For example, the Western and

Central Pacific Fisheries Commission (WCPFC) is a treaty-based organization established to conserve and manage tuna and other migratory fish stocks across the western and central Pacific Ocean. Article 30(2) of the Convention text reads in part as follows:

> In giving effect to the duty to cooperate in the establishment of conservation and management measures … the Commission shall take into account the special requirements of developing States Parties … in particular: … (c) the need to insure that such measures do not result in transferring, directly or indirectly, a disproportionate burden of conservation action onto developing State Parties, territories, and possessions …

Because of Article 30(2), some Small Island Developing States (SIDS) in the Pacific could potentially refuse to abide by the commission's conservation and management measures, based on a claim of Disproportionate Burden. The US State Department was concerned, since DB had never been defined and there was no internationally accepted way of confirming its existence or measuring its magnitude. Thus, the council decided to sponsor a workshop on the matter.

I flew to Santa Barbara to meet with Dale Squires, Leader of the Socio-economics Section of NOAA Fisheries, Gary Libecap of the Bren School of Environmental Science & Management, and Robert (Bob) Deacon of the U.C. Santa Barbara Department of Economics. The four of us created a workshop agenda and a list of participants. The council's chief scientist, Paul Dalzell, and I worked for a couple of months on planning and logistics. The council provided the venue, staffing, participant travel and per diem.

On September 18, 2014, the three-day Disproportionate Burden Workshop was gaveled to order in Honolulu by moderator Gary Libecap. It was a first ever international gathering of experts to consider the definition, measurement, and mitigation of DB. Twenty-two participants included economists, population scientists, and fisheries managers from as far away as the Indian Ocean, French Polynesia, Australia, and Europe. The workshop produced a generic process for defining and measuring DB, as well as suggested alternatives for avoidance and mitigation. I was selected to present the workshop results to a special preliminary session at the 11th Annual Meeting of the Western and Central Pacific Fisheries Commission in Apia, Samoa. My presentation was well-received, and there is now a more refined international understanding of Disproportionate Burden.

My years working with the council provided opportunities to associate with and learn from people of immense intellect and experience who spent long hours doing their best to make the world a better place. I am glad to have joined with them.

* * *

During my years with the council, Kitty and I became close friends and shared some personal adventures. In our thirties during a council meeting, we both agreed to stop smoking and replaced the nicotine with chocolate, specifically M&Ms. During the next year, we supplied each other with prolific quantities of M&Ms. After each gaining ten pounds or more, we were freed of cigarettes for the rest of our lives. I don't think either of us ever shed much of that extra weight, though I remain glad that we shed the smoking habit.

In Homer, Alaska, after a night's drunken crab fest in the company of Senator Ted Stevens, Kitty and I, along with Wads Yee and Peter Reed, chartered a boat to take us halibut fishing. Senator Stevens, wisely, did not accompany us. We were dressed only in city clothes, slacks, aloha shirts, and sports coats. A fifth person, a stranger, came along at the last minute. All I can remember about him is that he sat near the bow and periodically injected himself with a syringe full of unknown material. Luckily it turned out to be a calm, clear, and fairly warm day in the Gulf of Alaska. I marveled at the snowcapped beauty of volcanoes scattered on the horizon. We got dirty and cold but did catch some halibut and cod. Kitty boated the biggest halibut. The next day, still wearing the same clothes, Wads Yee and I crowded into a small pontoon plane for a day of trout fishing on Senator Stevens' private lake.

At a meeting in Puerto Rico, we were staying in a hotel that had a casino on the top floor. At some point, I and Svein Fougner decided to go gambling. I am not a gambler, know little about it, and do not enjoy it. Nevertheless, there I was playing numbers and colors at the roulette wheel. For some reason, I started being attentive to a weird, intuitive sense that came into my mind when it was time to select a color or number. I began winning rather consistently. As my winnings grew, patrons stopped at the table to watch. Some played the same numbers and colors that I chose. We were all winning. At some point I felt my weird, intuitive sense beginning to fade. After losing a few times, I walked away from that table with around eight hundred dollars. That was the first and last time in my life I ever played roulette. My few subsequent casino adventures have been losing affairs.

One Sunday in the Cook Islands, Kitty and I rented a motor scooter and rode tandem around the entire perimeter of Rarotonga Island. I drove while Kitty navigated, directed, and held on for dear life. Whenever we passed through a village, we made a point to stop and rest near a church. It made no difference—Catholic, Protestant, Mormon. The choirs were a match for anything I had ever heard. We couldn't agree on which village had the best sound, but we could agree that if they were combined, the result would give the Mormon Tabernacle Choir a run for its money. By the time we made it back to Avarua that afternoon, we were hungry and low on fuel. We hadn't realized that almost no gas stations or commercial establishments are open on a Sunday in the Cook Islands.

Several times over the years, Kitty and I and others have stayed at Aggie Grey's Hotel in Apia and visited Vailima, the home of Robert Louis Stevenson, on the Island of Upolu, in Samoa. We have hiked the trail to his grave atop Mt. Vaca and tried to imagine how it was that so many Samoans took part in his funeral that they passed his casket hand over hand the entire distance from his home to the top of that mountain. After departing Vailima, we have flown from Apia to Pago Pago in American Samoa and dined with our friend and council member Alo Paul Stevenson, the spitting image of his namesake.

Kitty was adept at injecting relaxation into formal occasions, no matter the situation or the stature of dignitaries involved. When she led, it was best to follow. As an example, one evening in Pago, American Samoa, five of us were walking to Soule's restaurant from our lodging at the Rainmaker Hotel. We had been in meetings for most of that day and were hoping for some drinks and dinner. Upon arriving at Soule's, we found it closed to the public due to a private function. The doorman said that the King of Tonga, Taufa'ahau Tupou IV, had arrived that day and was meeting with Tongans who resided in American Samoa.

"Oh, that's great," said Kitty. "We'll just drop in for a minute and pay our respects."

Despite the doorman's protest, we marched into the dining room in single file, Kitty in the lead. The King sat on a raised throne at the far end of the dining room. Even when sitting, his six-foot-five, four-hundred-pound frame presented an imposing figure. There must have been two hundred people eating at tables in that room, and every eye was upon us as our group of five snaked its way between tables toward the King. I was second to the last in line. Behind me was Jim Cook, a well-known Hawaii fisheries entrepreneur. In a guarded tone he said to me, "Dr. C, what are we doing? This is not very smart. You and I are the only *haoles* in the place." We kept on marching, right up to the pandanus mats and tapa renderings that covered the stage where the King sat.

There we were stopped by a person of apparent authority who asked our business. The King appeared to completely ignore our presence. Kitty gave the man her name and said that she just wished to pay her respects and those of council members who were currently meeting in Pago. The man then turned and addressed the King in the Tongan language. There was a moment of silence, as if the King were trying to recollect something. Then he suddenly focused on our group, Kitty in particular.

"Kittee, Kittee! Come, come! Executive Director Simonds, I believe." He motioned her onto the platform as if they were old friends. She stood directly in front of him without lowering her head or otherwise showing deference. He didn't seem to mind. Being so large of stature, his head remained above hers, even though he was sitting. We were introduced, and I shook the hand of a King. He was most gentle of touch for a man of his size. As we departed, Kitty invited him to attend our meeting the next day, but of course he didn't appear. We walked on down the street to Sadie Thompson's for the rest of our night's doings.

Upon the conclusion of meetings in American Samoa, it was our custom to visit Tisa's Barefoot Bar to unwind before flights departed. Tisa was quite a lady, but those stories are for another time and place.

* * *

My work with the council resulted in many adventures, one of which I'll relate here, as it typifies numerous similar experiences and reflects the Pacific way of things that became the bedrock of my life. On one early morning in the 1980s, Henry Sesapasara and I flew into his home Island of Tutuila, American Samoa. We had met a week earlier in Port Vila, Vanuatu, and then attended a United Nations Fisheries and Agriculture Organization (FAO) meeting in Apia, Western Samoa. That evening we were scheduled to depart from Apia to join a South Pacific Commission meeting in Noumea, New Caledonia. However, Henry, in typical fashion, had managed to spend all his council-allotted per diem, and now had no money left for the rest of our trip. In those days most islanders didn't carry debit or credit cards, so I had funded our eighty-mile flight from Apia to Tutuila with my American Express Card. We had just seven hours on the ground in Tutuila to check in with Henry's family and get money for the rest of his travels. I had agreed to come along because this side trip seemed more interesting than the prospect of spending the day at Aggie Gray's Hotel in Apia, waiting for our flight and Henry's return.

We were hauling luggage toward Henry's pickup truck in the airport parking lot when Henry asked, "Callaghan, can you loan me two hundred dollars?"

That was half my remaining per diem for the rest of our trip, and I had already paid for our tickets to get here; furthermore, as per the Pacific way, I was quite sure that the word "loan" could best be interpreted as "give." All that notwithstanding, between Pacific Island friends such a question can only be answered in the affirmative.

"Sure, Henry," I said as we loaded our bags into the truck bed. "I've only got twenties, is that okay?"

"Anything will do," he replied. "Thanks. I need to make some money for Noumea." I had no idea what he meant, but I didn't press the matter. The story would unfold in due course.

We stopped by Henry's house in Pago Pago to drop off gifts he had purchased in Apia for his wife and children. Those presents were likely the reason for his funding shortfall. Next, we rushed through a meal of taro, fish soup, and super-sweet lime ade. Guests are served food, no matter what else is on the agenda.

Then we drove straightaway to the clubhouse on the local golf course. There in progress were three or four well-attended tables of mahjong. I noticed a couple of Samoans, but most participants and bystanders seemed to be Chinese and Korean, probably workers or crew from the tuna canneries or fishing vessels.

Upon surveying the situation, Henry said to me, "Callaghan, I've got to ask you to wait outside. This may take me a couple of hours, so go to the snack shack by the kitchen and hang out. I'll be there as soon as I can."

"Okay," I said as Henry joined the group of bystanders at the mahjong tables.

The snack shack was empty, save for a beautiful brown-eyed Samoan waitress with a white plumeria over her ear. The flower faced forward, an inviting sign. Since I was the only customer, she sat with me at a table beside a giant Monkeypod tree. To her I was a curious newcomer whose origin and reason for being there were a mystery that needed to be solved. Over lime-infused Vailima drafts, I provided answers sparingly in order to extend our conversation. I have long since forgotten her name, but her shapely brown profile and welcoming smile still linger in the shadows of my mind.

Henry Sesepasara, unknown woman, Paul Callaghan, Manua Is., Am. Samoa, 1982

By midafternoon, Henry finally reappeared. "Callaghan, are you trying to make time with the management?" he said as he approached. Before I could answer, he was talking in Samoan to the girl. They apparently knew each other well.

"Here you go," he said as he handed me seven crisp fifty-dollar bills.

"This is much more than I gave you," I said.

"It's your investment return plus my plane ticket. I have enough for myself," he said, shaking a fistful of bills at me. "Now finish your beer, say goodbye to this beautiful lady, and let's get out of here. We need to make it back to Apia, and our flight for Noumea boards in two hours."

With considerable sweat and frenzy, and a modicum of uncertainty, we made it out of Tutuila and back to Apia, barely in time to board our six-and-a-half-hour flight to Sydney. No airport restrictions or TSA checkpoints existed in those days. Henry seemed to know everyone. I just followed along.

After spending several hours in Sydney's transit lounge, we boarded the three-hour flight to New Caledonia. The plane was full of Australian tourists headed to the beaches, restaurants and casino in Noumea. They loudly enjoyed the start of their vacations. Luckily, Henry and I were adept at sleeping in uncomfortable and noisy situations.

When I awoke, the sun had risen and the plane was on approach. As the wheels touched down, we whizzed past several vehicles with flashing red and blue lights. Taxiing toward the terminal, we passed lines of military vehicles and squads of French soldiers in battle gear. After some delay, we disembarked onto the tarmac and were immediately herded by soldiers into an empty hanger building. Some hundred-fifty passengers milled around while our luggage was delivered by truck and forklifted into a jumbled pile.

Word soon spread that the French Marines were quelling a Kanak uprising. The Kanaks were a mostly Indigenous group that advocated for New Caledonia's independence from France. Their methods were not always peaceful, and they represented a sizable portion of New Caledonia's population. Aside from reasons of colonial pride, France maintained control of New Caledonia because its mines produced the world's second largest output of nickel ore.

The thirty-mile-long road between the airport and Noumea town had been closed. We were stuck in this hanger with our suitcases until safe transportation could be arranged. The French military provided some food and water and allowed us to use the terminal restrooms, but there was no firm commitment as to when we might be transported to Noumea. The tropical midday heat mounted along with our anxiety.

After considerable searching, Henry and I were able to locate and extract our suitcases from the pile. That at least gave us something to sit on as time passed. By noon there was still no encouragement from the French soldiers as to our prospects. Excited holiday anticipation among the Australian passengers had faded into concerned discontent. Their unhappiness was further fueled when we were told that the Quantas flight was returning to Sydney empty. Any of us who wished to fly back for free would be accommodated. Some took the offer, but most remained in the hanger, hoping for the best.

Henry and I watched the Quantas plane depart as we sat on our suitcases in the shade near the open hanger door. "Well, Callaghan, what do you think?" mused Henry. "Are these Frogs going to let us go to town?"

"It doesn't look good. They're pretty much ignoring us. I don't believe the SPC will be holding our meeting if people can't get into Noumea," I said. "I wish we could just somehow get out of here, but not back to Sydney. I need a cold Vailima."

"You won't find Vailima in Noumea," said Henry. "The Frogs don't allow it. They want you to drink their local brew."

Just then an Air Nauru B-727 landed and rolled to a stop at the terminal. The boarding stairs dropped from the tail section, but no passengers disembarked. Soon a French officer was having an animated discussion with the plane's captain on the tarmac at the foot of the stairs. While they were conversing, a lone stewardess descended the stairs and walked from the plane into the terminal.

"Henry! I think I know that stewardess. She's Palauan and related to my wife, Nina."

I jumped up and hurried across the blistering hot tarmac toward the door that the stewardess had entered. Just as I got a few steps away, it opened and out stepped Eufrasia Remeliik.

"*Alii* (hello), Tochob," I said.

At the sound of her Palauan name, she stopped and stared at me, shading her eyes with her hand. It took a moment for her to focus. "*Baul san, ea kau, ke mekerang er tiang* (What are you doing here)?" she said.

"*Tochob, ak ouspech a ngesuo* (I need your help)," I said. "My friend Henry and I flew in early this morning. They won't let us go into Noumea town, and we're stuck in that hanger over there."

"Yes, we have three passengers who they won't allow off our flight," she said. "What can I do for you?"

"Where is your flight going from here?" I asked.

"Our next stop is Suva and then back to Nauru," she replied.

"Can Henry and I get on your flight and get out of here? I've got an AMEX credit card. Is there any way we can buy tickets on-board or in Fiji?" I asked.

"Well, the ticket office here is closed, and it's not normal procedure, but I'll ask the captain. Do you have luggage?"

"Yes, one each," I replied.

"Where are you located now?"

"In the shade of that hanger door over there."

"Okay, when I come down the stairs and wave to you, be prepared to hustle over and board. Just carry your suitcases up the stairs and we'll secure them inside the cabin. If I don't wave, or the stairs are retracted, I'm sorry. I couldn't get you on."

"*Ke kmal mesulang* (Thank you very much)," I replied. "We'll be ready."

Elated, I trotted back to the hanger. "Henry, I think we can go with them to Suva. Are you up for that?"

"Any place is better than here. Do you think Kitty will pay?"

"She has to," I replied. "It's not our fault that we can't attend the SPC meeting. We've got to get back somehow. Going through Fiji is probably no more expensive than going through Sydney."

"Yes, but she doesn't like to pay for foreign air carriers like Air Nauru."

"Don't worry, Henry, she'll pay. Quantas is a foreign carrier, and she paid for that."

"Okay, in Suva at least we can get you a Vailima and me some curry. What do we have to do?"

"If Tochob waves to us, we run to the plane and up those stairs with our suitcases. Hopefully the French soldiers won't stop us. Oh, there she is now, and she's waving. Let's go! We're out of here."

Once on board, Tochob seated us in the first-class section where she was the attendant. When I protested, saying that we couldn't pay for first-class, Tochob said, "Never mind. When you get to Suva, just pay for economy. They won't know." Then she continued in Palauan, "Hey, Mr. Paul, you didn't tell me that your friend was a good-looking Samoan."

I introduced them, and during the flight Henry spent inordinate time in the galley talking with Tochob. When we landed in Suva, Tochob disappeared through the crew line at customs. By the time we emerged, no one seemed prepared to accept payment, so we exited the airport and never paid Air Nauru a cent for our escape from New Caledonia.

It was nine or ten at night by the time the taxi delivered us to the Southern Cross Hotel, a budget place where Henry had previously stayed. When we checked in, one room for the two of us, Henry asked the desk manager, an Indian fellow, if there was a nightclub nearby where we could relax and drink a beer.

"Just walk over to Victoria Parade," he said. "There's a lot of them. The Purple Haze is popular these days."

"Can we exchange some US dollars for some Fiji money?" said Henry.

"Never mind," I said. "I've got five hundred Fijian left over from my last trip here. That should be more than enough. I've been carrying it around for a while, and I'd like to get rid of it."

We dropped our bags in the room and headed off toward Victoria Parade, the main drag. I no longer remember the name of the club that we eventually entered, but it was on the second floor, up a flight of narrow, poorly lit, wooden stairs. *No fire exits here*, I thought. We were led through the din and smoky haze to a table situated across the crowded dance floor from the band. Our waiter-es was *vaka sa lewalewa* in Fijian, *fa'afafine* in Samoan, *mahu* in Hawaiian; anyway, a transgender male. He was a bit aloof and sullen as we ordered two bottles of Vailima, the 750 ml. size.

Once seated, it became apparent that we were the only nonlocals in the place. All other customers appeared to be an assortment of Melanesians and Polynesians typical of Fijian society. I was certainly the only *haole* in the house, and Henry, though Polynesian, was likely the only Samoan. Our table was located in a conspicuous place, and I could feel eyes upon me. Over the years I had grown accustomed to that feeling, but still my senses remained attuned to potential trouble. Overconsumption of alcohol can bring out the worst traits in people. Apparently Henry felt similarly, as the history of Samoan-Fijian relations were not those of mutual admiration.

Nearby was a table filled with enticing young ladies about our age or a bit younger, some of whom sported welcoming flowers in their hairdos. When the band played, they danced with each other near our table. Their body language and flirtatious glances left little to the imagination. But Henry and I were not stupid Pacific tourists. We noticed that every so often the same two local men cut in and danced with the girls. It would be foolish, in this inebriated crowd, to attempt any interaction with those ladies before understanding how they were related to other patrons. All we could do was stoically observe, sip our beer, and fantasize a bit. The looking was in itself entertaining, and no one bothered us as we drank our beers.

I was eying the last swig in my bottle when our waiter-es appeared, asking if I needed another. Henry's beer was only half-consumed; he was never more than a social sipper, odd for an islander. I could tell that we'd both had about enough of this place. The crowded confusion, smoke, cha-cha-cha interspersed with rock was getting to me. "No," I said. "I think we're finished. We'll be on our way if you can bring us a check."

Without reply or smile, the waiter-es departed. In a few minutes he-she returned, placing in front of me a tray with a handwritten bill in it. The two beers were each $5 Fijian. I plunked a $50 Fijian note on the tray. The waiter-es grabbed it and turned to leave, then abruptly whirled around. "You blokes think you're funny, don't you? You best pay the bill and mind your manners," he said as he flopped the tray and my $50 note back on the table.

I was totally nonplussed. Henry jumped to the rescue. "We don't understand. What's the problem? It's not our intention to cause any trouble."

"Then pay with some real money," said the waiter-es in disgust.

"I don't understand? That's $50 Fijian," I said.

"That money's no good anymore, you twit," said the waiter-es.

"I got that money when I was staying at the Grand Pacific Hotel in 1972. It was Fijian money then. Why is it not Fijian money now?" My Irish temper was showing just a bit. I controlled it immediately. There was much to be lost by further upsetting this *fa'afafine*.

"It's no good now. They changed the currency. That's old money."

"Is this old or new?" I produced a $100 Fijian bill from my stash.

"That's no good either. What else can you pay with?"

"I've got an American Express Card, or I've got some American dollars," I said.

"We don't take plastic money," said the waiter-es. "I'll get the manager. Maybe he will take your US dollars."

The manager was a well-spoken Indian fellow. "Good evening, sirs. My employee tells me that you are trying to pay your bill with old money. We don't accept that anymore. If you want to exchange it, you'll have to go to a bank. If you don't have proper Fijian money, perhaps you can pay using US dollars. I believe you might be American?"

"Yes, I have US dollars and an American Express Card as well. Which do you prefer?"

"Oh, the American dollars will be fine," he replied.

I handed him a US twenty-dollar bill. Henry said, "Wait a minute, here's a ten. That's closer to the correct amount."

"I'm sorry, sir," said the manager, "but ten dollars US is not quite enough to cover the amount owed plus taxes and exchange fees. We don't provide change for American money, so I'll have to take this twenty-dollar bill as payment in full for your obligation. You are always welcome to return to our club, but please bring new Fiji money next time. Enjoy the rest of your evening, gentlemen."

"That guy just ripped us off," said Henry.

"Yes, but that's better than getting our heads bashed in by that *fa'afafine* and his or her friends. Let's get out of here."

As we descended the dingy stairs, Henry said, "Now we need to find some curry. I'm hungry."

"I'm up for that," I said. "I guess we can pay with American money. Your ten dollars should be enough. I only have twenties and fifties."

When we reached the street, we saw two Suva police officers, a man and a woman, standing under a street light. "Let's ask them where we can find some curry," I said.

As we approached the officers eyed us carefully. The man was at least six-foot-four, muscular, and physically fit. The woman, at close to six feet tall, appeared equally fit, but her demeanor seemed welcoming. They both wore blue uniform tops and eye-catching white *lavalava*(s) with deep chevrons cut into the bottom fringes. They carried no visible weapons other than a baton, but as we approached, I thought it would be very ill-advised to get crosswise with these two.

We explained our desire to find a restaurant that served good curry. The male officer did all the talking.

"You're visitors to Suva?"

"Yes," I said.

"Where do you stay?

"At the Sothern Cross Hotel."

"Where are you from?"

"America."

"What part of America?" he asked, looking closely at Henry.

"I live in Guam, and Henry here lives in American Samoa."

The male officer nodded with a quick lift of his eyebrows. The woman smiled. I judged that the interrogation was apparently concluded, but he continued. "That club you were just in is not the best place for visitors. Did you experience any problem?"

"No, everything was fine. We drank our beers, paid our bill, and left."

"You're lucky," he said, and then proceeded to give us directions to a "curry house" three blocks down Victoria Parade, then right, then left down an alley.

After walking past several rowdy clubs and intimidating people, we found the place. Inside we ate some of the best curry I've ever eaten. Our American money was accepted with a smile by the Indian proprietor, though we were the center of attention for employees and patrons alike.

Sometime after 1:00 a.m. we departed, fully satisfied and ready for a night's sleep. Waiting for us at the end of the alley stood the two police officers.

"What did you think of the curry?"

"It was exceptionally good. Thank you for your help," I said.

"We will follow you back to the Southern Cross, just to make sure all is well."

"Thank you very much, officers."

They nodded, and as we walked away, the woman said, "*Vanuinui vinaka e nomu volau* (Safe journey)."

The next day, Henry took a flight home to Pago Pago via Apia, and I flew to Nauru, spent a night in the Menen Hotel, then the next day flew to Guam.

The SPC fisheries meeting was never held. The French paratroopers suppressed the Kanaks in a matter of weeks, and after submitting a complete trip report, Kitty covered our travel and per diem.

*   *   *

The reader might wonder how it was that I was able to turn a three-year council appointment into a forty-year fishery management adventure. Here is how it came about.

In August of 1981, my term as a council member came to an end. The political winds in Guam had changed, and a Republican Governor, Paul Calvo, did not reappointed me, despite our shared first names. My last council meeting was in July of that year at the King Kamehameha Hotel in Kailua-Kona, just a mile from where I had begun council service three years earlier.

At that meeting, in addition to receiving a Resolution of Commendation, Chairman Yee appointed me to the council's Scientific and Statistical Committee (SSC). Parts of that council resolution are worth remembering:

> WHEREAS, Dr. Callaghan has consented to serve as a member of the Council's Scientific and Statistical Committee; and WHEREAS, Dr. Callaghan's expertise, dedication and service have greatly assisted in the work of the Council, and will continue to do so in the future notwithstanding that he, in this new position [SSC Chair], will not be remunerated, and notwithstanding that he is a mild mannered person who normally avoids situations of confrontation, such assignment will force him to deal with controversial, contentious, and difficult marine resource problems at times which to date, in his service with the Council, he has been able to avoid ...

The SSC was composed of fifteen scientists from the US mainland, Canada, Hawaii, and elsewhere in the Pacific Region. The committee included biologists, stock dynamic modelers, ichthyologists, mathematicians, oceanographers, statisticians, maritime lawyers, economists, and anthropologists. I was the youngest person in the room, surrounded by people holding degrees from Scripps, M.I.T., Cornell, Stanford, University of Washington, McGill, and the like. Within my first year of membership, I was designated SSC chair. In that position I served at the will of the council for an indefinite term and attended council meetings as SSC liaison, presenting SSC recommendations.

At SSC meetings I hid my anxiety as best I could while attempting to keep the surrounding egos focused on solutions to the agenda issues at hand. Initially some outspoken characters were exceptionally hard to keep on track. One was John P. Craven, Marine Affairs Coordinator for the State of Hawaii. John was a mathematician, known for his use of Bayesian search theory in the discovery of lost underwater objects, such as submarines, and the development of underwater mining techniques. Once John started talking, there was no choice but to retreat and listen. Yet somehow over time I was able to gain the members' cooperation, and at times a modicum of their respect. In any case, with the support of council members, and of course Kitty, I continued as SSC chair for thirty years.

Another SSC member who initially caused me angst was Salvatore "Sal" Comitini. Sal had been my dissertation chair, and I had been his research assistant. During that time, I had come to dislike him, so it was disconcerting to now find myself as his chair. I think he felt uncomfortable as well and thankfully didn't remain on the SSC for long after my arrival.

In almost all cases, SSC members did their homework, came prepared, listened across disciplines, and fervently believed in the council's conservation and sustainable use mandate. For years SSC members served without compensation, receiving only travel, per diem, and lodging. Most members looked forward to our meetings because they enjoyed the multidisciplinary interaction and intellectual challenge of providing real solutions to real problems. Though there was some turnover in membership, much camaraderie and interdisciplinary respect existed around the table. All recommendations were made on the basis of consensus, as determined by the Chair. I held only one vote during my thirty-year tenure as SSC Chair, and that was a vote on a resolution to never hold another vote.

During the last few years of my chairmanship, the scientific, policy and regulatory issues became more time-consuming and complex. In recognition, the US Congress decided that SSC members should be compensated for each meeting day at the rate of GS-15. Although seemingly reasonable, I don't believe that this change led to improved SSC productivity. However, it did have some unintended impacts on SSC member relationships. This was so because scientists who happened to work for federal or state agencies weren't allowed compensation, while compensation was paid to those who worked for universities or private institutions or were otherwise retired. I and others ended up donating significant portions of our pay toward funding SSC social functions that were held in conjunction with all our meetings. Often the most creative SSC work was accomplished after several glasses of wine during evening social gatherings.

As the years passed, my SSC reports to council meetings became increasingly complex. Sometimes I found myself presenting material that I didn't thoroughly understand. SSC members whom I had come to know and respect over the years had retired for one reason or another. I knew it was time to gracefully end this magnificent adventure, so in 2013, I relinquished the SSC chairmanship while remaining as a member and continuing to discharge my duties as Chair of the Finance and Administration Committee for the Central and Western Pacific Fisheries Commission. Finally, in 2017, I withdrew from most fisheries related responsibilities, calling an end to one hell of a rewarding and exciting time in my life.

I learned that successful chairing rests on knowing the material beforehand, anticipating difficulties and planning for contingencies. Kitty was a stickler for seating arrangements and an agenda order that contributed to productivity and reduced friction. There is a lot to be said for that. The council's SSC meetings and most multinational Pacific meetings operate by consensus. There is no voting. The chairperson decides when a consensus has been reached and declares the outcome, so it's critical that participants perceive the chairperson to be fair and open minded. In most cases a chair must avoid expressing personal opinion, but at times I stimulated discussion by appearing to lean toward an unpopular outcome. A chairperson must be a proficient listener, a judge of emotion and body language, alert to potential common ground and the possibility of compromise. On top of everything else, a chair must maintain order while not being perceived as autocratic. I can only assume that I became reasonably proficient at these skills, because I was asked to preside over meetings for many organizations during my thirty-five years in fishery management. Of course, there is also the likelihood that I got the jobs because no one else wanted the extra work. In any case, I enjoyed every minute of it, even those situations where a more articulate or informed participant rescued me from some dilemma or impasse.

*   *   *

The fishery council system was established under federal law to provide for the long-term sustainable use of marine resource stocks within US waters, while also protecting those bycatch and incidentally impacted species that could be threatened as a result of fishing activities. Further, the law was purposely written to favor US fishing interests over foreign interests, and to involve US resource users in the decision-making processes, the idea being that those most benefiting from a resource are likely to have an interest in protecting its long-term viability.

I feel certain that America's ocean resources would be in considerably worse condition today had the *Magnuson Act* not become law and the council management system not been initiated. Without the council's oversight, foreign interests would today completely dominate the harvest and processing of ocean resources, both in US waters and elsewhere in the Pacific. Targeted fish stocks would be in a much less robust condition, and incidentally impacted species such as turtles, sea birds, marine mammals, and sharks would be under much greater stress.

There are council critics, some of whom are my close and respected friends. A few detractors oppose all federal government regulation of fisheries. Other detractors are concerned that council membership is dominated by those who benefit from the resource—fishers, processors, and government agencies. They would prefer a council membership composed of environmentalists, ecology-minded scientists, and attorneys. Some detractors feel that the council has not done enough to protect marine resources, threatened species, and critical habitats. Some would like to see all commercial fishing eliminated within US waters. Their angst and frustration have at times led to personal antipathy toward council members, staff, and the scientists who advise council actions. Many critics are well-intended individuals, but in most cases, they haven't read the *Magnuson Act*, don't understand the council's federal mandate, propose no viable alternative, and are energized by emotion rather than factually based science.

This animosity has saddened me and at times caused me to question the value of my efforts to work within the existing institutional framework of resource management. But I believe we did our best, given the constraints we faced. We were sometimes blamed for problems that were beyond our control. For example, the council is often blamed for the overfishing and degradation of coastal marine resources that lie within three nautical miles of shore. These waters are under the jurisdiction of state and territorial governments, not the council. The council has often provided recommendations to state and territorial authorities, and frequently this advice has been ignored. The machinations of state-federal jurisdictional disputes and cooperative shortcomings are legendary in America's Pacific islands, but the council is not to blame for what has transpired within coastal waters.

Many council detractors also fail to understand that fishers under American jurisdiction harvest less than 3 percent of the annual Pacific-wide pelagic fish catch. The fleets of foreign nations catch 97 percent in waters beyond US jurisdiction. They are thus responsible for most overfishing, bycatch, and incidental damage to endangered and protected species. Forcing American fishers to endure onerous gear, seasonal, and quota restrictions puts them at an economic disadvantage relative to their foreign competitors, while resulting in little benefit to Pacific-wide fish stocks. The handicapping of American fishers reduces domestic catches, thereby stimulating US imports from the very fleets that are causing the most resource degradation. It's naive to believe that the "good example" set by American fishers will influence the actions of foreign fishers so long as those actions result in reduced profits. Multinational agreements along with the dissemination of ecologically beneficial, economically viable technology are the only meaningful long-lasting solutions. For better or worse, that Pacific-wide responsibility now rests with the twenty-six-nation Western and Central Pacific Fisheries Commission.

That said, I don't want to leave the reader with the idea that everything our council and Scientific and Statistical Committee did has turned out well. It has not. One stock that stands out in my mind is the Armorhead stock that inhabits the Hancock Seamounts in the most northwesterly part of the Hawaiian Islands. Prior to the *Magnuson Act*, the Armorhead and associated species were heavily fished by foreign interests, mostly Russian and Japanese. In its early years, the council allowed continued foreign fishing, but at a reduced rate with catch and effort reporting. This was a mistake. Belatedly, in 1986 the council imposed a complete moratorium on fishing in the area of the Hancock Seamounts. The fishery has remained closed until this day, and although the stock still exists, it has not recovered to fishable levels.

A second glaring failure was the Northwest Hawaiian Island Spiny Lobster fishery. The council implemented a Spiny Lobster Management Plan in 1983. The plan included numerous safeguards: permit requirements, size limits, gear restrictions, a ban on the harvest of egg-bearing females, logbook reporting, observer requirements, and the closure of all waters shallower than ten fathoms. This was not enough. Our assessments were wrong. The fishery had to be completely closed in 2000 and was never reopened. Although the lobsters may have recovered, the imposition of National Monument status over the entire Northwest Hawaiian Island area has eliminated any fishing and precluded investigative research as to the health of lobster and other fish stocks.

Certainly, the council system has not been a perfect steward of our ocean resources, but I am convinced that it has contributed to the betterment of Pacific Island societies and set an example for the wise and sustainable use of those fish stocks under American federal jurisdiction. My participation in that effort was a most rewarding experience; however, I remain pessimistic about the long-term health of marine resources. Proper national and multi-national management can delay the inevitable, but in the end, I believe that wild fisheries and their associated ecosystems are likely doomed from a combination of overfishing, pollution, and climate change. Efforts to protect, conserve and manage all natural resources, both terrestrial and marine, are laudable, but in many cases serve only to temporarily shift burdens and benefits from one social group to another. I fear the only hope for an improved outcome rests with a reduction in human population and a more equitable distribution of worldwide income.

Chapter 13

Government Service

It was shortly after noon on a Tuesday in the spring of 1982. The university maintenance crew had not yet gotten around to fixing the malfunctioning air conditioner, so my office door was open to the trade winds that provided some relief from Guam's humid heat. Students and faculty peered in as they passed, and I hoped that the open door would provide welcoming encouragement to anxious students who might otherwise be reluctant to seek help.

My classes were finished for the day, and I was sitting, feet up on my desk, eating a tuna sandwich while perusing the contents of a ten-day-old *Wall Street Journal*. My finance students were required to subscribe so that we might discuss pertinent articles in class. It didn't make much difference that the subscription was a victim of Guam's slow mail service. I was accustomed to reading old editions and had found that the delay actually helped me to maintain a longer-term investment perspective.

Having settled down to contemplation of interest rates and the yield curve, I was startled when in through the open door walked Herminia D. Dierking. Herm, as I called her, was an Accounting Professor, a member of a large influential Chamorro family, and in my eyes a most beautiful person.

"*Hafa-adai*, Doctor C. Are you busy?" she said, as her copper-toned body slipped into the chair beside my desk. Over the years, Guam was well-known for having placed finalists in several Miss Universe competitions. In my eyes, Herm fit the mold perfectly, despite being the mother of four children.

Yanking my feet off the desk and setting aside the sandwich and newspaper, I said, "What's up, Herm?"

"It's a shame that maintenance has not fixed your air conditioner. How long has it been?" she said.

"It's been about two weeks now. I've kind of lost track. But I've gotten used to it, and the door being open seems to persuade students to drop in."

With an impish smile she replied, "Yes, and I bet you devote considerable time to the prettiest ones."

I rolled my eyes, knowing that her observation was not unwarranted. "The question is at this moment, what can I do for you, my dear?"

"That remains to be seen," she replied. "How do you feel about the coming election?"

"Well, I don't know. I think my *pari*, Joe Paulino, is supporting Ricky Bordallo." It was best to be circumspect when discussing Guam politics with someone of unknown sentiment.

"So I have some tickets for Ricky's upcoming fundraiser on Saturday. Would you and Nina like to attend? It's at the Hilton Ball Room at seven—the dress is island formal. You do have shoes?" she quipped, looking at my flipflop-adorned feet.

"How much are the tickets?" I asked.

"A hundred dollars each," she said, a hint of concern in her soft brown eyes.

No matter the price, I couldn't say no, and she knew it. "Okay, I'll take two," I said as I reached for my checkbook.

"Make it payable to Bordallo for Governor," she said. "And make sure you bring Nina. Ricky wants Palauan community support too."

"I don't think Nina has anything planned for Saturday, but you never know," I said.

"Tell her that John and I will be there, and we've reserved seats for you both at our table." John Dierking was her attorney-husband, lucky guy.

She continued, "I think Ricky will win this time around. Calvo is weak in the south."

"That's what Joe says, and he should be a good judge of sentiment in Inarajan and Merizo. So don't worry, we'll be there," I said as I handed her the check.

"*Si Yu'us Ma'ase*, I'll see you at faculty meeting this afternoon at 3:30. Or had you forgotten?" she said as she floated through the door into the greenery of the campus walkway.

"*Adios esta*," I said as she disappeared.

Two hundred dollars poorer, I returned to the *Wall Street Journal* and my sandwich, pleased to be included in an important local grassroots movement.

* * *

That was the beginning of my short political career. At the behest of Herminia, I made several additional donations during the course of the campaign. Ricardo J. Bordallo won the election for Governor of Guam in November, and by January of 1983, Herminia had become Director of the Bureau of Budget and Management Research. My *pari*, Jose Paulino, was Director of Parks and Recreation, and I was Acting Director of Commerce.

I suppose the "Acting" designation deserves explanation. In November after the election results were certified, I received a phone call informing me that Governor-elect Bordallo would like to meet with me at nine o'clock the next morning.

When I arrived at his temporary offices in the Quan Building, a secretary greeted me. "Good morning, Dr. Callaghan. Please walk right in. He's expecting you."

Upon entering, I saw the Governor standing behind his desk, trim and dapper as usual. His open necked, long-sleeved dress shirt sported flashy gold cufflinks—a man of action. The tinge of greying hair around his temples provided just a hint of middle age where it disappeared under the frames of his oversized, horn-rimmed glasses.

With businesslike demeanor he welcomed me. "*Hafa adai*, Dr. Callaghan. Please come in. Make yourself comfortable," he said as he motioned toward the highbacked, brown leather chairs in front of his massive *Ifil*-wood desk.

"Thank you, Governor. Congratulations on your victory," I said as I slid into the seat.

"Yes, the people have spoken, and now we must produce results," he replied as he paced back and forth behind the desk. Without stopping and never looking directly at me, he said, "Some of my supporters tell me that you are an excellent economics teacher and well-respected at the university. They think you would be a good addition to my cabinet. Our family has also discussed your qualifications, and my brother Paul thinks highly of you, so I have decided to ask you to become Director of Commerce in my administration. What do you think of that?" He continued to pace while he waited for my response. Just like a discontented lion in a cage at the zoo, I thought.

The Governor-elect's offer was not a complete surprise. During the prior week, his brother, Paul Bordallo, had invited me to breakfast at a local restaurant. He and I had known each other for some time, as we were both avid fishermen and had served together on the Western Pacific Fishery Management Council in Honolulu. During breakfast, our conversation centered on fisheries management issues, but at one point Paul had mentioned that the Governor-elect was considering asking me to work in his administration, perhaps as Director of Commerce, and he wondered if I might be agreeable to that. I replied that I was certainly honored by such a thought and was interested in contributing to the betterment of Guam in any way possible. Paul had then mentioned that some family members, including Madeleine, the Governor-elect's wife, had reservations about appointing non-Chamorro cabinet members, so it was still unclear as to what the Governor might decide.

Despite Paul's advance notice, I was still unprepared and uncertain. I enjoyed teaching and was comfortable in an academic environment. I knew little about the administrative bureaucracy of Guam government and had no idea as to the duties of a director or the functions of the Department of Commerce. Furthermore, I was a relative newcomer to the Island, without Chamorro language capability, and without Indigenous family connections, other than those with the Paulino clan in Inarajan Village. As a director, I'd be at a disadvantage when it came to dealing with the Chamorro political, cultural, and social norms that permeated day-to-day government operations. Everything considered, I wasn't confident that I was up to the task of running a diverse agency of several hundred employees while functioning in an unfamiliar cultural environment.

"Governor, I'm honored by such an unexpected offer," I said. "May I please have some time to consider it? I'd like to talk things over with my wife, and I'd like to make sure that someone will be able to cover my classes at the university."

"Your wife is Palauan, isn't she?" he asked.

"Yes, Governor," I replied.

"Well then," he said, "she'll be the first Palauan member of Madeleine's *Y Inetnon Famalao'an*, the cabinet wives' organization. I suspect she'll like that. They do lots of good work for our Island. Why don't you come back tomorrow morning at the same time and let me know your decision. We have lots of work to do. It's not long before inauguration, and things are moving fast. I need to know that we can count on you as a member of our team."

The next day I arrived promptly on time but had to wait for an hour while others were ushered in and out. Joe Paulino and Herminia Dierking were among them, and so was Judith Guthertz, a fellow faculty member, who I had heard was being tapped as Chief of Police, the first ever woman to hold that position.

Finally, when it was my turn to enter, the Governor was standing behind his desk as he had the day before. "Good morning, Governor," I said as I sat down in the leather chair. "Today seems to be a busy day for you."

"Every day is busy. There is much to do," he replied. "So what is your decision about becoming Director of Commerce? Does your wife approve?" There was a slight suggestion of contempt in his voice.

I replied, "She feels that such a position is a great honor, sir, and so do I."

That of course was not completely true. Nina was not happy about having to undertake the social and political obligations required of a cabinet member's wife. Being the only Palauan among a throng of Chamorro women in *Y Inetnon Famalao'an* was not the least appealing to her. Almost certainly they would view her as their token Micronesian and their liaison to the Palauan and broader Micronesian women's communities, a responsibility that would be uncomfortable at her young age.

Despite these concerns, Nina was supportive. If I really wanted to do it, she was willing to try. The truth was, I wasn't sure I really wanted to do it. Up until then I had been a respected professor who maintained a low profile and socialized within the university community. Joining Bordallo's team would thrust me into the mainstream of territorial politics. There would be no more low-profile living, and little spare time to pursue the scuba diving and spear fishing I loved. My world would become much more crowded and much less private. Joe Paulino had already cautioned me that a directorship would not be an easy job for a *haole* Statesider.

While driving to the meeting that morning, I had concluded that I would rather not take the job. However, I couldn't bluntly say no to the Governor-elect. Outright rejection of his offer would be an affront. My experience in Palau had taught me that seemingly minor slights could have lasting consequences in small island communities. In the future the Governor's staff would scrutinize personnel actions closely, even those at the university. If I offended him, I and those who had recommended me would be diminished in his eyes, and worse, my friend Paul, the Governor's brother, would be equally offended. It was foolish to "burn these bridges." At some point either Nina or I might need help from Bordallo family members, many of whom occupied judgeships and prestigious professional positions. A negative response to the Governor-elect's offer would not be forgotten. My response had to be handled with tact, in a way that allowed him to save face.

While awaiting my turn in the outer office, I had tentatively settled on a course of action, and now there was no time for second thoughts. He came directly to the point. "So I assume you will accept the position. I talked with President Carter at U.O.G. She thinks you would be an excellent choice, and she assured me that the university can find others to teach your classes. So there is no problem at the university. So what is your answer?"

"Well, Governor," I said, "I think there is a person who would make a better Director of Commerce than I, if you're willing to consider him. His name is Anthony Quan."

The Governor continued his incessant pacing, stone-faced, without eye contact. There was no indication that he had actually heard what I had said. My heart was pounding as I forged ahead. "He comes from a solidly Democratic family, originally from Sumai Village. His older brother, John, is currently a Senator, and his mother owns this building we're in. I believe you know the family well. Tony has taught economics at the university in the past and is presently finishing his Doctorate in Economics at the University of Wisconsin. When he was teaching at U.O.G. we became close friends. I hold great respect for Tony, and I know he and his family are supporters of yours. I'm sure he would do a fine job as Director. Also, his wife is Filipina and well-connected in the Philippine community."

The Governor abruptly stopped, sat in his chair, and looked at me full on. He was clearly perturbed. "*Lanya*, you turn down a directorship by suggesting another person to take your place. That is a first. Most people would jump at the job. When is Quan going to finish his studies?"

"I'm not sure, Governor, but as you know, his mother runs the bridal shop downstairs. Maybe we can find out from her." I quickly added, "If you would like, I am willing to fill in for him until he gets back on-Island."

On my part, this whole thing was a spur-of-the-moment idea. I hadn't contacted Tony and had no idea whether he'd agree to take the job, let alone when he might be returning to Guam. But I suspected, knowing Tony's male ego, that he would grab the opportunity, and that would get me off the hook with minimal repercussions. At least that's what I hoped.

"All right then, my staff will contact you should we have further need of your assistance," said the Governor.

Those words were an invitation to leave, so I said as I got up, "I'm sure you'll find that Anthony Quan is very competent and up to the task, Governor. I'm willing to help in any way I can."

He didn't answer, but a few days later, David Shimizu, the Governor's Chief of Staff, called me, asking if I'd be willing to take on the acting directorship until Tony Quan returned from school. I said yes, and thus began my government service.

*   *   *

The acting designation turned out be quite fortuitous, since it freed me from legislative confirmation hearings and rigorous financial reporting requirements. In addition, it allowed me to retain a tenured faculty position at the university, thus ensuring my ability to return should the Governor decide to terminate my services—not an unlikely possibility in view of how things had unfolded between us.

In January of 1983, the week before I was scheduled to assume the directorship, I visited the Commerce Department offices located in the International Trade Center. There I met with outgoing Director Joe McDonald. We hadn't previously known each other, but I knew and liked his brother, Jim, who had managed the Toyota dealership that was once owned by Governor-elect Bordallo. Furthermore, it had not escaped me that McDonald was the middle name of the incumbent Governor, Paul McDonald Calvo, who had just lost the election. As in every Pacific Island, the personal, government and business relationships were so intertwined that one had to be cautious when speaking and dealing with local residents.

Our meeting went well. Joe was quite cordial. After introducing me to his secretary and immediate staff, he reviewed the many federal programs and grants administered by the department. Some US Economic Development Authority (EDA) grants were being audited and the expenditures challenged. These audits would fall into my lap, but Joe said that the problems were minor and I shouldn't worry about them.

Later, after taking over the department, I found that the problems were not so minor. For example, Guam had received an EDA grant to construct a Food and Drug Administration (FDA) certified processing plant for farm produce—pigs, chickens, bananas and the like. Subsequently, the money had been used to build a baseball stadium with restaurant stalls under the bleachers. Quarterly reports indicated that these stalls "processed" and served locally-grown foods. The auditors were not pleased.

The EDA had also funded construction of a fish hatchery that had never hatched a fish, and a farmers' market that sold mostly non-farm items to tourists. The list went on, and within a few months of becoming director, I became a frequent visitor at the Seattle Regional Office of EDA. There I experienced an eye-opening revelation about the federal bureaucracy. Regional EDA administrators were upset that they had been hoodwinked by unsophisticated islanders in a far-flung Pacific possession, but they weren't so upset as to risk appearing inept to their superiors in Washington. When push came to shove, they were willing to cooperate in order to smooth things over and sweep a few items under the rug. In due course the audit discrepancies seemed to evaporate. So much for my naive belief in the protections, oversight and accountability of federal agencies.

At one point during our conversation, Joe McDonald expressed his hope that I might continue to support a particular Headnote 3(a) project that he had been working on. Headnote 3(a), of 19 U.S.C.1202, of the US Tariff Schedules, allows products certified by the Director of Commerce as produced or processed on Guam to enter the United States duty-free. Joe said that he had been working with some importers to set up a coffee bean processing operation at the Commercial Port of Guam. He said that if things materialized as planned, the operation would create jobs and enhance Guam's economy. At the time I saw little reason to disagree.

Subsequently however, with the assistance of some Guam customs agents, I visited the "coffee processing operation" that was housed in a warehouse at the commercial port of Guam. One end of the building was filled with sacks of raw Honduran coffee beans. The beans had been shipped under a Honduran export certificate that indicated Hong Kong as the destination, yet here they were in Guam.

At the other end of the warehouse were pallets of colorfully repackaged beans, each bearing the inscription, "A Product of the U. S. Territory of Guam." These were being shipped to San Francisco under Headnote 3(a), with a Guam certificate-of-origin signed by the Director of Commerce. Clearly this coffee processing operation could better be described as a repackaging operation, more akin to smuggling than legitimate industry. It did not continue under my signature, and I have no idea whether Joe continued to sign certificates-of-origin after he was no longer director.

It took a few months, but eventually Joe McDonald's two Indian business partners were arrested, tried, and sent to federal prison for conspiracy to circumvent US Customs law. To my knowledge, Joe McDonald was never charged personally, although two corporations owned by him were charged, convicted and fined. So much for my naïve belief in the altruism of public officials.

*   *   *

My first week on the job provided additional eye-opening experiences. For example, Governor Bordallo's administrative staff informed all directors that we should purge our departments of non-permanent workers appointed during the previous administration, as well as all those who had supported incumbent Governor Calvo in the recent election. Based on personnel records, it was easy for me to determine who were political appointees, but I had no way of knowing who among the permanent staff had been Calvo supporters. Furthermore, I believed that employees should be fairly evaluated and judged based on their individual merit and ability to contribute to department needs.

I was quickly disabused of that naive notion by my Deputy Director, Henry Cruz, and the department's Personnel Specialist, Mary Chaco. They were both long-time government employees with strong political connections and strong family ties within the community. Between them they knew all the individuals involved and understood what needed to be done.

"Director Callaghan, you must get rid of these people or they will cause us lots of problems over the next couple of years," said Mary.

"But Mary, aren't some of them classified civil service employees? I can't just fire them for no reason."

"You leave that to me, Director Callaghan. That's my job. In some cases, we will have to reassign them in order to convince them that, as we say, the handwriting is on the wall."

"She is very skilled at her job," chimed in Henry. "You won't have to bother yourself with the process. Just give the okay."

During the next few days, the three of us reviewed the personnel files on Mary's list. In most cases I ended up following her advice. Some employees on the payroll had never shown up for work, save for paydays to collect their checks. Others had never shown up for work at all. Their checks were simply mailed to them. These severance decisions were easy, but some cases weighed on my conscience and still do to this day.

One of these was the case of Franklin Reynolds (a pseudonym). Franklin had been for some time Chief of the Customs and Quarantine Division. He was a classified civil service employee who had worked his way up through the ranks. Unfortunately, he had not been a Bordallo supporter, and the Governor wanted him out. I had nothing against Franklin, and probably could have worked with him; however, I knew that there were allegations of corruption and favoritism in the Customs Division, and these concerns were further reinforced when a review of payroll records indicated that three lower-ranked customs officers had received take-home pay higher than that of the Governor.

Wanting to get to the bottom of these issues and make appropriate changes, I told myself that Franklin represented the status quo and would likely be an obstructionist. It might be easier, I thought, to work with someone new. Henry and Mary were happy with this justification and suggested that I promote the deputy chief, Jessie Flores, to acting chief status.

"But what will become of Franklin?" I asked.

"Just leave that to Henry and me. As long as we have your direction to do so, we'll find another assignment for him," said Mary

"Well, okay," I said. "But make sure he's treated fairly."

Later I discovered that Franklin had been sent to a backroom office, where for months he transcribed data from old customs forms by hand. As far as I know, he remained there for the duration of my tenure at the Commerce Department. Not being certain that Franklin deserved such treatment, I allowed a potential injustice to proceed. For that I remain sorry. It has bothered me for many years.

One thing became clear during that first week: never get on the wrong side of an experienced personnel specialist. Mary Chaco knew her job well and had held a firm grip on it through several administrations. She knew every line of every personnel manual and every procedure and process for every action. If she wished to do damage, she could inflict infinite discomfort. If she was on your side, you won, at least most of the time. But, to my embarrassment, she met her match in the case of Fred Santos, the Public Market Manager.

The Public Market was located in Agana, on government land near the baseball stadium and the marina. The manager, Fred Santos, and his staff of eight were classified Department of Commerce employees. At the behest of Governor Bordallo, and with the vocal support of Guam's Chamber of Commerce, I proposed to privatize the market operation and terminate the employees, thus saving the government $180,000 annually. This action was not just a subterfuge to get rid of Fred and his crew. I honestly felt that there would be significant efficiencies and improvements realized should the market be privately managed. But Fred enlisted the aid of some senators, and a politically-charged battle ensued.

I found Fred to be a personable and competent fellow. He was for the most part well-liked by the stall venders at the market. Of course, there were some complaints about favoritism, but nothing more than would be expect in a nepotistic island environment. I actually liked Fred, but unfortunately, he had not supported Governor Bordallo, and he apparently had crossed Mary a few times as well, so he had to go. Mary and Henry said they could take care of Fred, but one thing led to another over the next year, until I found myself on the witness stand of Superior Court in front of Presiding Judge Joaquine C. Perez. Fred's view of the facts prevailed over Mary's paperwork. He retained his job, and with the help of some friends in the Legislature, proceeded to wall off his Market fiefdom from my oversight and control. By the ordeal's end, I actually admired Fred's tenacity and secretly wished him well. Several years later, Fred became General Manager of the Guam Mass Transit Authority. That pleased me.

*   *   *

When it came to the personnel matter of Rita Santos (a pseudonym), I stood my ground, firmly rooted in a sense of decency. Rita had been the Executive Secretary for the previous Director, Joe McDonald, and she was still on the job at seven-thirty in the morning when I arrived, anxious and excited, on my first day as Director.

My previous meeting with Joe McDonald had been the only meaningful transition effort initiated by the outgoing or incoming administrations. So at that early hour, I was surprised and happy to see a face that I recognized. The fragrant aroma of fresh brewed coffee hung in the air as Rita welcomed me. "*Hafa Adai*, Dr. Callaghan; congratulations on your appointment."

"Good morning, Rita," I said. "I appreciate you being here. I had no idea what to expect, and it's nice to see a face I recognize. Where am I supposed to hang out?"

"Your temporary office is right over here," she said as she led the way. "It will be another week before renovations are completed on the big office."

I was aware that Joe McDonald was still in the process of moving out from his palatial digs, an office that I would occupy after fresh paint and new furniture.

"Would you like some coffee, Dr. Callaghan?" Rita asked as I entered the temporary office.

"Yes, thank you. It smells good," I replied.

"Cream and sugar?"

"No, just black," I said. "I keep hoping that if I drink enough of that stuff my Statesider skin will get a little browner."

She smiled. "It's not the color of your skin that's important. It's the size of your Chamorro heart that counts most, Dr. Callaghan."

"I try my best to have an islander's heart," I said as she departed for the coffee.

While she was gone, I observed that the temporary office was clean and orderly, but drab and uninteresting. A window faced west with a view along Marine Corps Drive, five stories below. The cream-colored walls were bare and a bit smudged in places. Florescent light emanated from flush ceiling fixtures. I sat in the leather executive chair behind a grey metal desk that was piled with documents, all bearing colorful notation tabs and post-it notes. Across the room, near the door, a short couch hugged the wall. The only other furniture consisted of several grey, metal folding chairs, two of which were placed in front of my desk on the mottled grey vinyl floor.

Returning with the coffee, Rita closed the door and asked if she might speak with me privately.

"Sure," I said. "Let's sit and talk—that's if I can see you over the top of these papers." I pumped the side lever on the executive chair and slowly rose to a better perspective.

Rita sat on a folding chair, and I initiated the conversation. "It's nice that you're here so early, Rita. I'm an early morning person myself. My mind seems to work better in the mornings. So what do you want to talk about?"

"Dr. Callaghan," she said, "I know that it's normal for an incoming director to appoint his own secretary, but I would like to ask you to keep me on. I've been executive secretary for several directors at various agencies in Gov-Guam. I take shorthand and can easily keep notes and provide you with summaries of your meetings. I type over 130 words a minute and can translate from English to Chamorro and the other way around. I've been here at Commerce for five years now, and I know the people and projects in all our divisions. If you let me stay, I know I can be of help to you. I'm sure we can work well together. Please just give me a try. You won't be disappointed."

The transition team had provided me with almost no useful information regarding the day-to-day operations at Commerce, so I was well aware of her potential value. She knew what was going on in this organization of three hundred plus employees. All I knew was that Commerce handled an intimidating list of responsibilities, liaisons, and contacts, both domestic and international, and I would need all the help I could get.

"Rita," I said, "if you stay, I need to know that I have your loyalty and support. There is much that I don't know about this job. I'm new to government, and I don't speak Chamorro. I must know that I can count on you to always be watching my back and helping me out."

"You can count on me, Dr. Callaghan. I won't let you down. My husband doesn't have a job. He takes the kids to school and picks them up. My mother-in-law lives with us and helps out too, so I can come early and stay late. If you will just give me a try, I know things will work out between us. Please at least consider it," she pleaded.

"Well, all right," I said. "Let's give it a try for a couple of weeks and see how things work out. I'll be facing a lot of pressure to do otherwise, so don't let me down. I'm going out on a limb for you. I expect that you'll be 100 percent on my side at all times."

"Oh Dr. Callaghan, thank you so much. You can count on me for sure. Today you're only scheduled for a cabinet meeting at 2:00 p.m. But I suspect that your deputy, Henry Cruz, and the personnel officer, Mary Chaco, will want to see you as soon as they come in. I'll let you know when they're here. If you have any questions about those documents for your signature, just let me know, and I'll call the appropriate staff members to explain things."

Henry and Mary were upset with my decision to keep Rita because they felt that her allegiance would remain with the previous director, but I was adamant, and I was the boss, so there wasn't much they could do about it.

Over the next few weeks of briefings and twelve-hour days, I learned much about my department. We were responsible for collecting, interpreting, and publishing all Guam Territorial economic and demographic data, including import and export information and consumer price index estimations. We were the lead agency for conducting population, business, and agricultural censuses.

We were the point-of-contact for international agencies such as the Asian Development Bank (ADB), the U.N. Economic and Social Commission for Asia and the Pacific (UNESCAP), the South Pacific Commission (SPC), and U.S.A.I.D Pacific Region. We were the Guam grant administrators for the US Small Business Administration (SBA), the US Economic Development Authority (EDA), and the US Census Bureau (USCB). We administered the operations of Guam Customs and Quarantine and the Public Market. We were the government liaison to the Guam Chamber of Commerce and were responsible for providing analytical support to the Guam Economic Development Authority (GEDA).

Within a few weeks, I became more comfortable with my position and was slowly coming to grips with the political and social obligations of a Gov-Guam Director. One Friday at noontime, personnel specialist Mary Chaco stuck her head around the corner of my office door with a serious look on her face.

"Dr. Callaghan, are you busy? I have something important to ask of you."

"No, Mary," I said. "Come in. Have a seat. I'm just reading these regulations about Foreign Sales Corporations, and I need a break. What can I do for you?"

She remained standing and said, "I'd like you to do me a favor right now, Dr. Callaghan. Please go upstairs to the seventh floor and find room 755. Don't knock on the door; just walk in. When you get there, you'll see why I've sent you."

"Are you serious, Mary? What's going on?" I exclaimed.

"I'm serious! You'll see! Just please do as I ask," she replied.

"Okay, I'm on my way," I said as I tabled the corpulent volume of US Trade Regulations.

Soon I was standing in the seventh-floor hallway in front of a door designated only by the number 755. I knocked and immediately entered.

The image that confronted me was, to say the least, startling. Joe McDonald sat in a padded leather chair behind a bulky, cherrywood desk. Apparently the same desk and chair that he had occupied as Director. *Isn't that furniture government property?* I thought.

In front of Joe with her back to me was my executive secretary, Rita. Around the room were several people I had recently laid off or otherwise demoted, among them Franklin Reynolds. They were eating pizza and in the midst of conversation.

As those in the room perceived my arrival, mouths stopped. Heads turned. All eyes were on me. The stunned looks on their faces only served to amplify my own uncertainty. I wanted to turn and leave without saying a word, but my better judgment prevailed and I moved forward.

Joe was the first to react. "Come in, Dr. Callaghan. Have a chair. I've opened this office to take care of my ongoing consulting work. It's a step down from the Commerce Director's office, but it will do for now. How can I help you?"

Somehow, I summoned the courage to take one of the steel folding chairs beside Rita; turning it backwards, I sat with my forearms resting on top of the chairback. Without saying a word Rita slunk out of her chair. With head down, she went for the door. If she had a tail, it certainly would have been between her legs.

Joe spoke again. "What do you think of being Director? Is it all you had hoped it would be?"

"Well, I never really wanted the job in the first place," I said. "But I've learned a lot in the last few weeks. I heard that you had this place on the seventh floor, so I wanted to stop by and see what was going on and say hello."

"I'm just trying to earn a few dollars to feed the family," he said. "Most people would die to be given a directorship, and you say you don't want the job. I can't quite believe that."

"I'm just holding down the seat until Tony Quan gets back from school," I said. "I'd like to turn things over to him in the best shape possible."

"Yes, I heard he was going to take over. It'll be good to have a local boy in there," he said. "When does Tony get here?"

Ignoring his slight, I replied, "I don't know, but I'll be really glad when he does get here. He's much more suited to this life of local politics than I am."

"Well, from what I hear," Joe said, "you're quite comfortable signing politically motivated personnel terminations, so maybe you fit into politics much better than you think."

He had touched a painful truth and I could only respond with, "That part of the job certainly gives me no pleasure, Joe, and I'm sure you've also had to take similar actions during your years in government service."

With that, I stood and said, "I'd better be getting back now. Good luck with your consulting, Joe. If there's anything I can do from downstairs, don't hesitate to ask."

As I turned to leave, I saw that the pizza eaters had vanished, leaving behind several open boxes of uneaten pizza. "Can I have a piece of pizza to get me through the lunch hour?" I asked.

"Sure, take what you want," Joe said.

I left the room with my mouth full of peperoni and mushroom, and my mind in a state of upset and turmoil.

Upon returning downstairs, Rita Santos was nowhere in sight, and I found that personnel specialist Mary had placed Rita's termination action on my desk for signature, effective immediately. I signed it after due reflection as to my naive misread of island culture. I had presumed that Rita saw me as a gracious benefactor who had gone out of my way to save her employment, so I'd felt comfortable with her expression of loyalty, thinking it was motivated by gratitude and a sense of obligation. I had been wrong.

Chamorros are similar to other Pacific Islanders when it comes to interpersonal relations with outsiders. Unless the outsider has well-established, long-term local connections, Indigenous relationships always trump obligations to interlopers. From Rita's point of view, the consequences of her relationship with Joe and his family would last for a lifetime, whereas my support was transitory and could evaporate when, like all outsiders, I departed for greener pastures. Without some long-term connection to her future welfare, I should never have expected to be highest on her loyalty list.

Mary and Henry said nothing, and my friend Joe Paulino found me a replacement secretary, Fay Castro. Fay was properly connected to the Paulino and Lujan families, with whom I had close association. Fay never let me down, and although I haven't seen her in years, I know we remain friends to this day. I never saw Velma Santos again. Lesson learned.

*   *   *

As the days of my directorship progressed, there were further blows to my belief in the righteous nature of government service.

For various reasons, Customs and Quarantine Officers preferred working at particular locations. The larger ports of entry, such as the international airport and commercial seaport, were busier and provided more opportunity for overtime and shift differentials, whereas the smaller ports, such as the Navy and Airforce bases and the coastal small boat harbors, were quieter and provided a relaxed work environment. Some senior officers had spent years at the same location and had established relationships that provided an opportunity for corruption, favoritism, and excessive overtime.

In order to get control of the situation, I authorized new procedures that required rotation of assignments and equal overtime opportunities, irrespective of seniority. Customs officers were to be assigned to the various ports based on a biannual lottery. This would ensure the fair and frequent rotation of duty assignments. Some flexibility was provided by allowing officers to exchange assignments among themselves, with the approval of the Acting Chief of Customs, in consultation with Deputy Director Henry Cruz or me.

At the outset everyone agreed that the lottery system provided additional equity, but some senior officers weren't happy with their loss of control. Under the new rules, they had less opportunity to initiate favoritism, receive inducements, and control subordinates. Sometime later, the depth of their dissatisfaction would become apparent to me.

Another person unhappy with my changes at Customs was the Legislative Speaker, Carl Tommy Cruz Gutierrez. I don't know whether he and my Deputy Director, Henry Cruz, were related, but it's certainly possible. Keeping track of such family connections was a critical component of survival in government service on Guam. Those born and raised on islands learn from childhood to memorize family ties. Statesiders like me, unfamiliar with the entwined associations, can cope only by sticking to the written rules and attempting to act in accordance with our moral compass. I was luckier than many Statesiders on Guam because my wife was an islander and a member of the Palauan community. She had gone to great lengths to understand and memorize local Chamorro family interrelationships. Throughout our marriage, her advice was invaluable.

In any case, Henry had briefed me that the Speaker would be contacting me to ask that an exception be made for the assignment of a certain female customs officer. She had for some time been working at the Commercial Port of Guam. Under the new procedures, she was scheduled to work at Anderson Airforce Base. The Speaker wanted her to remain stationed at the commercial port. Further, Henry noted that the customs officer in question was rumored to be the Speaker's lover, and her daily commute to Anderson would be inconvenient.

I didn't tell Henry that I was aware of rumors circulating in the Palauan community that Speaker Gutierrez was involved in the importation of marijuana from Palau. It could be that Carl's inordinate concern over the work location of this particular customs officer was simply a desire that she remain available, close at hand, shall we say. It also could be that she was assisting him in nefarious import activities at the commercial port. Or perhaps she was simply a constituent whom he wanted to help for one reason or another.

When Carl called, I explained our lottery procedure and indicated that I was loath to make an exception based solely on an officer's travel inconvenience, especially since travel was a reimbursable expense. Furthermore, I didn't want to set a precedent, since there were other customs employees who might claim similar transportation difficulties. I suggested that she could exchange assignments with another officer in order to shorten her commute. He asked if she could exchange assignments with another officer in order to remain at the commercial port. I said I was sorry, but I felt we needed to rotate officers more frequently than we had in the past. The Speaker wasn't happy when he hung up the phone. Our relationship never improved. Carl Gutierrez went on to become Governor, and I forever remained low on his list of politically acceptable Statesiders.

*   *   *

About six months into my acting directorship, the phone rang one afternoon. It was the Governor's Chief of Staff, David Shimizu. He was calling from Manila in the Philippines to alert me that Governor Bordallo's entourage would be arriving at the Guam International Airport that evening. He asked that I arrange expeditious customs examination for the entire group. I knew that expedited examination was shorthand for no examination at all. Such treatment was commonly afforded to dignitaries holding diplomatic passports as well as the Governor, but not usually to his whole entourage.

I enquired from David as to why he was making this special alert. He replied that the Governor was bringing some plants and cuttings, Mango trees and the like, that he wanted to plant around Government House and in some parks. David and I both knew that plants, cuttings, and especially plants with roots in soil from the Philippines were absolutely not allowed to enter Guam. I was being asked to circumvent the law and ensure that the Guam customs officers were not put in the position of having to confiscate the Governor's plants.

I immediately began to consider how I might thwart the Governor's plan without it being obvious that I was responsible for doing so. Since Guam customs officers were authorized to enforce US Department of Agriculture regulations, I called the USDA representative on Guam. He assisted in training Guam customs officers and frequently worked with them during training sessions at the airport. I told him what was happening and suggested that he do some on the spot training at the airport that evening.

The plan appeared to work flawlessly. The federal officer intercepted the plants and held a training session, microscope and all, displaying to customs agents the microbes and insects that were detrimental to Guam's environment. After doing so, he locked the plants in the USDA office for safe keeping, until they could be transferred the next day to the Guam Department of Agriculture for incineration.

The Governor was furious. He didn't contact me directly, but he verbally tore into Henry Cruz by phone, getting him out of bed late at night. Next the Governor woke my friend Joe Paulino and demanded that he come to the Government House immediately. Joe was Director of Parks and Recreation, but the Governor knew of our close relationship, so island style, Joe became a proxy for the verbal lashing that was meant for me but could not be delivered directly.

The next morning Joe stopped by the incineration facility at the Guam Department of Agriculture. With the help of relatives who worked there, he rescued the plants as they arrived from USDA and delivered them to Government House. As far as I know, all the cuttings and trees, along with their accompanying contaminants, were planted at Government House and continue to grow there today. Furthermore, the USDA officer never learned the truth, but I'm sure that some Guam customs officers heard about what had happened. So much for the morale of hardworking customs agents who do their best to protect Guam from the introduction of pests and invasive species from abroad.

*　　*　　*

The economic statistics and demographic divisions at the Commerce Department seemed to function relatively smoothly. I understood the people and their work, and they understood me. The customs division, on the other hand, provided a never-ending source of angst. The following is one more example of the difficulties I faced as a nonindigenous administrator working within a close-knit island environment where personal relationships and reciprocity are highly valued.

One day after lunch, Henry Cruz walked into my office. "We've got a problem," he said.

That's odd," I replied. "We never have any problems when you're on the job."

He seemed not to understand my attempt at humorous sarcasm and reiterated, "We do have a big problem, Dr. C."

"So let's hear it," I said.

Taking a deep breath, he said, "Well you see, yesterday morning Officer Kermit Borja (a pseudonym) was on duty at the airport. About two hours into his shift, he told his supervisor that he had a doctor's appointment. The supervisor told him to take a Customs vehicle and return as soon as possible. What Borja actually did was drive to the Harmon Loop Hotel to meet his girlfriend for a little midday delight. Unfortunately, his wife surprised them in the hotel parking lot. Borja took off in the Customs vehicle, with his wife in pursuit. They raced all the way out to Yigo Village, where she ran him off the road. The Customs vehicle is totaled and Borja is in the hospital with minor injuries. Luckily no one else got hurt."

"Wow!" I said. "What about the girlfriend? What happened to her?"

Henry smiled. "She was really lucky that Borja's wife went after him instead of her. She got away, but she probably won't be visiting him in the hospital because the wife is maintaining twenty-four-seven guard duty."

"What do you think we should do with this guy, Borja?" I asked.

"I think we should give him at least a ninety-day suspension without pay. He's just an officer grade one, so we can't demote him," said Henry.

"Why the hell shouldn't we just terminate him?" I protested. "His actions were totally irresponsible and a horrible example for other officers. Shouldn't he pay for the vehicle?"

"The pickup is a total loss," said Henry. "Public Works says that it can't be repaired, and there's no administrative process by which we can force Borja to purchase a new one. And to make matters worse, Dr. C, Borja's wife is closely related to higher-ups in the Democratic Party, and Borja has been a staunch supporter of Governor Bordallo. I don't think we can terminate him without major repercussions."

"Shit, I don't give a damn if his wife is related to Saint Peter and his girlfriend is Mary Magdalene," I said. "He's got no business being a customs officer. Is this the first time he has screwed up like this?"

"No, his files show that he has taken sick leave several times without turning in doctors' excuses. He was probably meeting with the girlfriend. And last year he was written up for sleeping while on duty at the Navy base," replied Henry.

"Henry, write me a report that will support his termination and work with Mary to ensure that his termination is carried out properly according to the book. People can't act like this on my watch."

A concerned look crept onto Henry's face as he said, "Are you sure, Dr. Callaghan? This will cause me big difficulties."

"What do you mean, cause you difficulties? I'm not firing you. I'm firing Borja. All you have to do is the paperwork and follow the proper procedures," I said.

"You don't understand, Dr. Callaghan," said Henry. "Borja will go directly to the Governor through his most influential relatives. The Governor will ask me to fix the situation. My brother works in the Governor's office, and our father is employed at Public Works. Please don't terminate him."

At that moment I understood what Henry was trying to tell me. If I strictly followed the book and terminated Borja, there would be innocent people who paid a price as well. On this island, every administrative action I took, every decision I made, had personal ramifications that went well beyond what was superficially apparent. I recalled the difficulties endured by my friend Joe Paulino as he worked to rectify my decision to confiscate the Governor's plants. Joe came from a powerful family with many votes and significant influence. He could afford to defend me with the Governor and do what was needed to fix the situation. Henry was less well situated, less able to defend my decision, and more likely to suffer consequences.

"Wow, Henry, I hadn't thought of things that way," I said. "I'll tell you what, let me think about this for a couple of days. Meanwhile, you and Mary go ahead and prepare for a ninety-day suspension and tell Borja that I'm considering his termination. Meanwhile, keep me informed."

Two days later a young, well-spoken attorney named Philip Carbullido arrived at my office. He told me in an affable manner that he was a Democratic Party official and that he also represented Kermit Borja. He said that both party officials and the Governor hoped that I could see my way clear to not terminating Mr. Borja, since he had been a contributive supporter, and at present he was the only bread winner for his family of six.

I described Borja's conduct in detail and explained why I thought that such behavior warranted termination. Mr. Carbullido agreed with everything that I said but still requested leniency based on party affiliation, the Governor's request, and the Borja family's welfare. I said that I would give his request my fullest consideration when arriving at a decision. He thanked me and we parted on amicable terms. The next day I told Henry to go ahead with a letter of reprimand and a ninety-day suspension.

The intricate, invisible web of relationships that surrounded me became even more apparent when I found that Philip Carbullido's father was Francisco Chaco Carbullido. Mary Chaco was my personnel officer. Philip Carbullido's mother was Maria Salas Castro. Fay Castro was my secretary. Oh, and by the way, the young lawyer, Philip Carbullido, later became the Honorable Chief Justice of the Supreme Court of Guam.

Over the next few months things quieted down in Customs. There were few complaints and little necessity for punitive administrative actions. The lottery system for determining duty locations seemed to be working, and everyone seemed to be settling into the new way of doing things.

As Director, I had my own reserved parking stall in the customs area at the Guam International Airport. When I traveled off-island, I frequently parked my Toyota pickup there so that it would be easily available upon my return.

In this one particular instance, I was flying to Honolulu for a week of meetings. My friends Bill and Jane Williams had asked to borrow the pickup during my absence, so I had given them an extra key and told them to take it from the airport whenever they wished. A day or so after I departed, Bill dropped Jane off to take the pickup. When she exited the parking area and started down the hill toward a busy intersection on Marine Drive, she realized that there were no brakes. Only because of her deft maneuvering and use of the emergency brake was an accident averted. Upon examination, it was clear that the brake lines had been purposely cut. Apparently, some customs personnel were still unhappy with my more equitable duty assignment procedures.

* * *

As time went by, I became more confident and comfortable as a cabinet member. However, I stood out as a Statesider and the only trained economist, unafraid to express views that differed from those of the Governor. Most cabinet members were adept at telling the Governor what he wanted to hear because they valued their jobs and had few equivalent employment alternatives. Any contrary views on their part were either internalized or delivered in a circuitous manner, so as to avoid any hint of disloyalty.

I had adequate investment income, a tenured position at the university, and alternative career opportunities. Once a policy was established, I did my best to carry it out, but during policy formation, I openly expressed my opinion. The Governor was clearly uncomfortable with such independence and potential lack of loyalty. He seemed to have difficulty talking directly with me, usually expressing his wishes through friends like Joe Paulino or his Chief of Staff, David Shimizu. It was clear that Governor Bordallo eagerly anticipated the arrival of Tony Quan, whom he saw as being an agreeable "local boy" and a compliant "team player." As time passed there were increasing queries as to when Tony would arrive back on island. I didn't know, but I hoped it would be soon.

My direct, no-nonsense approach was not only disconcerting to the Governor, but it also caused the annoyance of some senators, not the least of whom was

Speaker Gutierrez. I have always found it difficult to tolerate people who mask their ignorance behind bombast and indignation. On several occasions during public hearings, I delivered blunt and cutting testimony that betrayed my lack of respect for some senators' level of competence.

For example, during one hearing I was asked to comment on a bill sponsored by Senator Frank Santos that increased the percentage rate of Guam's gross receipts tax. I informed the committee that the tax was both non-transparent and regressive, and therefore not a good way to tax people, no matter the rate. That provoked a tirade from Senator Santos, the essence of which was that the proposed increase was needed to balance the budget; it was the same equal percentage for all businesses across all goods and services; economists are too academic and impractical and "don't know everything." When he was done, I explained that the term "regressive" meant that the tax in question hurt the low-income poor more than it hurt the high-income rich, and that was the case precisely because the tax was a flat percentage on all goods and services. I then provided several examples to illustrate my point. Next, I commented that a non-transparent tax, like the gross receipts tax, benefitted politicians because the tax was hidden from the public and therefore those voters who paid the tax would be less likely to perceive the source of their pain, and therefore unlikely to blame legislators for their discomfort. Senator Santos walked out of the hearing.

After I had been Acting Director for almost a year and Tony Quan had not yet returned, Speaker Gutierrez introduced a bill that limited a director's acting status to ninety days. The bill passed, and not unexpectedly, the Governor signed it, saying that it made little difference, since he could reappoint me after ninety days if he wished.

Actually, I wasn't unhappy about the ninety-day window, since it provided some certainty and forced some action. Still, I was a bit ambivalent. On one hand I wanted to get back to the slower pace and comfort of the university. My body was beginning to revolt against the fast pace, long hours, and never-ending social requirements of the directorship. Christenings, weddings, village fiestas and funerals were an integral part of Chamorro society. The Governor's staff kept track of them and assigned cabinet members to attend. It wasn't uncommon for me to appear at five or six such functions on a weekend. At each there was copious amounts of rich, savory local foods. It was impossible not to avoid overeating. My favorite indulgence was *fritada*—pork or venison blood stew.

Paul Callaghan, Seattle, WA, 1982

On the other hand, there were department initiatives that I had begun and wanted to complete; however, in retrospect I must admit that I had become somewhat enamored by the privileges associated with being a director. When I traveled there was VIP treatment at island airports and first-class seating on flights to Pacific destinations. I had chaired the annual Fisheries Officers Meeting at the South Pacific Commission in Noumea, New Caledonia, and represented Guam at various Pacific-wide assemblies and workshops. Island leaders had begun to know my name, and I had developed region-wide friendships. On the home front I had come to expect and appreciate the differences paid to me: better and more prompt service at restaurants; invitations to celebrations and government functions; speaking engagements at Rotary Club and the Chamber of Commerce; reserved parking stalls; special treatment by government agencies, for instance, an easy-to-remember home phone number, 789-1200. Even Nina was beginning to enjoy her interactions with the Chamorro ladies of *Y Inetnon*

Famalao'an and the prestige that brought her within the Palauan community and at the university.

In January of 1984, before my ninety-day window had ended, Tony Quan finally arrived back on the Island. His confirmation hearing went well and he was soon sworn in as Commerce Department Director. Considerably relieved, I stepped into the role of Chief Economist with an office down the hall from Tony. There I focused on the task of compiling and publishing the "1983 Guam Annual Report" while at the same time working with Henry Cruz to support Tony and bring him up to speed on a range of issues. In the fall of 1984, I happily returned to teaching.

*   *   *

Despite becoming increasingly cynical as to the altruïsm of public service, my experience in government was both enlightening and worthwhile. The opportunity to be a big fish in Guam's little pond provided experiences and opportunities beyond anything that could have been possible had I lived elsewhere in America. During my time as head of the Commerce Department, I made regional ties that contributed to my success in other endeavors over subsequent years.

I owe much to that beautiful lady, Herminia Dierking, who facilitated my brief adventure outside academia into the world of politics. As Director of the Bureau of Budget, she controlled the government purse strings. While I was Director of Commerce, she often helped get critical allotments released and travel funding approved. I could go to her office with my problems, talk freely, and receive honest advice and counsel. She was masterful at persuading the Governor to say "yes" when he was prepared to say "no." Her advice to me was, "If you want something from the Governor, watch his body language. Don't bother talking to him when he's pacing back and forth. He only listens and makes decisions when he is standing still or sitting."

I watched with admiration as Herminia navigated her world of Chamorro male dominance and sexual harassment to become a respected multi-term senator in the Guam Legislature. God bless her departed soul. In March of 2008, I stood in line for an hour in the hot Guam sun, waiting to enter Dulce Nombre de Maria Cathedral for Herm's last viewing. At the casket, I wanted to reach out and put my hand on hers, but I knew what a commotion that might cause among the assembled dignitaries, so I just said, "Thank you, Herm" and walked on with my eyes dripping.

Jose (Joe) Eugenio Paulino smoked a lot of Marlboro cigarettes to calm his hyperactive personality and died of lung cancer in 1997 at age fifty-eight. He was just old enough to remember the Japanese soldier who lived with his family during the occupation of Guam, and how that soldier had cried when he hugged little Joe before going off to battle the American Marines. He never returned. Joe was my Guam godfather, my *pari*, one of the finest friends I ever had. When I arrived at the university, Joe took me under his wing. He helped me learn and navigate the island ways of Guam. When needed, he interceded for me among the Chamorro community. I owe much to Joe and his extended family, and I visit his grave each time I travel through Guam. The following is an excerpt from his funeral eulogy that I helped craft along with his sister, Patricia Quinata.

> Joe was first and foremost a Chamorro, he believed in his cultural heritage, and he understood it well, but he treated everyone he met as an equal human being and a friend. He had deep respect for cultural differences. He was tolerant and considerate of new ideas and ways of thinking. With Joe, everyone started out with a clean slate, a welcome heart, and a helping hand. Joe helped countless new-comers to better understand Guam and to better contribute to the community. He truly saw good in everyone. The door step of Joe's home has recorded the footprints of those from all over Micronesia who needed food, shelter, or help and found it in Joe's house. Many of them are now statesmen and leaders in their home islands. If you were to visit many Micronesian islands you would find that mention of the name Joe Paulino brings smiles and respectful acknowledgment to the faces of numerous people.
>
> For years, while a Professor at the University of Guam, Joe maintained office hours at a table in the cafeteria in order to be near the students. Both teachers and students would join him over coffee and the *Pacific Daily News*. Everyone who pulled up a chair at that table was always welcome and immediately included in the conversation of the day. Countless students, staff, and faculty were helped at that table. If Joe could not solve a problem, he would find someone who could. Everyone who ever sat at Joe's table is a better person for having done so.

As if Joe's death wasn't enough, in July of that same year, Anthony (Tony) Henry Quan passed away at age fifty-one of a rare genetic blood disease. Tony is buried in Guam Veterans Cemetery, in the village of Piti. Whenever I visit Joe, I try to also visit Tony. His family and I are still in contact. Risa, Tony's wife, a professor of linguistics, is now retired from the University of Guam. She never remarried and lives in Guam with her oldest daughter, Amanda. Ailene, the middle daughter, is an attorney living in New York. Caili, the youngest, is a ballet dancer and choreographer for Juilliard, Philadelphia's Ballet X, and other companies. We still keep in touch on the internet. Both Tony and Joe contributed immensely to the richness of my life. It's a shame that we couldn't have walked together into our sunset years.

In retrospect, the two valued lessons learned from my experience in government are the extent to which power corrupts, and the importance of maintaining one's perspective. Arrogance is a stealthy malady. It sneaks up on even the most well-intentioned person. Here and there empathy is lost, deference is misplaced, respect is forgotten, humility fades into condescension, integrity vanishes. As self-importance slowly ascends, one's perspective dims. The small pond appears bigger, and one's place in it more significant.

For a brief time in Guam, I lost perspective. Arrogance crept in, as it had once before in Palau when I was thought by some to be the son of Ibedul. For a time, I actually considered running for one of twenty-one seats in Guam's Legislature. Some non-Chamorros had successfully done so. Why not me? Thankfully, that little voice inside me screamed out, *No! That would lead to a complete loss of integrity, not to mention a disastrous physical lifestyle. You're a fine teacher, be happy with that calling.* As my mother advised, I listened to that little voice and have endeavored to avoid any revival of arrogance. I hope I have been successful.

It's worth mentioning once again that differences in cultural norms should never be judged as bad or good. They arise because of differences in history and environment and cannot be easily or quickly changed. When entering another culture, the outsider must adapt in order to have any possibility of contributive survival. The alternative is to be ineffective and ultimately swept aside. That is especially true in small Pacific Islands, and I suspect, in every small pond throughout the world. The trick is to adapt enough but not so much as to abandon one's bedrock principles. Few outsiders are able to achieve that balance.

Some final footnotes to all of this. On January 31, 1990, Ricardo Jerome "Ricky" Bordallo, Governor of Guam, at age sixty-two, after being convicted in

Federal Court of obstruction of justice and wire fraud, draped himself in Guam's flag, chained himself to a statue of Chief Kepuha on the busiest intersection in the capital city, and shot himself in the head with a .38 caliber revolver. It is said that Joe Paulino had been the model used for that sculpture of Chief Kepuha, the first Chamorro chief to be baptized a Roman Catholic by the Spanish in 1668. After Governor Bordallo's death, his wife, Madeleine Mary Zeien Bordallo, a Minnesota-born Statesider, went on to become Lieutenant Governor of Guam and serve eight terms as Guam's delegate to the US House of Representatives. Her father, Christian P. Zeien, had been for several years a teacher and administrator in the Palau school system. Nina was his primary nurse and care giver at Guam Memorial Hospital during a long illness and hospitalization prior to his death. Many of Nina's friends and relatives, as well as many of our respective students, became influential leaders throughout Micronesia and the American Pacific. As the years passed, Nina and I became increasingly entwined in the complexity of Pacific Island social relationships.

Chapter 14

Children

During the 1985–86 school year I took sabbatical leave, and Nina took leave without pay. We moved to an apartment in Honolulu with a magnificent, twenty-eighth-floor view of Diamond Head. The change was a welcome break in routine for both of us. We had never lived at such heights or had the convenience of our own swimming pool and tennis courts. Nina worked part-time at Straub Clinic Hospital while I took finance courses at the University of Hawaii Business School.

My interest in portfolio management and the trading of futures and options contracts overcame my distaste for scholarly toil, and I found myself sitting in graduate courses taught by Wall Street gurus, whose services were apparently supplied to the University by Goldman Sacks. These specialists taught classes on Mondays, Tuesdays and Wednesdays, returning to New York on the Wednesday night redeye flight and arriving back in Hawaii the next Monday morning—a horrendous schedule. Their compensation must have been princely given their opportunity costs.

The courses were rigorous. I worked hard to keep my head above water, and in the process learned a lot of financial modeling and probability theory, almost none of which would ever be of use to me on Guam. Yet from a personal perspective, I acquired sufficient understanding of portfolio management theory that my awe of Wall Street experts and their methodology was considerably diminished. Their models could account for and hedge against risk, so long as those risks remained similar to what had occurred in the past. But they were as blind as the rest of us with respect to the unexpected, never-happened-before kinds of risks—the shocks that occur three or four or five times in a lifetime. Preparing for those infrequent, unexpected risks was still a matter of intuition, experience, and luck. That realization gave me confidence that I was quite capable of managing a long-term portfolio of securities without the help of so called "Wall Street experts."

My intellectual improvement was not the only reason for our migration to Hawaii. Nina announced that she was pregnant and expecting in March. Initially, I was despondent and psychologically crushed. She had been in Palau for the prior summer, so I was certainly not the father. She said that the pregnancy had resulted from a one-night-stand with a Bank of Hawaii executive who was visiting Palau. I have never been sure of that explanation, but I took her word for it, got my ego under control, and decided to be the best father I could be.

Our move to Honolulu was thus prompted by a belief that medical services there were superior to those available in Guam. Nina saw the obstetrician regularly and had all the appropriate tests, including an ultrasound showing that the baby was a girl. That was especially good news from a Palauan perspective. Girl babies are important in a matrilineal society. We decided to name her Deureng Sarah Callaghan. The closest English translations of *deureng* are happiness, joy, bliss. Sarah McCrory Rodgers Callaghan was the name of my father's mother, who died before I was born.

We did all those things that expectant parents should do, including talking, reading, and singing to the baby as she kicked in the womb. By late March, Deureng had not yet arrived. Then one morning Nina said, "There's something wrong. I know it. She's not moving like she has been." That day Nina visited the doctor's office, and within a few hours she was on the operating table at Queen's Hospital for C-section surgery.

I was allowed in the operating room and watched as the baby was lifted from Nina's abdomen. The doctors called it respiratory distress syndrome. Deureng had placental fluids in her lungs and couldn't breath properly. She was rushed to the neonatal intensive care unit at Kapiolani Children's Hospital. I sat with her for four days while she struggled to hold on to life. At one point her little hand could squeeze my finger and I had high hopes she would make it into this world. But gradually her grip faded. By the time Nina was released from Queens Hospital, Deureng was leaving us.

It took some cajoling and a sizable monetary contribution before the Catholic priest from nearby Sacred Heart Church agreed to administer baptism and the Catholic last rites. In the afternoon of April 6, 1986, Deureng was taken off the ventilator and died in Nina's arms while we sat together under a stained-glass window in the hospital's chapel. We were both crushed. Nina was as distraught as I have ever seen her. Deureng is buried in the children's section of Hawaii Memorial Park Cemetery on Oahu, with a view of the Koolau Range. I visit her with flowers whenever I go to Honolulu. Had Deureng lived, I am sure that I would have been a proud father, and she would have been a contributive and respected member of her Palauan clan.

We spent that summer recuperating with Mom in Chester before returning to Guam in late August. There we jumped into our work with abandon, attempting to clear our minds and move on with life. It was a good year for me. I was once again recognized for excellence in teaching. This time the recognition came with an added bonus—my own personal reserved parking space. Toward the end of that academic year, after a laborious process, I was promoted to the rank of Full Professor with tenure, the top of the university pecking order. I was forty-four years old. Once again, I found myself to be a big fish in a small pond, trying not to lose sight of the fact that there existed bigger ponds containing much bigger fish. Over subsequent years I have had an opportunity to interact with some of those bigger fish. Many were impressive, some less so, their reputations having accrued from happenstance or the work of others. It seems that no matter the size of the pond, the trick is to maintain perspective and a modicum of humility.

*   *   *

Our home was located in Yona Village on a narrow, street known as *Chalan Ayuyu* (Street of the Coconut Crab). Our unofficial house number was 160. We had chosen it ourselves to fit in between those on either side. No one on Guam ever used numerical street addresses to designate location. There were no government-assigned house numbers and no home mail delivery. The only semi-accurate street maps were maintained by the cable TV company that grudgingly lent such information to the government when required. If a general description of our house location became necessary, "Yona, Camp Witek" would suffice, provided the person was old enough to know that Camp Witek had been a US Marine base during WWII. If specific directions were required, the wording would be something like this: "Go south through Yona Village on the main road until you reach the Yona Supermarket, a mom-and-pop store on the ocean side. Turn left at the first possibility after the market. That should be *Chalan Ayuyu*. It will dogleg to the left. Keep going until you see the house number 158. Then turn right, toward the ocean, down the steep concrete driveway. We are at the bottom on the right, number 160."

I mention *Chalan Ayuyu* because we had some interesting neighbors on that single-lane, partially paved, dead-end road, and many of those neighbors influenced my life in one way or another. Tom and Monica Flores Tinkham lived near the street's entrance. Tom was an English professor and Monica was a social worker and previous student of mine. Next door to them lived Robert (Bob) and Elaine Fuerst, both professors of psychology at the University. A little further down the road were Joe and Marion Murphy. Joe was the editor of Guam's daily newspaper, the *Pacific Daily News*. If you could get his ear over morning coffee or evening Irish whiskey, some distorted version of your thoughts might appear in "Pipe Dreams," his daily editorial column. Everyone on the Island read it. He did sometimes smoke a pipe.

Beyond the Murphys lived Harry and Kathleen Owings, both professors at the university, and next to them was Luchus (Lu) and Jo Eldredge. Lu was a marine biologist at the University Marine Laboratory. Their daughter delivered the *Pacific Daily News* every morning to everyone on Chalan Ayuyu. Our house was down a steep driveway between the Owings and Eldredge homes. Sharing the same driveway was Paul Lawlor, a local attorney. He hailed from Boston, had been a Peace Corps volunteer in Indonesia, and like Murphy and Callaghan, was partial to Irish whiskey. We had Chamorro neighbors as well, including the Mayor of Yona Village, Jose (Pedo) Terlaje, and several in-laws of the Cruz family, large landholders in the Yona Village area. It was a congenial and diverse neighborhood.

For several years Tom Tinkham and I walked together at dawn each morning before beginning our day at the university. In 2009, Tom unexpectedly died from complications related to a simple outpatient hernia repair. My reading at his funeral provides the best recollection of our time together:

> We walked and talked together, Tom and I, every morning on the road to Tagachan as the sun rose from the sea. Some days were rainy, cool and blustery, others warm and humid. It really made no difference; the walk was about 3 miles round trip and the company was good. We were kindred spirits, Tom and I. We

had both graduated from the University of Colorado only a year apart, during the Kennedy, Johnson, Vietnam War years, but didn't know each other at the time. We both joined the Peace Corps, hoping to make the world a better place. Our impact on the world was minimal, but our lives were forever changed and enhanced by that experience.

We walked and talked about the wonder of it all, how minor accidents and chance happenings had shaped the paths of our lives, paths that met every morning on the road to Tagachan as the sun rose from the sea. We talked of science and religion and politics, both insular and global, of linguistics, economics and social issues, of the weather and of many trivial things. In the process we learned a great deal from each other, and about each other. We revisited our youthful adventures. We compared our life experiences and an assortment of memories gleaned from some of the world's less traveled places. Upon reflection we agreed that our most valuable and enriching experiences had come upon us unexpectedly when we were engaged in something new that was a little out of the ordinary, or a bit risky.

On the road to Tagachan we discussed much about human cultural differences. We marveled at the richness of human diversity that surrounded our lives in Guam. We felt fortunate to be part of that mix, and we often reflected on how our lives had been so much richer, and so much more rewarding, than the lives of those Americans who had remained in the land of their birth.

Some days when the sun rose in a particularly beautiful way and the world around us appeared exceptionally magnificent, Tom and I would stop our trek to marvel at nature's perfection. We infrequently talked about the origin and meaning of life, because we were both of the mind that no earthly individual, ideology, or institution yet holds the singular answer to the truth of it all.

I will continue to walk every morning on the road to Tagachan as the sun rises from the sea. Tom was faster than I on the uphill, so

I'll quicken my pace in his memory. The walking I can handle, until I can't any more. It's the silence that will be hardest to bear. I'll miss my friend Tom, his insight, and his company."

For several years thereafter I walked our regular morning route alone. At sunrise I reflected on our time together and talked to Tom as if he were still striding beside me.

*   *   *

Sometime after Christmas in 1987, Bob and Elaine Fuerst invited the *Chalan Ayuyu* neighbors to a cocktail party on their veranda. They had a one-bedroom apartment attached to their house, and the gathering was to welcome a new tenant, Donald (Don) Soper. Don was a fellow faculty member and professor of marketing in the Business School. We all knew him, and it was a pleasure to now have him as our neighbor.

I have always been intrigued by the missing pieces of Don Soper's story. What I know is worth telling here. What I don't know, I leave to the reader's speculation, save for the observation that throughout the Pacific Islands there are migrants who prefer not to discuss their pasts.

What I know of Don's story starts in the fall of 1975. I had recently returned from doctoral studies in Hawaii and was loitering in the Dean's office, absorbing gossip from the secretarial pool, when in walked a well-dressed, distinguished-looking Caucasian man whom I judged to be in his sixties. In an assertive manner he informed us that his name was Donald Soper, he had recently moved to Guam from Southeast Asia, and he wanted to talk to the Dean about a teaching job. Being the only male in the room, he focused on me. "Are you Dean Perlosky?"

"No, sir," I replied. "I'm just a lowly assistant professor having a conversation with these beautiful ladies."

Ellen, the Dean's secretary, jumped in. "Can I help you, sir? Would you like to make an appointment to see Dean Perlosky?

"Well, if I must make an appointment, I will, but if he has time to see me now, that is preferable."

"I'll check his schedule. Give me just a minute," she said as she turned toward the inner office, leaving Soper standing at the counter.

I immediately asked, "What subjects do you teach, sir?" His demeanor was such that I intuitively felt the need to use the honorific "sir."

"Well, I'm pretty versed in marketing. At least that was my major at Harvard Business School. It's been a while, but I suspect that things haven't changed too much."

"Did you teach in Asia before coming to Guam? I asked.

"No, never taught before," he replied

Just then Ellen returned, indicating that the Dean would see him now.

Acting Dean Richard Perlosky was desperately in need of faculty members, since recruiting had gone poorly that year. So when Soper presented documentation of his Master's in Marketing from Harvard, he was hired. Few if any questions were ever asked about his previous job history.

Don turned out to be an excellent marketing instructor, well-liked by the students. Despite his demanding, authoritative, and boisterous exterior, we came to learn that he had a kind heart and a fine sense of humor. Each semester he told his introductory marketing class that he was about to retire, so he wanted to celebrate with a potluck party at the end of the semester. When the party day arrived, students went all out with entertainment and delicious home cooked foods. Don of course was not retiring, but told the same story to every beginning marketing class. He just enjoyed a good party, as did I and other faculty members who looked forward to crashing Don's end-of-the-semester feasts.

Apparently a confirmed bachelor, Don bought a small bungalow in the village of Dededo. There he lived with a young Vietnamese refugee named Luc, whom Don referred to as his house boy. The two of them were constant companions, Don paying for Luc's tuition and all other needs. At the time of the Fuerst's cocktail party, Luc had recently graduated with a B.S. in Management and had apparently moved on, so Don was now alone and downsizing into the Fuerst's *Chalan Ayuyu* apartment.

No one knew much of Don's past. Southeast Asia is a big place, and Don was never forthcoming about his former life, other than loud proclamations about his Texas roots, a heritage that was fully supported by the quality of his homemade chili and beans, but strangely not by his accent. At one point I had the opportunity to visit inside Don's bungalow in Dededo. One entire wall was covered with glass cabinets filled with sterling silver. There were platters, pitchers, goblets, plates and place-settings for at least twelve. When I asked about it, Don just muttered something about "old family silver." A few days later when I saw Luc, I jokingly said, "Hey, Luc, I guess you must spend some time polishing silver." He rolled his eyes as he replied, "Dr. Paul, you have no idea! I just get done and it's time to start over again."

On one hot Guam afternoon, I stopped by Don's office to visit and relax in his air conditioning. Don, in typical form, had grown tired of university inaction and purchased his own air conditioning unit that was larger, more reliable, and more efficient than those provided in other offices. During our conversation I complained about having to park and get out of my car to obtain a gate pass every time I entered Anderson Airforce Base. In those days the Business School was providing evening classes on the base, and I had also begun shooting trap and skeet there on the weekends. The entry pass procedure was becoming tiresome.

"Give me a few days and maybe I can fix that for you," he said as he slapped a clean piece of typing paper on the desk in front of me. "Write down your full name, date of birth, address, phone number, social security number and car license plate number."

While I was doing as he requested, I asked, "How do you have connections on Anderson Air Base?'

"I was in the Marine Corps for a couple of years. Maybe I can get you a permanent gate pass. I can't promise anything, but I'll try."

"Wow! Thanks, Don. If you can pull it off, that would be great," I said as I handed him back the information, which he placed on the corner of his desk along with a plastic card that he extracted from his wallet.

Just then Ellen, the Dean's secretary, stuck her head through the doorway and said, "Professor Soper, there's a DHL package for you at the Dean's office, and they want your signature."

"Can't they just bring it here?" he demanded.

"I'm sorry, Professor," she said meekly. "They're waiting for you at the Dean's office. They won't leave the package without your signature. You need to come right now."

"God damn, incompetent, inefficient idiots," he blustered. "Tell them I'll be right there. I'll be right back, Paul. Don't leave. I want to talk about tomorrow's faculty meeting."

When he had departed, I couldn't resist taking a look at the plastic card he had left on top of my information sheet. Along with alphabetical and numeric designations it read, Donald C. Soper, Colonel United States Marine Corps, Retired.

He soon returned with the DHL package, tossing it onto a table in the corner as he resumed his seat. "Don't see why they couldn't walk fifty yards down here," he muttered.

"Don, you were only in the Marine Corps for a couple of years? I thought enlistments were longer than that. Were you wounded in action?"

"No, after getting out I did some work for the government in Thailand and Malaysia. Now tell me, are you going to support my revised Marketing 300 course tomorrow at faculty meeting?"

His abrupt change of subject signaled that I should stop asking questions, which I did. But within two weeks I received in the mail decals for my pickup's bumpers that read, "Guest of the Base Commander, Anderson Airforce Base, Guam." Whenever I subsequently arrived at the base's front gate, I was waved in by the guards with a formal salute, as if I were a ranking officer or dignitary. Not only that, but I had full access to the Officers' Club and the adjoining liquor store. That base access permit was automatically renewed and mailed to me every year until September 11, 2001.

Don took early retirement after nine years at the university. By then he must have been well into his seventies. He left Guam telling us that he was moving to a small village in the Philippines where he was well-known and liked. He expected that they would take care of him into his old age, since for many years he had been funding the education of children from that village. Sometime in 2002, Don Soper was found beaten almost to death, somewhere in Manila. A chartered plane was sent from Houston to bring him home to Texas, where he died near his family. As a representative of our faculty, I wrote a letter of condolence to his brother and received back a pleasant but innocuous reply, hand-penned on expensive stationary, from his sister, Julia.

No matter how one might speculate as to the missing pieces of Donald Soper's life puzzle, he contributed to the Business School and the University of Guam. Whether or not that contribution balanced other questionable aspects of his life I cannot say. I am certain that some students remember him fondly. Others in the community may not. Luc still lives and works on Guam. I have never asked him about his time with Don Soper.

*   *   *

Having drifted a bit afield with Don's mystery, I now return to that evening cocktail party at the Fuersts' house. After dark, we guests were subjected to a slide show about Bob and Elaine's summer canoe trip. I normally hate to sit through other people's slide shows—my slide shows are of course always interesting. But in this case, I was fascinated by the wild country they had traversed near the Arctic

Circle in Northern Canada. At evening's end, I asked Bob to provide contact information for their guide service, Canoe Artic, in the hopes that I might book a similar trip for Nina and me. As he penned the address, Bob advised, "When you fill out the application form, make sure to lie about your age. They don't like to accept anyone over forty. You'll also need to provide a doctor's certification of ability to undertake rigorous activity. Oh, and if you can, go early in the summer, preferably in June, and you'll avoid the black fly season. There's nothing you can do about the mosquitos. They're a year-round wrecking crew."

As soon as we could get away in May of 1988, Nina and I flew to Chester. There, with Mom's help, we gathered together the clothing and items on the checklist provided by Canoe Arctic. Our guide was to be Alex Hall, the same person who had lead Bob and Elaine the prior summer. We removed the back seat of Mom's 1984 Plymouth Voyager and bought new tires for the almost three-thousand-mile drive from Chester to Fort Smith in Canada's Northwest Territories.

It was late May when we left Chester, the Voyager loaded with camping gear, packed in a way that allowed us to sleep onboard. Our objective was to reach Fort Smith by June 17, the canoe trip's inaugural day. Mom sent us off with a breakfast of bacon, eggs, and pancakes, as well as her hopes for a "safe and fantastic experience." Aside from our welfare, Mom's concern was for the safe return of her beloved Plymouth Voyager. She had managed to purloin a substitute rental vehicle for ten dollars a day, but clearly the Voyager's return, with us in it, was important. We promised to keep her "precious van" safe and well lubricated.

That first day we drove south to Reno, Nevada, and then east on US 80 through Lovelock, Winnemucca, and Elko to Wells, Nevada. There in celebration of our adventure's beginning, we spent the night in the comfort of a motel. The next morning, we started north on US-93, the Great Basin Highway. After passing through miles of high desert, small towns, and crossroads, we reached Jackpot, Nevada, 1,500 residents. Shortly after that, we crossed into Idaho, where the high desert and farmland continued. Then out of nowhere up popped Jerry Lee Young's Idaho Heritage Museum—lots of stuffed animals, Indian baskets, and obsidian arrowheads. Nina liked it. We then moved on to the relative metropolis of Twin Falls on the Snake River, population 21,000.

After camping for two nights at Craters of the Moon National Monument, we continued north on US-93 through green valleys, barren landscapes and mountain passes, eventually reaching Missoula, Montana, and the National

Bison Range. There we saw our first buffalos before proceeding onward through the Flathead Indian Reservation to Flathead Lake and Kalispell, Montana.

From Kalispell we headed up the Flathead River into Glacier National Park, where we spent three wonderful days camping on the shores of Lake McDonald. The park road had only recently been cleared of winter snow. We were one of the first vehicles to travel east over the Going-to-the-Sun Road past St. Mary Lake and onward to Canada.

At the border we crossed through the American side without stopping, but when we reached the Canadian Carway Guard Station, our problems started. I presented an American passport stamped throughout with visas and entries for places like Malaysia, Indonesia, Papua New Guinea, Philippines, Japan, Fiji, Vanuatu, and Palau. Nina had a Trust Territory of the Pacific (Micronesia) Passport with Guam, Palau, and US entry stamps. From the inspector's point of view, we seemed to be an odd couple on an odd excursion with an odd travel history. He may never have seen a Micronesian passport before.

In any case, the Canadian Border Services ordered us to park our car and turn the keys over to them, after which they questioned us separately in a nearby building. I gave them the phone number of Canoe Arctic in Fort Smith. I don't know if they actually called. They seemed most interested in whether we were carrying any firearms or large sums of money, and how we would pay for our expenses while in Canada. Why were we driving such a long distance when we could have flown to Fort Smith? When and how did we intended to leave Canada? Where exactly was our home residence—Yona, Guam? I explained our travel plans and showed them our booklet of traveler's checks and my American Express Card. That seemed to satisfy their concern about finances, but they still held us for about an hour while they rummaged through our car and belongings. Eventually we were sent on our way with an admonition to drive safely and enjoy our visit to Canada.

Then it was on to Calgary, Alberta, where we took the Trans-Canada Highway to Banff and Lake Louise, and then continued north on the Icefields Parkway to the Saskatchewan River Crossing and further on to Edson. From there we took a one-day excursion to Edmonton for the purpose of visiting the West Edmonton Mall, at that time the largest shopping mall in North America, a mind-blowing experience for a Micronesian woman and a guy from Guam. Then it was back to Edson and on north, always one eye on the gas gauge to ensure that the next source of fuel was within reach. As we went along, the landscape became increasingly austere, the settlements fewer and further apart. By the time we reached Peace River, there was only five hours of darkness each night, and we still had five hundred miles of dirt and gravel road ahead of us.

The days became even longer as we reached the town of High Level and passed on through places like Meander River, Steen River, and Indian Cabins. We encountered fewer and fewer vehicles on the road, and most nights we camped alone at government-sponsored camping locations. Upon crossing from Alberta into Canada's Northwest Territories, we followed the Hay River north through Grumbler and Enterprise to Hay River town itself, situated on the shores of Great Slave Lake, a huge body of water that stretched to the northern horizon. There we turned east for the last leg of our trip.

Fort Smith was located on the south shore of the Slave River, population less than 2,500. Being two days early for our scheduled meeting with Canoe Arctic, we spent time exploring the environs and the adjacent Wood Buffalo National Park, Canada's largest, over seventeen thousand square miles of forest, lakes, and animal life. Yes, we did see wood buffalo, close up too. Fort Smith was originally a French and English trading post and a portage site on the Slave River. The local Catholic church and mission school was still pastored by French Jesuit priests.

Early in the morning at a dock on the river, nine people and all our food and gear, enough for sixteen days, were packed into two de Haviland float planes, a Beaver and a Twin Otter. Nina and I were stuffed into the Twin Otter along with all the supplies. Sitting across the aisle from each other, we both had our own window. The aisle between us was filled with cargo, as were the seats around us. *We are lucky*, I thought, *we have two engines. Those other guys have only one, but this plane is no place for a person with claustrophobia*. Nina was horrified, but in typical Palauan form, showed no emotion and said nothing. We finally roared into the sky amid jolting turbulence as the water dropped away below us. Canoes were secured to the pontoon struts under each wing. I wondered how such a heavily loaded plane could fly, but fly it did, northeast for an hour or more. We flew over a vast wilderness world of islands, lakes, and rivers that stretched to the horizon. I had never conceived of such vast amounts of fresh water. Nina just assumed it must be salt water. We were about to enter a world radically different than anything either of us had experienced. Our tropical ocean knowledge was of no use in this place.

Upon landing, all gear, supplies, and humans were disgorged onto a white sand beach. After both planes had departed, we were left standing on the shores of what appeared to be a lake. Alex said this was the Thelon River. In the days that followed, I discovered that the Thelon River is better described as a chain of lakes connected by stretches of river. It runs some five hundred miles west to east across Canada's Arctic, eventually emptying into the Hudson Bay.

Alex had cached two canoes in the scrub forest near our landing site. His was a bit larger than the others, so Nina and I would ride with him. Because we had no previous canoeing or Arctic experience, Alex wanted to keep us close at hand. I no longer remember much about the other six people in our group. They were all male, experienced canoers, and in excellent physical shape. One of them was from Switzerland. He continually scandalized Nina by swimming in the nude each evening in front of our campsites.

Once the four canoes were loaded, we set off along the lake's edge until it narrowed into a channel with discernable flow. We were on our way for the next fourteen days. The Thelon River traverses the boundary between sparse boreal forest and treeless tundra. It was fortuitous that we rode in Alex's canoe, because he was close at hand to explain and call attention to things we might otherwise miss. Also, Alex's canoe led the way. That meant we were the first around bends in the river, giving us an opportunity to spot animals and birds before they took flight. Along the way we saw caribou, muskox, bears, moose, wolves, foxes, hares and ground squirrels, as well as geese of varying kinds, hawks, falcons, loons, terns and gulls. Fragile tundra plants covered much of the landscape. At one point Alex brought us to an abandoned wolf den. We were able to enter on hands and knees to view the tunnel system that housed the pack in winter.

The fishing was excellent. Nina and I both caught lake trout in the four-to-five-pound range. Grayling were abundant in the rapids near some of our portage sites. I caught a pike that measured from the ground to my armpit. All fish were released alive. Alex encouraged fishing but didn't cook them or allow fish to be brought anywhere near our campsites. "Fish smells bring bears. Bears bring big trouble. Wash your fishing gear carefully," he would say.

One night before crawling into our sleeping bags, Nina and I walked to the top of a knoll behind our campsite. At perhaps two hundred feet in elevation, it was the highest point around. There we sat in the golden rays of a sun that hung just above the horizon. A world of sparse trees and tundra spread out before us in all directions, our river meandering through the scene. The absolute quiet was unparalleled. A sense of terrestrial vastness permeated everything. I can remember thinking, *I bet we're the only human beings within hundreds of miles.*

Paul and Nina Callaghan with Alex Hall on the Thelon River, Canada, 1988

We sat there listening and watching for an hour while the sun grudgingly dipped below the edge of the world. It was almost midnight when we walked back to our sleeping bags in the twilight of an Arctic summer night.

Day after day we paddled on. Once we portaged because ice had clogged the river, twice we portaged to avoid rapids. Each night Alex set an intricate set of trip wires to arouse him should beasts meddle with our food stores. Each day led into the next, separated only by twilight. There were few if any spectacular landmarks or events. The lure of the northern Arctic rests in its austere vastness, its desolation, its wildness, its isolation from human impact. Although my time on the Thelon River was a worthwhile adventure, I would not return. It's enough to know that such a place exists and that I was privileged to pass through it. A lifetime would be required to gain the skills necessary for competence in that land, and I have only one life to live. I can only hope that the place will retain its wildness for the benefit of others.

Upon returning to Fort Smith in another overloaded bush plane, Nina and I headed back south the way we had come, this time venturing farther east to visit Yellowstone National Park and the Mormon Tabernacle in Salt Lake City. Two months had passed when we once again drove over the Lake Almanor causeway and back into Chester town. The Plymouth Voyager had logged some six thousand miles without a problem. Lee Iacocca and Chrysler Corporation had built a worthy vehicle. Mom was happy to once again have her children and precious van back home, with stories to tell.

Both Nina and I felt that our adventure to the Arctic Circle and back had been well worthwhile. We had gained a better understanding of northern North America—its history, people, and geography. However, along the way we had encountered no place that we would be willing to exchange for our Pacific Island world and lifestyle.

*   *   *

Nina and I spent the 1989–90 Christmas break traveling with Tom and Monica Tinkham in Thailand. Tom had lived there after his Peace Corps days in the Marshall Islands, so he knew the region well. We spent time in Chiang Mai and Sop Ruak and in the Golden Triangle where the Mekong River meets the Ruak River, and the countries of Laos, Thailand, and Burma (Myanmar) come together. We rode elephants into the mountains, staying for several days with the mountain people. There we chewed betel nut, ate unknown foods, and smoked more than a bit of opium. Nina fit in perfectly with the locals. They dressed her in local garb and took her with them across the border into Burma, a country that at that time was closed to Western foreigners. I remained behind. No amount of disguise could safely hide my size and skin color. It was with some relief that I saw Nina returning across that bridge with a basket on her head. I had envisioned the potential for an international incident that included ransom payments.

A major downside to this Thailand adventure was its timing. For almost a year Nina and I had been trying to adopt a child. We had applied through friends in Fiji and Palau, as well as with the Government of Guam. The associated applications, interviews, and home visits had been extensive. As luck would have it, on the day before our departure for Thailand, two Guam social workers appeared at our door. There was a Chamorro baby girl available for adoption. If we wanted her, we had to decide immediately and take custody within the week. In order to do that, we would be forced to cancel our trip, lose the money paid for tickets and deposits, and most of all, disappoint the Tinkhams, who had invested considerable effort on our behalf. Despite our pleas, the social workers were resolute. We had to do it that week or give up the opportunity. Sadly, we chose to give up the opportunity. The happy consequence of our choice was that the baby girl was adopted by a neighboring family and grew up to be a fine young lady, now a dance instructor in Eugene, Oregon. There are no secrets and no effective privacy rules in Pacific Islands.

Upon our return from Thailand, we were invited, along with the Tinkhams, to Bob and Elaine Fuerst's house for dinner. On this occasion we were the ones showing after dinner slides—a stimulating and artistic presentation of Tinkham and Callaghan adventures in Thailand. No one fell asleep, although Bob might have dozed a bit.

When the lights came back on and we had consumed a vanilla ice-cream-topped chocolate brownie, Elaine initiated a conversation that went something like this.

"We hear that you two are trying to adopt a child. Is that true?"

"Yes. I guess word gets around, doesn't it," I replied.

"Well, it turns out that my grandson, Robert, who's only eighteen, has just managed to get a seventeen-year-old girl pregnant. She doesn't want to get married, and they can't support a child at this point in their lives, so the girl, Yoshimi, is considering an abortion, or possibly putting the child up for adoption. I've encouraged her to choose the adoption alternative, but at this point I don't know what her decision will be. Robert just wants the whole problem to go away, one way or the other. So my question to you is, if Yoshimi decides to have the baby and give it up, are you folks interested in adopting it?"

Before I could reply, Nina jumped in, "Is it a boy or a girl?"

"We don't know yet. They haven't done an ultrasound."

Nina continued, "The father is your grandson. That's the Fernsler family that lives in University Apartments, right? Who's the mother?"

Nina, being a Pacific Islander, made it her first order of business to know the family lineages of every friend, acquaintance, and community leader. Her abilities in that regard astounded me. When it came to local people, she was a walking encyclopedia of lineage and history. Frequently her advice helped me to anticipate reactions and avoid pitfalls in community relationships.

"Yes," said Elaine. "The baby's father is my daughter's son, my grandson. The mother-to-be is a Japanese immigrant who attends JFK High School. Her name is Yoshimi Matsunaga. Both her parents are dead, and she lives with her older brother in Tamuning."

"Your grandson has Saipanese blood, doesn't he?" *How did Nina ever know that?* I marveled?

"Yes, that's right."

"So the baby will be mixed American, Saipanese, and Japanese?"

"Yes, that's right. Is that bad?" asked Elaine.

"Oh no!" said Nina. "That's good, especially if it's a girl."

I looked at Nina. She was clearly okay with the adoption idea.

"Sure, Elaine, we'll be happy to take the baby," I said.

"Whether it's a boy or a girl?"

After noting Nina's affirmative body language, I replied, "Yes, whether it's a boy or a girl."

My attorney and best friend, Bill Williams, prepared documents and handled all the in-person meetings. I paid for Yoshimi's medical expenses using Elaine as an intermediary. Anthony Robert Fernsler and Yoshimi Matsunaga and her brother legally relinquished custody, and Elaine Fuerst was designated the baby's guardian upon birth. I don't believe Nina and I ever officially met Robert and Yoshimi, but we did attend a cocktail party at which they were present. I can't recall if we were introduced. To my knowledge, they were unaware that Nina and I were the prospective parents. However, Guam being Guam, attempts at secrecy were rendered moot by the fact that Robert Fernsler's paternal grandmother worked in the Guam Social Security office. Upon processing the baby's Social Security application, all relevant information became known by all involved. I was fine with that. Nina was less so, but resigned to the realities of Pacific Island life.

Baby Matsunaga was born in Guam Memorial Hospital on February 7, 1990. Two days later, he was delivered to our front door by the Elaine and Bob Fuerst. It took almost a year to finish the legal work and change the birth certificate to read "Oldak Tane Joshua Callaghan." In the Palauan language, *oldak* is a verb meaning to join, bring together, or unify. In Japanese, *tane* is a seed or a source from which something evolves. The name Joshua was included at the request of Yoshimi.

Oldak's arrival changed our lives completely. In order to help care for him, Nina recruited two Palauan relatives, a younger sister, Akilina (Aki), and a cousin, Maria Fidelis Bacilio. Both girls were students at the university, Aki in social work and Fidelis in elementary education. Our family logistics and scheduling were complicated, but Oldak always had one or two people caring for him at all times. Unfortunately, he was a colic baby, crying incessantly. Few things could calm him. Sometimes a ride in the car worked, but the minute the car stopped, he would soon be howling once again. At night I found that I could quiet him by holding his body close to my chest in a pillow or blanket while walking. On some nights the two of us walked continuously for two or three hours, throughout the house, out the front door, up and down the driveway, sometimes along the road in our neighborhood. As long as I kept walking, he slept. When I stopped, it wouldn't be long before he was crying once again. None of us were getting enough sleep, and for a while household relationships became a bit frayed.

Akilina (Aki) Tewid, baby Oldak, Maria Fidelis Bacilio, Yona, Guam, 1990

Sometime around four months of age, Oldak's colic subsided, and we settled down to more regular sleep patterns. Still, the choreography of family life remained hectic. On top of her regular teaching responsibilities, Nina applied for and received a $700,000 nurse training grant from the National Institute of Health, the administration of which consumed much of her time. In addition to teaching four courses, I traveled frequently on fisheries-related matters. At the same time, the two girls had diverse educational requirements. Aki successfully completed college algebra, but her path was not easy, and the battle of wills during our nightly help sessions is still imbedded in my mind, and I suspect in hers as well.

Through all of this, Oldak grew up surrounded by love and caring. Certainly Aki and Fidelis were responsible for much of that. To my happiness, both girls subsequently graduated and have pursued productive lives of community service in Palau, Aki a social worker and Fidelis a teacher.

In May of 1990, Oldak was baptized in St. Anthony Church, Tamuning, the same church in which Nina and I had been married. He had four godparents. I chose Kitty Simonds and Rufo Lujan, a cousin of Joe Paulino and a member of a politically powerful and highly respected Guam family. At that time Rufo was Director of Guam's Department of Agriculture and Chair of the Western Pacific Fishery Management Council. Nina's choices were Fidelis and Peter Ruffatto. Peter was a young Statesider missionary type who lived in the Jesuit-sponsored Saint Ignatius House of Studies. Nina was a frequent contributor and visitor to that house and had many friends among the priests and young men who lived there while attending the university.

A child's christening is a major event in Guam society. Godparents remain enablers and supporters during a person's entire life. In celebration, we held a blow-out christening party at our house overlooking Ylig Bay. As per Guam tradition, Godfather Rufo's responsibility was to provide a pig for the event. Early in the morning on the appointed day, I drove to his house in Talofofo Village to transport the pig's carcass for roasting at the local bakery. Guam being Guam, the bakery specialized in pig cooking between batches of bread and pastry. When I arrived at Rufo's house, he was loading a 22-caliber rifle.

"Did you come for the pig?" he asked.

"Yes," I said. "Is it ready?"

"It will be. Come with me."

We walked behind the house to a pen that contained seven or eight pigs.

"Which one do you want?" he asked.

"Oh Rufo, I've no idea," I said. "I don't know anything about pigs. Whichever one you think will be best for the party."

Rufo called one medium-sized pig over to the fence. For some reason I still remember the name. "Bobo, come, come eat, Bobo." Expecting some treats, Bobo came dutifully to the fence; instead of a treat, he got a twenty-two bullet through the top of his head, dropping him dead on the spot.

"That one was Rufo Junior's favorite," said Rufo. "I'll have him clean it and scrape the hair off for roasting. If you come back around noon, it will be ready to take to the bakery. When does the party start?"

"We'll eat around seven, but you can come any time after five. Are you going to make Rufo Junior clean and butcher his favorite pig? Isn't that a little tough on the kid?" I asked.

"It's good for him to learn that the world doesn't present easy options; besides, he'll always remember his contribution to your son's christening," said Rufo. "Tell the bakery to deliver the pig at six-thirty. That way it'll still be warm when you serve." Rufo was never a person of tact, empathy, or compromise. I haven't seen him in years. He and Kitty Simonds eventually had a falling out over some council-related legal, audit, and personnel matters. They haven't spoken in years, and I was forced to choose between them. Given Rufo's recalcitrance and unpredictability, my choice wasn't difficult.

As an aside, I should mention that Rufo's brother, David J. Lujan, was the afore mentioned Larry Hillbroom Junior's attorney in his fight to gain his multimillion-dollar settlement as an heir to the Larry Hillbroom Estate. David Lujan subsequently became the court appointed trustee of Larry Junior's money. David and his family attended Oldak's christening as well.

The party lasted well into the midnight hours. About a hundred people signed the guest book and left a gift or monetary contribution for Oldak; even though he faded into sleep before dark and slept the night away, the guests enjoyed much good food and comradery. In the end, only the signatures of Rufo and Fidelis appear on the official baptismal certificate. There was space for only two signatures, and somehow church authorities felt that Rufo and Fidelis were the most appropriate. I suspect they were deemed so because Rufo came from an influential Chamorro family, and Fidelis had previously been a novice nun. Kitty and Peter had been practicing Catholics their entire lives. Kitty's brother was a priest, yet they weren't selected. I suspect that the Guam Archdiocese viewed Kitty as an unknown outsider from Hawaii and Peter as a Statesider with Jesuit affiliations, perhaps a bit too young and liberal for their conservative tastes. In any case, Peter left Guam that year, and I have lost contact with him; however, based on an internet search, it appears that he is a practicing attorney in the State of Washington.

When Oldak was about one year old, I happened to be sitting in our living room with my camera in hand. He had pulled himself to his feet and was supporting himself by holding on to the coffee table. I thought, *That's a nice picture*, and snapped one. Then without lowering the camera, I said, "Hey, Oldak, look at me," hoping he would face the camera for a second shot. But instead he came toddling toward me. I clicked the shutter and captured his first steps on film. After that he was off to the races, literally. He has never since done anything slowly.

*   *   *

Every summer without fail, we visited Chester for at least eight weeks, thinking it was important that Oldak know about the mountains, trout fishing, hiking, backpacking, and his Grandma Emma. Christmas and Easter holidays were usually spent in Palau, so that Oldak might learn about island living and get to know his Grandma Kasko and Grandpa Tewid, as well as his various aunts, uncles, and cousins.

In 1992 the three of us went to Bali for a couple of weeks along with Jim and Helen Cramer and their daughter, Rebecca. In 1995, Nina and I both took sabbatical leaves and our family moved to Palau for a year. I worked as an economic advisor in the office of Palau's President, Kuniwo Nakamura. Nina was contracted to design a nursing program for the Palau Community College. We lived in *Bekul a Tiul*, near the rest of Nina's family. Oldak experienced the ways of that extended family, attended Emmaus kindergarten, and cavorted in the jungle and mangrove swamps with his cousins, learning the Palauan language as he went along.

Some aspects of my work at the President's office are worth noting. About twenty-five people worked there in one capacity or another on a variety of issues. In order to enhance the flow of air conditioning, the spaces between desks were unencumbered. The few cubicles that did exist were open at the floor or ceiling. This configuration also enhanced the universal flow of information. Those who understood the Palauan language were "in the loop," privy to the phone calls and oral communication of others in the room. For this reason, staff meetings were seldom necessary, since everyone who should be "in the know" had already overheard or been told what was going on. Those who didn't understand Palauan were left in the dark, often finding out things at the last minute or not at all.

It was an exciting time in many ways. Just a year prior, Palau had received its "independence" from American trusteeship. It was now a fledgling nation with its own democratic constitution, a full-fledged membership in the United Nations, and all the associated domestic and international growing pains. There was much to do. The opportunity existed to pick and choose from laws, policies, and governmental structures that had already been tested elsewhere in the world. Well-intentioned advisors, mostly American and mostly lawyers, had come to

Palau to assist. However, it was clear to me that Palauans were going to undertake the doing and the learning in their own way at their own pace. Well-meaning foreigners, myself included, were used by the Palauans as pawns to defend against external pressures for change. I was treated a bit differently than most advisors because I had Palauan family ties and respected clan connections, as well as a past record of contribution. Also, I understood enough Palauan language to comprehend the ebb and flow of matters within the President's office.

My primary job was as liaison between the President's office and an Australian consulting firm that was drawing up the Economic Master Plan for Palau. The Palauans saw no need for such a Plan, but the US government required its creation as a prerequisite for aid funding. I became the middleman who read the drafts, explained them to the President's staff, and then delivered the unpleasant messages and criticisms back to the consulting firm. My immediate boss was a well-educated Palauan named Koichi Wong. He was a civil engineer by training and had been responsible for drawing up a land use plan. He didn't understand nor appreciate economic ideas, and felt that his land use plan was the only planning needed. I was never able to convince him otherwise. In the end I thought the Economic Master Plan contained much good advice for improving the Palauan economy. But like other plans before it, none of the recommendations were implemented. I suspect that was so because no Palauans were capable of implementing many of the recommendations, and Palauans were not about to bring in more foreigners to do the work.

For better or worse, much of my personal advice was also ignored. I pushed strongly for a value added tax (VAT) because of its equity and data generating benefits. Instead, an import tax was chosen because it was easy to collect, and VATs were not employed anywhere in America. I argued passionately against a Palauan only minimum wage because it would incentivize employers to hire less costly foreign workers rather than Palauans. Despite my concerns, a minimum wage for Palauans was adopted because it appeared politically correct and didn't negatively impact the existing use of foreign labor by established Palauan entrepreneurs. My cost-benefit analysis of electronic traffic lights at Koror's intersections showed that human traffic controllers would be more efficient and cost effective. Electronic traffic lights were installed anyway because they fostered an image of robust economies such as Guam and Hawaii. I tried to convince the Postal Authorities to encourage the patronage of stamp collectors because the full value of their purchases flowed directly into the treasury. I warned that Palau was issuing too many commemorative stamps. If this continued, philatelists would be discouraged from collecting Palauan stamps, and revenues would fall. No action was taken to limit new issues, and today Palau is known by philatelists as a "stamp mill" not worth serious collecting attention.

That year in Palau was a wonderful family experience for the three of us, that is if you discount our month-long bout with Dengue fever. Often we borrowed Grandpa Tewid's boat and spent weekends and holidays on the white sand beaches of secluded islands, caught fish, crabs, and lobsters, ate shellfish, cooked over open fires, slept under the stars. The air was salty and rich, having been cleansed over thousands of miles of ocean and oxygenated by the islands' dense tropical forests. The moonless nights were black and filled with stars, their view undisturbed by ambient light from human habitation. Oldak and I learned much from Nina about hunting and gathering and living off the bounty of a tropical land and sea. We watched day after day as the moon grew from a sliver to giant white ball, and then dwindled back again to a sliver. We saw firsthand how the moon and tides were related and how that relationship allowed Nina to predict the doings of creatures on land and in the sea. We saw the right time of year for harvesting wild nuts and fruits and the best ways to catch fish and crabs. In order to perfect such knowledge and skill, we would have to live the rest of our lives in Palau, something that was not to be our destiny. It is satisfying for me to know that such rich knowledge of nature exists among people who might otherwise, by Western standards, be considered ignorant.

*   *   *

I liked teaching and enjoyed interacting with students, certain that a knowledge of economic theory could help them better understand some of society's pressing issues. My enthusiasm likely contributed to my twice receiving excellence in teaching awards during the 1980s and 90s. However, several events during those years caused me to become disappointed with the university administration and disillusioned as to the institution's long-term academic integrity and potential growth.

Carol J. Cozan had been recruited to Guam as a high school teacher in the 1970s. Subsequently, she completed an M.B.A. and joined the Business School faculty as an instructor. In short order, Carol proved herself to be a fine teacher, and our Dean, Allen Leader, encouraged her to pursue doctoral studies. So in the 1980s, Carol went off to the University of Arkansas and by 1988 had completed a Ph.D. in Management. After returning to Guam, she filled the Deanship position in an acting capacity for a considerable period, during which time the Board of Regents delayed her permanent conformation.

Carol was a collaborative, consensus building administrator with high academic standards. As far as I was concerned, she was a pleasure to work under. Most faculty felt similarly, yet some on the Board of Regents believed that Business School deans should be masculine, and in Guam's case, Chamorro. As a result, Carol was never confirmed as Dean, and she never received the salary or recognition she deserved. Eventually in 1992, she chose early retirement rather than continuing to endure the not-so-subtle discrimination. Such treatment reflected habitual patterns of racial and gender bias throughout Guam's government. Carol's situation remained a source of continual annoyance to me, as I valued her friendship and respected her abilities.

Another irritant was the American Federation of Teachers (AFT). I felt that union policies protected incompetent teachers and degraded the effectiveness of traditional peer pressure, a foundation of academic excellence. Our employment contracts, negotiated by the union, did much to ensure union survival and influence, but little to improve the quality of student education or university excellence. The union's survival was largely dependent on laws passed by the Chamorro-dominated legislature; therefore, the union wasn't willing to take on the nepotism and racial, gender, political biases that affected university operations. In my mind the union was just another local institution that served to promote mediocrity and the status quo. I resisted joining and had little respect for its leadership.

In 1997, Guam's US Congressional delegate, Robert Underwood, and the university president, John C. Salas, had approved my attendance at a week-long United Nations Food and Agriculture Organization (F.A.O.) fisheries meeting in Santiago, Chile. There I represented Guam on the United States delegation. Upon my return, I found that the Governor had replaced John Salas for political reasons. The new university president was Jose (Joe) Taienao Nededog, a Chamorro and a retired Navy Lieutenant Commander who seemed not to have an academic or intellectual bone in his body. I knew of his background, since he'd been teaching management classes in the Business School, and I was not impressed. He had received his Doctorate degree from U.S. International University, now known as Alliant International University, certainly not a top-tier institution. As I expected, he attempted to oversee the university in an autocratic manner, as if he were running a military base. Needless to say, that style of management did not please many faculty members, me included.

In any case, I thought it proper to deliver to him the report of my trip to Chile, just as I would have done had John Salas remained president. At his secretary's invitation, I entered Nededog's office. He didn't look up from his desk as he said, "What do you want?"

"I wanted to meet you and congratulate you on your presidency and provide you a copy of the report of my recent attendance at the F.A.O. meeting in Santiago, Chile. Dr. Underwood and Dr. Salas asked me to attend, representing Guam. I returned this last weekend and thought you might be interested in what transpired."

"Leave the report with my secretary on your way out," was his reply.

I'm not sure Joe Nededog even knew who I was, nor did he apparently care to find out or engage in further conversation. I departed quietly, determined to show this person as little respect as possible during his tenure as president. From that point on, in public and to his face, I never referred to him as anything but Joe. I was told that he wanted to be addressed as Doctor or Mr. President, so I reveled in never doing so.

Jane Jennison Williams, the wife of my compadre, Bill Williams, had completed all course work leading to a Ph.D. in Anthropology at the University of Hawaii. Subsequently, she was hired by the University of Guam to develop, promote, and edit a social science journal. During a four-year period, Jane worked to create *ISLA Journal of Micronesian Studies* (the word *isla* in Chamorro means island). By the fourth year of its biannual publication, the journal had received international recognition as a quality, peer reviewed academic source for Pacific Island social science and historic research. Subscriptions and readership were growing, and because of that, the academic prestige of the University of Guam was being enhanced.

Those facts did not impress Joe Nededog or his Academic Vice President, Judy Guthertz. They refused to renew Jane's contract and placed a totally inexperienced Filipino women in charge of *ISLA*. I, along with Dr. Craig Severance from the University of Hawaii at Hilo and Dr. Don Rubinstein of the Micronesian Area Research Center, visited Judy Guthertz in her office to plead for Jane's job and the journal's continuation. Judy held a doctorate from the University of the Philippines in Public Administration. She had always demonstrated little respect for academic rigor and could be counted on to bend integrity for the sake of political expediency. Later she served several terms in the Guam Legislature, until voters finally saw reality. As we sat in Judy's office, an office filled with pictures and models of Volkswagen cars—she loved them and owned several—I knew there was no hope of salvaging *ISLA*. Joe had determined that the standards for publication were too high, and Indigenous faculty were not having their submissions accepted, so his solution was to get rid of the editor and, if necessary, the publication. Judy was Joe's lackey. We were not going to change her mind.

In a conversation a few months later, I asked Judy why they had fired Jane. Her response was, "Well, you know, Paul, we need to employ more locals." In subsequent correspondence with the university's accreditation body, Joe Nededog's administration was characterized as "an atmosphere of fear and intimidation." I certainly observed that to be the case, although, to my knowledge, I was never directly targeted.

By the end of 1997, I had come to believe that the term "insular university" was an oxymoron. It was clear to me that Chamorro political nepotism and racial and gender bias could never be eliminated as driving forces in University of Guam affairs. Unless fresh blood was brought in from mainland sources, the university was destined to remain a backwater substandard institution, university in name but insular and inwardly focused in viewpoint. I wanted to be challenged by my peers, not dragged down into intellectual mediocrity. As I became frustrated with my surroundings, my interests changed. I slacked off on the diligence of my classroom preparations. Academic politics began to grate on my psyche. I knew it was time to move on. For most faculty in my position, moving on meant transferring into an administrative position. Administration held little interest for me, especially under the current university leadership.

A review of my account at the Government of Guam Retirement Fund revealed that I could retire with thirty years of service. My retirement benefits would be just a few hundred dollars less than what I currently earned. Given that reality and my discontent with the institution's leadership, the choice became obvious. I retired in 1997 at the age of fifty-five. In 1998 I was given the honorary title of Professor Emeritus in Economics, but I never taught again.

Withdrawing entirely from university activities, I focused on family matters and fishing in my twenty-two-foot Yamaha boat named *Bedaoch* (*Noddy Tern* in Palauan). All my professional energy was directed toward fisheries management issues in conjunction with the Western Pacific Fishery Management Council and the US Departments of Commerce and State. For the next twenty years, these undertakings provided the main challenges and impetus in my life.

*   *   *

A year prior to my university retirement, something happened that almost put a premature end to this story. Oldak came home from day care with a high fever. It turned out to be chickenpox. Aki and Fidelis were no longer living with us, so Nina and I took turns caring for him. It was not an easy case. At one point he had convulsions and we had to soak him in a cold-water bath to lower his temperature. About the time he started to recover, I came down with severe abdominal pain. Knowing that I had never previously had chickenpox, I suspected that I had contracted it, but the symptoms weren't normal for chickenpox. Around noon, Nina drove me to the Seventh Day Adventist Clinic.

A doctor named Joseph N. Nozaki came to the car because chickenpox cases were not admitted into the clinic's waiting room. Despite my explanation that my son had just recovered from chickenpox, and my pointing out a lesion in my hair, the doctor diagnosed food poisoning and sent me home with pain pills. By ten o'clock that night, I was doubled over on the floor in pain. The pills were of no use. So off we went to the emergency room.

Guam Memorial Hospital was jokingly known as the place to go if you wanted to die. I was not happy about being there. In the 1980s I had an inguinal hernia repair performed at GMH. The operation took longer than expected, and I had difficulty regaining consciousness because of anesthesia irregularities. Unfortunately, GMH was our only option, unless one bought a plane ticket to Honolulu, which was an $1,800, seven-hour flight.

Doctor Olivia Cruz was on duty. She was a tyrant, feared by all nurses and hospital staff. However, when it came to that hospital, Nina knew it well and was afraid of no one. I can still hear Dr. Cruz yelling, "Put him in the storage room. No one with contagious chickenpox is coming into my emergency ward. Whose patient is he anyway? So get Nozaki over here."

With Nina's help, I curled up on the top of a dusty desk in the furniture storage room. She got me some zorrie from the car to use as a pillow. Dr. Nozaki didn't arrive until two in the morning. When he came into the storage room, I was shaking with fever, and the stomach pain was almost unbearable. During our wait, Nina had searched through the hospital and found an empty isolation room in the children's ward. Dr. Nozaki said I should immediately be transferred into that room, but first we had to pray. Though I could only sit bent over on the desk, we three held hands while he prayed for God's favorable intervention. Needless to say, I was not reassured and silently added a plea that I might find a competent physician to help me.

By sunrise I was ensconced in an isolation room of the children's ward. The controls for oxygen flow were located near the head of my bed. Once I discovered that more oxygen diminished my pain, I turned up the dial whenever the nurse left the room. The next nurse to arrive would readjust the setting. Upon her departure, I turned it up again. This game went on for a while until they discovered my ploy and moved the controls out of reach.

Sometime in the morning I was put in a wheelchair and shuttled through two floors and down the elevators to an ultrasound lab in the basement. *Oh well*, I thought, *so much for Dr. Cruz's attempts to keep chickenpox germs out of her emergency room.* I had just spread them throughout the hospital.

In the ultrasound lab, the technician pushed the device hard into my stomach area. I told him that if he did that again, I would certainly pass out from pain. He did it again, and I remember nothing much after that. They say I was in intensive care for five days with chickenpox throughout my inner organs. Nina let the family know that I was very sick and might not recover. Luckily for me, my cousin's wife, Helen Cramer, was doing work for the Center for Disease Control (CDC). She contacted doctors there, and they recommended an antiviral medication called Acyclovir. Nina hand-carried that information to the internist who had taken over from Nozaki. Surprisingly, there was Acyclovir available on Guam. Once it was administered, I began the long road back from the edge of nothingness.

As my internal organs improved, the pox made a last stand on the outside of my body. When I looked in the mirror, I wondered if my pus-scabbed face could ever recover. One night around midnight, Dr. Nozaki arrived in my hospital room and asked if I wanted to pray with him to thank God for my recovery. My response was not welcoming. We did not pray together. Later I quietly thanked God for my competent internist, my wife and child, my resourceful and caring cousin-in-law, Helen Cramer, and my intensive care nurse, Ruth Gurusami, a longtime friend who remains in Guam to this day, helping those who cannot help themselves.

*   *   *

In 1999 our family acquired a foster son. Nina's older brother, Seberiano (Seb) Tewid, and his wife, Lalo, both passed away within months of each other, leaving behind an eleven-year-old son named Lemal. According to Palauan custom, Nina and I were responsible for the support and care of Lemal upon the death of his parents. Nina thought of Lemal's arrival into our family as an obligation, one that must be carried out to the best of her ability, lest the Palauan community think badly of her. Lemal's success or failure in life would reflect directly on Nina's standing. I, on the other hand, thought of Lemal's arrival as a welcome opportunity to help someone in need. I wanted to be a substitute for the father he had lost, and to provide elevating opportunities and experiences that would add to the richness of Lemal's life. I did so out of love and concern for Lemal's wellbeing, not any sense of social obligation. I was often the "good-cop" for both Lemal and Oldak. Nina was frequently the "bad cop."

Lemal arrived at the Guam airport in late May, never having previously flown in an airplane or traveled outside Palau. Once in Guam, he was thrust into a world of bright lights, traffic noise, a knife-fork-and-spoon, sheets on a bed, English language, and rules of a time-regimented society. As if that wasn't difficult enough, within three days of his arrival, he and I flew to San Francisco and traveled to Chester in a rental car. Nina and Oldak were to follow in a week or two when Oldak's school recessed for the summer.

On the way to Chester, I drove through San Francisco and across the Golden Gate Bridge to Muir Woods, in the hopes that Lemal would be excited about the city, the bridge, and the towering redwood trees. Unfortunately, his overloaded sensory system allowed little more than a cursory understanding and appreciation. For much of the trip, he looked straight ahead, showing no emotion. Whenever we left the car, he stayed close beside me with a firm grip on my hand or my clothing. Upon arriving in Chester, he slept for twelve hours before Mom coaxed him out of bed with the smell of bacon and eggs over rice. For the next days, he was continually forced to assimilate newness. He had never before encountered cold or large daily temperature fluctuations, never seen a pine tree or a horse or a cow or a deer or any forest animals, never experienced long days and short nights, never ate potatoes, rhubarb, asparagus, artichokes or brussels sprouts.

Those first days in Chester with Grandma Emma cemented their relationship for the rest of Emma's life. Her empathy and concern for Lemal were apparent, and as per Palauan custom, he treated her with the utmost respect and care, watching attentively to see what he might do for her. On Mom's deathbed, she asked me to "always watch out for Lemal." I have tried to do so.

Despite Oldak having to learn that he was no longer the sole center of family attention, the two boys got along quite well. They cavorted together in the forest that summer, fishing, swimming, building forts, and getting gloriously dirty in the clean volcanic dust. Oldak taught Lemal much about life in America, and Lemal's age advantage provided the size and maturity to control Oldak's impulsive behavior. They made a good team, with Oldak leading the way, Lemal providing temperance and restraint. Given my proclivity to forget birthdays, anniversaries and the like, I was delighted that both boys had the same birthday, April 7.

Nina (Kilad), Lemal, Paul, and Oldak Callaghan, Yona, Guam, 1999

In the fall of 1999 when school commenced, Lemal attended the third grade at a small private Christian missionary school where we believed he could receive personal attention. That did not work out as well as we had hoped, so in the fall of 2000, both boys entered the fifth grade, Lemal at Harvest Christian Academy, and Oldak at St. John's School, the top two private schools on Guam. Oldak remained at St. John's through high school. After the eighth grade, Lemal transferred to Father Duenas Memorial High School, the alma mater of many young men from prestigious Chamorro families. Both boys graduated from those institutions in 2008.

Throughout their teenage years, the two boys and I spent a lot of time on the ocean in my twin engine, twenty-one-foot Force Marine boat named *Kerkirs* (*Black-Naped Tern* in Palauan). Both boys became certified open-ocean scuba divers and competent seamen with a healthy respect for the capricious ocean.

They learned much about trolling, bottom fishing, and handlining. They knew how to follow the birds to the mahimahi and tuna, how to set and retrieve an anchor from a hundred fathoms, how to use a sea anchor to maintain position, and how to set a nightlight for handline fishing. We sometimes traveled to distant seamounts where Guam was no longer visible on the horizon. They could find home with a GPS and a compass in the dark of night. Safety at sea was constantly on my mind. Sometimes without warning I threw a float overboard and yelled "man overboard." To the exclusion of everything else that might be happening around him, Lemal knew that his responsibility was to never take his eyes off that float while pointing in its direction with an outstretched arm. It was Oldak's job to maneuver the boat in the direction that Lemal was pointing until they had recovered the float. The gunwales of my boat were only knee high, and any of us could have fallen overboard at any time while handling large fish in rough seas.

Returning with anything less than three hundred pounds of fish was considered a so-so day. Of course, there were days of zero catch, but they were few and easily forgotten. The thousand-pound days are what stick in the memory of a fisherman and fuel his continued optimism. When the boys landed their first big blue marlin, in the eight-hundred-pound class, they took turns cranking the 14-0 reel. After more than an hour's hard work, we boarded that fish over the transom. In the process they learned to respect the power of such a large creature, especially when it's alongside the boat. I didn't carry a flying gaff, so securing a noose around the tail was critical. Gloved hands and unbent arms control the bill. A baseball bat to the head ends the struggle. Upon our return home, Palauan relatives arrived to clean and distribute the catch. Once again, our community respect as fishers was enhanced and reciprocal future assistance ensured. I seldom sold my catch but was always well compensated in-kind by those who received it.

* * *

Here it is appropriate to remember my friend and sometimes fishing companion, Frank (Frankie) Cushing, a person who was especially admired by Oldak and Lemal. Frank was born in 1944 in Bremerton, Washington. His family operated and participated in their own carnival/circus company. Everyone in the family trained for various acts. Frankie's mother, Marjorie Bailey "The Sky Lady" Cushing, performed the world's highest aerial act at the time, some 171 feet up on a sway pole. In 1950 their company was performing in the Philippines when they received permission from the US Army to entertain troops in Japan,

Okinawa, and Korea. They planned to transit to Japan via Guam, since they had been asked to put on a show there in conjunction with the Pacific Islands Fair.

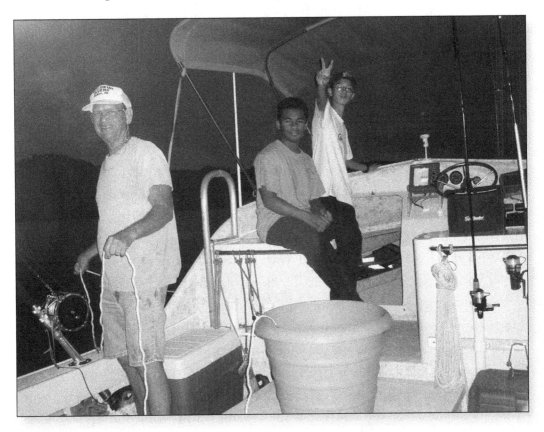

Frank Cushing, Lemal, and Oldak night fishing, Guam, 2013

The family arrived on Guam with minimal equipment, since most of it was being shipped through Hong Kong. Once in Guam, they set up a small show with a high dive tower and a couple of rides, but the operation was ruined by a typhoon, and on top of that, the Korean War broke out. Military and commercial shipping became inaccessible. They were marooned on Guam, but as they had always done, the Cushings made the best of it. They settled in and prospered. Frank and his brother and two sisters went to school on Guam. Everyone in the family worked to make ends meet.

Frank is a hands-on, practical, somewhat artistic person who loves nature—the forest and the sea and everything in them. He once told me that during high school classes, he daydreamed of fishing while looking out the window at the reefs of Tumon Bay, where he knew every crevice and cave. After high school, Frank tried college in California but decided that theoretical learning was not for him. Returning to Guam, he started a tropical fish collection and export business. In order to assist with that effort, his father built a twin outboard powered catamaran, made from fifty-gallon fuel drums. They sometimes used this platform for atulai fishing at night.

One night while fishing, Frank and his father were both asleep when the anchor gave way. They awoke to find that Guam was no longer visible on the horizon. For the next thirty-seven days they floated at sea, eventually ending up in the Babuyan Islands of the northern Philippines. There they waited for several weeks before being repatriated to Guam. Their survival was difficult, but not entirely surprising. It is well known that floating objects in the ocean attract fish. They had fishing and snorkel gear on board, so food wasn't a problem. Drinking water was the issue. Probably just one rainstorm made the difference between their survival and death.

With the onset of the Vietnam War, Frank was sure to be drafted, as were many young men in Guam. The Territory of Guam had the highest casualty rate of any state or territory in the US. So Frank did a very Cushing-like thing. He bought a one-way plane ticket to Saigon and got a job on a river boat delivering military supplies in the MeKong delta. The work was dangerous, but he knew boats and quickly learned the numerous intricate waterways. The pay was excellent, so he sent much of it home to the family. Frank thought that such work in the heart of the conflict would exempt him from military service. It did not. He was drafted, assigned to the 101st Airborne Division, and sent back to Vietnam to do the same thing he had previously been paid handsomely to do. Whatever happened during those years in Vietnam left Frank with PTSD symptoms. Upon returning to Guam, his alcohol consumption high, he went through two marriages and to this day has trouble sleeping at night.

For a while Frank experimented with longlining for tuna around Guam. He was the first to do so since Japanese efforts prior to WWII. He caught tuna but not in economically viable numbers. When I first became well acquainted with Frank, he was a marine technician at the University of Guam Marine Laboratory. There he took scientists out to sea in small boats to collect organisms and data for their various projects. Frank often knew more than the scientists about how to efficiently find and collect the desired animals, plankton or algae. What he didn't know he quickly absorbed from his learned passengers. That knowledge Frank was always willing to share with friends. He taught Oldak and Lemal how to build a "look-box"—a wooden box, the bottom of which is a pane of plate glass. At night when a light is hung at depth under the boat and the "look-box" placed in the water, it provides a crystal-clear, TV-screen-like view of the undersea world. Frank pointed out to the boys the various small crustaceans, eggs, and larval stages of animals as they drifted or swam by in the light. The boys were always in awe of Frank's knowledge, his simple explanations, and willingness to share what he knew. When I spoke, the boys were often slow to comprehend and act. If Frank spoke, Oldak and Lemal paid attention and moved quickly.

Frank's second marriage to a Palauan girl named Louise ended in disappointment when she left him for another guy. Several months after Louise had departed, I pulled into the yard in front of Frank's house. He had built that three-bedroom, two-bath, multi-story house himself. The parking area had flower beds decorated artistically with bleached white whale bones. I knew Frank was downhearted because of Louise's departure, so I hoped to cheer him up a bit and invite him to dinner at our house.

His workshop was in the back under the building, so I headed that way. Sure enough, there he was welding inside an aluminum boat that he was refurbishing.

When the sparks stopped showering, I said, "What's up, Frankie?"

"Callaghan! Grab the end of that iron bar and lift so I can finish this weld. Don't worry, I won't electrocute you, but close your eyes and enjoy the smoke. It's bad for what ails you, but it keeps the mosquitoes away."

On the hull he had painted in black glossy letters the name *Therapy*.

When the last sparks settled, I asked, "Is this boat your therapy?"

"Sure is. I've been working on her for two weeks now. It's good for the head. But what I really need is a rice cooker. What brings you around?"

"I just wanted to see how you were doing, and ask if you'd come to dinner tonight at our place. Nina's frying up some of those *atulai* we caught the other night. She said there'll be taro, papaya salad, pie and ice cream for dessert.

"Sure. What time?"

"About six or earlier if you want to sit on the porch and sip a few."

"You sip. I'm trying to reduce my consumption."

"No fun sipping alone. I'll see you around six then. By the way, I was just at K-Mart this morning, and they have a sale on kitchen appliances, including some fancy looking, totally automatic, Japanese rice cookers."

He gave me an impish smile and said, "At the moment I'm interested in the Philippine version. I'm going there next week to check out some possibilities. Hobson's wife has set me up with a lady. We'll see how it goes."

Feeling a bit stupid, it dawned on me that Frank was interested in a new female partner, not a kitchen appliance. He did subsequently go to the Philippines and find a wonderful, divorced lady named Ailene, and her two young boys. As Frank puts it, "I adopted two sons—and their mother." Oldak did some first-rate photography at their wedding in Guam.

Since marrying Ailene, Frank has been reinvigorated and become a superb father to those two boys. The four of them visited me in Chester during the summer of 2013. It has now been nine years since I've seen Frank and his family. I do miss them. Every so often when some task is completed but still not quite to my liking, I think of Frank's frequently repeated maxim: "Leave well enough alone."

* * *

The boys grew up in a multicultural, multifaceted environment. They learned from personal experience that race, color, creed, financial standing, and political persuasion provide irrelevant clues as to human character and worth. Their elementary and high school classmates were a diverse group of Asian and Pacific Islanders from Christian, Buddhist, Muslim, Hindu and Sikh families. Daily experiences taught Oldak and Lemal that people have different ways of thinking, different values, different expectations, and those variations matter a lot when it comes to communication, cooperation, and mutual understanding. Language skills are important, but empathy and kindness are crucial in multicultural group dynamics. Listening and astute observation are greatly more important than talking.

By the time Lemal and Oldak graduated from high school, they had experienced more cultural and geographic diversity than most people do in their entire lifetimes. They had been to Japan, Indonesia, and Australia as well as several Pacific Islands, including Hawaii, and of course to various parts of the United States. They had learned to know and appreciate a tropical sea with its surrounding island beaches and jungle forests. They had experienced magnificent night skies at twelve thousand feet while backpacking in the high Sierra. They had become Feather River trout fishermen, and mastered the shotgun skills required for trap, skeet, and sporting clay competitions. Most pleasing to me was that both boys could discern and appreciate the best qualities in all people whom they met. They treated everyone with empathy and respect, never letting me down when it came to interpersonal behavior. Whether it was with the most erudite or the most common, the wealthiest or the most destitute, conservative or liberal, male or female, old or young, I was most proud of their behavior toward others, and very proud to be their father.

Together Nina and I provided them with a variety of experiences so they might appreciate the world's diversity and understand that there is both good and bad in every human being, yet it is most propitious to focus on the good. I attempted to teach them by example in the hope that they might learn to do the same with others. Their mother provided an authoritarian approach, to which I added complementary and reasoned participation. With only a few exceptions, that combination seemed to work well.

I must admit that the boys' lack of interest and diligence in completing college studies has been disheartening for me. I'm afraid that the absence of a college degree will put them at a disadvantage in fields of endeavor for which they otherwise would be well qualified. In spite of that, I remain hopeful for their future and extremely proud of their integrity and sense of moral justice. Parenting is difficult. Perhaps Nina and I didn't always make the best decisions, but we tried, each in our own way, and from my point of view the results have been rewarding.

Those years when Lemal and Oldak grew up included some of the happiest years of my life. I was a child of older parents and then subsequently, in my fifties and sixties, became an older parent myself. The timing worked out well. I was semi-retired and financially secure, with a richness of experience and time to share with my children. In many Pacific Island societies, it's common for children to be raised by their grandparents. I can attest to the wisdom and long-term value of such customs.

Chapter 15

Divorce

It's hard to say when it was that things started to go awry. I suspect that work-related stress was an important factor. Nina had long been opposed to the Nursing School's attempt to offer a four-year Bachelor of Science degree. Most faculty were American-educated Caucasians who envisioned a nursing curriculum similar to that which they had experienced in Stateside institutions. Nina had been born and raised in an island environment that had few medical and public health resources. She knew that in such places, nurses are often the only medical providers and are called upon to deliver services far beyond those required of nurses working in a US mainland setting. Micronesian island nurses frequently make diagnosis, suture wounds, deliver babies, set and cast broken limbs, even prescribe and distribute medications. She felt that the proposed four-year Bachelor of Nursing program would produce graduates with too much theoretical learning and insufficient practical experience. These graduates would be unprepared to cope with outer island resource-poor conditions and would be attracted to leave the region for higher paying, less difficult jobs in the US and elsewhere.

Nina felt that given the University of Guam's geographic location, it should support a nursing curriculum that graduated exceptionally well-trained Licensed Practical Nurses (LPNs) and Registered Nurses (RNs) with the practical skills necessary to function effectively within the meager resources available in most Micronesian islands. Nina's opposition, coming as it did from the only Indigenous, well credentialed islander on the faculty, had not been received well by those who favored a US-style nursing curriculum.

Associate Professor Dominina (Kilad) Tewid Callaghan, MSN, MPH, Guam, 1995

I saw the logic in Nina's viewpoint, so I helped her to secure a $700,000 National Institute of Health grant for the purpose of assisting outer-island nursing students. As recipient and principal investigator of such a sizable grant, other faculty were forced to give serious consideration to Nina's views. They were not altogether pleased.

In light of this friction among faculty at the Nursing School, I wasn't surprised when in the mid 1990s, one of Nina's fellow faculty members took me aside, saying that she wished to share some concerns about Nina's state of mind. I politely listened, the gist being that Nina might be paranoid and delusional about nonexistent situations and problems in the Nursing School. After thanking the woman for forthrightly sharing her concerns, I dismissed her comments as just another symptom of what I understood to be constant faculty squabbling within the nursing program. At the time, I thought they just needed some tough male leadership—too many hens in the chicken coop. In retrospect, I should have been less gender-biased and more attentive to this woman's professional judgment.

At the same time in the late 1990s when Nina felt embroiled in stressful turmoil at the Nursing School, the university administration was being pressured by island politicians to establish an advanced degree in public health, a degree that would qualify Indigenous Chamorros for lucrative government positions in Guam's public health system. As was her nature, Academic Vice President Judy Guthertz seized the opportunity. Her Public Administration Department already offered a Master's of Public Administration degree. Why not tweak that program a bit to create a Master's of Public Health Administration degree? As fate would have it, the only faculty member in the university who held an advanced degree in Public Health was Nina. Because of her unhappiness with the Nursing School, it wasn't difficult for Vice President Guthertz to entice Nina's transfer into the College of Business and Public Administration. And I suspect that, given Nina's recently troublesome temperament, the Nursing School Director had every reason to support that transfer.

As a husband and retired Emeritus Professor, I did voice my opinion to all concerned that Nina's move was ill-considered. I saw no fire in her eyes for creating something new. Her sole focus was escape from the Nursing School in the hope of finding a better work environment. I felt that those new class preparations for a discipline in which Nina had little practical experience would be overwhelming. I also didn't trust Judy Guthertz. Her whole objective was to please the political establishment by delivering their requested degree option. A credible advanced degree program in Public Health Administration could not be sustained on Nina's capabilities alone. At least one terminally degreed faculty should be recruited, and I saw no effort being undertaken in that direction. Furthermore, Guam's government didn't have sufficient administrative positions in the Department of Public Health to accommodate many graduates. I was sure that it was Guthertz's intention to produce one or two or possibly three Indigenous graduates and then terminate the program, leaving Nina and some aspiring students in the lurch.

As I had expected, Nina came under more stress in her new position than had been the case in the Nursing School. On the surface she seemed to handle the pressure, but I noticed an increase in hyperactivity, insomnia, and what appeared to be more fervent religious zeal. In the end Nina got the last laugh on Judy Guthertz and everyone else. During the summer of 1999, the Guam legislature, in a budget-balancing move, passed a law giving five additional years retirement credit to those government employees who chose to retire before the fiscal year end. Nina walked away from the university with a comfortable pension and never looked back. When I say she walked away and never looked back, I mean that literally. For the next year and a half, the Public Administration Department tried to get Nina to clean out her office and return the keys. She never did, leaving behind art, plants, personal belongings, books, and academic records that were eventually trashed. As to how many graduated from the program, I have no idea, but as I suspected, it no longer exists.

*   *   *

Nina and I began the millennium both retired with decent pensions, two boys ten and twelve years old, two houses, two cars, and a boat, all debts paid in full. It seemed to be a situation in which Nina could finally relax, appreciate the fruits of her hard work, and enjoy being a mother. Unfortunately, that didn't happen. Her hyper manic states continued to come and go. Her insomnia increased. She no longer read books. Frequently she watched television until the early morning hours, sleeping little and dozing off during the day.

When Nina became involved with the Palau Women's Association and the Peleliu Club of Guam, I was hopeful that these activities would be good for her. And they were, for a while. She was instrumental in the clubs obtaining official non-profit tax status, and she was a leader in efforts to build a clubhouse on government land that had been set aside for community organizations. However, after a while her relationships with some club members deteriorated. The situation seemed similar to what had occurred at the Nursing School. My suggestions about empathy and moderation were of no avail. She was on the warpath about certain people in that association. There was no dissuading her, so I withdrew from discussions about club business, attributing their antics to a bunch of rival Palauan matriarchs engaged in a competition for pack dominance.

Nina's relationship with our neighbors in Yona Village also deteriorated. What I considered to be minor issues became major problems for Nina—everything from the location of property lines, to the responsibility for dog poop, to the ownership of breadfruit that hung over the fence, to the use of acceptable parking locations. At one point she got in a tiff with the mayor's wife over something. I can no longer recall the issue, but in Guam it is never a smart idea to get into a disagreement with a Chamorro village mayor's wife. There seemed no end to damaged neighborly associations resulting from Nina's lack of tact and uncompromising behavior.

It finally became clear to me that Nina was changing. Matters that in her earlier years she would have handled with graceful empathy, she now faced with tactless aggression. In most cases I was able to smooth over neighborhood flare-ups. However, I passed off her behavior as the norm for a Palauan matriarch passing through menopause, and I continued to hope that things would cure themselves over time. They did not.

Despite her volatile personality, Nina was a fine mother and excellent homemaker. Dust and dirt were not allowed to accumulate anywhere in our house. Food was always available. Rice, taro, and fish were the staples. The yard, with its various food-bearing plants and magnificent orchids, was well cared for. Clean laundry was always ready for the boys and me. Family body sanitation was a must, including daily bathing and flossing. Once a week Nina organized the boys into a bathroom cleaning and yard duty crew. Unfortunately, her approach to parenting was usually harsh and authoritarian. She continually instructed the boys, focusing on their faults, never giving praise. When I asked why she never gave compliments or praise, she would say, "Do you want me to tell those boys that they've done a good job when they haven't?" Perfection was Nina's idea of an acceptable job, and no one, including herself, ever quite measured up.

Lemal, Oldak, Nina, and Paul Callaghan, Yona, Guam, 2006

*   *   *

Lemal and Oldak both graduated from high school in 2008. That fall Lemal entered the University of Guam and moved into the dormitories. Oldak became a freshman at the University of Oregon in Eugene. Our house was empty, the demands of our daily routine diminished. I hoped that this quieter life would help calm Nina's anxiety. It had been a long time since I had seen her laugh.

Throughout most nights she was on the computer or watching television. Early in the morning she might get three or four hours sleep before starting off on some project, usually having to do with Palauan custom or women's affairs. The happy, bright-eyed, engaging and optimistic Nina I once knew and loved had evaporated in front of my eyes. Her world had become one of pessimism, darkness and paranoia. No matter what I said or did, she couldn't accept that anything was wrong with her. In her mind she was continually compelled to contend with the conspiracies of others.

My mother, Emma, had often encouraged Nina to write an autobiography. I can still hear Mom saying, "Nina dear, you must write about your life. It has been so interesting. I know you think it's nothing out of the ordinary, but most people would find it fascinating."

Palauans, like many Pacific Islanders, aren't inclined toward publicly venting private matters, much less doing so in a way that others might interpret as boastful or arrogant. No Palauans had ever written publicly about their personal lives. In Nina's mind, it would be extremely presumptuous of her to be the first to do so. I knew she was unlikely to ever take up the challenge herself, so I decided to give it a try. The effort consumed most of my spare time over a four-year period. I took breaks during summers in Chester and during my frequent fisheries-related work and travel. But whenever I was home on Guam, my daily ritual started with an early morning walk at sunrise, followed by several hours of secluded writing in my office/library.

That place was my sanctuary. From there my mind could wander afar. I will never again have a refuge to match it. From my desk, a panorama of Pacific Ocean stretched south and east to the horizon's curvature. The blues of sea and sky were continually transformed by the sun's angle and the shadows of clouds that morphed into every conceivable shape of white and grey. At times extraordinary rainbows spread their color before me. For a few minutes at the beginning and end of each day, the sky was transformed into fiery reds and golds that marked the sun's coming and going. My bookshelves were filled with a collection that brought together Pacific marine resources, economic theory, and the cultures of island people. There were artifacts and handicrafts from throughout Micronesia and the South Pacific, each with its own story and memory. Hawksbill and Green turtle shells hung on the wall, gifts from respected friends. My extensive seashell collection resided in a dark corner, away from damaging sunlight. There was one table dedicated to the tools and accoutrements for repairing fishing gear and making lures. Records in filing cabinets connected me with past students, some of whom were now leaders and professionals throughout the Pacific Islands. That room on the hillside above Ylig Bay was my place of thought and creativity.

For me, this attempt at non-technical writing can only be described as bittersweet creativity. Progress on Nina's story was slow. Some days it resulted in only a paragraph that would again be reconstructed the next day. Usually around noon, when I knew that Nina was awake with coffee in hand, I wandered down to the TV room for a conference about what I had written or intended to write. She was usually cooperative but skeptical of my efforts. She thought that nothing in her life seemed particularly interesting. Why would anyone spend the time to write about it? For me the writing turned into an effort of love, admiration and respect, feelings that I hold until this day. It was a way of reconstructing the old Nina, the Nina that had existed when I first met her. *Flight of the Dudek*, the story of Nina's growing up, was published by Amazon in 2012. Except for the typos, I am proud of it. I hope readers will find that it sheds light on a way of Pacific Island life that time and technology have erased.

*   *   *

Sometime in 2007, Nina decided to demolish the family's termite-ridden Palau house and to build a new one in its place. She insisted on forging ahead with the project despite the land title being in dispute. The Ibedul claimed ownership of much of Bkul a Tiull, the district in Koror where her family compound was situated. Perhaps because of my relationship with the Idid clan, or perhaps for other reasons, Ibidul did not contest the construction, so Nina hired an architectural firm to draw up plans, provide estimates and secure bids.

I favored the project but was concerned that Nina's unstable temperament and lack of experience in construction matters might lead to trouble if she alone were to supervise the construction. As luck would have it, a past student of mine, Kaleb Udui Jr., was at that time Chief Executive at the Palau National Development Bank. His administrative assistant was the same Tessie Faustino, who had years before lived with us in Guam while attending high school. With their help I secured an agreement that the bank would inspect and oversea the construction project. When payments were due, the bank would issue checks to the contractor from an escrow account that I continually replenished. For this service, the bank fee was 1 percent of the construction costs. That seemed a reasonable price to pay for not having to deal with Palauan contractors and Chinese workers in a country where building codes, permits, and contract law were nebulous or nonexistent. All went well for the first couple of payments, but then Nina accused the bank of not doing their job and cheating her. She fired the bank and the contractor and began doing things on her own. I was so upset that I completely withdrew from anything related to the project, including paying for it. Nina had sufficient funds to take care of that herself, so I just let her go her own way.

Two years later the house was still not completed to Nina's satisfaction, and she had managed to leave in her wake a number of disgruntled contractors, subcontractors, friends and relatives, at least one of whom sued her in Palauan courts. She of course counter-sued. As her husband, I was not immune from being an unwilling party to these legal battles, so I kept my head down and for a while stayed far away from Palau. Eventually the two-story building was completed, although Nina continued to complain about shoddy workmanship and materials. It had a one-bedroom one-bath apartment upstairs, exclusively for Nina, and four bedrooms and two baths downstairs, for family members. However, for some reason Nina became irritated with the family and locked them out, renting the downstairs to the employees of a foreign firm. This had the unpopular result of introducing foreign strangers into the family compound and into the otherwise all-Palauan neighborhood of Bkul a Tiull.

That house construction ended up causing considerable pain for all concerned, but upon its completion, it was one of the finest houses in Bkul a Tiull. I don't know what it looks like today, or who's living under its roof. I do know that Nina's brother, Nino, and his family live next door. Nina's sister, Aki, lives in a separate house behind. Nina spends most of her time in Guam. To my knowledge, Ibedul has not pursued his claim to any lands in Bkul a Tiull, but it remains a possibility that he may do so in the future. I wish that somehow I could have made the outcome better for all involved.

*   *   *

In late 2008, I had become concerned enough about Nina's state of mind that I began searching for assistance. At the time there existed only two qualified psychologists and one psychiatrist available to the civilian public on Guam. They worked almost entirely for the government and seldom took on private patients. As a long-time nursing teacher, Nina knew them all personally. She was not willing to consider having an evaluation, and if she were somehow forced to do so, she possessed a background in psychiatric nursing that could allow her to mount a convincing performance as to her competence. Whenever I attempted to talk with her about her state of mind or the possibility of psychological evaluation, she became extremely defensive, accusing me of being part of a conspiracy to silence and sideline her.

Initially Nina's paranoia was focused on people and institutions outside our immediate family. But beginning in 2009, I more frequently became the object of her suspicion and mistrust. Her unhappiness with the Callaghan Family Trust provides an example.

In the early 1990s when Oldak arrived in our lives, I established, at considerable expense with a top flight Honolulu law firm, the Callaghan Family Trust, along with associated wills and health care directives. The Trust incorporated all of our separate and community property. I was the designated Trustee for the community property and my separate property; Nina was designated Trustee for her separate property, primarily her brokerage and bank accounts. Following my father's sage advice, we had never maintained joint accounts during our married life.

In the event that one of us should pass away, the other automatically became Trustee of the entire Trust and could draw on it for their needs. Should we both pass away prior to the boys reaching the age of forty, the Bank of Hawaii Trust Department would become Trustee and administer the Trust for the benefit of Oldak and Lemal. If the boys were under eighteen at the time of our passing, Kitty and John Simonds were designated as guardians.

One morning Nina and I were having our normal morning coffee conference when out of the blue she said, "I don't like the Callaghan Trust. It's your way of controlling our money so that I don't get any."

"Bun, it's a way of avoiding probate expenses and making things easier for you when I die. After I'm gone, you and the bank will be in charge of everything. The lawyers explained that to you in Hawaii."

"Don't honeybun me. I don't care. I want it gone. You're using that Trust of yours to hurt me. It benefits you and the boys but not me. I don't trust the bank or you. I want my own separate accounts."

"You already have your own separate accounts within the Trust. Nobody except you can do anything with your Merrill Lynch account or your savings and checking accounts, or your UOG retirement money."

"But those accounts say Callaghan Family Trust. I want them to say Dominina K. Callaghan. I don't want to be part of this Trust of yours. I don't trust you or the lawyers or the bank. How do I withdraw my money from your Trust?"

"All right, I'll show you what to do, but you're making a big mistake."

"So you say, but I'll be proved right. You wait and see."

I prepared a registered letter for her signature that informed me, as Trustee, of her desire to withdraw from the Trust and directing me to change the titles on her separate property into her name only. I reluctantly helped her do as she wished, though I am quite sure she had received legal advice to the contrary. The Callaghan Family Trust of course remained operative with me as Trustee of my personal property and our community property—cars, boat, residence, and real-estate holdings. I continued to file joint tax returns and pay all taxes, insurance, license, and permit fees.

Initially thereafter calm prevailed, and Nina appeared happy with the outcome. However, now that her brokerage account was listed in her sole name, she started receiving contacts and "advice" directly from Merrill Lynch account representatives, who saw her high six-figure account as a potential source of commissions. They had no idea what a hornets' nest they were playing with. Within a year Nina had created so much angst at Merrill Lynch that she was given one month to move her account to another firm, or Merrill Lynch would close the account, sell the securities, and mail her a check for the total proceeds. To my horror, Nina chose the latter course of action, placing the proceeds in a local bank account that paid a pittance of interest.

*   *   *

Throughout 2010 I made several trips to Chester. Mom was now ninety-nine years old, and her body was beginning to fail, though her mind remained as solid as ever. After Dad died in 1974, Mom sold everything in Livermore and moved to a small house on Lassen Street in Chester, just eight miles from her beloved mountain cabin. During winters she lived in Chester town. Otherwise, she could be found, as she put it, "out in the mountains."

Until recently Mom had been a model of longevity. She had snow-skied into her mid-eighties, and spent summers alone at her cabin well into her mid-nineties. There from May through October she lived without electricity, using propane lights, stove, and refrigerator, pumping water from Willow Creek, gathering and splitting her own wood for fireplace warmth, and swimming twice each day in the North Fork's fifty-degree waters. Although she held a driver's license that didn't expire until her one hundredth birthday, she had recently decided it was time to stop driving. That decision was a demoralizing blow to her sense of independence, but she persisted with an ever optimistic and inquisitive outlook. Using her one operative eye (the other eye had been blinded in the 1980s as a result of failed cataract surgery), she read each weekly edition of *The Economist* magazine, cover to cover, and religiously watched *PBS News Hour* each night.

Now Mom had reached a point where her body was a frail wisp of its former self. Unable to take her morning walks or drive to the store or post office, she was pretty much housebound. During the Summer of 2010, Nina, the boys, and I visited Chester for two months. We took Mom on drives to some of her favorite places: Domingo Springs, where for years she had collected drinking water; Feather River Meadows, where she had camped with her parents and grandparents as a six-year-old in 1917; Willow Lake, where she always enjoyed the spring wildflowers and birdlife. We drove through Lassen Park to Hat Creek, where her mother and father had honeymooned in 1904, traveling on horseback all the way from their Manton Ranch. On one trip around Lake Almanor, Mom pointed out a hillside where as a teenager, Charlie Jorey, a Swiss immigrant and local postman, had taught her how to ski. We took her to the gold rush mining town of La Porte, where my great-great-grandfather once lived before he was charged with murder and ran from the law, never to be heard of again. That story can be read in Mom's book, *The Road through Rabbit Creek: A Search for Gold in Old La Porte*.

I think she enjoyed that summer, although our family life was a bit hectic for her liking. I know she appreciated Nina, Oldak, and Lemal. Their respect and reverence for the elderly had been instilled into them at an early age. We took Mom out to dinner at her favorite restaurants and made sure she regularly got to Char's Beauty Shop, where she could catch up on the town gossip. The ladies at Char's had given Mom a ninety-ninth birthday party and were planning a one-hundredth town-wide blowout. Mom was not pleased, telling me that she would attend out of respect for those who had gone to the trouble of organizing it, but she much preferred not being the center of such attention. In her words, "Getting old is not for sissies, and I've been lucky enough to persevere. There is no need to remind me of it."

In September Nina and Lemal returned to Guam, and Oldak returned to school in Oregon. I kept Mom company until mid-October, when I flew to a fishery meeting in Honolulu and then on to Guam. During our time together, we discussed current affairs and reminisced about my childhood and hers. I hold fond memories of those chats, though many specifics have departed my memory. I do recall her admission that she was ready to die. All her lifelong friends and relatives were gone, and the daily difficulties of living were becoming so challenging that life no longer held much enjoyment. She spent a lot of time that fall lying on the captain's bed in the kitchen, looking out the window with a view of the pond and meadow, watching the leaves put on their red and gold colors before wafting down to cover the ground. She knew every species of bird at the bird feeder and could predict their annual migrations. "Soon the snow will come and they'll all leave except for the Juncos. They'll stay with me for the winter. I hope someone can help me put seed out for them."

When I departed, others stepped in to help Mom. Jan Jensen, as he had for years, took care of all physical work around the house and the cabin. The cheerful ladies of K.J.'s Cleaning Service arrived twice a month. Dick and Patti Caywood, the owners of Peninsula Market, delivered groceries upon request. Susie Brumett spread her vivacious optimistic joy into Mom's life while providing daily help with cooking, laundry, and personal needs. Colette Cozort, who lived across the street, and the Daugherty family next door could be counted on in an emergency. My cousin, Jim Cramer, visited from his home in Davis for a night or two every couple of weeks. Mom valued his visits, and he, her company. Mom's mental acuity, wisdom, and knowledge of history were well-respected in Chester. Having first arrived there as a teenager in 1927, she had seen many changes. Community members like Laura MacGregor and Joan Sayre periodically stopped by to pay their respects and learn a little something about what they didn't know.

Nina flew from Guam to help Mom in early December 2010, and I came a few weeks later. We spent the holidays together. It was a cold and dismal. Mom was never a fan of Christmas season, but she maintained an upbeat attitude despite the difficulties of daily living. "It takes me more than an hour to get dressed each morning," she would sigh. "The hardest part is the damn shoes and those shoe laces." She refused all offers of help. "I'll do it myself no matter how long it takes, but I refuse to emerge from my room in a nightgown and slippers like some floozy. It's bad enough that Susie has to help me take a shower." Each night she watched the *PBS News Hour* while sitting in a low, upholstered armchair. When the news was over, it was all she could do to rise up out of that armchair. She rocked back and forth to gain momentum for the effort. If she didn't succeed, she would try again and again until she was standing on her own. If anyone offered to help, she would say, "No, thank you. I must do this on my own."

Before I departed in January of 2011, Mom said to me, "Paul dear, Nina doesn't need to come here to take care of me. I can get along fine on my own with the help of Suzie and Jan. I feel Nina has changed some. Is she under a lot of stress? I worry about her. She seems harsher and more strident than she used to be." Not wanting to burden Mom with my concerns about Nina's state of mind, I replied, "Don't worry, Mom. She's just a Palauan matriarch going through menopause." Those were the only words ever exchanged between Mom and I regarding Nina's mental health. I returned to Guam in mid-January of 2011.

On March 2, 2011, I received a call from Dr. Vincent Natali, Mom's doctor in Chester, saying that Mom was hospitalized with a bladder infection, and I should make plans to get to Chester as soon as possible. Shortly afterward, Jim Cramer called to say that he and Helen were already in Chester with Mom, and things didn't look good. That night I caught a flight out of Guam via Tokyo to Honolulu and San Francisco. After traveling for almost twenty-four hours and gaining a calendar day by crossing the International Date Line, I reached Mom's room in Chester's Senica Hospital. She was clearly down but happy to see me. We held hands and talked for several hours. She wanted to know about the status and wellbeing of Nina, Oldak, and Lemal. I told her everyone was healthy and doing well, though I knew the boys were having difficulties with college, and Nina's mental condition appeared to be worsening. She knew I wasn't being completely candid. Mothers know those kinds of things. "I worry about Nina and those boys," she said, "especially Lemal; he has had a hard row to hoe. Keep an eye on them for me." By evening, I had been awake for some thirty-six hours. "Paul dear, you go get some sleep," she said. "Come back in the morning. Don't worry, I'll wait for you." She was smiling, so I took her words as a joke.

The next morning, March 3, 2011, I had breakfast with Jim and Helen before arriving at the hospital around eight. When I sat down beside her bed, Mom was pale and didn't open her eyes. "Hi, Mom. I'm here," I said as I reached under the covers and found her hand. A faint smile crossed her face and she gave a light squeeze, which I returned. Within a few minutes, her hand became cold. I held it with both of mine in a vain attempt to keep it warm. Soon her arm and the rest of her body became cold. I felt her legs. They were cold too. I called the nurses. They took care of the rest. Mom died two months shy of her one hundredth birthday, just in time to avoid attending that birthday party organized by the ladies at Char's Beauty Shop.

One might ask how someone could die of a bladder infection in this modern day of antibiotics. The answer, it appears, is that Emma and Dr. Natali had an understanding. Unbeknownst to me, Mom suffered from a vaginal prolapse that resulted in her having frequent urinary tract infections. She had reached a point where she was tired of taking antibiotics and didn't want to undergo surgical repair at this point in her life. When the infection flared up this time, she was ready to die and told Dr. Natali, no antibiotics and no life-prolonging or resuscitation measures. When I arrived at the hospital, I had seen him in the hallway. Among other things, he said to me, "When you go home tonight, tell the nurses to turn off the oxygen." I thought nothing of it and did as he requested. That's probably why Mom was close to the end when I arrived the next morning. Dr. Natali and Mom had been friends for years. He had once been a Jesuit seminarian and a comrade of several Jesuits I had known in Micronesia. Dr. Vincent G. Natali gave much to the people of Chester and the surrounding area, my mother included.

As executor of Mom's will and Trustee of the Emma Callaghan Trust, I remained in Chester doing those things necessary to settle an estate. We couldn't bury Mom until the ground had thawed at the Chester cemetery. Toward the end of May, we held a catered memorial gathering in-lieu of the centennial birthday party that Mom had avoided. Nina and Lemal flew in from Guam. Oldak came from Eugene, Oregon. Many people from the surrounding area arrived to pay their respects, socialize, and watch a PowerPoint presentation of Emma's life. Some relatives and friends drove hundreds of miles to be there. Numerous respectful thoughts and memories were shared aloud by family and guests. Nina was particularly distraught and unable to finish her remarks. I rescued her at the podium. On that day I was particularly honored to be Emma Callaghan's son.

* * *

I made several trips between Guam and Chester over the next twelve months in order to close Mom's estate and care for the house and cabin. Often these trips were planned to coincide with fisheries management related work in Hawaii or elsewhere in the Pacific. By May of 2011, life with Nina on Guam had become more difficult. I was becoming a culprit in her delusional worldview. For instance, I was informed that during my absences, Nina was spreading conspiracy fabrications to various government officials and friends. Among these fabrications was her delusion that the Navy was attempting to force us out of our property in Yona because they wanted to carry out some secret operations below our house in Ylig Bay. According to Nina, I had previously been, and probably still was, a C.I.A. operative who was now involved in assisting the Navy in this nefarious plot.

As time passed, Nina accused me of being a party to this and other conspiracies and questioned the purpose of my frequent travel and work for the Federal Government. "I know you're doing more than just Fisheries Council stuff," she would say. "I don't know what you're up to, but I'm going to find out, and when I do, you're going to pay for it." All my protestations and logic to the contrary had no effect on her conviction.

I knew of one auntie and one niece in Nina's family who suffered from mental illness, and neither of those cases had turned out well. When Nina brought up the possibility that someone might be poisoning her food, I became concerned for my safety. It was likely that her thinking would soon progress to the conclusion that I was poisoning her food. At that point there was no telling what she might do. When I felt the need to lock my bedroom door at night, I knew it was time to leave Guam for a while.

In the spring of 2011, I was still working diligently on Nina's life story and had cajoled her into proofreading the draft manuscript. Her comments and additions had been relevant and helpful. Though she viewed the project with some skepticism, our collaboration on the book continued to go smoothly. I was even able to satisfy her demands that I leave out some events and change some character names to better conform with her current preferences for certain family members over others. Because of this, some truths and incidents had to be left on the cutting room floor, but overall, I had made progress toward completion of a final draft. In the hope of giving Nina some breathing room and defusing the poison food issue, I decided to take what documents I needed to Chester and try to finish the book there. Perhaps if I went away for a while, things between us might calm down. At least it was less likely that I could be accused of poisoning her from a distance.

By the beginning of August 2011, things had gone well in Chester. Nina's story had been titled *Flight of the Dudek*. It had been proofread and an artist had been hired to create illustrations for each chapter. I had acquired copyright protection and a Library of Congress designation. Create Space, an Amazon subsidiary, had agreed to publish. The book was on its way to fruition, and the mountain living had refreshed my body and mind.

On August 14 I received a letter from Guam attorney William Pesch, indicating that he was representing Nina, who wished to proceed with a divorce.

It had been my intention and expectation to live in Guam and remain married to Nina for the rest of my life. Given my knowledge of Nina's state of mind, I wasn't totally surprised by her action, but I was saddened. An excerpt from my return letter to Attorney Pesch reads as follows:

> I am really sorry and quite sad that Nina feels as she does. From my point of view we have had forty-one years of happy, productive, and mutually beneficial marriage. During that time, we've raised two boys, worked together to improve our economic and social standing, and had a lot of fun along the way.
>
> If a divorce will provide Nina with greater happiness, then I certainly hope that it can be accomplished in a cost effective and amicable fashion. To that end I propose working with you and Nina to draft a mutually agreed upon settlement agreement.

I provided all materials that Attorney Pesch requested, as well as my suggestions for distribution of the joint and separate property. There were no debts or liabilities at the time. After reading the draft divorce settlement, Nina fired him and hired attorney Jeffery Cook. I then provided Attorney Cook with the same documents and the same suggestions for settlement that I had previously sent to Attorney Pesch. In October, when I returned to Guam, Mr. Cook, Nina, and I met in his office to go over my suggested settlement. I suspect that Attorney Cook privately told Nina that he believed my offers were fair and in fact quite generous. But she refused to accept them, saying that I was hiding some assets and not providing enough income for her to continue living the lifestyle to which she was accustomed.

During our meeting, Attorney Cook made it clear that he represented Nina's interests, not mine. He recommended that I seek my own legal counsel. So reluctantly, I searched Guam for an attorney to represent me. It soon became clear that Nina had already contacted many top law firms in regard to our divorce or the Callaghan Family Trust or her house construction in Palau. Conflict of interest rules prevented those firms from serving me as a client. Even the firm of my long time friend, Bill Williams, was precluded from representing me because of previous work on our joint behalf. Eventually in late November 2011, I found Attorney Jon Visosky, who agreed to represent me. He did a fine job, removing much burden from my shoulders.

Subsequently, Nina went through several more attorneys. She even fired one during a court hearing. Judge Bordallo was not amused, giving Nina quite a lecture and sixty days to agree upon a settlement or appear back in court with a new attorney. He further assigned us to meet with an arbitrator in hopes that we could settle prior to the sixty-day deadline. I was hopeful, since the arbitrator was retired Judge Richard Benson. Nina had known him since arriving on Guam as a teenager. I thought she would certainly listen to his advice. She did not, but I believe he tried in private to convince her that my offered terms were fair and favorable.

Since my return to Guam in October, Nina and I had continued to live under the same roof. Our relationship was, on the whole, quite amicable. After years of doing so, we were quite able to live together. We did, however, spend a lot of time apart with differing schedules, and I continued to eat separately and sleep alone at night with the door locked. In our conversations, I tried to stay away from any subjects that I knew might trigger her delusional rants. In her mind I had become the cause of all problems, and her attorneys had been too incompetent to discover my supposed devious behavior.

Once I had hired Jon Visosky and saw how deftly he interacted on my behalf, I knew that I had adequate legal representation and could now leave Guam knowing that my interests were protected. I hired a moving company to pack a few personal items, and in December 2011, I departed Guam for Chester. Simply moving to another residence on Guam was not an option. I felt we needed complete separation from each other—out of sight, out of mind, I hoped. Guam is too small a place to accomplish any degree of anonymity.

With sadness I left behind a wife of forty-one years, numerous friends, and a lifestyle that comprised community and regional respect. Gone was my house and office/library with a million-dollar view, my archive of Pacific economic and social literature, my fifty-year collection of irreplaceable Pacific art, craft, and furniture, and a shell collection gathered by my own hands. I knew that those Pacific-related possessions had no place in Chester. Pretty much everything we had built and collected during our married life I left behind for Nina. She would continue to be a Pacific person. I would have to change.

Upon my arrival, Chester was drearily cold with snow on the ground. I was homesick, sad, and demoralized. I lay on Mom's couch in the kitchen, looking out the window at the snowflakes drifting down onto a quiet, white world, wondering how the rest of my life might unfold. After fifty years in the Pacific,

I had left so much behind. None of what I had learned in the Pacific was of any use to me in this place. For weeks I remained in a depressed and remorseful state of mind. Had I done the right thing by leaving Nina? She was sick through no fault of her own. It was totally unfair that such a malady had befallen a hard-working, creative, intelligent person like her. I told myself that my continued presence in Guam would not have made things better for Nina. She simply had to come to her own realization that there was something wrong with her. Until that happened, no one could help. My presence would do nothing to hasten that recognition. It wasn't like I had left her destitute. She had relatives to watch out for her and plenty of financial resources. In time, without me around to blame, she might improve. That said, my Catholic upbringing made guilt a hard burden to dispel.

The old five-room Chester house with its single-pane windows and drafty sills seemed continually cold to my tropical bones. The kitchen table near the oil stove became my center of indoor living. At night I slept in Mom's old twin bed, in what had been her bedroom next to the building's only bathroom. Furniture arrangements throughout the house remained as they had always been. Everything, from the 1940s electric mixer to the manual can opener mounted on the wall, reminded me of Mom. I talked to her as if she were still lying there on the captain's bed in the kitchen, sharing with her my sorrow and frustration at what had happened between Nina and me. Those one-sided conversations did a lot to soothe my mind. My tears flowed often, but I could hear Mom saying, "Paul dear, you've done the best you can. That's all anyone can ask. Go on with your life. You've had a fascinating one so far. There's no reason that further adventures can't lie ahead of you."

That winter of 2012 was a low point for me, but I managed to busy myself, cleaning out Mom's personal effects and getting Nina's book ready for publication. Neither activity was particularly uplifting to my psyche, but the myriad of winter chores and some cross-country skiing did provided relief, as did internet correspondence and visits from cousin Jim Cramer. His counsel and support have always been of great value to me.

As spring approached, the nights became shorter and the days warmer. My spirits revived as did my workload of Pacific fishery management obligations. Departure from Guam had not diminished those responsibilities, and I was soon flying frequently between Sacramento and Hawaii. Friends in Hawaii who knew of my flexible lifestyle began asking me to look after their homes while they were away on vacation. John Sibert and Pierre Kleiber were fellow members of the council's Scientific and Statistical Committee. They and their wives, Karen and Nan, had beautiful homes on the mountainside of Saint Louis Heights overlooking Honolulu. For weeks at a time I lived in luxury, drove their automobiles, and got to know the city's environs. Meanwhile, Kitty Simonds provided an office for me at the Fishery Council headquarters.

As life in Honolulu expanded, my departures from Chester became longer and more frequent. The work and lifestyle in Honolulu provided the Pacific connections and tropical living I craved. By January of 2013, I had rented an apartment in St. Louis Heights near the Kleiber and Sibert residences, purchased a car, and settled in at the Fishery Council office. My apartment was in a quiet location with a panoramic view of Diamond Head, but its one-bedroom configuration was a bit odd. The washer and dryer were located at eye-level in a narrow bedroom that barely allowed space for a standard bed. To enter and exit the unit, one had to negotiate thirty-six stairs. That provided healthy exercise, as did my morning walks on the mountainside. I loved that apartment at 1649 Bertram Street and spent six memorable years there. It was a perfect hangout for a bachelor.

Though I maintained legal residence in California, my return trips to Chester were primarily for seasonal maintenance of the Chester house and cabin. During my absences from Chester, both Jan Jensen and Susie Burmett cared for things, just as they had when Mom was alive. Their help made possible my transition to Hawaii living, and I remain grateful for their continued friendship and reliable assistance.

On August 8, 2013, I was in Chester when the Stipulated Interlocutory Judgement of Divorce was ordered and signed by Judge Bordallo. His original sixty-day ultimatum to Nina had stretched into more than a year. During that time, Nina had plowed through several attorneys and thousands of dollars in legal fees. Yet after all the machinations, costs, and personal pain of this drawn-out process, the final results were essentially the same as those I had initially offered to Attorney Pesch. Nina got all the real estate, household furnishings, and autos in Guam and Palau, debt free. I got the real estate, household furnishing, and autos in California. We split our combined retirement incomes, 60 percent for her, 40 percent for me. She kept her personal investment holdings, and I kept mine. Despite her continuing protests to the contrary, I felt satisfied that I had left Nina financially secure, a dignity she well deserved after the many good years we spent together.

Though I continue to hold respect for Nina and concern for her wellbeing, I have not contacted her in recent years. Until she is ready to seek help, I'm sure that contact will only open wounds that time has begun to heal. Oldak and Lemal, who both now live in California, do maintain some contact with their mother, and Nina's brother, Nino, keeps in touch with me. In my view, our divorce was a sad affair, a great loss for us both, a loss I now have managed to put into the background of my life. November of 2020 would have marked our fiftieth wedding anniversary.

Chapter 16

Hawaii

My six-year stint in Honolulu was entwined with a romance that changed the direction of my life. It all began when I was seventy years old. I was in Honolulu to chair a Scientific and Statistical Committee meeting. Recently, I had published *Flight of the Dudek*, my account of Nina's life. The book had been partially edited and illustrated by a woman named Margaret, who had been raised in Palau and other Micronesian Islands, but who now lived in Honolulu. Margaret and I had known each other for more than forty years; having mutual friends and meeting occasionally, we remained on the periphery of each other's lives until the book project brought us together. Margaret's cultural insight and knowledge of the Palauan language had made a valuable contribution, so it seemed fitting that I should ask her to celebrate the book's publication.

Punctuated by the Waikiki Friday night fireworks, we dined together in a restaurant atop Honolulu's Ilikai Hotel. That evening led to fervent correspondence and eventually to Margaret visiting Chester during the spring of 2012. There I hoped to introduce her to my mountain home and come to better know her during some hiking and biking adventures. Our time together went splendidly. The excitement seemed just as it had been in my twenties, and so apparently it was for Margaret. That week together was an uplifting and blissful experience. We swam in cold river water, hiked to mountain lakes, biked through pine forests, and sat together watching natures marvels. I fell in love, and Margaret seemed to indicate a similar attraction for me.

I was not the least deterred by her revelation of an ongoing eight-year relationship with a live-in-partner named Martin. At the time she enumerated his shortcomings and indicated a desire for change. So in my view, change it would be. I felt certain that Margaret would not be happy living full-time in Chester's mountain environment. If we were to be permanently together, our life would have to be based in Hawaii or another Pacific Island, and that was fine with me. Pacific Islands had been my home for most of my life. Within a few months, I moved more permanently to Honolulu.

Before leaving California, I told my cousin Jim Cramer that I could not believe this was happening to me at my age. "It's too good to be true," I said. "I can't be this lucky. Something must be wrong, but I've got to go to Honolulu and find out." As always, Jim was supportive but circumspect, preferring to focus on the practical aspects of my departure: mail, bill payment, yard maintenance, a ride to the airport.

Upon my arrival in Honolulu, it appeared that Margaret and I both had high expectations, but gradually over the next few weeks, Margaret became unsure. Intimacy between us faded, and our relationship progressively declined. My euphoria had apparently been premature. Margaret was uninterested in a full-time partnership that involved immediate change in her existing lifestyle or living conditions. I had no idea how to deal with her apparent change of heart. My forty-three years of married life had dulled the skills and judgment necessary to bolster our relationship. I made blunder after blunder. The harder I tried, the worse matters seemed to get.

I was miserable and had no idea how to resurrect the situation. Anguish kept me awake at night and distracted during the day. It was bewildering that such a seemingly perfect relationship could have gone so awry. We both understood and loved the Pacific, Micronesia, and Palau in particular. Our views were socially progressive. We were both concerned about conservation, global warming, income distribution, recycling, universal health care, education, uncluttered simplicity, exercise and proper nutrition. We abhorred conspicuous consumption, wasted resources, war, big money in politics, corporate and human greed. We were separated by only three years in age, and it seemed to me that we were happily capable of supporting each other through the difficulties of old age. Money was not an issue. She had some and I had considerably more. In my mind we were a perfect couple. Our combined strengths had the potential for boundless contributions to numerous causes.

During distressed and sleepless nights, I mulled over what had gone wrong. Why did it happen? How was it that I had so blundered, when things had started so beautifully and seemed so perfect? I felt that Margaret had given me false hope during her visit to Chester. I had taken a risk and made the hard choice of moving to Honolulu. Now when it was her turn to make hard choices, she was apparently unwilling to give up a comfortable lifestyle to take a chance on me. I felt betrayed and foolish for having misjudged the situation. My work and friendships at the Fisheries Council were the only things that dissipated my depression. So I threw myself into those activities, hoping that time might provide a path forward.

Over the next three years, Margaret and I continued to maintain a friendship, periodically dining and attending events together. For me, our outings provided a range of emotion that ran the gamut between excitement, enjoyment, and sorrow. The uncertainty, lack of encouragement, and pain of rejection weighed upon me, but for a long time I held to the hope that she might have a change of heart. Eventually I had to give up that hope.

Everything in my life has worked out for the best. This episode would likely be no different, I thought. Despite the loss of Margaret, my coming to Honolulu had resulted in productive work at the Fisheries Council, new friendships, and countless satisfying experiences, but there remains to this day a sense of loss and a nagging desire to better understand what happened between Margaret and me, and why.

*   *   *

In that regard, it's worth relating a religious experience that helped me come to grips with my emotions regarding Margaret.

During our time together, she had introduced me to Quaker Friends Meeting. Her family had been respected members of that Society, and Quaker philosophy had permeated Margaret's upbringing. At this point in her life, it seemed to me that Margaret's involvement in Friends' activities was driven by a nostalgic sense of obligation rather than any perception of spiritual benefit. On the other hand, I found Meetings for Worship to be an interesting contrast to my Catholic upbringing, and for a time I became a regular Sunday attendee.

My mother had always taught the benefits of solitude and self-reflection, undertaken in the stillness of a forest, on the bank of a running brook, or the edge of a grassy meadow. The noise and dynamics of Honolulu City offered few such venues, so the quiet of Friends Meeting on Sundays provided a welcome opportunity for introspection and contemplation.

There I sat in my customary wooden chair, on the periphery of the circle of Friends. It was one of those hot, humid, windless Sundays that often beset

Honolulu during September. The louvered windows of the stately, wood-paneled meeting house were wide open, but the only air circulation came from overhead ceiling fans, too few in number to do much good.

As prelude to an hour of silent reflection, we sang the prescribed refrain:

*"In calm cool silence once again we find our own accustomed place
among our brethren, where yet we may hear the still small voice,
the still small voice, the voice that reached the prophet's ear."*

Tranquility settled over the group as I squirmed for comfort in the unyielding chair. Some last-minute arrivals entered the room, among them Margaret. Confident strides carried her across my field of vision to a soft-backed chair beside the far wall. There she sat, eyes closed, body erect, greying blonde hair hanging slack behind. Her placid countenance betrayed no hint of her disposition.

What I most admired about Margaret was not superficial; it was her magnificent intellect, her conviction and tenacity that bordered on the stubborn, her creative artistic talent, and her clarity of expression, both written and oral, in Palauan and in English. For me she was an angel of perfection, but alas, I apparently was not so for her.

Other than noise from an occasional car in the street, the Meeting's tranquility was unbroken and its serenity enhanced by a symphony of song birds perched in shade trees that engulfed the building. For most of my life I had been aware of a small voice within me. I wasn't sure if it was the same small voice that others sought to hear at Quaker Meeting, but it had served me well, sometimes warning, sometimes reminding, sometimes prodding, but always dim and easily dismissed. Experience had taught me not to ignore that tiny sound of wisdom as it fought its way into my consciousness.

With eyes closed I lamented Margaret's lack of interest in my permanent company. Self-pity surged. I'm too old, too disagreeable, too inept. I snore. I can't dance. I'm slow of wit compared to her. She is three years younger, sensual, good looking, outgoing, effervescent, and very smart. I've botched everything that I've tried with her. It's hopeless, yet I care too much to stop trying and hoping.

"Stop moping. Get over it," said the voice within.

But we have similar backgrounds, similar likes and dislikes, mutual friends, similar political and social beliefs, even similar tastes in food. She's the most perfect, most amazing woman I've ever met.

"Isn't there anything annoying about her?"

Well, I've noticed that some of her resolute opinions are rooted in principled emotion rather than analytical rigor. It bothers me that she feels comfortable with simple, static answers to complex, dynamic problems, answers that reflect her view of "common sense." She sometimes fails to appreciate the multidimensional complexity of issues, weighs information based on its source rather than its validity, and sometimes displays an aversion to thoughtful consideration of opposing views.

"Her partner Martin must meet her needs."

I'm sure that Martin is a really smart guy. A botanical expert, I understand. He likely provides benefits to her life that I could not. In fact, he must be a kind and supportive person because she has been with him for a long time and apparently has chosen not to leave him on my account.

"So if she did leave him on your account, would you feel good about that?"

No, probably not. Martin must love her and value her company. I don't like being the cause of hurt for anyone.

"That's the real you talking. Are you always happy when you're with her?"

No, sometimes I'm uncomfortable or insecure. When that happens, I don't always use the best words to precisely reflect my feelings. She can pounce on these faux pas, with little consideration for my underlying intentions and sincerity.

"Words are important. She can't read your mind."

I know, but at times it seems like she doesn't want to try. It seems to me that sometimes she's short on empathy, a bit self-serving, a bit mechanical. She almost never admits a mistake or appears to engage in any introspective self-evaluation. When uncomfortable or challenged, she can be harsh-tongued and hurtful.

"I thought she was perfect?"

I guess no one is. She fears change and demonstrates an inordinate avoidance of risk and uncertainty. For example, the nearest vehicle must be more than a block away before she'll cross the street. The risk of damage to her social standing among Palauans weighs heavily upon her. In fact, her fear and uncertainty as to Palauan acceptance of our relationship may well be a reason that she is unwilling to move away from Martin.

"She might have reason for such fears. Anything else?"

She cares a lot about the integrity of the process leading to an ultimate goal. This is especially so regarding environmental and conservation issues. For me, it's the attainment of the ultimate objective that counts most, not the process of getting there. It doesn't matter to me what compromises are made along the way, so long as the resulting gains outweigh the incremental costs.

"You think like an economist. She apparently thinks like an artist. You both see the world differently. Do you expect that her annoying traits will change over time?"

I guess not. People don't change much at our age. But being with her is so interesting, fulfilling and enjoyable. I'm sure I can endure, circumvent, or ignore her annoying behaviors. They are more than balanced by her positive traits.

"Really? How sure are you?"

Well, I guess I must have some annoying characteristics that bother her.

"Yes, perhaps she doesn't feel a need to adjust to your annoying mannerisms. Look at things from her point of view."

Okay, her present life isn't perfect, but it's full of satisfying activities that nurture learning and creativity. Her situation isn't lavish, but it is comfortable, predictable and secure, at least in the short term, and she's not by nature a long-term thinker. Her partner, family, and friends provide sufficient emotional support. She lives and works in her Pacific world. Its people and history are her life, her strength, her art and her persona.

"And what addition do you bring to her life?"

Not much I guess, a conversation now and again and financial support that would allow her freedom to do more of what she loves doing. But I guess I'd bring her a whole suite of new considerations and stresses while not providing much of value in return; in her view, my costs probably outweigh my benefits.

"Aha, she doesn't need you. She thought she did, but she changed her mind. Get on with your otherwise interesting life."

Okay, I guess she likes the idea that I remain a friend and patron because that relationship comes with some gain to her, few difficulties, and little risk or obligation.

"And I thought you were looking for an American partner. Is she American?"

Initially I thought so. She looks American, and in many ways acts American, but as I've gotten to know her, I understand how her behavior reflects a complex Islander-American-Quaker mix. Quaker philosophies of simplicity, peace, integrity, and equity are intertwined with Micronesian attitudes of indirectness, obligation, status, control and manipulation. Some of those ideas conflict and she's burdened by having to choose among them depending on the situation.

I guess I failed to appreciate how much of her persona is rooted in Islander psyche. Based on my experience in Palau, women think of men as useful and sometimes valuable accessories to be pulled closer, pushed away, traded, or discarded as need be. In a Palauan marriage, obligation and responsibility trump all other emotions. Margaret is much that way. She pulls me toward her when she needs company or patronage and pushes away when my presence disrupts or threatens her order. In Chester she made light of Martin's importance. I interpreted that behavior in a way that supported my own hopes and dreams, thus leading to overinflated expectations regarding the depth of our relationship. I see that now.

"Well then, you best take your dream elsewhere."

Just then I realized that much of the hour had passed, and I wondered if others around the meeting room were having equally productive conversations with a "small voice."

Across the room, Margaret continued in statuesque meditation. She was still beautiful to me, but a little of her perfection had faded. That Sunday at Quaker Meeting marked the beginning of the end of an emotional rollercoaster I never expected to experience at my late age in life. However, I can confirm that love in old age feels exactly as euphoric as it does in youth. The pain of rejection is no less hurtful, save for the likelihood that it might be the last time around.

In retrospect, this affair with Margaret provides a reminder that empathy is a critical interpersonal skill. If I had better appreciated Margaret's position, I might have acted differently, and things might have turned out differently. If I had listened more keenly, I might have heard more clearly. At the time I could only appreciate my own position. I had left California, moved to Honolulu, rented an apartment, bought a car, found employment, and looked for real estate to accommodate us both. I thought that level of commitment should certainly alleviate any of her concerns. At the time it seemed simple to me—you say goodbye to Martin; we find a house and hire a moving company. We live together. I now realize that Margaret's position was not so simple. I failed to appreciate the relatively high level of sacrifice and risk that was required on her part. I rushed when she needed a slower pace. She pulled away when I needed calming encouragement. Both of us misjudged the other.

The following analogy strikes me as being apropos. At one time or another we have all attempted to assemble a jigsaw puzzle. While searching through the pile of pieces, we find one that appears to be the right color, size, and shape to fit perfectly into a particular void. With anticipation and excitement, we place the piece in the intended space. Shockingly, it does not quite fit. Our judgment was wrong. It almost fits, but no matter how the piece is manipulated, it's ever so slightly unsuitable. Perhaps if enough pressure is applied it can be forced into place. That attempt results in further dissonance, so we become exasperated, tossing the piece back into the pile, only later to pick it up again for a second try.

At some point we're forced to admit our mistake, and eventually another piece is found that slips perfectly into place. In the end, the recalcitrant piece also finds its proper home in the order and symmetry of things.

I still care deeply for Margaret, but time and distance have clarified my perspective. We still maintain a friendship, and it's comforting to have a friend who shares and understands my Pacific Island past. A tinge of sadness and pain still remain whenever I think of her. I continue to believe that we could have had much happiness together and accomplished many good works for Micronesians and Palauans in particular. I could be wrong, but I believe that our respective reputations within the Palauan community would have been enhanced had we joined together. The vast majority of our island and Stateside friends would have applauded our togetherness, and those who had reservations would eventually have accepted us. An opportunity lost, or perhaps a pitfall avoided.

It strikes me that when people are relatively young, a square peg can be forced into a round hole, with lasting benefit. Over time, after wear and care, the peg becomes a little more rounded and the hole a little more square. However, when people are old, there's not enough time left to amend rough edges and overcome differences.

*   *   *

I've told and perhaps belabored the story of Margaret and me because it marked a significant turning point in my life. Without her at my side, there was no hope of recovering any semblance of my previous island-oriented Western Pacific life. The experiences of almost fifty years would have to be put aside. Ways of thinking and acting would have to change. I would transition in Hawaii and ultimately return to California, to the place where it all began, to a small mountain town, to a culture in which I had forgotten how to feel comfortable, to an unaccustomed environment, to an empty house, to people who had no understanding or interest in the world from which I had come. I would begin anew, a transformation not of my choosing and one undertaken with reluctance in my mid-seventies.

As to my Quaker connection, it too fell away. I liked what I saw during my short time with the Society of Friends. Those members whom I encountered were socially well-intentioned, thoughtful and intelligent. They espoused values that I believe are critical components of a meaningful and productive life. Their rejection of creed, ritual and formality is refreshing, and their ethnic and gender inclusiveness is admirable. Besides that, their positions on war, incarceration, climate change, family planning, immigration and equality were in line with mine. My withdrawal from their association had little to do with ideology but was largely driven by my reticence to participate in their cumbersome, inefficient, communal organization structure.

Quaker governance embodies an emphasis on unanimity and consensus. Everyone is accorded the right of expression. I have spent much of my professional life involved with international and domestic organizations that require consensus resolution. I know it to be a slow, cumbersome process that demands engagement, empathy and compromise. The issues under consideration must be of sufficient import to justify the required time-consuming engagement. In my mind, the issues considered at Quaker Friends meetings for business and social concerns were quite trivial and not worth the time and energy required to reach consensus. I found the deliberations unsatisfying, became impatient, and gradually withdrew. As a footnote, I can see that impatience has been a shortcoming throughout my life—a shortcoming that may have cost me dearly in various endeavors.

In any case, if Quaker Friends meetings were held near Chester, I would be tempted to return to regular Sunday appearances, and I recommend Friends meetings to anyone of a progressive intellectual bent, no matter their prior religious affiliation—Christian or not.

*   *   *

From 2013 through 2017, I worked full time at the council office on Bishop Street in Honolulu, contributing to the council's Scientific and Statistical Committee as well as a subcommittee of the Western and Central Fisheries Commission. In those capacities I traveled to places like Pohnpei, Bali, Samoa, Fiji, Philippines, Japan, Guam, Palau, the West Coast, and Washington, D.C. At international meetings I frequently represented Guam, and because of alphabetical seating, I came to know some delegates from French Polynesia and Indonesia, my left and right table mates. When I sat on the Commonwealth of the Northern Marianas delegation, Canada and Cook Islands were my adjacent associates. Life was full of stimulating activity that kept my mind from focusing on the sadness of my divorce and the frustration of the Margaret affair.

When not attending off-island meetings, my daily routine consisted of an early morning walk to the top of St. Louis Heights, granola and blueberries for breakfast, a fifteen-minute drive to the council office, lunch in Honolulu's business district, and a drive home in the evening after rush hour.

Paul Callaghan, Kitty Simonds, and Doy Farwell (stenographer), Honolulu, 2016

There had often been sufficient food and drink at council functions to negate the need for dinner; if not, I stopped at Good Earth Market on King Street for groceries and vegan takeout. My studio apartment in St. Louis Heights was a place of solitude and comfort, its view of Diamond Head a constant reminder of my good fortune.

In March of 2015 I had recently returned to Honolulu after two weeks of skiing in Vail, Colorado with my college fraternity brother, Neil Dunbar. I felt fine and had taken my usual early morning walk, eaten breakfast, and driven to work. When exiting the elevator on the fourteenth floor, I realized that my right side was numb from the top of my head to my toes. The council staff immediately transported me to the Straub Hospital emergency room. Upon admission, I was subjected to forty-eight hours of tests and observation under the assumption that I had suffered a mild stroke. During the evaluation process, it was determined that I had not suffered a stroke but did have significant coronary artery blockage.

Following a failed attempt to stent the blockages, on May 4, 2015, I underwent coronary bypass surgery. In the few days prior to that operation, I was forced to consider the possibility of death. It was comforting to reflect on a satisfying life and the knowledge that the most important things had been tended to. Those matters left undone would simply be someone else's problem. I was upbeat and resigned to my fate on that morning when Pierre Kleiber dropped me off at the Straub Hospital intake door. This would be another of life's adventures, one like others that I had faced alone.

Irish luck prevailed once again. The operation was pronounced a success, and my life continued, notwithstanding a painful recovery process, during which the council staff visited often. Margaret brought Palauan food and Pacific news. Other friends and neighbors assisted, and Oldak came from California to help during the first phase of my homebound recovery.

When Oldak was forced to return to his job in California, I was as yet unable to lift any weight or drive a car, and had trouble negotiating the thirty-six stairs to and from my apartment. I could not lie down. All sleep had to be accomplished in a sitting position. Fortunately, I was able to enlist the help of a young Palauan man named Eluang Michael, the nephew of Martha Dever, the wife of my friend Dr. Greg Dever. I would judge that Eluang was in his late twenties, a quiet, gentle, caring person who had been discharged from the US Army after suffering injury to his feet and legs. He never told me what had happened to him, but he walked with a slight limp and at times I think was in considerable pain. In any case, Eluang chauffeured me around, helped with shopping, and did whatever else needed doing. We talked some about how much he liked the Army and wished that he could have remained in the Service. After being discharged, he had gotten several jobs, but they hadn't worked out for one reason or another. I paid him for his help, but perhaps not enough.

After my recovery, I saw Eluang a few times. One night Margaret and I took him out to dinner because we thought he might be lonely living in the Devers' house in Palolo Valley. The Devers spent much of each year in Palau, leaving Eluang to care for their Palolo home. In 2020 Eluang committed suicide, PTSD and depression, they said. He was a fine person and a great help to me when I was in need. I wish that I had paid greater attention to him when he was in need.

* * *

My dream of finding a loving and congenial partner did not end with Margaret. I had spent over forty years living with the same person in a mutually beneficial relationship that embodied little overt affection. Determined to find something more, I began an eHarmony internet search. On that site there appeared to be three categories of available women my age: those seeking a replacement for a recently deceased partner, with the intent that their lives continue just as before—restaurants, country club golf, duplicate bridge, and travel; those whose financial situation would benefit from an additional contribution; and those who had been single for some time and were seeking a compatible partner with whom to share the ups and downs of life. I focused on the latter group, with emphasis on education, geographic proximity, age similarity, and political compatibility—no smokers, heavy drinkers, religious zealots, or dog, cat, and horse lovers.

After tapping the delete button hundreds of times, I met Victoria, an attorney working in the State of Hawaii Adjutant General's office. Victoria had recently been blown to Hawaii by unfavorable political winds in her home state of New Mexico. She was looking for companionship to help her learn about the Pacific and better enjoy Hawaii. I was looking for companionship to take my mind off my divorce and Margaret, so Victoria and I enjoyed each other's company for a couple of years in a platonic relationship, until Victoria moved back to her home in Albuquerque. We still correspond, and I value her friendship greatly. She lifted my spirits and provided delightful camaraderie during a depressed time in my life. We shared some fun times together and some disconcerting ones too. Our favorite hangout was the Kahala Mall, where we went to movies, ate, and just cruised around. I will never forget the night of the 2016 presidential election. After seeing the movie *The Eagle Huntress*, Victoria and I walked out from Ward Theater to find that Hillary Clinton had lost the election to Donald Trump. Victoria, being a staunch progressive democrat, was deeply shaken. I was equally upset, to the point that I managed to bounce my little Ford Fiesta car over the center strip while turning left onto Ala Moana Blvd.

For some reason, I have no idea why, Victoria didn't completely fill that void in my life that needed filling. She was an amazingly congenial and interesting person. Her social and political ideas were similar to mine. She was even a semi-practicing Catholic, who likely could have drawn me back into the Catholic Church. Yet for me, Victoria was another puzzle piece that didn't quite fit. I do look forward to hearing from her. She holds a dear place in my heart, and I wish her the best of everything. But she was not the permanent partner I was seeking. And in fairness, she might well have felt the same about me. We never discussed intimate or long-term considerations.

I continued to push the eHarmony delete button until one day, up popped Suzanne Lee, an artist from Portland, who according to eHarmony's screening algorithm had the right characteristics—a post-graduate education, roughly my age, a liberal outlook, a non-smoker, no religion, no pets. In early November of

2014, I was in Chester and decided to drive the nine hours north to Portland for a visit. On the way I stopped in Albany, Oregon to stay the night with an old-time fishing buddy, Bob Saylor. We had spent countless hours on the ocean together in Guam, but I hadn't seen Bob since he moved to Oregon to be closer to his wife's family. It was midafternoon when I drove up in front of Bob's house. He immediately came out.

"*Hafa adai*, Callaghan. What brings you to this neck of the woods? Don't you know that Californians aren't welcome in Oregon," he said as he gave me a big hug.

"I'm on my way to visit a lady in Portland," I said as he finished crushing the wind out of me. Bob is a big guy.

"Well, that explains everything. Who is this lady, and how do you know her?"

"We met on the internet. She's an artist who lives in Portland, a place called Sellwood. Do you know where that is?"

"Sure, it's part of southeast Portland on the Willamette River."

"How long does it take me to drive there from here?" I asked.

"Oh, about an hour to an hour-and-a-half, depending on the traffic."

"So I guess I'll get out of your hair sometime tomorrow afternoon, if that's okay?"

"Good!" he said. "That'll give us time to get caught up. I've been doing some halibut and albacore fishing on the coast—got some stories and gear to show-and-tell. Come on in. Make yourself at home. Denise is at the store. She'll be happy to see you."

Bob and I had a great visit—mostly nonstop fish talk. He had originally arrived in Guam from Southern California to pursue aquarium fish collecting. His business thrived for several years, collecting live species from Guam's reefs, holding them in his warehouse filled with salt water tanks, and then shipping them to worldwide aquarium customers. Eventually it became clear that Guam's reefs were too small to support continued profitable harvests, and Bob grew tired of spending days underwater, breathing stale air from scuba tanks. So he reengineered his business to provide swimming pool maintenance and repair. By the time he left Guam, Bob and his crew of mostly Micronesian workers were caring for a large percentage of the Island's swimming pools, and there were many, given the number of hotels and resorts on the Island. He and I each had a fishing boat, so sometimes we fished on mine and sometimes on his. All I can say is that we caught a lot of fish together and saw a lot of white water over the bow.

Upon arriving at Suzanne Lee's house in the late afternoon, I found her behind the house in her studio, dressed in Levi's and a paint-stained, long-sleeved shirt. She was on her hands and knees on top of a table, cutting a piece of metal with a hacksaw. *This is a positive sign*, I thought. *She's not a milk-toast, TV-watching, slippered widow. She's wearing boots.*

Without changing position, Suzanne said, "Hello, you must be Paul. Can you hold the end of this while I finish cutting?"

Eventually we accomplished a more formal introduction, and she invited me into her house. The two-story, two-bedroom, one-bath unit was a collage of color, form, and function, both inside and out. In the basement was a separate one-bedroom rental unit. Suzanne was a good-looking lady, not overweight but well filled out in the right places. She was vibrant, self-assured and congenial, clearly used to being independent.

During the next couple of days, we drove into the Columbia River Gorge, hiked to some waterfalls, visited Maryhill Museum, ate at restaurants and talked a lot. She had been married and divorced twice and had raised her only son mostly as a single parent while working as a teacher, cook, and public artist. For many years she taught at the Oregon College of Art and Craft, while at the same time cooking for the Oregon Medical Association. As a way of providing outdoor experiences for her son during summers, Suzanne had cooked for a family-owned group of ranches in Wyoming, twelve miles south of Cooke City, Montana—the B-4, RDS and the L-T, where Hemingway had often spent time. Although the numbers varied, on any day there might be forty hungry mouths to feed, including family, wranglers, farm hands and guests. Getting supplies and provisions meant a trip over the Beartooth to Billings, Montana, 120 miles of torturous mountain road. All in all, I came away from that three-day visit quite impressed with a unique and interesting lady who laughed a lot and seemed to enjoy my company.

Over the next three years, I continued to see Margaret, Victoria, and Suzanne, in between fisheries-related work and travel, as well as periodic maintenance trips to the Chester house and cabin. I had written off the possibility that Margaret might give up living with her partner in order to hang out with me, but the two of us occasionally met at lunch or dinner for discussions about our mutual experiences and friends. Sometime in 2017, Victoria's contract with the State of Hawaii expired and she returned to Albuquerque, where she now works for the

New Mexico State Government. I was sorry to see her go, but her departure served to somewhat simplify my hectic life.

Suzanne and I kept up a liaison between Portland, Chester, and Honolulu. Given my numerous commitments, life became frenzied, but also fulfilling. In January of 2017, Suzanne and I took a three-week art-oriented tour of Thailand and Vietnam along with ten folks from the Portland-Seattle area. I was one of the few non-art-oriented persons in the group, a most enlightening experience. After that trip it was clear to me that Suzanne and I were pretty well suited for each other. It was time to start thinking about retiring from Pacific life and responsibilities. Chester would now be the place I called home, and Suzanne would be a big part of that new life.

Suzanne Lee and Paul Callaghan, Honolulu, 2016

*   *   *

My six years living in Honolulu provided a most comfortable and satisfying life transition. Honolulu is a relatively small city as cities go, but it's special in many ways. When the trade winds blow, the air is clean and fresh, the temperature welcoming, and the rainbows over the Ko'olau magnificent. The population hails from all corners of the Pacific world. Life is a bit slower than most cities. Human beings have time to relate with one another. I enjoyed my memberships and frequent attendance at the Hawaii Symphony, the Honolulu Museum of Art and Bishop Museum. There was usually something of interest happening at the Doris Duke, Manoa Valley, or Diamond Head Theaters. On weekends I could easily book a flight to the Big Island of Hawaii for a visit with old friends like Craig Severance, Bill and Jane Williams, Peter Black, and Pat Bryan.

Friends Meeting followed by a drive to the Kailua Sunday Farmers Market or a relaxed brunch at the Manoa Tea House and a visit to Doris Duke's Shangri La could richly fill an entire Sunday. On Saturdays I shot skeet at the Koko Head Skeet Club. There I discovered that redneck conservative values are not exclusively the province of Caucasian America, though the Hawaiian version is a bit Asian-nuanced. My favorite upscale restaurants were the Hau Tree Lanai, Duc's Bistro, and Michel's at the Colony Surf. I often ate at the Dew Drop Inn or picked up take-out from the Diamond Head Market. Fresh fish was readily available at Nico's and Kinney's near the Honolulu Fish Auction. Aside from the Margaret affair, life was about as good as it gets during those years in Honolulu. Thanks to the kindness of Kitty Simonds and the energy of council staff, I was kept busy and engaged in productive pursuits. I owe Kitty much and can never overstate her rich contribution to the fabric of my life. She was an anchor during turbulent times, always a trusted friend and respected leader. I miss our informal chats over a glass of wine at day's end.

Chapter 17

The Last Stop

In 2018, I demolished Mom's old house in Chester. With Suzanne's architectural and artistic assistance, along with the fine workmanship of Broglio Construction, we built a new home in its place. Having retired from my Pacific fisheries responsibilities, I sold my car, closed out my apartment, and departed Honolulu in February of 2020, just ahead of the COVID Pandemic. Suzanne and I now live in Chester on five acres of forest and meadow land with a stream running through.

Our lives rotate between Chester, Portland, and Cascade Head on the Oregon coast. There in partnership with five other Oregonian families, including Senator Jeff Merkley, Suzanne owns a four-story pole house that was designed by Bill Church and built in 1972 by University of Oregon architecture students. The house overlooks the sea in a spiritual place where the Salmon River enters the Pacific Ocean. It's a cold ocean, much different than the tropical seas of my past. I find it less friendly and a bit foreboding. Though beautiful in its own way, I'm not drawn to it as I was to the tropical sea, but it's the closest I get to the ocean these days.

Most of my friends and acquaintances remain scattered among a myriad of Pacific byways. There are those whose names do not appear in these pages but hold a place of fondness in the neural niches of my mind. I often wonder how they are doing and hope we will meet again at some point.

About twenty-five years ago in Guam, I took up the shotgun sports of skeet, trap, and sporting clays. I still shoot competitively in my age group and hope to continue as long as my eyesight and physical reaction capabilities remain intact. When I do well in a tournament, I think of my dad, Joe. He would be proud of my shooting, though aghast at the waste of ammunition and the price of everything these days. His conservative investment training has served me well over the years. At this point there are more than sufficient funds to care for myself and others, while additionally being a bit extravagant at times.

Suzanne and I get along well and laugh a lot. Being around her is comfortable and relaxing. There are no rough edges as there were with other women in my life. As time has passed, we've become an integral part of each other's lives. Suzanne has helped me to reintegrate with Stateside American life. I value her companionship, and I expect that we will be together for the rest of our time on this earth. This puzzle piece fits perfectly. She's a keeper, and every day she shows me that I am as well.

In addition to our house in Chester, I still maintain the cabin on the North Fork of the Feather. It remains much the same as it has throughout my lifetime. Some things, thank God, don't change much. I hope to maintain it for a while longer. We don't stay there overnight much anymore, but we do spend days when I often sit on the porch and reminisce a bit.

*   *   *

It's afternoon on one of those warm fall "Indian Summer" days. I'm sitting in a director's chair, feet propped up on the cabin porch railing. Suzanne is in the kitchen. A smell of food is in the air, and our dinner table is set by the fireplace. For the moment, I'm enjoying the day's last warm rays of sunshine while sipping a glass of Jameson Irish Whiskey. The drink's origin reminds me that at eighty years of age, I'm the last of my Irish Callaghan line. I hope my forbearers are not upset. Oldak will carry on the name if not the genetics.

Within sight, many of my childhood markers are still recognizable, though there are some subtle changes. The forked trunk of the nearby Jeffrey pine is no longer as equally balanced as it once was. At some point in the last few years, winter snow and ice broke the top off the left fork, though the tree itself continues to grow, healthy and strong. Near the tree's base, the lava outcropping has changed little, though a marmot family hasn't occupied that place in years. The strewn logs, runways of my childhood playground, have rotted away to dust. Only I know where they once lay. Below in the gorge, the sound of flowing water is as it has always been, yet I can discern minor changes in the river's course—banks washed away, boulders moved, channels shifted. The old growth forest across the canyon survived the Dixie Fire of 2021 and remains intact. Save for a few fire-singed underlings, the scraggy topped sugar pines and grizzled yellow pines still reach to the sky in stately majesty. They have watched over the cabin for its entire existence and observed my progression from babyhood to old age.

The waterfall and swimming hole are much the same as they were in my youth, though the pool is shallower and wider at its downstream end. Forest growth has blocked my view of the grassy beach, but I can still clearly see the lava rocks where Mina Anderson sat fishing each morning at dawn. She would be sad to know of today's meager spawning runs of Rainbow and German Brown. Their passage upriver has been hindered by a diversion dam, built in the 1970s near Chester to protect the town from seasonal floods. Few spawners can make their way around it.

My favorite old yellow pine in the entry road, the one that Mom saved from harvest sixty years ago, fell to the ground last winter, having been ringed by pine beetles—their numbers enhanced by a warming environment. The tree's ring count confirms its birth before our nation was founded. I'll use its limbs for firewood this fall and winter, their warmth a fitting evocation of our lifelong relationship.

Warming weather has led to lighter snow packs and less precipitation. In the winters of my youth, the cabin was buried in ten feet or more of snow each winter. Now it's lucky to see two or three feet. The river and its tributaries have lost volume and become warmer. Along the banks, moisture-absorbing alder bushes have replaced the water-conserving willows. I continue to pump the cabin's non-potable water from Willow Creek, but its flow is only half that of my youth. During the early 1980s, government and private interests killed off the beaver populations on the river and at Willow Lake, the headwaters of Willow Creek. This has distorted the ecology of the watershed and destroyed much trout habitat.

In turn, the diminished fish stocks have had an observable impact on dependent species. No longer do I hear the feisty call of kingfishers. Osprey and eagles seldom visit. The ouzels are fewer in number and no longer nest in the rock cliffs at the swimming hole. Fewer Merganser duck families chase minnows in the shallows. The river otters have departed to more hospitable locations downstream in Lake Almanor. It has been a long time since I've heard or seen a frog or a yellow and black water snake. We played with them when I was a child.

Warming temperatures have expanded the ranges of some species into higher altitudes. In my childhood we never saw ravens, wild turkeys, or Asian doves around the cabin. Now we do. The ravens are particularly destructive, preying on small rodents and robbing the nests of native birds. The forest is drier than it was in my youth. There are fewer macro fungi, mosses, and wild flowers. The lumber industry has purposely eradicated porcupines, because they sometimes girdle and kill trees. There seem to be fewer chipmunks and squirrels than there used to be. I haven't seen a fisher or a marten since my childhood, but there are still a few bobcats to be seen every so often, and mountain lions still follow the deer migrations, though I just as soon not see one of them.

Despite the changes around me, this seat in the sun is comforting and restful. The forest smells are as they have always been. The sugar pine that Mom planted as a seedling and faithfully watered has grown to almost a foot in diameter, on its way to becoming a forest giant. Domingo Springs, where we get our drinking water, still gushes with purity, its watercress garden as lush as ever. The cabin itself is little changed. There's still no hot running water. One wall holds seventy-five years of butcher paper trout silhouettes, representations of fish caught by me, my children, and others, all witnessed with the signatures of grandparents, parents and friends. The hand-built rock fireplace still throws out warmth. The doorjambs record annual height records of me and my children as we grew from babyhood. The loft still provides a place of refuge for young visitors. There are a few improvements. The wooden ice box has been replaced with a propane refrigerator, the kerosene stove and lighting are now propane fueled, and a septic system with indoor toilet has replaced the outhouse.

It's pleasing to realize that I accomplished much of what my parents encouraged me to do in life. I have traveled roads not commonly taken, learned to understand and appreciate people from faraway places, maintained my integrity, and tried to make the world a little better place for others. I think my parents would be proud. Anyway, I hope so, as I intend to be buried in the Chester cemetery alongside them.

I have now come home, full circle, to the place of my beginnings. For me, Chester is the last stop. It's a comforting place to hang out, and I'm lucky to have Suzanne as my partner. She makes every day an exciting adventure. God willing, we may still have more time for fun together. My day-to-day acquaintances here in Chester know little about my previous life, so there are no companions with whom to reminisce. In some ways that's good. My focus is directed toward matters current and future, a healthy vantage to maintain in old age. Life here is simple and uncluttered. At the moment, my objectives are a refill of this whiskey glass, a stoked fire, and dinner with Suzanne.

*   *   *

Having returned to my mountain roots, my good fortune continues. I feel blessed and satisfied with the way life has turned out, and I'm ready for the sunset of my story.

Each day in Chester town I walk the half mile from our house to the Post Office. There's no home delivery of mail in Chester. On the way I pass the Corner Store, where as a child I played on the wood floor while Mom bought our groceries. Back then we maintained a charge account and paid by the month. The place is now a cash and carry liquor store with a couple of gas pumps outside, but the same wooden floor inside. The gas station used to be across the street next door to Ida (Dinty) Moore's Fly and Tackle Shop. That gas station is now a coffee shop, and Dinty is buried in the Chester Cemetery near Mom and Dad.

The Chester Post Office is where most community relations take place. People greet each other, gossip, read death notices, and post lost and found alerts. The ritual of politely holding the front door open for others is strictly observed. When old-time Chester residents see or hear my name, the conversation often goes something like this:

"Oh! Are you Emma Callaghan's kid?"

"Yes."

"Your mother was a great lady. Did you build that new house on Lassen Street?"

"Yes."

"So are you going to stay and live in Chester?"

"Yes. That's my plan."

"So where have you been all these years?

"Oh, here and there, just going with the flow."